CARTOONS AND ANTISEMITISM

CARTOONS AND ANTISEMITISM
Visual Politics of Interwar Poland

Ewa Stańczyk

University Press of Mississippi / Jackson

The University Press of Mississippi is the scholarly publishing agency of
the Mississippi Institutions of Higher Learning: Alcorn State University,
Delta State University, Jackson State University, Mississippi State University,
Mississippi University for Women, Mississippi Valley State University,
University of Mississippi, and University of Southern Mississippi.

www.upress.state.ms.us

The University Press of Mississippi is a member
of the Association of University Presses.

Any discriminatory or derogatory language or hate speech regarding race, ethnicity,
religion, sex, gender, class, national origin, age, or disability that has been retained
or appears in elided form is in no way an endorsement of the use of such language
outside a scholarly context.

Copyright © 2024 by University Press of Mississippi
All rights reserved

∞

Library of Congress Cataloging-in-Publication Data

Names: Stańczyk, Ewa, 1981– author.
Title: Cartoons and antisemitism : visual politics of interwar Poland / Ewa Stańczyk.
Description: Jackson : University Press of Mississippi, 2024. | Includes bibliographical references and index.
Identifiers: LCCN 2024016326 (print) | LCCN 2024016327 (ebook) | ISBN 9781496851499 (hardback) | ISBN 9781496851505 (trade paperback) | ISBN 9781496851512 (epub) | ISBN 9781496851529 (epub) | ISBN 9781496851536 (pdf) | ISBN 9781496851543 (pdf)
Subjects: LCSH: Antisemitism—Poland—History—20th century. | Jews—Poland—History—20th century. | Jews—Caricatures and cartoons—History. | Jews—Press coverage—Poland. | Antisemitism—Caricatures and cartoons—History. | Antisemitism in art.
Classification: LCC DS146.P6 S73 2024 (print) | LCC DS146.P6 (ebook) | DDC 305.892/4043809034—dc23/eng/20240506
LC record available at https://lccn.loc.gov/2024016326
LC ebook record available at https://lccn.loc.gov/2024016327

British Library Cataloging-in-Publication Data available

CONTENTS

Acknowledgments vii
Abbreviations ix
Introduction 3
Chapter 1: The Voice of the State 16
Chapter 2: Local Struggles 46
Chapter 3: Against Antisemitism 85
Chapter 4: Hidden Identities 120
Chapter 5: Satire for the Masses 152
Conclusion 199
Notes 207
Works Cited 245
Index 259

ACKNOWLEDGMENTS

Writing a visual history of any kind leaves one indebted to the many people who preserve the ephemeral sources that make that history. In the course of researching this book, I was privileged to meet a number of dedicated archivists, librarians, curators, and art historians whose expertise and enthusiasm became the driving force behind this study. I would like to personally thank Paulina Pilcicka at the Museum of Caricature in Warsaw who patiently guided me through the archival collection of the museum, provided me with secondary literature on political cartoons, and helped me fill in the many blank spots in my story. Her vast knowledge of "who was who" as well as her friendly demeanor made my repeated visits to the museum not only conducive of original research but also enjoyable. Agnieszka Reszka at the archives of the Jewish Historical Institute in Warsaw introduced me to the Papers of Józef and Ernestyna Sandel, and Zuzanna Benesz-Goldfinger at the JHI Arts Department talked to me about the surviving drawings of Mendel Reif. Katarzyna Błesznowska-Korniłowicz, Mateusz Senczyno, and Tomasz Weresa at the archives of the Academy of Fine Arts in Warsaw regaled me with stories about the academy and, apart from providing me with student documentation of those who later became caricature artists, recommended additional reading on the history of their institution. Both Iwona Pilucik at the National Archives in Kraków and Katarzyna Król at the archives of the Jan Matejko Academy of Arts in Kraków pointed me to relevant record groups and answered numerous queries. Katarzyna Król was also generous enough to send me scans of interwar student files at a time when the reading room was closed to visitors. Anna Dziedzic at the University of Warsaw archives kindly assisted me in obtaining permission to reprint a photograph from the university collection. Librarians Magda Klikowska-Janik at the Józef Piłsudski Regional and Municipal Public Library in Łódź, Aneta Lewandowska at the Łódź University Library, and Daniel Biedrzycki at the National Library in Warsaw scanned dozens of illustrations for me and did so with admirable speed and fortitude. My student assistant Weronika Wasilewska aided me with preliminary library research in Poland.

The project received generous funding from the Polish National Agency for Academic Exchange (NAWA), which enabled me to spend an uninterrupted period of eight months in Poland between November 2022 and June 2023 as the *Polonista* fellow. I owe a special debt of gratitude to NAWA's wonderful staff members Renata Cieniak and Mariusz Czech, who supported me throughout my stay in many matters big and small. My time at the host institution, the Department of Cultural Studies at the University of Łódź, provided me with an ideal respite from a busy teaching life and allowed me to focus entirely on research. I am especially grateful to Dorota Golańska, who made my stay possible, and to Agnieszka Rejniak-Majewska, who gave me a warm welcome on my first day in Łódź, helped me with practical matters, involved me in the research activities of the department, and, when needed, provided me with solitude to write the bulk of this book. The monthly seminar of the Polish Association of Cultural Studies proved to be a vibrant and provocative forum where I could discuss my work. I would like to thank the colleagues who read chapters, asked probing questions, and provided helpful comments following my talk in May 2023. I thank, in particular, the discussant, Małgorzata Domagalska, and seminar participants Katarzyna Anzorge, Łukasz Biskupski, Agnieszka Rejniak-Majewska, and Tomasz Majewski.

My appreciation also extends to the staff at the University Press of Mississippi who took interest in this project from the start and provided me with generous page space to expand the manuscript. I am grateful to Lisa McMurtray, Michael Martella, Todd Lape, Katie Turner, Joey Brown, Amy Atwood, and Jordan Nettles for their good nature and patience. The feedback of the two anonymous readers helped me look at the drawings with a fresh pair of eyes and make this book better.

A number of colleagues and friends supported me in the writing of this book in other ways. Some provided much-needed diversion; others read chapters, looked at the cartoons with me, and offered suggestions for archival research. I would like to thank, in particular, Kasia Błażewska, Alex Drace-Francis, Iwona Guść, Kalina Kupczyńska, Diederik Oostdijk, Kees Ribbens, Ola Sikora, and Michał Turski. I am also grateful to Randall Bytwerk for answering my query about visual propaganda in Nazi Germany.

Last but certainly not least is the family: I thank my husband for bringing joy and wisdom to my life. And I thank my mother, Weronika, most of all.

ABBREVIATIONS

Camp of National Unity (Obóz Zjednoczenia Narodowego, OZN, Ozon)
Christian National Party (Stronnictwo Chrześcijańsko-Narodowe, SChN)
Communist Party of Poland (Komunistyczna Partia Polski, KPP)
National Democracy (Narodowa Demokracja, ND, Endecja)
National Party (Stronnictwo Narodowe, SN)
National Radical Camp (Obóz Narodowo-Radykalny, ONR)
National Radical Movement (Ruch Narodowo-Radykalny, RNR)
Nonpartisan Bloc for Cooperation with the Government (Bezpartyjny Blok Współpracy z Rządem, BBWR)
Popular National Union (Związek Ludowo-Narodowy, ZLN)
Polish Peasant Party "Piast" (Polskie Stronnictwo Ludowe "Piast," PSL Piast)
Polish Socialist Party (Polska Partia Socjalistyczna, PPS)
Union of Young Poland (Związek Młodej Polski, ZMP)
Union of Independent Socialist Youth "Life" (Związek Niezależnej Młodzieży Socjalistycznej "Życie," ZNMS "Życie")

CARTOONS AND ANTISEMITISM

INTRODUCTION

On 24 November 1928, during a Sejm (Polish parliament) session, Polish Jewish MP Yitzhak Gruenbaum presented an antisemitic caricature to his fellow deputies. The drawing portrayed a German man wearing a spiked helmet, the Pickelhaube, associated with the Prussian Army. When turned upside down, the illustration revealed a denigrating representation of a Jewish person. As he showed the drawing to his Sejm colleagues, Gruenbaum alerted the audience that the image had brought about a violent attack on a Jew, before citing specific publications in the country that perpetrated similar instances of hateful caricature and reporting. Listing this and other cases of anti-Jewish activity and discrimination, Gruenbaum argued that they "undermined the rule of law [domestically] and sullied the reputation of Poland [abroad]."[1]

The cartoon displayed by Gruenbaum in the Sejm was by no means a novelty to local audiences. Antisemitic caricature had been present in the Polish lands since at least the mid-nineteenth century, but it was only in the beginning of the twentieth century that widespread anti-Jewish imagery emerged in the print media.[2] The influx in the first decade of the twentieth century of Litvaks and of Russian- and Yiddish-speaking Jews from the territories of the former Grand Duchy of Lithuania into large cities such as Warsaw and Łódź led to an escalation of antisemitic sentiment. It was around this time that the Polish right-wing press established some of the lasting tropes of Jews as provocateurs, disloyal noncitizens, and ruthless exploiters.[3] Following establishment of the independent Polish state in 1918, antisemitic portrayals became a trademark of many mainstream satirical magazines, such as *Mucha* (*Fly*), *Szczutek* (*Fillip*), and *Żółta Mucha* (*Yellow Fly*). Some outlets made it their raison d'être to combat the so-called Judaization of Poland, using the cartoon format as part of that supposed struggle. These included such far-right magazines and newspapers as *Samoobrona Narodu* (*National Self-Defense*), *Kurier Poznański* (*Poznań Courier*), *Pod Pręgierz* (*Under the Pillory*), and *Szabes Kurier* (*Sabbath Courier*).[4]

Following the death of Poland's de facto leader Józef Piłsudski in 1935, the antisemitic discourse of two major ethno-nationalist forces, the National Democracy (Endecja)—by then rebranded as the National Party (SN)—and its youth offshoot, the National Radical Camp, intensified further. Mob violence followed, including pogroms in Grodno and Przytyk as well as antisemitic riots in Odrzywół, Raciąż, and Suwałki in 1935 and 1936 respectively.[5] The final years before the outbreak of the Second World War were marked by intensification of the economic campaign against the Jews, escalation of physical attacks in the universities, and widespread calls for Jewish emigration, among others.[6] All of these events were reflected in the political cartoons of the time and discussed on all sides of the political spectrum.

Well-known illustrators, such as Kazimierz Grus, Paweł Griniow, Edmund Heydak, Włodzimierz Bartoszewicz, Kamil Mackiewicz, Bogdan Nowakowski, Julian Żebrowski, Marian Walentynowicz, and Maja Berezowska, all had a history of drawing antisemitic cartoons.[7] Grus, in particular, specialized in this type of content, contributing vilifying portrayals of Jewish people to *Szczutek*, *Kurier Poznański*, *Żółta Mucha*, and *Szabes Kurier*, among other magazines.[8] He was also the author of an antisemitic comic strip, "Ucieszne przygody obieżyświatów" ("The Enjoyable Adventures of Two Globetrotters"), published by *Orędownik* (*The Spokesman*) in 1936. In it, two impoverished protagonists, Prot and Gerwazy, fought numerous Jewish villains, including smugglers, human traffickers, communists, and greedy shop owners, who supposedly dominated the country to the disadvantage of ethnic Poles.[9]

Visual content was, no doubt, the easiest way of spreading and affirming negative stereotypes, particularly in this society that still had widespread illiteracy.[10] The Catholic press, too, contributed to that wider trend, employing caricature and other anti-Jewish visual content.[11] The end of the 1930s, in particular, was a period of heightened antisemitic propaganda and was also when the "Jewish question" appeared in satirical magazines most often.[12] According to scholar Dariusz Konstantynów, such content was meant to mobilize the people to support the battle for *odżydzanie Polski* (de-Judaization of Poland) in which Endecja's founder Roman Dmowski, the young fighters of the National Radical Camp, and ethno-nationalist journalists had participated for years. Many of the publications mentioned above could thus be seen as alternately condoning and encouraging violence.[13]

Left-wing political and social groups were not absent from this debate, publicly protesting the rising tide of antisemitism. In 1935–1936, the Polish Socialist Party physically confronted the pickets and fighting squads of SN. In a similar way, the Communist Party of Poland appealed to all antifascist groups in the country to combat the "pogrom atmosphere" as well as calling all Polish and minority workers to form special defense units within trade unions. Another leftist organization, the League for the Protection of the Rights of Man and the Citizen, warned in the beginning of 1936 that antisemitic discourse was a way of diverting public attention from more pressing political and economic issues. Similarly, in the industrial city of Łódź, a grassroots group was established by workers, students, and clergymen to combat expressions of antisemitism and associated propaganda in the media.[14] Print media in Yiddish (including the Zionist *Haynt* and Folkist *Der Moment*) as well as some liberal leftist magazines in Polish, such as *Szpilki* (*Pins*) and *Wiadomości Literackie* (*Literary News*), also participated in these efforts.[15] These outlets used visual and verbal satire to protest the discriminatory policies and violence in Poland and to warn against the fascist threat in Europe more generally.[16]

POLITICAL CARTOONS AND THE "JEWISH QUESTION" IN POLAND

Scholars have shown that political cartoons have been a useful vehicle for voicing various political agendas, from anti-state dissent to state-sponsored propaganda.[17] Due to their traditional national focus, visual culture such as this has been also said to contribute to the transformation of national identities, while mobilizing citizens to undertake a struggle for various topical causes.[18] According to Chris Lamb, historically, most great cartoonists were passionate about improving their societies, casting a jaundiced eye on everything they considered unjust and in need of reform.[19] More generally, cartoonists have been romanticized as the guardians of free speech who are the first to recognize and challenge internal and external threats that endanger democratic values.[20]

Although the study of antisemitism has been a burgeoning field for quite some time, less attention has been paid to how twentieth-century visual culture proliferated anti-Jewish sentiment and, in so doing, participated in the ethno-nationalist project.[21] Even less consideration has been given to political cartoons in Eastern Europe, and the research that does exist has focused mostly on the Cold War and the associated international power struggle.[22] Historians, generally, have been slow to incorporate political cartoons into their analyses.[23] Richard Scully and Marian Quartly argue that while written sources tend to be subject to in-depth critical analysis, historians treat cartoons either as supporting evidence or ornamental material that is presumed to be self-explanatory.[24] But as work in the field shows, for nearly three centuries now cartoons have been an important "instrument for the formulation and expression of public attitudes and emotions."²⁵ According to Thomas Milton Kemnitz, cartoons "remind the historian of the importance contemporaries placed on seemingly insignificant events and of the relation between these occurrences, popular attitudes, and public opinion."²⁶ As some of the more recent debates around the medium suggest, political cartoons and caricature can also provide useful material with which to study multicultural societies and the social tensions inherent to such societies.²⁷ Analyzing such material historically—that is, in the context of contemporary discourses and opinion sources of the day—can also help shed light on how print media and visual culture contribute to the spread of political ideology.²⁸

This book seeks to examine how Polish interwar illustrators and editors responded to a variety of interrelated issues surrounding the so-called Jewish question. Focusing on five major satirical weeklies of the 1930s, from far-right outlets to the antifascist magazines of the liberal left, the book argues that political cartoons became instrumental in communicating both reactionary and radical content in ways that, though not necessarily novel, were not available to other types of journalistic work. Utilizing the pictorial metaphor, exaggeration, and ironic detachment typical of the medium, interwar illustrators were able to voice political commentary more succinctly and forcefully than their colleagues elsewhere. In doing so, they pursued a unique mode of politics that was both intellectual and artistic. Because it went hand in hand with the unprecedented spread of satirical print media and a drive toward urbanization and modernization, this visual politics could now reach a growing number of readers. These audiences were predominantly urban and middle class, and the artists often responded to metropolitan concerns around integration and interfaith mingling. What they also did is to employ the figure of the Jew as a rhetorical crutch with which to reflect on wider social, economic, and political issues.

This book analyses those portrayals in their specific historical context as well as discussing the political economy surrounding their production and dissemination. Thus, rather than looking at the caricatures in isolation, the study links the magazines and their output to the economic, political, and personal factors that shaped the satirical media industry. These factors include the identities of the producers, sources of funding, and the impact of state censorship on the operation of a specific outlet, among others. Paying special attention to the people behind the magazines, this book underscores the need for deanonymization of the producer. Here, interwar caricatures emerge not only as a window into the various uses of satire and political debates of the day, but also as important sources with which to examine a whole generation of political commentators—illustrators, writers, and editors—some of whom came of age in the independent Polish state and actively cocreated the political landscape of that state. In its focus on these historical actors, the book shows that antisemitic caricature was as much about the artistic conventions and political climate of the time as it was about the individual creators and their vision of political journalism.

Speaking more broadly, *Cartoons and Antisemitism* reconstructs what the late interwar media *told* their readers about Jews and how this fit in with wider discussions surrounding the minority question. Thus, rather than exploring what contemporary audiences made of that content and how caricature affected the reality on the ground, a difficult task in its own right, this study maps the existing satirical discourses and provides a tentative diagnosis as to their impact on the state of interwar democracy and its rapid decline on the eve of the Second World War.

SATIRICAL WEEKLIES IN INTERWAR POLAND

The first examples of caricature in the Polish lands can be traced back to medieval art, including the famous altar of Veit Stoss in St. Mary's Church in Kraków, which used caricatural representation. In the sixteenth and seventeenth centuries, caricature largely developed as an anonymous art form, with only a few names, such as Maciej Morawa and Teodor Konica, surviving in the annals of the medium. In the two centuries that followed, visual satire became a common feature of the ascending print media, while during the Partitions, particularly in the second half of the nineteenth century, many famous painters, including Aleksander Gierymski, Jan Matejko, Juliusz Kossak, and Stanisław Wyspiański, pursued caricature drawing.[29]

The establishment of the Polish state in 1918 provided favorable conditions for the development of full-fledged satirical magazines and brought about an unprecedented flourishing of the medium of political cartoon. Scholars estimate that between 1918 and 1939 there were more than two hundred satirical and humor weeklies in the country.[30] Most of them were either short-lived or locally bound, and the actual number of outlets that were truly influential was much lower. Historians of Polish satire assess that only up to twenty-five weeklies were distributed more widely.[31] This was a fast-changing sector, and comparable fluctuations were typical for much of the other periodical press. Overall, the numbers of print media outlets were fairly high: in 1932, a total of 1,831 titles were available in Poland. This figure increased to 1,855 in 1933, 1,859 in 1934, and 2,186 in 1935.[32] This large number of newspapers and other periodicals was not that surprising considering Poland's population had reached thirty-two million by 1931. Approximately twenty-two million declared Polish to be their first language, and many others were bilingual or trilingual.³³ The rise of literacy and the steady increase in the urban population, from just above six million in 1921 to nearly nine million in 1931, contributed to the emergence of a new generation of readers.³⁴

Print media were easily accessible to Poland's interwar population. According to media historian Andrzej Paczkowski, toward the end of the 1920s one million daily newspapers were sold in Polish, Yiddish, German, Ukrainian, Russian, and other languages spoken in the country.³⁵ In 1938, this figure had doubled, with the actual number of readers being potentially much higher.³⁶ The average cost of a newspaper was between five and fifteen groszy.³⁷ Satirical weeklies were more expensive, ranging on average from twenty to thirty groszy, with lower rates available for quarterly subscribers.³⁸ In comparison, the monthly salary of an average worker came to around two hundred zloty per month.³⁹ Thus, while reading the cheaper dailies was affordable and enabled readers to keep abreast of current affairs, satirical weeklies provided a more exclusive form of political commentary that was often combined with light entertainment.⁴⁰

Three cities were the hub of interwar visual satire in Poland: Warsaw, Lviv, and Kraków. The early interwar scene was dominated by the Lviv-based *Szczutek* (1918–1926), which brought together Poland's most talented artists such as Kazimierz Grus, Kazimierz Sichulski, Kamil Mackiewicz, Józef Doskowski, and others.⁴¹ *Szczutek* was crucial in negotiating the transition to the independent state in November 1918, as seen in Poland's first serial comic strip, *Ogniem i mieczem, czyli przygody szalonego Grzesia* (*With Fire and Sword or the Adventures of Mad Grześ*, 1919), which told the story of the consolidation of Poland's borders between 1918 and 1920.⁴² When *Szczutek* closed down, the space was filled by *Cyrulik Warszawski* (*The Barber of Warsaw*) (1926–1934), a magazine that brought together many liberal and progressive writers and illustrators, notwithstanding the funding it received from the Sanacja government.⁴³ In 1935, young illustrators from Warsaw established a new liberal magazine called *Szpilki* (1935–1939, 1945–1994), which continued the liberal tradition of *Cyrulik*, becoming one of the major liberal magazines of the interwar period.⁴⁴

These publications coexisted with two other magazines that had a more popular profile. The first of those, *Mucha* (1868–1939, 1945–1952), had militant anti-tsarist beginnings, being funded under the Russian imperial rule. After the establishment of independent Poland in 1918, it followed the official state line, irrespective of successive changes in government.⁴⁵ The second magazine, *Wróble na Dachu* (*Sparrows on the Roof*) (1933–1939), which operated in Kraków and was distributed nationwide, had a more commercial profile. It avoided overt attacks on both the government and specific political figures, its chief concern being to maintain high sales by providing light entertainment.[46] This list can be supplemented with ephemeral publications that were distributed both nationwide and at the local level. Two right-wing magazines discussed in this study, the Warsaw-based *Szarża* (*Charge*) and the provincial *Pokrzywy* (*Nettles*), were such ephemera. Despite being short-lived, they were the chief satirical magazines of the antisemitic right, with a strong political profile and an ambition to counteract the liberalizing forces of *Szpilki* and others.

The 1930s was the golden age of the Polish satirical press. Scholars estimate that the three major magazines of the time, *Szpilki*, *Mucha*, and *Wróble*, which make up the bulk of the material studied here, had a joint circulation of approximately 100,000 copies per week.[47] These figures tend to be tentative, however, and largely different from numbers recorded in the recollections of interwar magazine editors and illustrators, who often cite lower numbers.[48] What is certain, however, is that both *Mucha* and *Wróble* were mainstream middle-of-the-road magazines that enjoyed the greatest popularity. The leftist *Szpilki* was popular with liberal urban intellectuals, selling relatively few copies, while *Szarża* was aimed at the ethno-nationalist reader. Despite catering to audiences of different ideological persuasions, the latter two were addressed to a politically engaged reader. *Pokrzywy*, which had the lowest circulation, was the only magazine focused on smaller towns and villages, specifically in the conservative region of Greater Poland. It was also the only satirical magazine established with the exclusive goal of fighting the so-called Judaization of Poland, being modelled on similar nonsatirical periodicals and newspapers.

Each magazine published the work of a different set of artists, many of whom specialized in particular themes. *Wróble*, for example, could pride itself in working with the leading illustrators of the time, including Mieczysław Piotrowski (1910–1977), Karol Ferster a.k.a. Charlie (1902–1986), Bronisław Schneider (1915–1943), and others. *Szpilki* tapped into the pool of younger antifascist artists, such as Eryk Lipiński (1908–1991), Mendel Reif (1910–1942), and Jakub Bickels (1911–1944). *Mucha* collaborated with established conservative illustrators, including Stanisław Rydygier (ca. 1890–ca. 1958), Bronisław Fedyszyn (1900–1940), and Władysław Leski (1907–1969). Much of the visual satire of the time was anonymous, however, and it is no longer possible to identify many of the artists. This is also the case for all of the original cartoons in the antisemitic *Pokrzywy* and, to some extent, in the ethno-nationalist *Szarża*, although the latter did work with talented artists of the younger generation, such as Julian Żebrowski (1915–2002). In general, *Wróble* and *Szpilki* were a magnet for Poland's most accomplished illustrators, the former providing ample space for drawings as well as a steady source of income, and the latter building the liberal credentials of many young artists of the time. The cartoons in *Mucha* and *Pokrzywy* were generally of a lower standard and often hateful, which made anonymity an understandable choice on the part of their artists.[49]

ANTISEMITIC DISCOURSE IN INTERWAR POLAND

The mid-1930s marked a radical shift in Polish politics. In the words of historian Ezra Mendelsohn, "violent anti-Semitism made a dramatic reappearance."[50] This development stemmed from a combination of factors, including economic stagnation and the rise of right-wing authoritarianism. The death of Piłsudski in 1935 played a part in the escalation of anti-Jewish sentiment. During his life, Piłsudski was able to hold extreme antisemitism in check despite facing a powerful political force, that of Endecja and, later, its radical youth offshoot, the National Radical Camp, which considered Jews "an alien, mafialike race" who "were to be excluded from any form of assimilation."[51]

Following Piłsudski's death, his own movement, Sanacja, grew increasingly divided over the "Jewish question." On 7 February 1937, the Camp of National Unity (Ozon) emerged from Sanacja, calling for intensification of the ongoing struggle against Jews with a view to reducing their number in Poland. Citing overpopulation and economic crisis, as well as arguing that Jews were inherently "foreign" to the Polish nation, the group gave the green light to bottom-up efforts aimed at eliminating Jews from various sectors of the economy, culture, education, and industry.[52] The emergence of Ozon and further utterances from the ruling camp also put an end to the traditional view of Sanacja as protecting the Jews or even being a "puppet government" controlled by the Jewish minority.[53]

Although the mid- to late 1930s was a period of virulent and widespread antisemitism in Poland, manifestations of anti-Jewish sentiment were present throughout the interwar years.[54] According to historian Paul Brykczynski, a novel brand of antisemitism had already surfaced during the elections of the early 1920s when "Endek [those associated with Endecja] politicians and journalists constructed an entirely new and starkly concrete narrative of a Jewish conspiracy to take over the very government of Poland, in alliance with the Polish left."⁵⁵ Research on anti-Jewish discrimination and violence shows that the 1920s was a decade when such sentiments were consolidated, particularly among the ethno-nationalist youth.⁵⁶ The exclusive and anti-pluralistic nature of Polish nationalism and Polish Catholicism has often been cited as a major contributing factor.⁵⁷ At the same time, scholars show that Endecja's vilifying of the Jews originated much earlier, during the Revolution of 1905, when the traditional national enemy of Russia was replaced with the Jews and the Polish left.⁵⁸ These findings are corroborated by historians of Polish visual culture who, likewise, view 1905 as the turning point in portrayals of the Jewish population in the Polish lands.⁵⁹ Correspondingly, research on antisemitic cartoons shows that the 1920s brought a proliferation of anti-Jewish imagery in the Polish media before reaching its peak in the mid- to late 1930s.⁶⁰

Between 1937 and 1938, the highest number of Jewish-themed drawings appeared in the antisemitic *Pokrzywy* (more than 20 percent of all illustrations), followed by the liberal *Szpilki* (approximately 9 percent) and the commercially minded *Wróble na Dachu* (4.4 percent). Although the pro-government *Mucha* devoted fewer illustrations to the Jewish minority (2.6 percent), its frequent focus on the foreign policy of Poland (7.5 percent) as well as on broader international developments (28.9 percent) often invited reflections on the so-called Jewish question.⁶¹ Among all of Poland's ethnic minorities, Ukrainians and Germans included, Jews attracted the most attention from Polish caricaturists. The representations of Jews were more affecting and incendiary than portrayals of the other two ethnic groups, which reflected wider political realities and existing debates at both top-down and bottom-up levels.⁶²

Despite their mirror-like qualities, interwar cartoons were hardly a passive medium that merely reproduced the reality. In fact, as historians of the medium propose, due to "their emotive nature, their relative immediacy and their many-layered meanings," cartoons potentially helped "crystallise attitudes" as well as expressing "the thinking of a broad segment of society."⁶³ It is true that almost no historical sources exist to elucidate the impact of such cartoons on interwar audiences and, conversely, the impact of the reading public on the artists. We have no way of knowing what readers thought about the content presented in those magazines and how it affected their actions. The scarce and fragmented documentation that exists about interwar media contains no survey results or other evidence that would help us understand this. However, what this study demonstrates with certainty is that the satirical output of the time can be a useful yardstick with which to measure the manner, extent, and frequency of anti-Jewish reporting and its entanglement with other pronouncements on the topic, be they official statements or nonsatirical journalism.

SOURCES AND STRUCTURE

This book studies interwar cartoons from five Polish-language weeklies, *Mucha*, *Pokrzywy*, *Szpilki*, *Szarża*, and *Wróble na Dachu*, as a way of exploring how the so-called Jewish problem was portrayed by illustrators on different sides of the political spectrum. My choice of these five magazines was determined by their visibility among other satirical print media of the day and the intensity of their involvement with the topic. The variety of portrayals and drawing styles seen in these five magazines was meant to cater to the tastes of a cross-section of the Polish-speaking majority. Although "it is difficult at times to decide whether the artist is influencing the public or the public the artist," as one scholar argues in another context, the cartoons analyzed here imply a dialogic relationship between readers (as elusive as they may be), the cartoonist, and the political forces in place.[64] Being dependent on both sales and state censorship, interwar illustrators of all political persuasions engaged in a complex balancing act involving these different actors.[65]

The division of chapters by magazine is also motivated by how the five periodicals approached satire. For *Mucha*, which ventriloquized the hegemonic discourse, humor served as a weapon against those who undermined the interests of the state, the "state" being equated with the government. *Pokrzywy* believed in the coercive function of satire, calling local inhabitants by name to change their Judeophiliac ways and pursue nationalist interests. To the leftist artists and writers behind *Szpilki*, satire was a means to show the ugliness of antisemitism and a way to imagine a reality without it. In contrast, *Szarża* hoped to fight communism, Sanacja, and the Jews. It did all these things but in ways that were often imprinted with the double perspective of its Jewish editor who was forced to operate incognito. *Wróble na Dachu* placed commercial success above all else. Despite offering quality satire, it was politically noncommittal, veering between antifascism and occasional mild anti-Jewish stereotyping.

None of these magazines existed in a void, and, like political cartoons in other countries, the visual culture of interwar Poland was pervaded with intertextual references. These references alluded not only to political figures and topical issues of the time. They also built upon existing discourses in daily newspapers and the periodical press, by either advocating or disputing specific viewpoints. Some of the magazines in question, most notably *Szpilki*,

Pokrzywy, and *Szarża*, were also in an implicit dialogue with each other. One way of entering into that dialogue was to deliberate over the social role of satire. The freedom to produce satire, whether the visual or textual kind, was seen by those authors and artists as an important civil and political right. Irrespective of their ideological persuasion, most of the five weeklies professed a shared commitment to satirical expression, viewing it as an important facet of democracy. Except for the progovernment *Mucha*, the creators behind all of these magazines agreed that state censorship brought about a demise of satire in addition to endangering democracy and free speech.

Aside from tackling political content in ways that were discrete to Poland, the cartoons analyzed in this book also engaged with transnational modes of representation. It is true that only a few of these weeklies proliferated Christian anti-Judaism that had been present in European visual culture since the Middle Ages.[66] However, other tropes such as those of "Judeo-Communism" or "the worldwide Jewish conspiracy," which had emerged in the nineteenth century and quickly became the hallmark of antisemitic caricature elsewhere, were more widespread in Poland. This would suggest that satirical magazines of the time, even the most antisemitic ones, aspired to more topical satire and avoided outdated themes such as deicide and blood libel. Instead, it was the radical right-wing newspapers of the time, including *Szabes Kurier* and *Pod Pręgierz*, that provided a platform for such portrayals.

This book shows that the political cartoons of interwar Poland also operated within a broader transnational framework of representation. It analyzes those tropes against the backdrop of wider antisemitic discourse as well as providing a tentative discussion of commonalities between Poland and other states. The book argues that, although the various debates on the "Jewish question" were closely tied to the political and cultural sensibilities of the interwar republic, many representational strategies used by the illustrators were global and could be understandable to readers elsewhere. As such, following historians in other national contexts, this project emphasizes the need for more transnationally oriented studies of cartoons.[67] It demonstrates that anti-Jewish drawings too can be subject to such an analysis and that national studies such as this could be a starting point for further inquiries into the topic.

Cartoons and Antisemitism consists of five chapters of analysis. The book begins with an examination of anti-Jewish caricatures in the progovernment *Mucha* magazine in chapter 1. *Mucha* was a national magazine, with reporting focused predominantly on foreign policy efforts to find territories for Jewish settlement, a plan meant to lead to a mass Jewish exodus from Poland. This content was accompanied by more "folkloric" representations of Polish

Jews. While perpetuating what one scholar described as "weak antisemitism," *Mucha*'s portrayals normalized anti-Jewish stereotyping and presented it as a supposedly harmless and permissible lighthearted entertainment.[68] The chapter shows that its long-term editor in chief, Władysław Buchner, was central to enforcing such an editorial line, while perpetuating a style of satire that was becoming anachronistic in the print media of the interwar era.

Chapter 2 takes us to the geographical stronghold of right-wing satire: the region of Greater Poland. Using the case study of the *Pokrzywy* magazine, the chapter discusses how the provincial print media strived to effect change from the bottom up by mobilizing the local people to boycott Jewish enterprises and shaming those ethnic Poles who patronized Jewish businesses. The chapter shows that the magazine disseminated some of the most venomous antisemitic caricatures of the day, combining ad hominem attacks on local citizens with global tropes of Jews as dangerous exploiters, conspirators, and communists. While the former portrayals were the creation of local amateur artists, the latter were most likely illegal reprints from foreign antisemitic outlets. Combining local vignettes with transnational visual tropes demonstrates that, despite its focus on provincial affairs, the people behind the magazine were also cognizant of and eagerly embracing global trends in antisemitic representation.

Focusing on the progressive magazine *Szpilki*, chapter 3 demonstrates how Jewish and non-Jewish artists and journalists joined forces to protest the overwhelming climate of hate in the country, as well as drawing attention to international threats such as the rise of fascism. The chapter argues that, despite functioning in a milieu that was becoming increasingly authoritarian and dominated by the divisive rhetoric of the far right, the magazine was able to carve out spaces of satirical freedom, testing the limits of state censorship and, effectively, sustaining democratic thinking.

Chapter 4 questions the ideological intentionality on which much antisemitic representation is believed to hinge. It does so by analyzing a short-lived ethno-nationalist magazine, *Szarża*, which hoped to fight the alleged Jewish control over Polish art, culture, and economy, while surreptitiously hiring Henryk Szpigiel, a highly skilled editor in chief of Jewish ancestry. The chapter argues that traces of Szpigiel's double perspective can be found in the magazine, making it a conflicted commentary on Polish-Jewish cohabitation. Importantly, the chapter demonstrates that the history of *Szarża* adds a new perspective to our knowledge of the actors and motivations behind the antisemitic satire of interwar Poland.

Chapter 5 unpacks the idea of satirical impartiality by examining a popular nonpartisan weekly from Kraków, *Wróble na Dachu*. The chapter discusses how the ethnically and politically diverse staff of *Wróble* approached antisemitic discourse, from militant drawings that attacked the perpetrators of anti-Jewish violence to stereotypical portrayals of Jews that, like *Mucha*'s drawings, normalized antisemitism. Shying away from political partisanship and establishing entertainment as its raison d'être, the magazine was able to bridge various viewpoints as part of its supposed neutrality. In its attempt to appeal to a cross section of Polish society, the magazine also reflected the myriad perspectives that existed on the "Jewish question" within Polish society more generally.

The conclusion brings together the various strands of my argument and emphasizes the centrality of individual artists and editors in the making of the visual politics of the time. It also underscores how the political cartoons produced in Poland participated in global debates about the supposed Jewish threat and the rise of fascism, as well as documenting the ebbs and flows of domestic debates. The conclusion shows that, in the interbellum, unlike today, political cartoons played an especially important role in creating affective communities of artists, editors, and the ever-elusive readers, who were passionate about the visual medium and trusting in its ability to bring about radical social change.

Chapter 1

THE VOICE OF THE STATE

In September 1934, the Polish Association of the Publishers of Daily and Periodical Press in Warsaw received an announcement of the death of Maria Buchnerowa, née Pajewska, the wife of Władysław Buchner, association board member and long-term editor of the satirical magazine *Mucha*. Buchnerowa, who passed away on 31 August, was described as "a woman of higher mind" (*kobieta o umyśle wyższym*) who was steadfast in supporting her husband in editorial activities and maintaining a proper observance of publishing standards. Buchnerowa was a true literature lover too, who was always eager to advise her companion on how to capture a specific piece of news using an appropriate literary genre. Above all, she was a compassionate person, sensitive to human misfortune and always ready to help those in need.[1]

By the time his wife passed away, Buchner was seventy-four, having been the editor of *Mucha* for forty-six years. Born in 1860, he had begun his journalistic career in 1882, working for several newspapers and weekly magazines of the time, before acquiring *Mucha* in 1888 to become its publisher and editor in chief.[2] By the mid-1930s, his militant years were long over. The revolution of 1905, which constituted the heyday of his activity as a satirist, brought him fame and recognition in the profession. It was around that time that the magazine, which had originated in Warsaw, then part of the Russian Empire, turned into a hub of anti-tsarist satire, making Buchner a victim of repeated attacks. To avoid censorship and persecution by the authorities, in 1906–1907 the magazine appeared under a number of conspiratorial titles, such as *Motyl* (*Butterfly*), *Wróbel* (*Sparrow*), *Kukułka* (*Cuckoo*), *Kruk* (*Raven*), and *Bąk* (*Bumblebee*), all drawn from ornithological and entomological vocabularies, while the editor himself was forced to escape persecution to the more liberal city of Kraków, then under Austro-Hungarian rule.[3]

After establishment of the Polish Republic in 1918, the weekly welcomed the political reality for which it had fought under the Partitions, gradually becoming the mouthpiece for the Sanacja government.[4] Having outlasted the tsar, Buchner saw it "a natural duty of every publisher" to engage in "strenuous work for the state."[5] It comes as no surprise, then, that after the death of Marshal Piłsudski in 1935, *Mucha*, like other state-aligned outlets, continued to support the authorities, despite their gradual shift toward authoritarianism.[6]

With his wife and intellectual companion gone in 1934, Buchner was forced to shoulder editorial responsibilities alone, with his son Władysław Buchner Jr. occasionally featuring in official records as deputy editor.[7] This was a family enterprise through and through, but one in which Buchner Sr. played a central role. In an annual statement sent to the Polish Association of the Publishers of Daily and Periodical Press in 1937, Buchner's assistant declared that *Mucha* had only one member of the editorial staff, presumably Buchner himself, and one administrative employee, most likely the author of the statement. Four illustrators working for the magazine on a noncontract basis contributed drawings "for cash."[8] Such a small portfolio of contributors, combined with an aging editor in chief, meant that by the mid-1930s there was no longer scope for satirical experimentation. Every issue of the magazine bore the imprint of the editor's traditionalist tastes and style of satire. Conservative at best, the magazine offered no space for new ideas and ideological ferment, maintaining instead the political status quo. Nevertheless, *Mucha* commanded the respect of many. It had been in existence since 1868, having won an established place in the market and boasting high sales figures of approximately thirty thousand copies per week.[9] This made it well positioned to become Sanacja's mouthpiece, a special role in a satirical landscape in which both the socialist left and the ethno-nationalist right were intensely critical of the government.

Throughout the mid- to late 1930s, *Mucha* pursued Sanacja's agenda with consistency, reporting on domestic and foreign policy issues in a regime-friendly manner and adjusting the tone of its journalism to the ebbs and flows of official discourse. Adhering to Buchner's own political proclivities, the magazine professed a strong distrust of the Soviet Union and an ambivalent attitude toward the international community, the League of Nations included. Above all, *Mucha* provided steady coverage of the so-called Jewish question. It discussed the widespread calls for Jewish emigration, the ongoing persecution of Jews in other European states, and the supposed threat of a mass refugee crisis following intensification of anti-Jewish persecution in fascist Italy, Nazi Germany, and elsewhere.

As the government's efforts to engineer a mass exodus of Polish Jews deepened in the second half of the 1930s, Buchner followed suit with relevant representations of the group meant to persuade readers that Jews were fundamentally different from the Christian majority. Like the government,

Mucha's editor believed it was possible to resolve the "Jewish problem" in the international arena, using diplomatic means, as well as domestically by employing softer tactics of discrimination and deterrence. While it is difficult to assess the persuasive qualities of such satire without audience research since no surveys exist that could illuminate the impact of interwar cartoons and satirical writing on contemporary readers, *Mucha*'s coverage of the "Jewish problem" adds an important dimension to the existing discussion of interwar antisemitism. It points to the pervasiveness of milder forms of antisemitism in the public sphere, not only in their capacity to propagate negative stereotypes but also to normalize condescending portrayals of Jews as the unwanted minority to be expunged from the country. *Mucha* thus pandered to the tastes of those readers who might have wished for a "de-Judaized" Poland but saw "de-Judaization" as an issue of internal and foreign policy, rather than a patriotic obligation of all ethnic Poles.

MIGRATION, PALESTINE, AND JEWS AS "EXPORT PRODUCT"

Mucha's editorial policy on migration mirrored the government's preoccupation with finding a distant territory for Jewish settlement, whether in Madagascar, a common topic of discussion at the time, or elsewhere. The magazine often reported on the ongoing talks with Western powers, which Sanacja and its sympathizers saw as a necessary step to resolve the so-called Jewish question. In 1938 alone, when such discussions reached their apogee, the magazine published nearly ten cartoons on the putative Jewish emigration. This was supplemented by a host of literary material, such as epigrams, anecdotes, and satirical poems pertaining to the topic. Like some of the other satirical magazines, *Mucha* also reported on the Madagascar plan in early 1938, immediately after results of the fact-finding mission to the island were made public in Poland.

Those references to the so-called Madagascar plan were highly topical. Already in 1936, the Polish Foreign Ministry had entered into talks with the French minister of the colonies, Marius Moutet, about the possibility of setting up a colony on the island and transporting Polish Jews there. The following year, in spring 1937, the Polish government sent a fact-finding mission to the colony to examine the possibilities of mass Jewish settlement.[10] Although the mission's findings were far from encouraging and Polish Jews themselves were apprehensive of the project, the putative Jewish colony in Madagascar became a widely discussed topic in the media. Right-wing

1.1. The Exchange of Colonial Products, from *Mucha*, 7 January 1938, 4.

outlets, in particular, presented the plan as both highly realistic and necessary to resolving a variety of problems, from the supposed overpopulation of Poland to widespread poverty.[11]

In a cartoon published on 7 January, *Mucha* presented the Jews as Poland's chief export product, a comparison used by the magazine twice more that same year. The cartoon portrayed personified France and Poland, Marianne and Polonia, respectively, exchanging colonial and national products (Figure 1.1). Marianne's gifts are plentiful. They include wine, grapes, tangerines, dates, sardines, and other goods. Polonia has only one export product—Jews. The Jew she is portrayed handing over to Marianne wears traditional garb: a black rekel and a kashket. The Jewish man is much smaller than the two women, a visual strategy that *Mucha* applied in other drawings too.[12] In March 1938, to address ongoing talks with the League of Nations concerning the worsening situation of European Jewry, *Mucha* published a similar cartoon that depicted a member of the Polish delegation passing a basket full of Jews to John Bull, a popular personification of Britain. The caption underneath reads: "This is our main export product for the years to come."[13] The same visual trope was used again in December 1938 in a cartoon showing a representative of the Polish government in the company of John Bull and Uncle Sam (Figure 1.2). Here the Polish official is drawing the two other men's attention to his basket of Jews as he lifts the cloth covering the basket. Alluding to the rise of antisemitic measures in Germany and the ensuing refugee crisis, the Pole is asking the two allies why they are concerned only with the fate of German Jews and not the fate of his "kiddies" (*pociechy*).[14]

The use of national personification was a common visual strategy for *Mucha*'s illustrators, even though the practice was being discontinued as old-fashioned by other magazines of the time.[15] Scholars show that some of the figures above had been present in caricature since the eighteenth century. In Britain, for example, John Bull came to be connected with a variety of domestic and international issues, from taxation to national defense.[16] Similarly, the combining of figures such as Uncle Sam and John Bull in late nineteenth-century American culture symbolized Anglo-American cultural and economic links, including what leaders of the day saw as a "co-leadership of global civilization" and "imperial internationalism."[17] Marianne, too, appeared in a range of contexts. For instance, historian Douglas Klahr argues that one German magazine used this allegorical figure around the time of the First World War to "project not only German attitudes toward France but also France's attitudes toward its societal decline, which was routinely aligned in the French press with issues of gender."[18] Historians of the political cartoon, including those working in such contexts as Germany during the First World War, Bulgaria and the Soviet Union in the 1920s, and the Netherlands in the Second World War, show that national personification was widespread in those countries too.[19] Importantly, scholars of the contemporary cartoon demonstrate that national personifications continue to fare well with present-day cartoonists and audiences.[20]

The enduring transnational popularity of national personifications notwithstanding, toward the end of the 1920s appeals were made to phase out the practice.[21] Well-known illustrators of the time viewed personifications as obsolete and advocated for their abolition. For instance, caricaturist David Low argued in 1937 that artists needed to abandon both anthropomorphic personification and animal allegory in their portrayals of nations and be

1.2. The Jewish Question at London Conference, from *Mucha*, 2 December 1938, 1.

more attuned to the changing spirit of the times. He contended that "New models are required for a world which, as it annihilates time and space with its speed machines, its sound machines, its vision machines, is annihilating also regional peculiarity." Low admitted nonetheless that to engender new visual symbols would be difficult because the various peoples were becoming increasingly similar and—to use today's language—"globalized." At the same time, he was adamant that "to perpetuate the old ones is to perpetuate confusion."[22] The majority of Polish cartoonists kept abreast of these innovations, and *Mucha* was one of the few remaining magazines to use personification until the outbreak of the Second World War.[23] Discussing interwar cartoons many years later, historians of Polish caricature described *Mucha*'s prolific use of personification as aimed at streamlining the message. At the same time, they were clear that *Mucha*'s use of such symbols was somewhat ingenuous.[24]

Aside from using transnational figures such as Uncle Sam, Marianne, John Bull, and Polonia, *Mucha* personified the Polish nation by drawing existing political figures. For example, a cartoon published in June 1938 presented Poland's foreign minister Józef Beck in a chef's hat, holding a cooking pot with a single Jew in it (Figure 1.3; see also this book's cover). The caption reads: "Let it go into the world. We don't like this dish."[25] The cartoon commented on domestic developments, specifically the "thirteen theses" passed by Sanacja's offshoot Camp of National Unity. The thirteen theses were approved during the group's meeting on 19–21 May and could be described as the Polish equivalent of the Nuremberg Laws of 1935. Specific theses proposed to reduce Poland's Jewish population, pass legislation that would decrease the number of Jews in certain professions, and retain the status of Palestine as the chief destination for Jewish immigration as well as securing new territories for settlement through diplomatic channels.[26] The Camp of National Unity, also known as OZN or Ozon, argued that the proposals were conceived to protect national interests and ensure "Poland's strength and greatness."[27]

While all four of these cartoons intimated that Poland's ambition to relocate Jews was an international issue, *Mucha*'s illustrators recognized that the international community did not necessarily share that sentiment. The two images presenting Polish Jews in a basket, in particular, emphasized the Allies' reticence to accept this unlikely gift as well as stressing the perceived incompetence of Roosevelt and Chamberlain in resolving the issue.[28] All four cartoons used a single Hasidic man to represent the whole population, turning the people into a suggestive visual stereotype meant to evoke religious traditionalism and lack of assimilation into mainstream Polish society. The man was also presented as an inanimate object of trade to be marketed to outside buyers because the product had no appeal to domestic consumers. Such representations mirrored Sanacja's approach to Poland's "Jewish question" as a problem of the international community rather than an issue that should be resolved internally.

Mucha's cartoons, including those discussed above, responded to bureaucratic arrangements within the Polish government that reflected the way Jews

1.3. The Anti-Jewish Decree of OZN, from *Mucha*, 10 June 1938, 3.

were seen by interwar Polish policymakers. Until Piłsudski's death, domestic matters surrounding Polish Jews were overseen by the Ministry of Interior, while issues relating to emigration were administered by the Consular Section of the Ministry of Foreign Affairs. This changed in 1935 when the entirety of Jewish affairs, both internal and external, was handed over to the Foreign Ministry.[29] Such administrative arrangements signaled the government's demarcation of the Jewish issue as the domain of international politics and heralded future plans to remove the Jewish population from Poland by means of diplomacy and organized emigration.

Mucha's satire mirrored the government's approach to the issue in yet another way. As many countries, including the United States, had curbed immigration from the early 1930s as a response to the economic crisis, Palestine (under the British mandate) continued to absorb the largest proportion of all Jewish immigrants, including those from Poland. In 1931 and 1932, Polish Jews were granted more than half of the overall number of entry certificates. This number dropped to a quarter in 1935 and 1936 as a result of the mass Jewish emigration from Germany.[30] After 1936, the flow of immigration into Palestine was reduced significantly following restrictions on entry introduced by the British as a reaction to Arab unrest.[31] *Mucha*'s reporting on the deteriorating situation of Jews in Europe tended to focus on these developments, rather than addressing the more urgent need of containing the spread of antisemitism in specific European states, Poland included. One cartoon by artist Bronisław Fedyszyn presented Palestine as a stronghold with a sign that says, "No room." It depicts John Bull leaning over the wall of the fortress, smoking a pipe and looking pensive, as desperate Jews from Czechoslovakia, Germany, Poland, and Romania demand entry. The caption warns that this is "Israel's new wailing wall."[32]

The cartoon is clearly critical of Britain. After all, this was the time when Polish officials continued to appeal to the British to open Palestine to Jewish colonization.[33] Due to the ongoing Arab unrest, these requests were not being honored. On the surface, Fedyszyn's drawing, and the humanity he affords to each and every one of his characters, appears to be sympathetic to Europe's would-be emigrants. They are a mix of traditional and assimilated Jews, suggesting the artist's attempt to avoid simplifications. Their frantic-looking faces and eyes wide open in apprehension show people in distress; their small suitcases that bear the names of different countries are meant to signify the few possessions they have brought with them. This is an evocative image of people in need of a homeland. Nevertheless, placing Polish, Czech, German, and Romanian Jews side by side is at odds with the supposed sympathy afforded to them by the artist. Such composition of the group would suggest that *Mucha* made no distinction between Poland's attempts to "de-Judaize" the country and the corresponding practices of full-fledged authoritarian regimes such as Nazi Germany, emerging dictatorships such as Romania, and post-Munich Czechoslovakia, victim of a recent Nazi invasion.[34] If compared with *Mucha*'s other cartoons on this topic, including one titled "The Colonies," which praised Hitler's methods of "dealing with the Jews," it can be presumed that to *Mucha* (as to many in the government) these were commendable practices worthy of emulating in Poland.[35]

There was a specific reason for *Mucha*'s mild approach to Hitler. As a pro-Sanacja outlet, *Mucha* supported the official line of nonaggression toward Germany, as approved by the bilateral treaty on 26 January 1934. This included the press accords of 24 February 1934 that stipulated the media follow similar rules.[36] Any content considered anti-German as well as representations that were offensive to Hitler personally were flagged by the German authorities, who recorded a steep rise in anti-German rhetoric in 1935.[37] Although the main focus of such complaints was on the Polish daily press, textbooks, and maps, some satirical outlets were targeted too.[38] However, unlike regular censorship by the Polish state, which led to confiscations prior to the issue hitting newsstands, such interventions usually happened ex post facto following criticism from the German legation. Despite being aligned with the state, *Mucha* was not immune to such interventions. On 18 November 1936, the German embassy in Warsaw demanded that an issue of *Mucha* from 11 September 1936 be retracted due to a supposedly belligerent cover representing the German chancellor.[39] Subsequently, the Polish Foreign Office requested that the Ministry of Interior confiscate the issue retrospectively.[40] Although the issue had by then been released and read, and the response from the German legation was belated, the symbolic value of such a retraction should not be underestimated. It was a way to caution the outlet and ensure that similar representations were avoided in the future.

The Polish-German nonaggression pact impacted Polish public life in yet another way: paired with the rising antisemitism in the Sanacja camp, it played a crucial role in the evolution of the government's anti-Jewish policies later on, in the second half of the 1930s.[41] *Mucha*'s cartoons from the late 1930s illustrated the various strands of this growing sentiment. Like its illustrations, the satirical poems and anecdotes published by the magazine were also vocal about the intention of the authorities to ensure a mass outflow of the Jewish population. As one satirical composition advised: "You need to be clever and cunning with the Jews. Mind you, when Haman wanted to drive them out, they stayed, but when Pharaoh wanted to stop them, they fled. Why not try Pharaoh's tactics? Who knows, these might work in Poland."[42] In the words of another, although "Jews eagerly bought old junk," it was hard to "pawn off" Madagascar on them, even though it was "as old as the world."[43] Persuading the Jews to leave, whether for Madagascar or another location, became one of *Mucha*'s chief endeavors.

Although unusual locations, such as Madagascar, attracted much attention from the media and some sections of the political establishment, the government continued to view Palestine as the primary destination for the presumed Jewish immigration.[44] After the Peel plan had been announced in July 1937, recommending the partition of Palestine into Jewish and Arab territories as a way of solving heightening tensions in the region, Poland's foreign minister, Józef Beck, repeatedly appealed to the League of Nations to expand the Jewish section into the Negev with access to the Red Sea.[45] In that respect, the ambitions of the Foreign Ministry overlapped with the goals of Revisionist Zionists who sought mass Jewish settlement in Palestine.[46] In 1936, the Revisionist Zionist leader Ze'ev Jabotinsky had approached the Polish government to request support for his "Evacuation Plan," which was to result in the departure of 1.5 million Jews for Palestine over the course of ten years. The Foreign Ministry responded favorably. Up until the outbreak of the Second World War, the government offered military training to Betar members, facilitated their illegal immigration to Palestine, and advocated for Jewish settlement in Palestine in the League of Nations.[47] Between 1936 and 1939, Polish authorities also exported weapons and military equipment to Palestine to support Jewish struggle against the Arabs.[48] These largely clandestine efforts to back Jabotinsky's organization were, by no means, at odds with the international proclamations by the government that highlighted the supposed threat posed by Jews to Polish national interests.[49]

The situation in Palestine, and in particular the Arab revolt against the British authorities and the Yishuv (the community of Jewish residents in Palestine prior to the establishment of Israel in 1948), which had gone on since 1936, was touched upon by *Mucha* too. In its largest and most evocative cartoon on the topic, called "The Palestinian Trotting," the Arab rebellion was depicted through a metaphor of harness racing. Here John Bull is portrayed as a jockey on a saddled horse, with a representative of the Yishuv sitting in the sulky. "Even the world's most famous jockey cannot ride this furious Arab mare!" complains the Jewish man in the sulky.[50] Indeed, the Arab horse in the cartoon is unruly, neither of the two men being able to control it. This and two other drawings that alluded to the revolt showed growing skepticism about the possibility of resuming Jewish immigration to Palestine. The second cartoon presented two middle-class Jews looking at a painting of a Palestinian Arab man. The man in the painting is portrayed wearing the keffiyeh head cover, baring his teeth, and taunting the viewer with a jambiya dagger. In the accompanying conversation, one of the men asks the other why he purchased the painting of that "scary Arab." The other responds: "To discourage myself from going to Palestine."[51] Skepticism as to whether the Palestinian plan was at all feasible was also expressed in a cartoon set in a kosher restaurant on Nalewki Street in the heart of the Jewish district in Warsaw, showing two Jewish men worrying that the revolt might bring about an influx of Jewish Palestinian refugees into Poland.[52]

Unlike some of the earlier-discussed images, the three drawings on Palestine presented mostly middle-class Jews. The second cartoon was particularly interesting in that regard. The painting's owner is an affluent man, indicated by his pot belly, flamboyant suit, and fashionable shoes. Using such physical characteristics and clothing style to portray acculturated Jews was not exclusive to the Polish print media. As scholar Julia Secklehner shows, Viennese interwar magazines also featured the stereotype of the "moneyed assimilated Jew of the haute bourgeoisie."[53] Cartoonists in other regional contexts applied a similar visual trope to connote the stereotype of greed, gluttony, and cosmopolitanism. Nonstandard bodies such as these constituted thinly veiled social critique, adding another layer to the written message.[54] *Mucha*'s cartoon thus echoed the idea of Jewish influence and wealth, possibly with the aim of cautioning the pro-Sanacja readers that Jews might not be leaving the country after all. As another cartoon in *Mucha* summarized this concern, Jews will outsmart the international community in the end: they will hide behind the various immigration plans and remain where they have always been, that is in Poland, for a thousand years or more.[55]

As leftist and antifascist outlets of the day were ringing alarm bells about the growing discrimination against Jews in Poland and elsewhere, the editors of *Mucha* seemed to have remained oblivious to the fragility of the existing political order. The above-mentioned cartoon that prophesied that Jews would outmaneuver everyone else only to stay in Poland was published only seven months before the outbreak of the Second World War. The legacy of the editor's late wife and intellectual companion, Maria Buchnerowa, who had been known for her benevolence, was sorely missing in these commentaries, reflecting an observation by the poet Czesław Miłosz who remarked many years later that Polish antisemitism in the late 1930s was so blinding that it made it impossible "to clearly realize the danger of war."[56]

JEWISH REFUGEES FROM AUSTRIA AND GERMANY

On the eve of the Second World War, several European states revised their citizenship laws with a view to forcing out some of their Jewish inhabitants. On 28 December 1937, an authoritarian and antisemitic government was appointed in Romania under the leadership of Octavian Goga. In January 1938, a royal decree was passed that invalidated all citizenship documents issued to Romania's Jews after the First World War. In effect, 225,000 Jews, 36 percent of the country's total Jewish population, lost their citizenship.[57] The situation was closely followed in Poland, which shared its southern border with Romania. Polish ethno-nationalists were alarmed by the situation, fearing the influx of Jews from Romania into Poland.[58] Right-wing groups, national conservative workers, and merchant associations were said to organize meetings in which they discussed banning putative refugees from entry.[59] They demanded that the government close the Polish-Romanian border.[60] As early as the first week of January, nationalist newspapers cited Czech media that supposedly reported on the arrival of "two trains" of Romanian Jews in the Subcarpathian town of Užhorod.[61] This news was denied by Prague.[62] The Polish government issued a statement saying that "Immigration into Poland is regulated by very precise rules aimed at the protection of labor" and that "the number of Jews—Polish citizens—inhabiting Rumania [sic] and enjoying the right to return to Poland at any time is very small."[63] Given the ongoing calls for the boycott of Jewish businesses in Poland, the statement's focus on protecting the labor market came as no surprise. It was meant to reassure the public that Poland's borders were sealed and no further "threat" to the national economy was expected. The discussion surrounding the issue turned out to be short-lived, disappearing almost completely by mid-March. It was, however, hysterical and obsessive—something that even Jewish outlets were quick to ridicule.[64]

Despite attempts by the authorities to quench the discussion throughout much of January, *Mucha* still chose to comment on the issue during that month. In a cartoon published on 21 January, illustrator Bronisław Fedyszyn portrayed a Jewish Romanian couple trying to cross the border into Poland. As the guard warns them, "Entry to Poland's forbidden!," the couple exclaims, "We're not going to Poland but to Nalewki Street!"[65] Here the Romanian crisis was used as a rhetorical crutch to comment on Poland's own traditional community inhabiting the Jewish district of Warsaw. In the words of one scholar, ethnic Poles often complained that walking in Nalewki was "like being in a foreign country."[66] In a similar vein, the Polish press depicted it as a place where people "dressed, spoke and acted differently."[67] What *Mucha* seemed to be saying, then, was that the district would always remain a foreign territory, irrespective of whether it was inhabited by Polish or Romanian Jews.[68] However, by no means was the cartoon solely a way of poking fun at the unassimilated members of the Jewish community. In fact, the couple in Fedyszyn's image were well-to-do, as their elegant coats, fur collars, and hats implied. They had travelled to the border on foot and were met by the Polish patrol at a remote mountain crossing. This image of unwanted immigrants arriving at a poorly guarded crossing echoed the enduring idea of the enemy at the gates, with the border as a danger zone that was under assault.

The magazine toyed with the image of state borders in another cartoon devoted to the refugee crisis caused by the Nazi annexation of Austria in mid-March 1938. The drawing by Stanisław Rydygier repeated the earlier visual formula: it portrayed a conversation at a border crossing between a guard and the arriving Jews. The group consists of eight people, six men and two women of various ages, who claim that they now "wished to become Polish patriots."[69] The new arrivals are portrayed as relatively wealthy and, although it is intimated that they are travelling from Vienna, their suitcases bear the names of three other locations: Moscow, Berlin, and Bucharest. The figure at the forefront, a portly man from Austria, dressed in a checked suit and a long coat, adheres to the stereotype of a prosperous *Westjude*. This is also the case for his companions, all of whom are "cravat Jews," wearing fashionable attire of the new bourgeoisie, as opposed to the caftans and kashkets of the traditional *Ostjude*. In Rydygier's rendition, these were true European citizens who, unlike their Orthodox counterparts, were the embodiment of modernity. And yet, the diversity of the group and their modish fashions also insinuated they were drifting cosmopolites, an idea deliberately at odds with their declarations of wishing to become Polish patriots.

Rydygier's cartoon was a topical response to one socialist journalist's proposal that Poland accommodate fugitives escaping neighboring countries.[70] Published in July 1938, the drawing was also a commentary on the ongoing debate about Polish citizens living abroad. On 18 March, only six days after the annexation of Austria by Nazi Germany, the Consular Section of the Polish Foreign Ministry proposed a controversial bill to revoke the citizenship of any Pole who had resided abroad for an uninterrupted period of five years, which it claimed severed their connection to Poland and the Polish nation.[71] The Sejm approved the bill two weeks later.[72] Wiktor Tomir Drymmer, who headed the Consular Section, admitted years later that the bill caused much debate and was often criticized as antisemitic.[73] Despite protests from the World Federation of Polish Jews, the measure was implemented, affecting hundreds of thousands of Polish Jews living in Austria, Germany, Italy, and the Free City of Danzig.[74] Austria alone boasted a Polish Jewish diaspora of approximately 25,000 people who were affected by the new law.[75] Between 1 January and 15 April, only 792 Polish Jews from Austria were permitted to return to Poland.[76]

The cartoon by Rydygier sought to rally support behind the decree and, possibly, prepare the public for a new ordinance on citizenship that was in the offing. The representation of Jews returning from Moscow, Berlin, Bucharest, and Vienna and vowing to turn into Polish patriots also repurposed the traditional antisemitic trope of Jews as opportunistic side-switchers. As scholar Tatjana Lichtenstein argues in the context of interwar Czechoslovakia, viewing Jews as nationally indifferent or opportunistic in matters of national belonging was not rare among nationalist groups and could both stem from and be fueled by anti-Jewish sentiment.[77] Here too *Mucha* doubted the sincerity of patriotic declarations by the putative arrivals, presenting their will to return as driven by practical considerations.

Although the magazine commented on these events only sporadically, its textual content was also unsympathetic toward Jewish refugees. One anecdote, entitled "Birth rate" published in April 1938, deliberately inflated the numbers of new arrivals. A make-believe report from the Statistical Office recalled the following conversation: "'In March Poland recorded the highest birth rate. The population increased by 80,000 people.' 'Why so many?' 'The Jews arrived from Austria.'"[78] Given the discrepancy between the actual number of Polish Jews living in Austria and the figure cited, it is fair to say that *Mucha* engaged in moderate fear-mongering. As with any joke, *Mucha*'s readers must have realized they were being fooled. All the same, the absurdity of the anecdote encouraged the reader to suspend reality-testing and take the only tangible detail of the story—the eighty thousand arrivals—at face value.[79]

Toward the end of 1938, Polish Jews living abroad were to face a much graver ordeal. Since April 1938, Nazi officials had been considering a mass expulsion of Polish Jews from Germany. They demanded assurances from Poland that those expelled would be accepted. The Polish government refused, and, in September 1938, the Polish Ministry of Interior Affairs announced a new decree requiring that all holders of Polish passports abroad receive an endorsement stamp prior to 30 October 1938 or the passport would become void. Wishing to prevent mass return of expatriate Jews, Polish consular officials in Germany tended to refuse to grant stamps to Jewish passport holders. The Third Reich followed these developments closely, aware that the Polish government would attempt to prevent forced repatriation.[80]

Between 27 and 30 October 1938, the Gestapo, on orders from the German Foreign Ministry, arrested nearly twenty thousand Polish Jews in Germany and Austria and transported them to the Polish border.[81] The deportees were dispersed in a number of locations along the border. The largest group of approximately eight thousand people was concentrated in the border town of Zbąszyń, where a refugee camp was established by a Jewish aid organization, the Joint Distribution Committee (JDC).[82] While some refugees found shelter with relatives or were allocated accommodation in Warsaw by Jewish relief agencies, many remained stranded in Zbąszyń until the outbreak of the Second World War.[83] Several men who were deemed stateless were sent to the Bereza Kartuska Internment Camp, a high-security facility aimed at political prisoners and known for its harsh conditions, including hard labor and the use of torture. The government was said to intern the stateless persons as a way to discourage further attempts at illegal entry.[84]

In the first two weeks after the *Polenaktion*, as it was called by the Germans, the Polish press was forbidden from reporting on the Zbąszyń camp.⁸⁵ However, toward the end of the year, the Ministry of Foreign Affairs gave clear instructions to journalists that the events may now be used to argue for "the urgency of Jewish emigration from Poland."⁸⁶ From mid-November 1938 onwards, when the ban was lifted, print media of various political persuasions began to discuss the situation at the border. Polish Jewish outlets drew attention to poverty, dire living conditions, and anxiety among the refugees.⁸⁷ Socialist newspapers emphasized the cold-heartedness of the Nazi regime whose policies had caused the situation.⁸⁸ Some of those who visited the camp described the magnitude of human tragedy they witnessed. In the words of one journalist, the camp was an inferno, and utterly "shameful" to all Poles. It was filled with downright misery, the scale of the suffering being so great that it made the situation "unreal."⁸⁹ Right-wing and moderate conservative outlets devoted much less attention to the crisis.⁹⁰ If they did, they commented very little on the struggles of the refugee population. Instead, they chose to report on the growing frustration (and even aggression) of the deportees, as well as the pressure the crisis put on local services and the supposedly demoralizing effect the refugees had on the people of Zbąszyń.⁹¹ Some of these reports expressed hope that ongoing talks with Germany would bring the crisis to a close.⁹²

In response to this humanitarian emergency, *Mucha* chose the strategy of silence. It did not devote a single cartoon to the events, while its epigrams and anecdotes only indirectly touched upon the issue. Given the seriousness of the situation, the few satirical texts that did appear seem cruel and insensitive. Only one week before the deportations, *Mucha* mocked the purported Jewish skill of escaping danger, preferably to the safe haven of Nalewki Street where one could live peacefully into old age.⁹³ In early January 1939, the magazine ironically called the Jews in Zbąszyń a "friendly gift from Germany."⁹⁴ The following month, it mocked Jews for having served the Germans so faithfully, only to be deceived by their "cousin."⁹⁵ Although few and far between, these short, and supposedly humorous, texts showed clear contempt for the victims of expulsion.

Given the profile of the magazine, it is not surprising that the role of the Polish government in aggravating the situation remained unmentioned. What *Mucha* could not say was that the crisis that unraveled in Zbąszyń was a clear example of the ineptitude of the government's foreign and internal policies.⁹⁶ After all, the situation was caused directly by the decree on the nullification of Polish passports, which the German government had anticipated and to which it reacted with speed and cruel efficiency. For the pro-Sanacja elites, the events led to a growing sense of helplessness toward the actions of their Nazi counterparts and a deeper awareness that Poland's "demographic issues" were nowhere near as important to the international community as they were to the domestic actors.[97] The apathetic reaction from *Mucha*, which resembled the indifferent response from the right-wing press, can also be read as an expression of utter surprise. As we have seen, the feared mass influx of Romanian and Austrian Jewry had been averted. This particular crisis, which the government had thought to have anticipated, was not.

GREED, EXPLOITATION, AND THE PURPORTED LACK OF ASSIMILATION

Although much of *Mucha*'s reporting on the Jewish question focused on foreign policy and required a degree of political literacy on the part of its readers, some of its Jewish-themed content could also appeal to a less demanding audience. In fact, the magazine replicated many long-standing antisemitic stereotypes. This included representations inferring Jewish people's greed and their supposed exploitation of the ethnic Polish economy. Portrayals of Jews as oblivious to Polish mores and unable to become part of the Polish culture were also common. These tropes were uncomplicated and required no prior knowledge of international politics. Publishing such cartoons enabled the magazine to bridge the gap between an educated, politically conscious reader and a less-sophisticated mass reader. In its reporting, *Mucha* was able, then, to oscillate between what Andrei Oișteanu described as "intellectual" and "folkloric antisemitism."[98] It was perhaps this ability to indulge different tastes that made it into a popular and well-selling magazine.

The stereotype of Jews as exploiting the national economy or engaging in shady business activity appeared in *Mucha* at least on a monthly basis, whether in visual or textual form. With government plans to Polonize the country's economy well underway, such content reinforced the stereotype of Jews as the enemy within, acting to the detriment of Polish national interests.[99] Disseminating such content was undoubtedly a useful way of garnering popular support for the ongoing economic boycott and securing political legitimacy for the government. One cartoon in March 1938, in particular, was representative of the notion of Jews as exploiting the national economy. It depicted a Jewish man milking a cow with the name "Poland" written on its body (Figure 1.4).[100] As in English, the Polish phrasal verb *doić kogoś* (to milk somebody) implies that one tries to take advantage of someone or get as much benefit or profit from something as possible. Here, too, *Mucha*

1.4. This Is How It Should Be in Poland, from *Mucha*, 25 March 1938, 8.

suggested that Jews abused the system and took unfair advantage of the Polish economy, wrecking the livelihoods of ordinary Christian citizens.

At the visual level, the artist used contrast to drive the message home. Here the figure of the Jew, dressed in a heavy caftan and high boots, is placed alongside an image of a barefoot peasant, idly playing a recorder under a nearby tree. In the distance, a road sign points in two directions: Poland and Madagascar. A man with a knapsack on his back and a woman with a baby strapped to her chest are shown walking out of the country, heading toward Madagascar. Their hunched backs and the few belongings they carry convey an image of extreme privation: these are the Christian Poles who are forced into exile by Jewish greed and exploitation. The caption tells us that the cartoon is an imaginary take on "how things should be in Poland according to Jewish MPs." Not only is the cartoon imputing certain ideas to Jewish representatives in the Sejm; it also tells us that those supposed visions are wrong. Visual contrast plays an essential role in proving the spuriousness of these proposals and highlighting, by the law of reversal, the official credo that it is the Jews, not gentile Poles, who must leave the country. Visual clues tell the audience that the unshod shepherd belongs in the bucolic landscape around him as his undisturbed music-making, folk clothing, and bare feet are all signifiers of his being native and in tune with the surroundings. In contrast, the Jewish man is out of place with his environs, his heavy caftan and boots marking him as foreign. Even the cow, a symbol for the misused motherland, looks at the Jew with despondency.

Mucha's commentary on the supposed exploitation of the country by Jews was also consistently pursued in its satirical writing. A rhymed witticism published in another issue that same year reinforced the above ideas. "Poland is our mother," Jews were quoted saying. Asked why, *Mucha* responded for them: "Because she always lets them suck her dry."[101] Elsewhere, the editors argued that every Jew "would like to live in Palestine, have fun in Paris, and do their business in Poland only."[102] Here the derogatory Yiddish loan word *geszeft* was used to describe Jewish business.[103] *Mucha* was no doubt skilled in spreading half-truths and using them to promote the official economic policy of *swój do swego* or "patronize your own." In that, the magazine resembled right-wing outlets that blamed the growing poverty in the country on "Jewish capitalism" and "Jewish monopolies."[104] It is true that some large business owners were Jewish and that they controlled substantial sections of the economy, such as the publishing and book markets.[105] At the same time, the widespread boycott affected many small merchants, artisans, and the urban poor, who were forced to rely on international aid. It is estimated that, in 1937 only, the JDC donated just under a million dollars to be redistributed among Polish Jews affected by the discriminatory policies.[106] While some of the cartoons discussed in this chapter would suggest that the editors were fully aware of the heterogeneity of Poland's Jewish population, including economic disparities within the community, *Mucha* chose to ignore that knowledge when convenient. Where financial matters were concerned, the magazine preferred to conceptualize the Jew using the centuries-old trope of a shylock, a Jewish money-lender, who was "naturally" good with money.[107] However, here the medieval usurer tended to be replaced with the more familiar figure of a savvy capitalist skilled at acquiring wealth.[108] As one *jeu d'esprit* by *Mucha* instructed the reader: "Jews are like sponges. They suck in the money so if you squeeze them, the money will flow."[109] According to another one, "money is the life-blood of the nation" and Jews were the most "full-bloodied nation" of all.[110]

The stereotype of a resourceful Jew was accompanied by visual portrayals that depicted Jews as prone to engage in illegal business activity. In one cartoon, *Mucha* represented a conversation between two small-time merchants talking about the possibility of entering into a business venture together. The men are shown against the backdrop of Jewish shops, most likely in Nalewki Street, that sell down feathers and carbonated water. "Salomon, would you like to start a business venture with me?" asks one of the men. "Thank you but last year I was already locked away for six months," responds the other.[111]

To *Mucha*, Jewish business was, by definition, a dishonest enterprise, deceit being ingrained in the economic culture of local Jews. Here the reproach went beyond the sole content of the captions. According to art historian Matthew Baigell, the visual formula of two people engaged in a conversation against the background of a Jewish store was a common way to convey a critical commentary on Jewish business practices. Using the case of American cartoons, Baigell shows that such representations already existed in the nineteenth century.[112] Alongside textual material, in America such content strove to demonstrate that "for Jews honesty and a sense of morality are irrelevant in business enterprises."[113] This was no different for *Mucha* and Poland. Witticisms on the alleged Jewish penchant for *szachry* (swindling) appeared in the magazine too, mimicking reports on the "Jewish *szacher macher*" in right-wing newspapers.[114] In addition, the magazine published supposedly historical pieces meant to prove that criminal tendencies were entrenched in the Jewish nation. As one such "historical" anecdote argued, the crimes of human trafficking, smuggling, and usury were common among local Jews prior to the First World War.[115] The text also implied that Jews were inescapably averse to "sensible work" (*sensowna praca*).[116]

These examples show that *Mucha*'s artists and writers built upon a wider body of antisemitic satire that spanned several historical periods and transcended national borders. Concomitantly, such representations were an expression of deeply local mentalities and approaches to commerce. In fact, aside from revealing obvious hostility to Jews, those portrayals also bore the imprint of folkloric stereotyping of trade. According to anthropological research conducted by Alina Cała in rural Poland in the 1970s and 1980s, elderly peasants who still remembered the multiethnic communities of interwar Poland considered trade to be the unquestionable Jewish domain. However, in comparison to farming, trade had a bad reputation. It was disparaged as a supposedly deceitful activity and "idleness" (*próżniactwo*), which required no specific effort or skill. To those peasants, only physical labor could merit the title of "real work."[117]

Of course, *Mucha* was not completely off the mark. Some Jews, like those of many other ethnic groups, ethnic Poles included, did engage in criminal activity. This was reflected in the Yiddish press that thrived on sensational content. According to historian Eddy Portnoy, it reported on "Everything from the highest levels of literature, philosophy, politics, and science to the lowest levels of beggary, poverty, pimpery, prostitution, and inept stupefaction."[118] However, what made *Mucha* different was its almost exclusive focus on the (perceived and actual) transgressions, vices, and faults of Polish Jews. The suspension of disbelief that accompanied satire enabled the magazine to use salacious news and make sweeping generalizations about the group as a whole. These generalizations were not entirely harmless. According to one historian of the period, Jews were often discriminated against in the legal system. More often than not, court cases involving Polish and Jewish defendants resulted in harsher punishments being imposed on Jews, while crimes committed on Jews were not always systematically investigated.[119] To blame such state of affairs on satirical cartoons would be an exaggeration; but it is true that persistent stereotyping in the media hurt the group's interests, demonized them in the eyes of the general population, and created a discursive culture in which negative portrayals and typecasting were not only condoned but applauded.

A similar approach to antisemitic stereotyping was visible in *Mucha*'s portrayal of Jewish mores. The magazine liked to present Jews as undeveloped and having backward habits. In particular, its cartoonists were fixated on personal hygiene. In 1938, three cartoons were published on this topic. In one, two Jewish men are shown at the Polish seaside, reluctant to bathe in the sea (Figure 1.5). The dialogue underneath reads: "Mr Sztynkfus! Why are you not getting in?" / "Oh, you mustn't do that at once if you didn't interact with the element for a year, neither in the river nor in the bathtub."[120] The name Sztynkfus ("Mr. Stinky Foot") was meant to symbolize the Jewish ghetto where, according to some contemporary media, dirt and bad hygiene were rampant.[121] The two men are in a swimsuit and swim trunks, enabling the cartoonist to reveal big chunks of their bodies. The image was clearly inspired by nineteenth-century ideas on anthropometric differences between various population groups. The two men, although different from each other, were both given the stereotypical "Jewish body." Both have thick, black, curly hair, prominent stubble, ample body hair, fleshly lips, and large noses. Sztynkfus, moreover, was given thick eyebrows, bow legs, and antelope eyes, all hallmarks of a fin-de-siècle antisemitic representation of the Jew.[122]

Mucha's illustrators employed the hooked noses, large lips, and thick curly hair in yet another cartoon set at the seaside. The drawing presented a conversation between a man and a woman (Figure 1.6). In it, the man boasts about his new rental apartment, which includes a bathtub. In response, the woman asks innocently, "Does this mean you can swim?" Aside from replicating the stereotypical Jewish facial features, the cartoon poked fun at supposed Jewish backwardness. Here, the woman is presented as unfamiliar with modern conveniences, such as the bathtub, and ignorant as to their purpose.[123] When compared to another beach-themed cartoon published in the liberal *Szpilki* that same summer, which commented on the alarming news about Christian-only bathing area being introduced in the popular

1.5. At the Polish Seaside, from *Mucha*, 1 July 1938, 7.

1.6. On the Beach, from *Mucha*, 29 July 1938, 6.

vacationing area of Puszczykowo in Greater Poland, *Mucha*'s drawings on this topic seem petty, if not deliberately oblivious to the growing discrimination against Jews.[124]

Mucha was not the only satirical magazine to comment on seaside resorts. Other outlets employed similar illustrations of Polish beaches jam-packed with Jewish bodies. Illustrators such as Kazimierz Grus and Julian Żebrowski portrayed Jewish vacationers as "the plague," lying down in the squalor of discarded eggshells and banana peels. In a similar vein, their bodies were depicted as a muddled collection of oversized paunches, buttocks, noses, and feet. Art historian Dariusz Konstantynów notes that such a style of drawing was meant to infer that Jews were not only different but also degenerate, repulsive, and frightening.[125] Given that this was a time of poverty and economic crisis, images of oversized bodies were also a comment on the indecency of those who had the luxury to overindulge. Having said that, the trope of Jews trying to overtake gentile beaches was not exclusive to the interwar period nor to Poland. Similar representations of odd-looking Jewish bodies also appeared in nineteenth-century beach drawings in Britain and the United States, as well as in spa caricatures in Bohemia and elsewhere.[126] More generally, calls to counter the spread of Jewish tourists in holiday resorts were typical for both the fascist discourse of the interwar period and earlier representations of summer resorts as gentile spaces in which Jews were unwelcome.[127]

Discussing the use of exaggerated bodily features, scholar Chris Lamb says that "editorial cartoonists sometimes walk a fine line between exaggeration and ethnic stereotyping, which reflects the seamy side of the profession's history and the biases of those who work in the profession."[128] *Mucha*'s illustrators crossed that line eagerly and cherished their freedom to perpetuate ethnic stereotypes. In that, they were different from some present-day cartoonists who find bodily tropes ineffectual and likely to detract attention from the main message of the cartoon.[129]

Aside from commenting on Jews in seaside resorts, *Mucha*'s artists also raised issues of personal hygiene. One cartoon in early 1938 depicted two Jewish men talking about how one of them had been described by an acquaintance as *brudas* (a slob), an insult that eventually resulted in a court case. The affront was not untrue, the conversation suggested, but the plaintiff planned on bathing prior to the hearing to prove the slanderer wrong.[130] In this cartoon, *Mucha* was able to capitalize on two stereotypes—that of supposed Jewish uncleanliness and that of slyness. The caricature was not particularly imaginative as far as the pictorial content was concerned; it used a visual design present in many other drawings in the magazine, namely, an image of two men absorbed in a conversation. This was a one-size-fits-all formula that enabled the editor to match the illustration with a variety of captions on Jewish issues, depending on the need of the moment. Such an approach was hardly surprising given Buchner's unadventurous editorial style and the fact that he was *Mucha*'s sole editor, responsible for a lot of the writing and contracting work, both of which precluded regular to-and-fro exchanges with the few commissioned illustrators. Working with fixed pictorial scenes such as these could reflect the need for efficiency in an office that was short-staffed and, after 1934, deprived of the helping hand of Maria Buchnerowa. Buchner mirrored the lackluster matter of the cartoon above in his textual satire on dirt and hygiene. This included a joke on how the tablecloths needed to be grubby to make a restaurant truly Jewish.[131] In another short composition, he argued that one should be able to use the tablecloth as a menu, "reading" the stains and spills the same way one would read the *carte du jour*.[132] Above all, Buchner's satirical texts and cartoon captions portrayed Jews as smelling of various foods, including onions, as well as drinking astonishing amounts of water after having eaten herring.[133]

Even though *Mucha* made no explicit reference to the so-called *foetor judaicus* (Jewish odor), its insinuations of filth and bad hygiene suggested that Jews smelled bad, whether from the lack of soap and water or the foods they consumed. In that, *Mucha* replicated long-standing olfactory stereotypes that, according to one scholar, "were used to anchor beliefs about Jewish otherness from the medieval through to the modern period."[134] Whereas in the Middle Ages the trope was used predominantly in discussions of religious difference, in *Mucha*'s modernized interpretation, body odor was an issue of national development or a lack thereof.[135] As modernity (and bathtubs) relegated smells to modern sewage systems and deodorized the bourgeoisie, Jews allegedly continued to lag behind, having missed the modernity boat.[136] Such observations were not completely innocuous. Throughout history, olfactory stereotypes have been used to justify exclusion and persecution.[137] In the Third Reich, the supposed *foetor judaicus* became one of the tenets of genocidal policies, and Hitler himself was said to believe that Jews had a distinct body odor that could never be eradicated.[138] In *Mucha*, these stereotypes served as clear othering devices. Specifically, they were meant to suggest that Jews were fundamentally different from ethnic Poles or, at least, oblivious to local mores. As some of *Mucha*'s cartoons and satirical texts demonstrated, its editor likely believed that, despite being citizens of the Polish Republic, Jews could never be assimilated. In that, he was no different from European fascists of the time who viewed Jews as fundamentally alien and culturally incompatible with their national populations.[139]

This alleged inability of Jews to adapt to local mores was also seen in cartoons on other themes. While many of the drawings discussed above were meant to appeal to the sense of sight and smell, other portrayals focused on hearing. In particular, the magazine employed the common trope of Jews as being, in Sander Gilman's words, "unable to truly command the national language" of the country in which they lived.[140] One example was a cartoon depicting a conversation between the editors of two dailies: the pro-Sanacja *Gazeta Polska* (*Polish Gazette*) and the Polish Jewish *Nasz Przegląd* (*Our Review*). The cartoon commented on a statement by Bogusław Miedziński of *Gazeta* who reportedly said that "Jews and Poles lacked common language."[141] While the statement was meant to be metaphorical, the cartoon depicted Samuel Hirszhorn, one of *Nasz Przegląd*'s journalists, asking Miedziński whether the language used by his newspaper was the same as that of *Gazeta Polska*. *Mucha*'s answer was negative.

As Sander Gilman puts it, "Within the European tradition of seeing the Jew as different, there is a closely linked tradition of hearing the Jew's language as marked by the corruption of being a Jew."[142] In other words, throughout history, Jews were seen as using a corrupt variant of the standard language or "littering" the language with foreign influences.[143] Antisemitic stereotypes aside, *Mucha*'s targeting of *Nasz Przegląd* was not coincidental. The daily was actively involved in discussion of the so-called Jewish question in general and critical of the government and its anti-Jewish policies in particular, which made it vulnerable to attacks such as this. And yet, unlike what *Mucha* might have suggested, *Nasz Przegląd* was a well-respected Polish-language newspaper, valued for its economic and political analyses and read not only by many Polish-speaking Jews but by the ethnic Polish intelligentsia.[144]

All the same, the question of language was a real one, as was the associated stereotyping. From the late eighteenth century onward, Polish assimilationists called for the linguistic Polonization of Polish Jews.[145] By 1931, when Poland's population reached 32 million, more than 8 percent of the overall populace named Yiddish as their mother tongue.[146] Many native Yiddish speakers spoke Polish poorly or with a recognizable Yiddish accent.[147] It was those speakers of Polish that *Mucha* ridiculed, either in cartoons such as the one above or in its regular column "Poseł Winersztok ma głos" (Member of Parliament Winersztok Takes the Floor). The column, written by Buchner, offered commentary on current affairs from the perspective of a fictional Polish Jewish MP.[148] Winersztok talked about "ghetto benches" in the universities, supposed Jewish communist activity, the Madagascar plan, the possibility of war, the importance of Jewish MPs in the Sejm, the growing anti-Jewish atmosphere in Poland and beyond, racial laws in Italy, and the resulting expulsions of Jews, among other issues.[149] The column mimicked spoken language and was ridden with pronunciation errors, grammatical and lexical mistakes, and infelicities of style. It contained occasional words from Yiddish too.

The fictional Winersztok was not a native speaker of Polish, and his speech was meant to evoke what was called in old German *mauscheln*—to speak German with a Jewish accent.[150] Polish also had a verb for it, *żydłaczyć*, which in itself was a deeply derogatory term.[151] According to the Polish Jewish writer Michał Głowiński, *żydłaczenie* equaled "bad Polish" that was embellished with nonexistent idioms drawn from Yiddish, as well as "a peculiar, unrepeatable accent, a special intonation and an extended melody to a sentence."[152] *Mucha* used *żydłaczenie* for a reason. Although written from a supposedly Jewish point of view, Winersztok's speeches were aimed at ridiculing the vocal members of Polish Jewish community and undermining the cause they fought for, including social equality.[153] Implicitly, however, the magazine was also saying that Jews could not assimilate. In concocting Winersztok's speeches, Buchner told his readers that Jews were mangling the Polish language and had no understanding and appreciation of the national heritage.[154]

Buchner's columns, although largely exaggerated, record a linguistic phenomenon that was well known to interwar readers, Warsaw dwellers included, who were familiar with Yiddish-inflected Polish. That way of speaking disappeared almost completely after the Second World War, having been left unrecorded and undocumented.[155] As Yiddish entered the "postvernacular" phase, to use Jeffrey Shandler's term, and was reinvented by successive generations of Yiddish speakers and their heirs, the Yiddishized Polish disappeared with the annihilation of Poland's Jewish community.[156]

As editor in chief, Władysław Buchner was behind much of the content discussed here, as the one both writing and commissioning the work. Only two generations removed from his Jewish grandfather Abraham Buchner, Władysław fashioned an authorial persona who was seemingly detached from that heritage. And yet, the obstinate spirit of Abraham, who died in 1869 when Władysław was only nine, was somewhat present in the activities of the editor of *Mucha*. A teacher in the Rabbinic School in Warsaw and author of numerous Hebrew textbooks, Abraham Buchner was critical of both Hasidism and the anti-Hasidic Orthodoxy, calling for abolishment of the cheder and establishment of a universal system of schooling. His freethinking approach to the Bible as well as the conversion to Christianity of his elder son, Józef, in 1842 caused an uproar in Warsaw's rabbinic circles. By the time Władysław was born, all of Abraham's children, including Władysław's father, had been baptized.[157] On the surface, *Mucha*'s editor chose not to dwell on his ethnic background, but his approach to traditional Jewry was shaped by his upbringing in a learned home where tradition was something to confront, rather than hold in reverence, and where assimilation and education were considered the primary values.

Nevertheless, Buchner's personal background and motivations do not assuage the potential impact such reporting could have had on the interwar public. Although no research exists to prove this, it would be no exaggeration to say that, in a country weakened by economic crisis, disseminating the stereotype of the Jew as conniving, dishonest, and outlandish could potentially aggravate existing ethnic tensions. At the same time, *Mucha* did not see its publications as hateful. Following the official discourse, it considered the ongoing struggle against Jewry an expression of patriotism and, even more so, a national duty. Antisemitism was thus presented as a rational choice rather than a manifestation of jingoistic hate.[158] "Do Poles hate Jews?" asked one poem published in the summer of 1938. The answer was seemingly straightforward:

> Is it hate to de-Judaize the cities,
> Is it hate to value your own trade,
> Is it hate to work for the industry,
> to prevent the Vistula from becoming the Jordan?
> Is it hate to have your own culture,
> Is it hate to push the Homeland forward,
> Is it hate to apply medicine to the wound,
> Where is hate here, let me ask you.[159]

Both this and some of *Mucha*'s other satirical poems and epigrams are far from sympathetic. Many of them are cruel and, when read with hindsight, could be interpreted as foreshadowing the events to come. Commenting on various antisemitic proposals, one light-hearted comment maintained that there was nothing wrong with wearing "yellow patches" (*żółte łaty*) since in Poland almost every Aryan wore mended clothing.[160] Yet another satirical dialogue advocated for a Jewish ghetto to be created in Warsaw since, in the words of its fictional interlocutor, "all my creditors were Jews."[161] Further, *Mucha* posited that there had never been a single Jew who did not profit from war.[162] These observations date back to the autumn and winter of 1938, revealing blatant insensitivity to the existing discrimination and an ostensible obliviousness as to the growing threat of war.

However, *Mucha*'s antisemitism, at least its visual content, could be described as relatively "weak." Despite the commonness of its anti-Jewish reporting, the magazine was not as rabidly antisemitic as some of its contemporaries; neither was it particularly sympathetic toward the Jewish plight. Its anti-Jewish satire, particularly the visual type, was tenacious but not exceptionally fervent. Unlike some far-right publications that excelled in discrediting Jews and did so in ways that bordered on extreme, *Mucha*'s antisemitism was of the half-hearted type. Several commentators of the time, editors and illustrators alike, were thus right to remember *Mucha* as "non-descript," derivative, and devoid of *cięty dowcip* (sharp wit).[163] Nonetheless, as one scholar warns, such "softened content," which is "ostensibly geared towards entertainment," could still play "its role in the shaping of public opinion."[164]

Indeed, those purportedly humorous depictions were by no means harmless. Paired with the stronger textual content, they condoned violence and created acceptance of instances of grassroots antisemitism.[165] While it is impossible to say if this reporting was representative of how ethnic Poles felt about Jews, it was certainly illustrative of what government officials might have thought but were afraid to say openly. The poetic license that came with satire enabled the magazine to voice opinions that state officials would not dare utter in public, despite sharing the same basic sentiments. *Mucha*'s push for mass Jewish emigration, its calls for ending the supposed Jewish control of economy, and its sensory antisemitism all bore the imprint of the contemporary climate of hate.

That only a few of *Mucha*'s artists signed their drawings is telling.[166] The biographies of those we can identify can be summarized in a few lines. Bronisław Fedyszyn, one of *Mucha*'s most prolific artists, who provided cartoons to the magazine in 1932–1939, was self-taught and received no artistic education in the family home.[167] He trained as a cellist in the Warsaw Conservatory and, in addition to his work as illustrator, performed in the Polish Radio chamber orchestra from the late 1920s onward. In 2013, many of his antisemitic cartoons, drawn in the 1930s, were included in an exhibition of anti-Jewish caricature organized by the Jewish Historical Institute in Warsaw.[168] He died in Warsaw on 22 January 1940.[169] Stanisław Rydygier (born as Rüdiger) was the son of painter and caricaturist Bronisław Rydygier (1858–1929). Following in the footsteps of his father, who worked with *Mucha* in 1926–1929, Stanisław begun to work for the magazine in 1929, continuing until the outbreak of the Second World War. Emulating the style of his father, he employed black ink in most of his drawings as well as using the contrasting plates of white and black.[170]

Studying *Mucha* today reveals the content to which progovernment readers of the time were perennially exposed. Such content had the power to reinforce negative stereotypes and strengthen existing ideological positions on both international and domestic issues. *Mucha*'s representations of Jews were dismissive, to say the least, comprising all tricks in the antisemitic rule book, including vilification, scapegoating, and victim blaming. The rise of fascist regimes in Europe did not alter *Mucha*'s reporting. Like many other outlets of the time, the magazine recorded the warning signs of the impending world war, and speculated on the effects that such war would have on Poland's Jews, but chose to ignore them in favor of advocating narrowly defined national interests. As the next chapter will show, other satirical magazines went much further, using satire to bully their readers into adopting the antisemitic mindset and wearing the label of "anti-Jewish" as a badge of honor.

Chapter 2

LOCAL STRUGGLES

On 11 December 1935, the commissar of criminal police for the district of Kalisz in the province of Greater Poland wrote a letter to the chief prosecutor concerning a certain Władysław Siepka, a priest in the village of Stawiszyn. The letter reported that, since his arrival at the parish in 1934, Siepka had made himself known as a staunch supporter of the National Party (SN) who spread racial hate as well as making statements causing social unrest. In a sermon in November 1934, Siepka maintained that Jews and Freemasons ruled the country, while honest people were being imprisoned. In January 1935, he criticized local authorities for deploying additional police units at the market; according to the commissar, the units had been called in to prevent a pogrom brewing in the area because of Siepka's agitation. In July 1935, the priest appealed to his flock to build a Catholic, and not Jewish, Poland, and on 8 December 1935 he encouraged his congregation to paint anti-Jewish slogans on public buildings. That same night, unknown perpetrators vandalized building fronts with graffiti that called for the boycott of Jewish businesses. The letter noted that Siepka's campaigning had caused a rift between Christian and Jewish inhabitants of the village, as well as leading to instances of anti-Jewish violence and property destruction.[1]

The example of Father Siepka was not an isolated case of direct anti-Jewish politicking undertaken by SN members in the district of Kalisz. Young agitators were known to be travelling across villages and towns in the region, talking to the inhabitants, and disseminating both antisemitic and anti-Sanacja content.[2] They spread leaflets among schoolchildren that called on them to refuse to share classrooms with Jewish schoolmates, as well as urging them to dissuade their parents from purchasing goods from Jewish sellers.[3] Importantly, SN shock troops picketed in front of Jewish shops and stalls at the market, terrorizing customers who chose to patronize non-Christian businesses.[4] Such direct action, which was by no means exclusive to the Kalisz area, was accompanied by related coverage in the print media. SN-aligned publications tried to outdo each other in promoting the idea of an ethnic

Polish economy and the eventual "de-Judaization" of the country as a whole. Greater Poland, more generally, was a traditional stronghold of SN, and many of its major publications, such as the Poznań-based outlets *Pod Pręgierz* (*Under the Pillory*) and *Orędownik* (*The Spokesman*), originated in the area.

The region gave rise to the only long-running satirical magazine in the country that was exclusively created to push anti-Jewish propaganda. Named *Pokrzywy*, the magazine not only reported on local ethnonationalist efforts to "de-Judaize" Poland but actively contributed to that struggle, sometimes in ways unavailable to their fellow campaigners on the ground. Historians of Polish caricature suggest that because its title alluded to the Nazi satirical magazine *Die Brennessel* (*The Burning Nettle*), it is possible that the magazine was modelled on hate publications in Germany and elsewhere.[5] It undoubtedly drew on similar daily publications in Greater Poland that, although not satirical per se, consisted of similar content and professed parallel political views. *Pokrzywy*'s first issue was published on 1 June 1937. This was at a time when economic struggle against Jews was intensifying and official attempts to orchestrate mass Jewish emigration were proving to be largely ineffective. Despite sharing some of the same goals with the Polish Sanacja government, the editors were critical of the authorities and of what they considered to be the ineptitude of the state in resolving the "Jewish question."[6]

Pokrzywy offered a more radical solution to the alleged Jewish domination of economic life. Not only did it employ antisemitic satire, exaggerating supposed Jewish vices; it also attacked and shamed ethnic Polish patrons and helpers of the Jews. According to historian Olaf Bergmann, in 1938, as much as 20.5 percent of *Pokrzywy*'s caricatures were devoted specifically to the "Jewish problem."[7] Despite using some of the same antisemitic tropes as the progovernment *Mucha*, this magazine was far removed from the political agenda of its pro-Sanacja counterpart. Instead, it was a firm supporter, if not mouthpiece, of the National Party, which, as we have seen, considered establishment of a Catholic Polish national state its main political goal. The party was also likely the main source of funding for the magazine, allowing it to survive until the outbreak of the Second World War.[8]

Unlike the national *Mucha*, *Pokrzywy* was a regional magazine. It was established in Kalisz and was deeply embedded in local affairs, covering events in the surrounding towns of Sieradz, Pleszew, Jarocin, Ostrów Wielkopolski, and Krotoszyn. It was Kalisz, however, that boasted the largest Jewish community in the voivodship; this came to 25,000 people in August 1939.[9] Aside from covering events in the region, the writers occasionally ventured out to report from the nearby industrial city of Łódź, which was known for its strong socialist movement and a sizeable Jewish community. In those reports, Łódź was the antithesis of what *Pokrzywy* wished Kalisz and other surrounding towns to be.

Analyzed in retrospect, this magazine's local flavor is precisely what makes it interesting. Because it responded to municipal politics and bottom-up economic practices, *Pokrzywy* is an excellent source with which to analyze how the antisemitic media campaign unfolded at the local level. In commenting on local affairs, the magazine's editors gave special importance to satire. Its creators believed in the corrective function of humor and thought that a public appraisal of both individual and collective failings was critical to maintaining a healthy nation and to the building of a "better tomorrow" (*lepsze jutro*).[10]

ECONOMIC BOYCOTT, *SHABBOS-GOYIM*, AND THE CREATION OF A NATIONAL ECONOMY

From the very first issue, *Pokrzywy* devoted significant attention to the goal of the formation of a national economy. The editors clearly believed that, to effect change in the country as a whole, they needed to get local affairs in order first. As with any new periodical, the first issue presented, if implicitly, the mission of the magazine. The issue was meant to offer readers a taste of *Pokrzywy*'s worldview and show where the editorial team stood politically. The tellingly titled doggerel "Dobroczynna pokrzywa" ("The Beneficial Nettle") did just that. The verse began with discussing the benefits of the humble nettle before moving on to *Pokrzywy* (the magazine) and its tasks. Although sometimes despised, the verse claimed, the common nettle offered a wealth of healing properties: it purified the blood and lungs, alleviated rheumatism, and reduced fever. A light spanking with the nettle was said to expunge human vices too. This "spanking" was to be *Pokrzywy*'s main weapon. The editors pledged to defend the "rights of the nation" by rhetorically spanking those who dared to patronize the shops of the "sidelock wearers" or "peyot wearers" (*pejsaci*), as opposed to supporting "their own."[11] In the pages that followed, the editors handed out their first smacks.

The first issue made the municipality of Kalisz its main target. The council was said to ignore Polish businesses and provide a variety of jobs to Jewish companies. These included printing and the delivery of office supplies. *Pokrzywy*'s editors maintained that lower prices should not determine procurement decisions and claimed that the reduced cost would be reflected in the inferior quality of print and paper. To make things worse, they maintained, such decisions undermined the position of the Polish employee.

Jewish typesetters were able to keep their jobs, while ethnic Polish typesetters were forced out onto the streets, which left them "hungry and miserable." To emphasize the perceived necessity of protecting the ethnic Polish economy, the editors asked rhetorically: "Where are we? In Poland or in Palestine?"[12]

Like many other pieces published in *Pokrzywy*, this particular article was far from humorous. It was serious in tone, devoid of witticisms and double entendres, and hardly breaking new ground as far as satire went. A rhymed slogan, placed at the bottom of the article, summarized the author's main thoughts: "Kupuj towar u Rodaka! Buduj Polskę dla Polaka!" (Buy goods from your countryman! Build Poland for a Pole!). This was accompanied by the "Black list of Judeophiles," published on the same page, which was soon to become a regular feature in the magazine. The list provided names of ethnic Polish shop owners who patronized Jewish suppliers; it also named individuals who frequented Jewish shops.[13] The final page contained advertisements of Christian businesses, from food wholesalers to photographic studios.

The appeals to frequent ethnic Polish shops were to pervade *Pokrzywy*'s issues for months to come. This was visible in the textual content, including rhymed verse and editorial pieces, as well as in the visual matter. Both types of content explored the motivations of ethnic Poles for patronizing Jewish shops. According to one doggerel, Jewish traders were popular with Christian customers because they were cheaper, offered goods on credit, and were open to haggling. By contrast, gentile shopkeepers had fixed prices and required cash payments. The verse maintained that, despite "bowing beautifully" and entertaining their patrons with sweet talk, Jews tampered with weighing scales and had a general tendency for swindling and dishonesty; blunt verbs such as *oszwabić* (to cheat) and *orżnąć* (to rip off) appeared here. Importantly, the doggerel criticized Jews for trading on Sundays and, as such, having an unfair advantage over their Christian counterparts.[14]

While that particular verse was a general examination of certain tendencies the editors believed to be present in their immediate environment, other content provided concrete examples. In one of its articles from the field, covering the situation in the town of Zduńska Wola in Central Poland, *Pokrzywy*'s reporter complained that ethnic Poles were a minority there, only 40 percent of the total population, while the rest comprised Jews and Germans of the Evangelical Church: "One feels sad on entering the town. The Jewry has proliferated omnipotently around here. They trade noisily on their dirty premises and act defiantly as if they were at home."[15] While building on the long-rooted antisemitic tropes of Jewish boisterousness and filth, the article also condemned Jewish traders for working on Sundays and inviting their customers to use the back entry as a way of bypassing the official holiday. One Jewish bakery, owned by a man called Liwerant, was said to be jam-packed.[16] The report told of the few Christian shops found outside the main market square; those were said to have a tidier appearance but lacked board signs designating them as Christian businesses. The stated purpose of the article was to rally support behind the Polonization of Zduńska Wola, which was described as having a "strategic location" and being an important transportation hub. This was accompanied by a roughly drawn cartoon portraying Liwerant standing in front of his bakery and inviting customers to use the back entry, while a large sign at the front says, "Today is Sunday. Closed."[17]

Like the majority of the original drawings in *Pokrzywy*, the cartoon of the bakery in Zduńska Wola was produced by an unskilled anonymous artist. The six people in the image, both customers and the shop owner, look unnatural, their gestures stilted and faces devoid of expression. The figure of Liwerant himself is lifeless, resembling a motionless cardboard shape displayed at the shop front to attract customers. Although his arms and hands point the regulars to the back entry, his body is stock-still, lacking the usual fluidity of human motion. Liwerant's clientele look similarly expressionless, their angular shapes and undefined fingerless hands a likely result of the illustrator's inexperience.

Zduńska Wola was not the only town to be criticized as lagging behind in the so-called de-Judaization of trade. Kalisz too was presented as a site of ongoing economic struggle, despite SN's managing to gain a foothold in the anti-Jewish boycott in the local area. On 9 July 1937, SN's Economic Department (*Wydział Gospodarczy*), in cooperation with its fighting squads, drew a thick white line that divided the marketplace, Rynek Dekerta, into Jewish and Christian sections. Jewish merchants refused to recognize the ghettoization by declining to trade in the two weeks that followed. Members of the Polish Socialist Party (PPS) also expressed their outrage at the situation. Meanwhile, the head of the Kalisz *kehilla* and a councilman for the national Association of Small Merchants and Traders, Josef Mosze Heber, along with other representatives of the Jewish trading community, intervened with Poland's prime minister, Felicjan Sławoj Składkowski, who acted as an MP for the Kalisz area.[18]

This was not the first time Heber had asked Składkowski for help. In June 1936, a similar request for assistance from the prime minister resulted in Jewish traders from Kalisz being able to continue trading at the markets of Greater Poland. This time, however, Heber's efforts were to no avail.[19] On 1 August 1937, *Pokrzywy* published a scathing cartoon that depicted Heber awarding medals to socialist and progressive activists who protested the ghettoization.[20] Some months later, the magazine published a short article arguing that local Jews did not deserve half of the market but should have only 12 percent of the space, which corresponded with the percentage of Jews in the district of Kalisz.[21] The cartoon showed ten male characters against a backdrop of market stalls and city buildings in the distance. In it, Heber wears a long black coat and a kippah, while the gentile men are in suits with badges showing their political factions, such as PPS or BBWR (for Nonpartisan Bloc for Cooperation with the Government), sown on the lapels. Above the party insignia is an embossed star of David, meant to stigmatize each of the men as unpatriotic helpers of Jews who have departed from the path of national loyalty. The drawing is clearly the work of the same caricaturist who produced the picture of Liwerant discussed above. Once more, the maladroit human figures show little complexity as far as contour lines, detail, shading, and individual features are concerned. The image looks flat and lacking in perspective. Importantly, the usual pithiness of the cartoon medium remains unexploited. The drawing is literal and, except for the stars of David that are meant to criticize the pro-Jewish allegiances of the protagonists, it has no visual metaphors. This is a simple scene that can hardly be described as satire. In the cartoon's unusually long caption of seven lines, the socialist defenders of the Jews are described as devotees of "Israel" who love it more than their own nation.

Politicians like those portrayed in the cartoon were used as justification for why the antisemitic campaign had to continue. In August 1937, Endek units placed a banner calling for *Kalisz bez Żydów* (Kalisz without Jews) across one of the town's main streets, Kanonicka Street. Two young Jewish sportsmen, who were also PPS members, Łajzer Kleczewski and Jakub Gelbart, removed the sign clandestinely.[22] This did not deter local SN activists. In November 1937, *Pokrzywy* announced a Week of Propaganda, organized by the National Party, to take place from 8 to 19 December to raise awareness of the ethno-nationalist program of the "Polonization" of Kalisz. The event's organizing committee was said to consist of several Catholic clerics as well as other members of the local community.[23] The editors believed that, in the course of the next two years, "the Jewish bastion will fall and all economic units will be taken over by the Poles."[24] The article further explained that patronizing Jewish businesses harmed the future of the Polish nation and constituted an act of national betrayal. The author ended on a menacing note: "Albo my—albo oni!" (Either us or them!).[25] Indeed, the region of Greater Poland was famed for its Weeks of Propaganda, organized by SN's Economic Department. Not only were the events aimed at promoting Christian trade but at mobilizing ethnic Polish traders to join anti-Jewish protests.[26]

Pokrzywy's editors firmly believed that acquiescent local authorities were crucial to the success of the project. The city of Poznań, in particular, was seen as the most advanced in the top-down policies and bottom-up practices of "de-Judaization." Its mayor was admired for displaying a "progressive" outlook, as exemplified by his support for the boycott. More specifically, the writers mentioned a circular in which the president purportedly asked each and every civil servant to see to their moral duty of favoring Christian shops over Jewish businesses. "When will the same happen in Kalisz?" they asked wistfully.[27]

Throughout its short existence, *Pokrzywy* was a vehement critic of town mayor Ignacy Bujnicki, who took office on 1 May 1937.[28] Since 1928, Bujnicki had been connected with the BBWR, which encompassed several smaller parties, including those of ethnic minorities. He was also involved in a number of charities, such as the Red Cross.[29] It was perhaps his engagement with minority groups that made him disliked by ethnonationalist pundits. *Pokrzywy*'s editors, too, deplored his inclusive politics. One cartoon presented Bujnicki in the company of the community head, Josef Mosze Heber, and two other people as he removes a sign in the town center that calls for the boycott of Jewish businesses.[30] The drawing, made by an artist calling himself "Marek," showed the mayor balancing on a ladder supported by a single Jew, as Heber and another man beg him to be careful. Unlike some of the other cartoonists working for the magazine, Marek used visual symbols to convey a hidden message. The clever metaphor of a shaky ladder, in particular, was meant to warn Bujnicki that, unless he was cautious, his associations with the Jewish community in Kalisz could lead to his downfall.

In reality, Bujnicki and Heber were natural allies. Heber was active at both local and national levels, as his numerous attempts to intervene with the prime minister on behalf of Kalisz's trading Jews show.[31] He was also vocal about the worsening situation of Jewish merchants in the country, which made him a convenient target of antisemitic attacks in the local media.[32] Bujnicki was concerned about the increased activity of SN in his town and the worsening security situation in the area. *Pokrzywy*'s editors understood that and published a report of Bujnicki's official visit to the city of Poznań that described the mayor's unease at the sight of SN activists who chanted proboycott slogans.[33] Another cartoon imagined Bujnicki as a young boy with sidelocks, alluding perhaps to his mother's maiden name, Koerner, and communicating in a thinly veiled manner that the mayor had Jewish roots.[34] Yet another caricature undermined Bujnicki's patriotic credentials, doubting his status as a veteran of the Polish-Soviet War.[35] When Bujnicki disputed the latter information, the magazine's editors were forced to apologize and admit that the mayor did indeed volunteer to fight in 1920.[36] Unsurprisingly, the municipal office made a point of ostracizing the magazine and refused to invite it to major social events in the city, a fact that the editors bemoaned in the months to follow.[37]

Personal attacks such as these were *Pokrzywy*'s forte. Not only did the editors repeatedly chastise the municipality for patronizing Jewish businesses; they also rebuked local MPs for their supposedly harmful philosemitism. One cartoon targeted Feliks Karśnicki, formerly of BBWR, later of Ozon, who was said to "have a weak spot for the Jews." According to the magazine, the administrator of Karśnicki's estate was Jewish, and many of the official events he organized were staffed by Jews. The cartoon offered one example. It presented the MP posing for a Jewish photographer called Engel. The drawing portrayed Karśnicki standing proud and tall in front of the camera, his figure twice as big as that of Engel. It could be that, by introducing the contrast, the anonymous artist, who signed his work "jimski," was intimating that Engel flattered his customers, possibly with a view to cajoling them into business-related favors. This interpretation was corroborated by the lengthy caption, which explained that Karśnicki employed Engel to cover an event commemorating the anti-Russian January Uprising of 1863, organized by the Association of Former War Volunteers of the Polish Army of which he was the president. The caption ended with an appeal to Karśnicki, requesting that he stop embarrassing his home party Ozon, which only two months later issued the anti-Jewish "thirteen theses." To *Pokrzywy*, Judeophilia, or *żydofilstwo* as its editors condescendingly labeled the phenomenon, was a dangerous predilection that poisoned the national spirit.[38]

The magazine's editors expected full commitment from everyone claiming to support the national cause. Their message was clear: hypocrisy would not be tolerated. In one piece of engaged journalism, the writer denounced a Sanacja MP, Wacław Budzyński, for having double standards. The parliamentarian was said to visit the town of Zduńska Wola to promote his new political group, Jutro Pracy (The Tomorrow of Work). The group endorsed an ethno-nationalist ethos, including the "de-Judaization" of Poland, while Budzyński himself was a staunch advocate of removing Jews from all sectors of the economy. Reporting on the event in Zduńska Wola, the writer ridiculed Budzyński for "commencing his national work" in the region by printing leaflets in the local Jewish printing house. The local Endek supporters allegedly derided him for this, and the meeting turned into a complete fiasco, much to the satisfaction of the journalist.[39]

It was not only public figures who were admonished in the magazine. Ethnic Polish shop owners became its target too. According to *Pokrzywy*,

Dwulicowość niektórych kupców polskich

Nie chodźcie do żyda, nie fatygujcie się, ale wszystkie drobne kwoty składajcie u mnie, a ja odniosę je za was całym workiem do żydowskiej hurtowni!

2.1. The Two-Facedness of Some Polish Merchants, from *Pokrzywy*, 21 November 1937, 3.

even Poles who supported the boycotting campaign tended to frequent Jewish wholesalers. One cartoon portrayed a shop front bearing the sign "Sklep Chrześcijański" (Christian Shop) as well as an exclamation "Do not buy from the Jew!," while a scene unfolding in the side alley depicted a Jewish supplier, Dawid Perle, bringing a new delivery of goods to the store (Figure 2.1).[40] Rather than a dig at a specific business, the cartoon was most likely a criticism of the widespread practice among ethnic Poles of using Jewish suppliers. The picture bore all the hallmarks of *Pokrzywy*'s usual approach to visual politics. It was a simple rendition of an urban scene, based on a similar concept as the drawing of the Liwerant bakery. In both, the artist chose to depict the establishment as a corner shop, giving the viewer a look into the side entrance where the stealthy acts of national disloyalty were being perpetrated. Despite its conventional setting, this was a deeply political cartoon that showed there were difficulties to the existing economic struggle. While in this case the name of the Christian shop, which supported the Jewish wholesaler, was not disclosed, some of *Pokrzywy*'s textual content was less discreet about the specific business owners who obtained their goods from Jewish suppliers. Often their names and the exact locations of their shops were mentioned as a way of marking the individuals as unpatriotic and shaming them into changing their ways.[41] *Pokrzywy* had an uncompromising stance on the issue: sacrifices had to be made for Polonization of the economy to be accomplished.

In the same way they shamed retailers for providing a lifeline for Jewish wholesalers, *Pokrzywy*'s editors discredited individual customers who purportedly patronized Jewish businesses. One article from the provincial town of Pleszew criticized a local teacher named Piaczyński who was said to have purchased a fur coat for his wife from a Jewish woman in Kalisz.[42] Another editorial reported that the head nurse in a care home in the town of Ostrów sold her cow to a Jew and bought another one from him.[43] According to a report from Kalisz, a "Mr Buczkowski who is building a house on Piekarska Street procured roofing felt from Szachtl the Jew."[44] Yet another piece claimed that, in Kępno, the daughter of a Mr. Piwoński was a regular at Schwarz's shop.[45] Similarly, a report from the town of Sieradz stated that a well-known restaurateur in the Poznański Hotel, Józef Rubaszek, bought everything from Jews. He allegedly bought a radio worth 600 zloty, as well as a carpet, tablecloths, and tableware. He was also thought to procure meat from Jews on a regular basis. *Pokrzywy* advised Rubaszek to start wearing sidelocks and leave for Palestine. The text further implied that, unless he complied, Jews would take full control of the country and Rubaszek's own children would end up being their servants. The piece ended on a menacing note: "Unfortunately, there are more idiots (*matoły*) like that in Sieradz and we will write about them in our next issue."[46]

But the magazine's readers were in for a surprise. The next issue included a statement from Rubaszek in which he denied all the allegations, claiming that the information was fabricated by an "enemy" of his who sought revenge. He maintained that he was an upright citizen who only patronized Christian shops and supported the national economy. *Pokrzywy*'s editors reported being pleased that the situation in Sieradz was not as bad as they had first assumed.[47]

The boycott did not focus on trade only; it hoped to inhibit Jewish presence in all sectors of the economy and industry. One area of *Pokrzywy*'s intervention was the labor market. The magazine stigmatized individuals who purportedly dismissed ethnic Poles in favor of employing Jews. One issue criticized a hospital in Kalisz for sacking a Christian midwife and continuing to employ several of her Jewish colleagues.[48] Elsewhere, a pharmacy of Nowicki in a small town of Burzenin was rebuked for employing a Jewish pharmacist.[49] In yet another issue, the local village of Ceków was blacklisted for delivering milk to a Jewish, rather than Christian, dairy.[50] Calls for the "de-Judaization" of whole professions, such as the judiciary and apothecary, were also issued.[51] These coincided with the introduction of the so-called Aryan paragraph by an increasing number of professional and academic associations nationwide, which prohibited Jews and persons of Jewish descent from membership in said organizations.[52]

To what extent those reports targeted real persons is difficult to determine. The local character of the magazine and the specificity of personal details, including addresses and names of businesses, would suggest that, irrespective of their veracity, *Pokrzywy*'s denunciations referred to existing individuals. That those reports were based on hearsay and malicious finger pointing is more than certain. In a period of heightened antisemitic campaigning and ongoing economic boycott, any association with Jewish traders and suppliers could be potentially damaging, particularly to ethnic Polish retailers who relied on customers from across the political spectrum. At the same time, the examples mentioned here would suggest that some gentile traders and customers were somewhat indifferent to such politicking. Rather, they were economically minded and strategic in their spending decisions.[53] While the actual reach and influence of public shaming in the print media are difficult to measure, *Pokrzywy*'s editors seemed to firmly believe in the corrective, if not coercive, function of their content. In an oft-reprinted cartoon, the magazine depicted a Jewish man and his Polish helper escaping from a whipping with nettles (Figure 2.2). The former is being punished for plotting to bring about the demise of the Polish nation and the latter for treason. The punishing hand executing the sentence holds a bouquet of the stinging plant, ready to spank everyone who disobeys. The composition of the drawing, consisting of the two supposed offenders and the disembodied albeit intimidating arm closing in on them, was meant to alert readers as to the power of the magazine. No one could escape the stinging of *Pokrzywy*'s satire. The caption above the image reads: "*Pokrzywy*—the menace of Jews and *shabbes goyim*."[54]

Unlike the majority of caricatures published in the magazine, which were drawn in square or rectangular frames, this image was frameless, perhaps to convey the infinity of *Pokrzywy*'s reach. Also, the artist of this caricature was more capable than the others: both the faces and clothing of the characters contain a fair amount of detail, their movements are more fluid, and there is a greater sense of perspective, atypical for the local artists. It is likely that the image was pinched from a foreign antisemitic magazine, possibly even the German *Brennessel*.[55] Such publications would have been available to those who sought them out, considering the number of ethnic Germans in

„Pokrzywy" — postrachem żydów i szabesgojów.

Patrzajcie! — Od „Pokrzywy"
Ucieka ledwo żywy
żyd i jego obrońca...
Dość nam już tej hołoty,
Wyżenim ich za płoty,
Niech nam nie ciemnią słońca.

2.2. Nettles—The Menace of Jews and Shabbes Goyim, from *Pokrzywy*, 1 September 1937, 6.

Poland and the efficient circulation of German-language print media among Germans living outside Nazi Germany. Importantly, both the title and the motif of the punishing nettle were what the two publications had in common, requiring no additional modifications on the part of the Kalisz staff and making the image instantaneously usable.

Terrorizing those who interacted with Jews was not exclusive to *Pokrzywy*. According to Joanna Michlic, in ethnonationalist print media "political parties, social organizations, and individuals who opposed anti-Semitism were as a rule labeled as traitors of the Polish nation and servants of the Jews. Such individuals were commonly referred to as 'shabbes goys' (*szabesgoje*), 'Jewish servants' (*żydowskie pachołki*), and 'Jewish uncles' (*żydowscy wujkowie*)."[56] *Pokrzywy*, too, used these terms, in addition to "Jewish aunts" (*ciotki żydowskie*) and "Jewish henchmen" (*żydowskie wojtki*).[57] These terms, as well as the equally crude *żydofile* (Judeophiles), were particularly widespread in other publications that pledged to safeguard Christian traders and to nationalize the economy. The Poznań-based daily *Pod Pręgierz*, for example, listed names of people who maintained business contacts with Jews and supported the Jewish cause, including charities for refugees escaping Nazi Germany.[58] In some issues, photographs of local *szabesgoje* were published on the front page of the newspaper to stigmatize such individuals.[59] In a similar vein, the Catholic press criticized Polish firms for maintaining business contacts with Jewish contractors. Newspapers published didactic stories in which Jewish products were presented as "enemy" products of inferior quality.[60] According to Ronald Modras, a historian of antisemitism, the Catholic press "experienced no moral difficulties in encouraging the boycott," viewing "the boycott as an aspect of their obligations to church and state. It was not a contradiction to Christian charity but a consequence of it."[61] Readers of such publications were asked to keep those principles in mind as they went shopping or used professional services.

It is not known to what extent *Pokrzywy* and other publications were successful in persuading the general public to change their daily economic practices. What is certain, however, is that the anti-Jewish boycott, which intensified in the second half of 1937, created practical obstacles to supporting Jewish businesses. Members of Endek units and of the far-right National Radical Camp (ONR)-Falanga picketed Jewish shops and started scuffles to prevent customers from entering.[62] OZN's youth section, the parafascist Union of Young Poland (ZMP), organized and funded picket lines outside Jewish businesses. The organization also took action against Catholic merchants who continued to collaborate with Jews, among other activities.[63] Like Falanga, ZMP adhered to a militaristic ethos, and its members were uniformed. It was popular with youth and grew in size rapidly, from forty thousand members in autumn 1937 to sixty thousand in spring 1938. Boycotting activities organized by these organizations often turned into unrest and brought terror to the streets, effectively dissuading Poles from frequenting Jewish stores.[64] In many communities, the picketing and physical attacks on Jews and their customers led to shop closures and made it "virtually impossible to carry on business."[65] Many traders reported feeling terrorized and fearing for their lives.[66]

Following countless calls to boycott Jewish businesses in 1937, *Pokrzywy*'s economic campaigning subsided in early 1938. One cartoon in January 1938 presented the shop front of a certain "K. Mühlstein" declaring bankruptcy. The shop, which had sold textiles, is surrounded by cannons bearing the names of Christian firms that had banished the Jewish seller from the market. Before the cannons stands Mühlstein himself, talking to a fellow cloth trader, Lejba Siemiatycki, who would soon share the fate of his colleague, having already filed for insolvency. The extended caption informed readers that the sustained anti-Jewish boycott in Kalisz was finally beginning to bear fruit.[67] It is likely that the cartoon referred to real-life businesses since Leon Siemiatycki was indeed a Kalisz trader, actively involved in local affairs.[68] The two men were drawn realistically, rather than as pictorial types employed in so many cartoons in other magazines, including the progovernment *Mucha*. Dressed in clothing that is neither too extravagant nor too modern, the two traders are clearly locals, known to customers in Kalisz. The local anchoring of the magazine as well as its usual drive toward realism meant that the likenesses of Mühlstein and Siemiatycki avoided the caricatural tone of *Mucha*'s portrayals, which relied on generalized traits and vices. That publication's strategy of personifying supposed Jewish shortcomings made for a persuasive visual idiom that could potentially help distance the reader from the real person. Despite being equally hateful in intention, *Pokrzywy*'s focus on familiar subjects did not allow for such detachment, forcing the reader to make a specific ideological choice.

Once Mühlstein and others were gone, part of *Pokrzywy*'s mission was complete. Its portrayals were not mere propaganda. Even though many of the other nationalist outlets continued to support a proboycott agenda up until the outbreak of the Second World War, 1937 saw a drastic decline in the number of Jewish-owned shops across Poland. According to a survey of one eastern Polish region, in 1932 Jewish retailers constituted 92 percent of all shops in the area. In 1937, this figure had dropped to 64.5 percent. A similar trend was seen nationwide. Although industry was more resilient to the boycott, an increasing number of ordinary Jews experienced economic hardship and even abject poverty.⁶⁹ This was no different for Kalisz.⁷⁰ Like many other communities in Poland, Jews in Kalisz had already been weakened by unemployment and economic difficulties of the crisis years, and the community was marked by desolation, hopelessness, and growing suicide rates.⁷¹ Paired with hostility and increasing physical violence, the boycott provided the final blow to many small business owners.

Deliberately oblivious to the human cost of its ongoing hate campaign, *Pokrzywy* nonetheless continued on the same antisemitic path. The magazine lived by many of the principles that it promoted—for example, by commissioning advertisements from Christian businesses only. This practice was consistently upheld from its founding in 1937 to its final issue in August 1939. The message that communicated this in an admittedly tautological manner read as follows: "Wydawnictwo przyjmuje ogłoszenia *wyłącznie tylko* od firm chrześcijańskich" (The publisher accepts advertisements *exclusively only* from Christian companies).⁷² The announcement appeared on the final page of each issue.

In the two years of its existence, *Pokrzywy*'s callous portrayals of Polish Jews also came to encompass the tropes of Jewish threat and domination. Both were meant to flag the damage that Jews were supposedly wreaking on Poland.

JEWISH DOMINATION

In *Pokrzywy*, the tropes of Jewish threat and domination tended to overlap with the theme of ruination that Jewish presence was said to cause to the Polish state in general and the Polish economy in particular. This alleged Jewish domination was understood predominantly in spatial terms. This manifested in two ways. First was the highly symbolic idea of the supposed Jewish control over the Polish national spirit. Second was *Pokrzywy*'s more tangible conception of public spaces as dominated by Jews. This was exemplified by the magazine's depiction of day-to-day Polish-Jewish encounters in urban spaces. The Polish national realm, whether in its symbolic or physical dimension, was thus portrayed as being polluted by the Jews and in urgent need of reclaiming by Christian Poles. By no means were these ideas new. The conviction that the Jewish national spirit was not only inherently alien but also inimical to the Polish soul was deeply rooted in the national thought of Romanticism. Chief representatives of Polish antisemitism believed that the only way of eradicating this supposedly damaging influence was to separate Jews from the rest of the population.⁷³ By the late interwar period, that separation did not denote merely ghettoization; its ultimate goal was a complete removal of Jews from the country.

That some of *Pokrzywy*'s antisemitic representations were rooted in national symbolism, both nineteenth-century and earlier, is clear from the visual tropes used by the magazine. However, *Pokrzywy* provided an altered and modernized version of those symbols to address current social and political anxieties and to hint at the ongoing public debates. In September 1937, the magazine published a cover cartoon entitled "Jewish dreams." The cartoon centers around a Jewish man in traditional garb, plucking the two-headed Russian eagle and casting a menacing glance at the Polish coat of arms—a white crowned eagle—displayed on the wall. "I wish I could ritually slaughter the white eagle," the caption below reads, "the same way I slaughtered the black Russian one" (Figure 2.3).[74] Not only was the man an embodiment of the so-called Judeo-Bolshevik threat that was now supposedly consuming Russia; he was also an internal enemy with a desire, if not a concrete plan, to derail Polish affairs. The Jewish dreams in the title were thus the dreams of domination.

The drawing was created by an artist who understood the purpose of the caricature medium. The illustrator named "Alfa" drew the figure of the Jew in a clearly exaggerated manner: his open mouth, pointed teeth, sinister gaze, and long thumbnail were meant to underscore the alleged threat posed by the Jewish population. Like the cartoon of the stinging nettle spanking the Jew and his Christian helper, this image was by an artist who paid close attention to detail. This is seen in the facial expression of the subject, the folds on his coat and trousers, and the shading and use of line on the plucked body of the slayed bird. Although far from accomplished, the drawing reveals more visual nuance than the caricatures portraying the protagonists of local affairs that were likely done by nonprofessional artists, possibly SN activists, from Kalisz. The global theme of the cartoon that could be applied to different national contexts would point to a mature artist of sorts, suggesting that the illustration was borrowed from a foreign antisemitic publication and adjusted to fit the local context, notably through addition of the Polish eagle in the top left corner and context-specific captions. Such borrowings were not that uncommon in the Polish print media of the day. The sources of the reproduced illustrations were rarely given; sometimes the signature of the original artist was removed to suggest it was created by a local artist and avoid possible copyright claims.[75]

Pokrzywy's choice of the theme of slaughter could also be read as an allusion to the ongoing debate on the *shechita* or ritual slaughter. Throughout much of 1936, the Polish Sejm discussed a controversial bill that stipulated that animals should be rendered unconscious before slaughter. Since Jewish

2.3. Jewish Fantasies, from *Pokrzywy*, 27 September 1937, 1.

law prohibited stunning animals, the legislation would effectively mean an end to the kosher meat industry. Rightly so, the Jewish media considered the proposal to be antisemitic.[76] In a similar way, Polish Jewish MPs criticized the anticonstitutional nature of the bill and argued that the proposed ban would affect many Jews for whom ritual slaughter and the sale of kosher meat were their main source of income.[77] In the end, the bill was passed, and the new law took effect on 1 January 1937. Although it permitted exemptions for groups whose religion required a different method of slaughter, it was a Pyrrhic victory for both parties. For Endeks and other antisemitic pundits, animal rights advocates included, the debate was by no means finished. They continued to demand a complete ban on the *shechita* up until the outbreak of the Second World War.[78]

Reference to the contemporary discussion on immobilizing and stunning animals appeared in another cartoon in 1937. Once more it was used as a metaphor to describe bigger issues, in this case the perceived harm that Jews were believed to bring to other nations. Entitled "The Jewish Slaughterhouse of Nations," the cartoon portrayed a Jewish abattoir in which a cow is led to slaughter. Blindfolded with a hammer and sickle headband, the animal was to represent all Christian nations that were blinded by Communism and then brought to be "slaughtered" like cattle, with Russia and Spain named as chief examples. According to the caption, Poland was in danger of suffering a similar fate.[79] This competently drawn cartoon, which used the motif of *shechita* to draw attention to other topics, not least so-called Judeo-Communism, was a reproduction from the German weekly *Der Stürmer*, as the signature of the artist, Fips, indicated. Fips was a *nom de plume* of Philipp Rupprecht (1900–1975), the chief illustrator for *Der Stürmer*, who joined its staff in 1925 and remained with the magazine until 1945.[80] Throughout his career, Fips produced thousands of cartoons that had global resonance, employing antisemitic tropes that would have been recognizable to audiences in Germany and elsewhere.

Pokrzywy made use of caricatures by Fips at least five more times, and the slaughterhouse cartoon reveals all the trademarks of his usual drawing repertoire.[81] Like the slaughterhouse character, his Jews are typically overweight, unshaven, and bent-nosed, as well as having protruding lips, large teeth, and drooping posture. These representations were meant to suggest that Jews were, by nature, ugly. To prove the documentary value of its caricatures and emphasize that these were not solely the artist's impression, *Der Stürmer* employed doctored photographs that reinforced this imagery. It was the magazine's editorial policy to retouch such photographs to make Jewish subjects look unappealing: noses were enlarged and facial expressions distorted, all in an attempt to strengthen the stereotype. Unlike *Pokrzywy*, which

2.4. Jews and Communists Are Devising the Annihilation of the Christian World, from *Pokrzywy*, 25 October 1937, 2.

had no access to such advanced technology, *Der Stürmer* enlisted mixed visual media in spreading the antisemitic message. Readers responded with enthusiasm, claiming to have seen Jewish types just like the ones depicted by Fips.[82]

The slaughterhouse cartoon was not *Pokrzywy*'s only reference to the so-called Judeo-Bolshevik threat. The trope appeared in the magazine a few more times, but the uses were neither particularly persuasive nor imaginative.[83] The most striking of those cartoons warned that Jews were plotting the destruction of Christian civilization and it was not too late to come to one's senses and recognize the enemy within. The drawing represented the Polish nation standing on top of a rock and facing the abyss, as Jews and communists await their fall (Figure 2.4).[84] Evoking Romantic imagery, including literary classics such as Juliusz Słowacki's *Kordian* in which the main character delivers his patriotic soliloquy standing atop a mountain, the motif of the rock was meant to appeal to the national imagination, tying the patriotic imagery to the fear of the Other. While this image was also likely to be a foreign import, its use by *Pokrzywy* demonstrates the transnational reach of the symbolism of Romantic nationalism, which remained relevant across state borders and could be seamlessly transferred between national contexts.

Similar national symbols that could have had transnational resonance appeared in another cartoon. In it, the illustrator employed the metaphor of homeland as boat in a tempestuous sea. In the Polish context, the cartoon could be read as an allusion to the well-known *Eight sermons before the Sejm* (1597) by the Polish Jesuit Piotr Skarga, which criticized the greed and self-interest of Sejm representatives, calling them to take responsibility for the national future. Describing the country as a ship in danger of sinking, Skarga argued that the fatherland needed the immediate attention of its citizens in order to survive. Although *Eight sermons* was virtually unknown in Skarga's time, it became all the more relevant after the last Partition of Poland in the late eighteenth century. It was then that the text became part of the national canon, providing an important corpus of national symbols and imagery on which to draw in the coming decades.[85] In *Pokrzywy*'s cartoon, the boat sails under the banner of the National Party, the strained faces of its crew conveying the difficulty of the task at hand (Figure 2.5). The four men are being tested: their labored motion, downcast gaze, and bulging muscles intimate that only determination and unity will defeat the enemy. In the sea below, six Jewish and communist "sharks" encircle the vessel and bite into its oars. Although outnumbered and unsure of the future, the SN men persevere. The cartoon is no doubt a battle cry, one meant to stir the reader and provide a stimulus to action. Despite the perils of stormy sea, the caption also exudes confidence:

> Tighten your arms! Stiffen your shoulders,
> And Poland will be liberated—we'll break the necks of the enemies,
> Though the storm roars around us, we'll lift up our heads!
> The time of tempest will not scare us, our hands are strong.
> Although the wind breaks the sails, be joyful, brothers![86]

Both the image and the poem were meant to reassure the reader that, unlike the sixteenth-century Sejm representatives of Skarga's Poland, the ethno-nationalist activists of the present appreciated the gravity of the situation. Their strength and enthusiasm were to herald victory over the threat of Judeo-Communism. But the cartoon was important for another reason. Published on 15 March 1938, the day of the Anschluss, it signaled a purported danger of Jewish refugees escaping Nazi-dominated states, the same way as some of *Mucha*'s cartoons from that period did.

Although the criticism of Soviet Communism was fairly widespread in the ethno-nationalist press of the period, constituting a response to contemporary

2.5. The National Ship in Battle, from *Pokrzywy*, 15 March 1938, 1.

events such as the ongoing Great Terror, the idea that Jews attempted to undermine Christianity and reduce their gentile counterparts to slavery was more anachronistic and hearkened back to the *Protocols of the Learned Elders of Zion*, a notorious forgery of the previous century. Written in France in the 1890s, supposedly on orders from the tsarist regime, and circulated widely after the First World War, the text posited that Jews colluded in a global conspiracy and aimed to command all possible sources of power. Using money, socialism, pornography, alcoholism, humanism, and other tools, Jews were said to seek an all-encompassing world domination. The text speculated that, after their successful revolution, the Jews would eliminate all religions but Judaism.[87]

Several of *Pokrzywy*'s cartoons and texts built on those ideas. In the mode of the *Protocols*, one cartoon pictured a "Jew—the Eternal Revolutionary," equipped with the Talmud and a volume of Karl Marx, spouting slogans of equality, brotherhood, and the freedom of religion (Figure 2.6). The caption underneath reminded the reader what many other cartoons only implied: the Jew "dreams of ruling the world and thus he overturns and destroys the

2.6. Jew—the Eternal Revolutionary, from *Pokrzywy*, 15 July 1938, 10.

established order of Christian nations. Marxists and Freemasons are his allies. The struggle against Jewry is the struggle to liberate the Christian spirit."[88] The visual elements of the cartoon, which was far more detailed than other drawings published by the magazine, further demonized the figure. With a hooked nose, goatee, sidelocks, bulging eyes, and barred teeth, his face exudes malice and evil. This, as well as his bare hairy legs and arms and torn clothing, brought to mind the medieval portrayals of Jews as the agents of Satan. In the words of one historian of antisemitism, such representations were meant to present Jews as "seeking to entrap innocent believers and entice them away from their Christian faith." Those portrayals, which depicted the Jew as "embodying the will of Satan," enabled medieval Christendom to "inaugurate an inexorable process of dehumanization."[89] The *Protocols*, too, linked Jews to the devil and the Antichrist; it was this very association that inspired modern antisemites to construe Jews as wielding considerable power over national and international affairs.[90]

Like some of *Mucha*'s cartoons discussed in the previous chapter, this portrayal bridged folk and intellectual antisemitism. In a state with a large Roman Catholic population and an extensive system of cultural symbols in which Jews were often cast in the role of the antithetical Other, anti-Jewish portrayals such as these were bound to resonate with audiences. According to anthropologist Alina Cała, the belief that Jews colluded with the devil and possessed superhuman powers survived in the Polish countryside well into the 1970s, superseding the events of the Second World War and the Holocaust.[91] Although these findings might not reflect the views of all ethnic Poles of the interwar period, they indicate that medieval-style antisemitism was deeply ingrained in the national stereotyping of Jews. At the same time, the "Eternal Revolutionary" cartoon could also have a global resonance. Its focus on dehumanizing the Jewish body was a trademark of many German cartoons of the time that were reproduced by *Pokrzywy*. Given how different it was from the drawings by local SN artists, this caricature was most likely the work of an outsider artist and additional evidence of the derivative character of the magazine.

To *Pokrzywy*, as to other creators of antisemitic content, the idea of purported Jewish domination was a capacious one. It could range from inferences that Jews have colonized the whole world to various depictions of the influence they were said to exert over the Polish economy. For example, one cartoon by Alfa depicted a cheder in which the teacher is teaching his young pupils the geographical location of Palestine. When asked where the Jewish colonies are, the melamed responds plainly: "That's the rest of the world."[92] The caricature was drawn by the same, most likely foreign, artist who produced the image of the slayed eagle discussed earlier. The teacher was the same man, as his lanky frame, sidelocks, sly leer, below-the-knee trousers, and oversized slippers suggest. Implying that the idea of Jewish power was instilled in Jews from a very young age, the cartoon was clearly one of *Pokrzywy*'s showpieces since it was rehashed the following year.[93] Another cartoon on this topic depicted Polish Jewish representatives of the judiciary, banking, and several industries joined in a celebratory dance, while a poverty-stricken gentile watches the scene in silence. Derogatory terms such as leeches, swindlers, and thieves appear in the caption.[94] The magazine's textual content, too, spoke of foreign agents (*obca agentura*), cartels, and plots aimed at taking over Polish industry.[95]

Given the local character of the magazine and its chief preoccupation with bottom-up antisemitic activism in the Kalisz region, such transnational concerns could seem oddly out of place, despite going hand in hand with ethnonationalist debates around the so-called de-Judaization of Poland. The editors of *Pokrzywy* clearly understood that to make the supposed Jewish threat seem more real, they had to operate with familiar locations, in the same way their cartoons, poems, and articles on the economic boycott did. Thus, the metaphorical representations of Jewish dominance that could seem distant, if not abstract, to readers from Kalisz were often interspersed with references to concrete towns and cities in the region.

The city of Łódź loomed large in *Pokrzywy*'s rehashing of the canard of Jewish domination. Located approximately 115 km from Kalisz, Łódź is marginally closer to Kalisz than the region's capital, Poznań. To *Pokrzywy*, Łódź was the antithesis of Poznań. A textile center that emerged on the wave of industrial capitalism, driven largely by Jewish and German entrepreneurs, Łódź was an obvious target. To add insult to injury, the city was a stronghold of the Polish Socialist Party, and its municipality had been governed by socialists since the 1936 election.[96] Even in the early years of the newly established state, Łódź was vilified by the right-wing press as the city of Jewish profiteers exploiting the impoverished Polish masses.[97] The Endek Poznań, with its strong ethno-nationalist following, stood in sharp contrast to everything that Łódź represented. This was basic mathematics. In the nineteenth century, Greater Poland and other Prussian lands had a lower percentage of Jews than other regions.[98] In 1939, Jews constituted only 0.3 percent of the total population of the Poznań district.[99] By comparison, in Łódź, Jews comprised one-third of the overall population, making the city the second largest Jewish community in Poland after Warsaw.[100]

In *Pokrzywy*, Łódź was represented as controlled by the Jewish "kings of cotton," stretching their tentacles across the city to enslave the ethnic Polish poor. One conspicuous cartoon portrayed two male figures emerging from

2.7. The Cotton Kings of Łódź, from *Pokrzywy*, 15 September 1938, 4.

the smoking chimneys of the city (Figure 2.7). Their exaggerated faces bear the hallmarks of both medieval and nineteenth-century antisemitism. Their elongated noses, for example, are meant to signify racial difference.[101] Their menacing sneers and large pointed ears symbolize their supposed malevolent nature. More importantly, the smoke from which the two figures emerge was drawn to resemble tentacles that envelope and threaten the city.

The caption below the image, written in the Yiddishized Polish of *Mucha*'s Winersztok, further emphasized the evil intentions of the industrialists, including their plans to turn Poles into slaves.[102] The cartoon was meant to reflect the economic reality of the city. According to the 1931 census, 77.4 percent of Łódź's textile factories were owned by Jews. They featured prominently in trade, crafts, and the liberal professions too, and only a small percentage of the city's Jewish population were blue-collar workers.[103] What the magazine did here, then, was to translate the preponderance of Jews in the industry and other sectors of the city's economy into the language of antisemitism.

The cartoon did so by employing the visual models of global antisemitism used in other contexts, including nineteenth-century America. Historians of American Jewry and art have pointed out that, in the American print media, wealthy Jewish families such as the Rothschilds were presented as spreading eight tentacles across the world to intimate their controlling of global affairs.[104] The trope of tentacles, in particular, was aimed at dehumanizing the subjects and enhancing the hate-mongering effect of such visuals.[105] The trope of octopus tentacles survived the Second World War and has continued to be used throughout much of the twentieth and twenty-first centuries, in such disparate examples as Soviet Cold War propaganda in the 1950s, the Greek Junta's anti-Zionist reporting in the 1970s, and contemporary conservative discourses surrounding Hungarian-born Jewish American billionaire George Soros.[106]

In *Pokrzywy*'s view, Łódź was not only completely dominated by wealthy Jewish industrialists but also provided a breeding ground for Communism (*wylęgarnia komuny*), an ideology that was purportedly a lifeline to the Jews. According to another cartoon on the topic, Łódź had to be "disinfected" in order to cut off that source of support (Figure 2.8). The drawing presented local representatives of the National Party spraying a building overrun by pests, a collection of cockroaches and maggots with names of coalition parties, PPS, KPP (for the Communist Party of Poland), and Bund, printed on their backs. The insecticide used here consists of a powerful mixture of two ethno-nationalist magazines from Greater Poland: *Pokrzywy* itself and its Poznań-based ally, *Orędownik*. As they spray the house front, the men hope they will also bring down the Jew who watches the scene unfold from the rooftop.[107]

The cartoon was, no doubt, the magazine's response to the municipal government elections that took place that same year. In Łódź, the left was victorious with the united front of Polish, Jewish, and German socialists and communists gaining 46.3 percent of all votes. Although this was a narrow defeat for National Democracy, it made the party finally realize that the people's front was a threat that needed to be taken seriously.[108] These sentiments were very much present in *Pokrzywy*'s cartoon: the disappointment of defeat and

Mecenas Kowalski: Wyżej kolego po tym żydowskim robactwie!
Stary Czernik: Dobiorę ja się i do góry. Ale najpierw trzeba przepędzić pepesy, tę wylęgarnie komuny i podporę żydowstwa. Braknie podpory—to i żyd z dachu spadnie z samego przestrachu.

2.8. The Disinfection of Workers' Łódź, from *Pokrzywy*, 1 September 1937, 3.

the resolve to renew a struggle against any ideology that undermined the ethnonationalist cause.

This drawing was manifestly a work of a local amateur artist; the stiff triangular bodies of the subjects, their ill-defined faces and hands, the distorted sense of proportion, and asymmetrical placement of the building were

LOCAL STRUGGLES 73

Żydowska dżungla na teatralnej widowni

Pewien nieznany człeczyna	Ale rozpacz go opadła,	Tak go zewsząd wzięto w koło,
Przybył do Łodzi z Konina	Kiedy przy nim Sura siadła,	Że uczuł się niewesoło,
I wprost nadały go bogi	I uczuł mocne oparcie	A zapachy cebulowe
W gościnne teatru progi.	Na ramionach tłustej Salci	Odurzyły jego głowę.
Tu odetchnie i ożyje,	Szmul Pomeranc pchnął go brzuchem	Wreszcie usnął i nie wiedział,
Polska sztuka się opije,	I zapitał tuż nad uchem:	Że w żydowskiej dżungli siedział
I w wytwornym otoczeniu	„Co szi panu nie podobi?	Odtąd na wspomnienie Łodzi
Odda się błogim marzeniom!	Niech pan damu miejsce zrobi!"	Od zdrowych zmysłów odchodzi.
		satyr.

2.9. A Jewish Jungle in Theatre Audiences, from *Pokrzywy*, 15 July 1938, 12.

emblematic of several other drawings on local topics. By comparison, the earlier image presenting the "cotton kings" of Łódź was more characteristic of foreign caricature, which tended to operate with the easily transportable tropes of Jewish control and domination. The latter themes, although recognizable to the readers of *Pokrzywy* and falling in line with the wider agenda of economic struggle, stood out among the visual renditions of day-to-day life in Kalisz that were more common, and therefore relatable, to local audiences.

Some of the magazine's other references to Łódź were focused on the visibility of Jews in public spaces and were meant to emphasize what many on the right saw as an uncomfortable coexistence. One portrayal, drawn in a three-panel strip, depicted an anonymous Pole from the provincial town of Konin who has travelled to Łódź to get a taste of its cultural offerings (Figure 2.9). On his arrival in the movie theatre, the man is besieged by three other spectators, ostentatious Jewish characters whose oversized bodies, Yiddishized Polish, flamboyant clothing, and unpleasant body odor impose on the man's personal space.[109] The Salomeas and Szmuls of this particular strip constitute an omnibus of visual, olfactory, and auditory antisemitic tropes. In contrast, the befuddled Pole has an unassuming persona: he is an everyman from the provinces who is starved for culture, something he is eventually denied. The ordinary setting of the scene was meant to convey the authenticity of the story, while the allusions to Polish culture that the Konin man was prevented from savoring implied that this very culture might in fact be under threat.

The image itself provides only some of the aforementioned information, but the rhymed poem underneath fleshes out more detail about the encounter. What the comic strip cannot say using the visual means, the verse can spell out for the reader. This includes the supposed names of the Jewish characters, the smells they exude, and their heavily accented Polish. Thus, if analyzed solely in visual terms, this is a generic story that can be easily transferred from one national context to another, providing yet another example of the transnational circulation of specific antisemitic tropes, not least loudness and gaudiness. It is the poem that gives it a local flavor and makes the narrative potentially identifiable. The drawing style itself surpasses *Pokrzywy*'s usual lay offerings as well as departing from its typical focus on real-life subjects. Although they are given specific names, such as Szmul Pomeranc, the Jewish protagonists presented here are, in principle, stereotypes, being pigeonholed as the larger-than-life *Westjude*. Such typecasting, although appearing occasionally in *Mucha*, was never of interest to *Pokrzywy*'s in-house illustrators, who preferred to focus on realistic scenes that were of importance to the ongoing economic boycott. This would suggest that the strip was one of the numerous borrowings from the foreign press, intimating an ambitious editor who wished to share wider European offerings with his readers.

Like the strip above, the magazine shared the common consensus among right-wing pundits that Jews beset public spaces, spaces of leisure included, and that this "occupation" required an immediate action. Alarmist news about the rising numbers of Jews in specific areas, whether on Nalewki Street in Warsaw, the city of Lviv, or the seaport of Gdynia, were recurrent, as were the comparisons of such localities to Palestine. "There are more Jews here than in Palestine," the magazine would comment gloomily, rehashing the tone of similar wisecracks published in the progovernment *Mucha*.[110] This was accompanied by calls to readers to familiarize themselves with the "enemy." In a serial ad promoting a new Yiddish-language textbook, the magazine appealed to its regulars, "Learn the Jewish language! Knowing the enemy is half the battle won!," before encouraging them to purchase the book and the accompanying Yiddish-Polish dictionary.[111]

While it is unclear whether this ad was to be taken at face value, assuming that antisemitic audiences would learn Yiddish required a leap of faith and could have possibly evidenced the ad's satirical intentionality, some of *Pokrzywy*'s other pronouncements were graver in tone, suggesting a perceived urgency of their anti-Jewish proclamations. Like the cartoon about the aftermath of local elections in Łódź, many representations used comparisons to disease to intimate how deeply Jews had penetrated into the tissue of the state and how difficult it might be to remove that unwanted presence.

Żydowskie wrzody na gospodarczym organiźmie Polski

Społeczeństwo polskie czeka na operację

2.10. Jewish Tumors on the Economic Organism of Poland, from *Pokrzywy*, 1 May 1938, 11.

A cartoon published in May 1938 was representative of that. It depicts a Polish man in a doctor's office (Figure 2.10). His bandaged head, hand, and feet hide malignant lumps as the title, "Jewish tumors on the economic organism of Poland," imply. Each of the swellings represents one sector of the economy: banking, trade, crafts, and industry. Next to the patient stands the "doctor" clad in a surgeon's apron, wielding a sharp, long, pointed knife. In the same way the tumor-ridden parts of the body bear inscriptions pointing to a specific branch of the economy, the doctor is a metaphor for the hoped-for change in government, from Sanacja to the National Party, which was to bring about a cure to the body economic. "Polish society is awaiting surgery" is the caption below the image.[112] Aside from alluding to the old canard of Jewish control, the cartoon could also be read as part of preelection campaigning before parliamentary elections that were to take place in autumn that same year.

The idea that Jews were a foreign organism that fed on the Polish body was also expressed through use of the parasite comparison. In one text, Jews are likened to "disgusting lice" that hold on to non-Jews as though they are a sheepskin coat. "Whoever wishes to get rid of the lice must burn the coat," the text recommends.[113] In another text, a rhymed poem entitled "Poland the Superpower," author Artur Lorek recommended that, to restore Poland's position as superpower, one had to put an end to the Jewish "parasitic scum" (*pasożytnicza menda*).[114] Elsewhere, the same author warned against the "Jewish swarms" (*żydowskie mrowie*) and "Jewish mob" (*tłuszcza żydowska*) that were supposedly overtaking Polish cities.[115]

According to historian of medicine Paul Weindling, in the nineteenth century, antisemitic scientists in Germany and Austria used the metaphors of ulcers, growths, parasites, and insects to describe Jews, particularly the *Ostjuden* who were fleeing pogroms in Russia.[116] This is when, to quote Weindling, "Hereditary biology and bacteriology cross-fertilized with loathing of Jews as an alien culture and religion to generate a biological stereotype of the Jewish race as pathogenic."[117] During the First World War, anti-typhus campaigns conducted in Polish cities by German medical staff were focused predominantly on Jewish districts as the main sources of the disease; the growing number of delousing facilities were seen as crucial to the effort.[118] Later, in Nazi-occupied Poland, posters that conflated three words "Jews—Lice—Typhus" were used to justify the creation of the ghetto as a means to contain the spread of a supposed epidemic.[119] In the words of anthropologist Hugh Raffles, these time-honored narratives would find "fulfilment at Auschwitz," whereby the "discourses of hygiene . . . but also specific technologies, identifiable personnel, and particular institutions initially dedicated to the eradication of disease, shifted rapidly and quite seamlessly to the eradication of people."[120]

Pokrzywy's calls to cut out the "Jewish tumor" did not end here; they were accompanied by more general appeals to expel Jews once and for all. "They'll find somewhere to go," said the anonymous author A. L. nonchalantly, as though to address the wider European and domestic debates about the possible destination for mass Jewish emigration.[121] Another publication by A. L. asked rhetorically, "Is there not enough space in the Sahara desert?," before proposing that Jews should prove their ingenuity and turn it into a land of milk and honey.[122] In yet another text, A. L. demanded that the government resolve the issue of Jewish emigration immediately and act "according to the will of the nation."[123] Responding to nationwide debates on the subject, including those ongoing in the pro-Sanacja *Mucha*, these points suggested that the magazine attempted to expand its scope and, possibly, establish itself as an influential actor in the national discussion on the "Jewish question."

POKRZYWY AND SATIRE

That *Pokrzywy*'s editors saw the magazine as an important actor in that debate is certainly visible in its self-referential content. Although *Pokrzywy* had a strong sense of mission and an ambition to spread its antisemitic message far and wide, these features were not necessarily compatible with its profile as local magazine. Nonetheless, the editors firmly believed that theirs was a brand-new approach to satire that should be emulated by other magazines in the country. This affectation was, of course, part of the magazine's publicity and a way to position it in the wider context of satirical print media of the time.

Analyzing the issues of *Pokrzywy* published between its establishment in June 1937 and late 1938, the second year of its operation, I found more than twenty such self-referential, and admittedly self-congratulatory, passages in which the editors discussed the goals of the magazine, expanded on their understanding of satire, attacked competing outlets and liberal figures, and bewailed the destruction wreaked on satirical weeklies such as theirs by state censors. From the very first issue of the magazine, *Pokrzywy*'s editors made it clear how they defined their publication's role as a satirical magazine operating in a very particular social and political milieu. In a long editorial, the creators of *Pokrzywy* extolled the virtues of laughter and criticized the bitterness and lugubriousness of Polish mentality in the postpartition period. They blamed the national literary tradition, including the Romantic poets Mickiewicz and Słowacki, for proliferating the imagery of graves, gallows, and crosses. Juxtaposing the gloomy Polish faces with the "sunny laughing 'gobs' of the average American," the editors proposed that the national tendency for sadness and melancholy stifled the creativity of the "Polish soul." Satire, they argued, allowed for the spread of optimism and taught critical thinking, which Poles, "as the proverbial nation of poets," had not yet learned. The editors thought it their task to educate the people through laughter and pointed to the collective vices in an attempt to mobilize the nation and improve its future.[124] The "Beneficial Nettle" doggerel, discussed near the beginning of this chapter, made it clear that economic struggle against Jews was an important part of that national activization.

The ambitious goals described in the editorial were somewhat inconsistent with the actual content of the magazine, which was mostly devoid of the usual referentiality and depth of accomplished satire. In that, the content of *Pokrzywy* was no different from much of conservative satire elsewhere in the world. According to American political cartoonist Paul Conrad, "conservatives don't have a sense of humor."[125] Those who study humor in other contexts argue that conservative comedians are rare.[126] Similarly, communication scholars maintain that satire is the unquestionable liberal domain. According to one study, liberals have a higher tolerance for ambiguity than political conservatives, with conservatives tending to process messages literally as well as lacking appreciation for irony.[127] Writing about the contemporary dearth of conservative satire, those scholars maintain that this:

> is not merely about conservatives' reluctance to challenge governing institutions or the existing social order. Conservative political voices today often do both of those things. Instead, the lack of conservative satire likely stems from differences in the vehicles and rhetorical forms that liberals and conservatives use to issue such critiques. For conservatives, humor is simply not their preferred vehicle.[128]

A similar point can no doubt be made about interwar Poland, where antisemitic satirical magazines were often short-lived and less important to the political right than the corresponding dailies that had a similar purpose but were more serious in tone and more widely read.

Despite its humorless character, *Pokrzywy* (and the like-minded daily press) seemed to have been fairly successful in achieving its other aim, that of disrupting and eventually eradicating Jewish activity in the region. As early as the sixth issue, the magazine's editors boasted about how they were able to keep Jews and their helpers awake at night, while also revealing that they themselves had become objects of harassment by those they had criticized: "In their fight against *Pokrzywy*, the enemies of national ideas and selfless work for the state use all means at their disposal to free themselves from the unpleasant criticism. Slander, insults, blackmail, threats, stealing staff with bribes, terrorizing colporteurs—this is the weapon used by . . . [our] opponents."[129] While the magazine did not disclose who those "adversaries" were, it is possible that it attracted critique from local politicians, including Kalisz president Ignacy Bujnicki. Eight weeks into the magazine, the editors spoke proudly of how "the 'Nettles' have blossomed" (*"Pokrzywy" zakwitły*) and the publication had become the most-read magazine in the Poznań and Łódź voivodships, as well as in the Kalisz region.[130]

While I have found no evidence to confirm these claims, it is possible that the claim to high readership in Kalisz was somewhat accurate, given it was the only satirical magazine in the Kalisz area. At the same time, archival sources pertaining to SN activities in the region mainly list two local outlets, *Orędownik* and *Wielkopolanin*, as the most influential publications in the area.[131]

The magazine's editors also discussed the various forms of harassment experienced by its staff. These annoyances ranged from fairly negligible issues, such as the municipal authorities' failing to invite the magazine's representatives to important local events, to more serious matters, including public attacks by local newspapers or even legal proceedings accusing *Pokrzywy* of slander or the colporteurs being molested by an unnamed uniformed representative of the fascist Falanga group.[132] These events aggravated the editors, eliciting a series of strongly worded responses. One such response alluded to an article in the local newspaper *Echo Kaliskie* (*The Kalisz Echo*) that attacked *Pokrzywy*'s acting editor Bazyli Bożko, a Ukrainian from the Kiev area, for taking actions against the interests of Poland by publishing critiques of the Polish clergy. *Pokrzywy* delivered a cutting riposte: the journalist in question should instead scrutinize his own actions; after all, he had invested in the Jewish cinema "Oaza," while Polish cinemas suffered substantial loses.[133] The editors pledged to seek satisfaction in court.[134]

While it is not clear whether a lawsuit ensued, soon enough *Pokrzywy* itself became engulfed in two separate court cases. Neither of the cases involved Jewish plaintiffs, but the proceedings concerned offensive satire all the same. In their report on the first case, which took place in the provincial town of Ostrów Wielkopolski, the magazine's editors praised the "factual and well-thought-out defense" by their lawyer, who argued that all cultured and freedom-loving nations have set great store by satirical writing and imagery, accepting it with humor and without resorting to criminal prosecution.[135] In their commentary on the second case—in the town of Krotoszyn, in which the editor in question was eventually acquitted—the editors bragged about their own "noble gesture" of handing out a pot of nettles to the accuser as a peace offering at the end of the trial.[136] Given the antidemocratic nature of the magazine, including its hate speech, such pronouncements were not only deeply hypocritical but also indicative of the inherent bigotry of those behind *Pokrzywy*.

Like many other satirical magazines of the time, *Pokrzywy* fell victim to state censorship. In 1938, at least four issues were confiscated by state censors: issues 12, 15, 16, and 17. In each case, the magazine distributed a second printing of the issue, which was amended to meet the requirements of the censor. Issue 15, published on 31 August 1938, in particular, was redesigned to demonstrate the workings of censorship: blank spots marking the expurgated material were reproduced with the word "Skonfiskowane" (confiscated) in place of the original content. Judging from the title of the first bowdlerized piece, "Przed wyborami" (Before elections), one can presume it was a poem about the upcoming parliamentary elections in November 1938, possibly criticizing the Sanacja government, a practice not uncommon in the nationalist *Pokrzywy*.[137] The second piece was a cartoon: only its title and caption were reprinted, suggesting that the objectionable content may have been critical of Germany, with which the Polish government had signed a nonaggression treaty the previous year.[138]

Repeated confiscations and the associated necessity of issuing a second printing put many periodicals in serious financial trouble. In 1932, the Polish Association of the Publishers of Daily and Periodical Press conducted a survey of its members nationwide that showed censorship was becoming increasingly erratic. Confiscations rarely abided by any set rules. They took place without due notice or explanation. They were inconsistent, favoring some outlets over others, often permitting similar content to be printed in one publication, while penalizing another. Importantly, provincial censorship offices were believed to be stricter and less predictable that those in large cities.[139] It is clear that these problems affected *Pokrzywy*. The magazine persevered nonetheless, being cognizant that such practices were not exclusive to Poland but rather plagued the print media in many other European states. In the editorial for issue 15, the writers argued that good political satire was on the brink of extinction, a development that was detrimental to the public interest. The piece maintained that despite the official pronouncements of civil liberties and republican democratic values, the concerted attack on satire undermined these very principles.[140] In this respect, *Pokrzywy* shared the liberal views on freedom of speech professed by many other publications of the time, including the leftist magazines that were both antistate and antifascist. Despite spreading antisemitic content that was deeply racist, antidemocratic, and anticonstitutional, *Pokrzywy*'s editors, like their liberal counterparts, viewed themselves as being at the forefront of a struggle against an increasingly authoritarian state.

Nonetheless, such views did not mean that the magazine's editors saw the liberal leftist outlets as their allies. Quite the contrary, they were consistently disapproving of such publications, including the Polish Jewish newspaper *Nasz Przegląd*.[141] They also occasionally attacked high-profile representatives of the liberal left, such as the renowned Polish Jewish poet Julian Tuwim,[142] and polemicized against left-wing journalists and writers. One such polemic was directed at PPS activist and writer Wanda Wasilewska whose article on Jews in the region of Polesie, published in the liberal magazine *Wiadomości literackie*, greatly incensed the editors of *Pokrzywy*. Wasilewska's article was part of *Wiadomości*'s survey of the "Jewish question" in Poland. Written as a Marxist critique, her article drew attention to exploitation of the working masses, Jews included, by the ethnic Polish landowners of the eastern region of Polesie and praised Jewish resourcefulness and hard work in the area. The *Pokrzywy* editors said that Wasilewska had written an "incredibly disgusting" piece of "Jewish propaganda," which they also considered deeply anti-Polish.[143]

While the *Pokrzywy* editors provided no further detail as to why Polesie was such an important site of national struggle, their reaction needs to be placed in a wider context of interwar debates about the region. Since the 1920s, the swampy area of Polesie was seen as a possible locus of a state-funded melioration project designed to provide a solution to existing demographic issues. Although the project never came to fruition, it was a hotly debated issue at the time. Among other possibilities, Polesie was considered one solution to the overpopulation of Polish cities and a possible site for Jewish settlement.[144] It is possible that Wasilewska was writing precisely from that perspective. Applauding the ingenuity of the region's existing Jewish inhabitants, whether restaurant owners or farmers, she made a compelling case for the importance of Jews for the flourishing of Poland's borderland territories and implicitly advocated for the inclusion of Jews in debates about the future of the region.

Aside from responding to specific proposed projects like the Polesie one, *Pokrzywy*'s editors also commented on the surrounding media landscape more generally. Although their own content was not particularly highbrow, the editors set a high bar for which publications were worthy of praise and which were not. In particular, the editors held tabloid newspapers in low regard, especially if they sprang from Jewish-owned media conglomerates. One cartoon attacked the Łódź-based *Express Ilustrowany* (*The Illustrated Express*), describing it as *szmonces* (shmontses, nonsense) and a "Jewish newspaper for stupid women."[145] The newspaper was part of the Republika media corporation, which sold other popular titles and had the stable financial backing of some of Łódź's most successful textile owners. As a publication that dealt with light content, *Express Ilustrowany* was, unlike *Pokrzywy*, both widely read and largely impervious to state pressures. Such successful titles were no doubt a thorn in *Pokrzywy*'s side, especially given the fact that, as one op-ed divulged, the magazine suffered from a lack of funding.[146] State confiscations and slander cases depleted *Pokrzywy*'s scarce resources even further, forcing the magazine to ask for donations.[147]

While the editors never spoke explicitly about how, in their opinion, *Pokrzywy* featured in the wider context of the print media in Poland, they exuded an air of self-importance as well as embellishing their own achievements in running a widely read and far-reaching satirical magazine. For example, they proudly followed and reported on *Pokrzywy*'s supposed readership further afield, as one photograph of a devoted reader posing with a newspaper stand in what was supposedly Warsaw was meant to show. Interestingly, the stand displayed *Pokrzywy* alongside other far-right outlets, including *Samoobrona Narodu* (*The National Self-Defense*), *Orędownik*, and *Front Aryjski* (*The Aryan Front*), signaling the "specialized" profile of the distributor.[148] The editors clearly were proud of their magazine being included in the pleiad of Poland's right-wing periodicals and, whenever possible, emphasized its affinity with such publications. For instance, one issue of the magazine extended heartfelt congratulations to Kalisz-based *Orędownik* correspondent Stanisław Kotarski who had received his fiftieth fine for spreading antisemitic slogans. The accompanying cartoon portrayed Kotarski wearing a regal cape consisting of sewn-together fine notifications, while the caption below explained that "in these hard times even such prosperity was rare."[149]

Aside from applauding the antisemitic activity of their coconspirators in other periodicals, *Pokrzywy*'s editors also bragged about how their own satire was anathema to Jews, *shabbos-goyim*, and philosemites. According to one cartoon, which repeated the magazine's go-to imagery of stinging nettles that encroached on and irritated a half-naked Hasidic Jew, *Pokrzywy* was a highly effective "anti-Jewish cure."[150] Variations on the theme appeared in other cartoons, including one showing a naked Orthodox Jew escaping a nettle tickle from a Polish man dressed in a folk costume of the Kraków region, and another one that presented a Jew and his gentile helper escaping from a nettle lashing.[151] The name of the magazine thus provided a continuous source of references and "witty" wordplay. There were also other attempts to exaggerate the actual impact of the magazine. One cartoon portrayed a school in Kalisz where pupils supposedly read *Pokrzywy* before class and advocated the introduction of a new subject called *pokrzywologia* (nettlelogy), which would be a useful antidote to Judeophilia.[152]

If we are to believe the various self-referential content, the magazine was serious about advancing satire in Poland and countering the restrictions to free speech imposed by state censorship. That its hate rhetoric stood in sharp contrast to those very values, including the democracy-inducing role of caricature, was never acknowledged by the magazine's editors. Like many ethnonationalist outlets of the time, *Pokrzywy*'s editors saw the national work as superior to any other form of public engagement, considering their own activity a vehicle for social and political change. Despite sharing many similarities with nationalist newspapers from Greater Poland, such as the previously mentioned *Pod Pręgierz* or *Orędownik*, which were also involved in the economic boycott, *Pokrzywy* stood out for its commitment to satire and widespread use of caricature. Its editors firmly believed in the corrective function of what they saw as humor, hoping to shame ethnic Poles from the local area into the ethno-nationalist mindset as well as stigmatizing Jews as a dangerous "mob" that was taking over the country. Although it is not clear what the actual reach of the magazine was and how its impact compared to nationalist work on the ground, *Pokrzywy*'s constant financial problems and its lack of artistic talent suggest that this influence did not stretch beyond a narrow base of SN readers.

Unlike cartoons in more recognized satirical magazines in Poland, *Pokrzywy*'s drawings were never signed, and their authors remain unknown. Judging from the amateurish quality of many of these images, nonprofessional artists were creating illustrations out of ideological conviction, rather than for financial gain. They were conversant with local realities and serious about representing the world as they saw it, displaying a preference for true-to-life depictions over visual metaphors. Alongside the images made by local staff, some of the more vicious cartoons were illicit reprints from German antisemitic magazines of the time. Such a blend of local vignettes and globally resonant portrayals showed that, despite *Pokrzywy*'s focus on provincial affairs, the people behind the magazine were abreast of the wider trends in antisemitic representation. By adjusting some of the images and rewriting captions to match their small-town milieu, they enthusiastically endorsed the existing models of caricature and paid heed to the German masters. Like Siepka the priest, whose national work caused concern to district police and brought joy to *Pokrzywy* itself, the editors hoped that spreading such portrayals would be a catalyst for fundamental social change.[153]

Of the 25,000 Jews recorded living in Kalisz in August 1939, only 2,225 survivors returned to the city in the aftermath of the Second World War. Those who survived the war in the USSR constituted the largest group of returnees (1,655 people).[154] The ethnic Polish president of Kalisz, Ignacy Bujnicki, a frequent object of the magazine's satirical attacks, was shot dead by the Nazis in November 1939.[155] No records exist of the people involved in the magazine, other than the names of the consecutive editors listed at the back of every issue (Wincenty Sierakowski, Bazyli Bożko, and Stanisław Arasimowicz), and their publishers (Jan Wojciński, Stefan Jaroni, and Narcyz Kajzer). It is possible that, like many of their ethnonationalist colleagues, some of them went on to defend the country in September 1939, fighting the Germans whose satirical models they had once been keen on emulating.

Chapter 3

AGAINST ANTISEMITISM

In the summer of 1991, Eryk Lipiński, one of the original founders of the interwar satirical magazine *Szpilki*, received a letter from Jerusalem. The letter announced that Yad Vashem: The Holocaust Martyrs' and Heroes' Remembrance Authority had decided to confer on him the title of Righteous Among the Nations.[1] In the six years that had preceded the decision, multiple witnesses and survivors sent in testimonies of the support that Lipiński and his then-wife, a fellow *Szpilki* cartoonist Anna Gosławska, had extended to Jewish friends and strangers in German-occupied Warsaw. According to a notarized letter by survivor Lida Birsten, the couple provided her with care and friendship after she had lost all her family members and was forced to live under a false identity.[2] Close acquaintances remembered how the homes of the Lipiński couple and their relatives became refuges for Polish Jews where no one was ever refused help.[3] Fellow artists, including *Szpilki*'s Jakub Bickels, were among those who were given shelter. Others were reported to have been rescued from the Warsaw ghetto and supplied with forged documents produced by Lipiński, an activity for which he was later arrested and sentenced to several months in the Mokotów prison.[4]

The support network that arose around the couple during the Second World War was a continuation of their work as caricaturists in 1930s Poland. *Szpilki*, the magazine to which they both regularly contributed, was the chief antifascist satirical periodical of the interbellum, its satire an important means of protest against contemporary antisemitism. The magazine provided a rare example of social and political criticism against various actors of the time; this was voiced in a political milieu that discouraged liberal thought and punished attempts at radical commentary with censorship and confiscation.[5] In its programmatic antifascism, *Szpilki* also distanced itself from other satirical print media that were generally hostile to Jews and hesitant to criticize Nazi and fascist exploits in Europe and beyond. By ridiculing common tropes in the antisemitic debates on migration, the economy, and education, among other subjects, *Szpilki* contributed an important perspective to the deeply polarized public discourse of the late 1930s in addition to reflecting on the social role of satire in late interwar Poland.

Eryk Lipiński, one of *Szpilki*'s founding members, recalled how the idea for the magazine was born during a get-together with Zbigniew Mitzner (1910–1968) in late autumn 1935 in Warsaw's Szwajcarska café, a common meeting place for interwar artists. Lipiński was a student at the Academy of Fine Arts, while Mitzner was a young freelance journalist working for socialist newspapers. In their late and midtwenties respectively, the two men envisaged *Szpilki* as a decisively leftist and progressive magazine that was to oppose the current Sanacja regime.[6] Recalling the founding of the magazine fifty years later, Mitzner said that at the time "the control over satire" could be found "in the streets," so all that was needed was a bold idea.[7] This was certainly true, and the establishment of the magazine was easy; but given the magazine's links to PPS and its anti-government profile, the authorities immediately flagged it as dangerous—the first issue was heavily censored. The editors went ahead with the issue nonetheless, including placing blank spots in place of confiscated pieces. According to Lipiński, this was an excellent advertisement for a new publication such as theirs.[8]

The first group of caricaturists who worked for *Szpilki* prior to the Second World War included Franciszek Parecki (1913–1941), Bohdan Bocianowski (1911–1983), Anna Gosławska (1915–1975), aka Ha-Ga, who later became Lipiński's wife, Zenon Wasilewski (1903–1966), Karol Baraniecki (1911–1986), and Jakub Bickels (1911–1944).[9] Established writers and poets such as one of *Szpilki*'s cocreators, Andrzej Nowicki (1909–1986), as well as Stanisław Jerzy Lec (1909–1966), Leon Pasternak (1909–1969), Konstanty Ildefons Gałczyński (1905–1953), Tadeusz Hollender (1910–1943), Janusz Minkiewicz (1914–1981), and Światopełk Karpiński (1909–1940) all contributed texts from early on.[10] The magazine promoted new talent too, including authors Zuzanna Ginczanka (1917–1944) and Jerzy Kamil Weintraub (1916–1943) and illustrators Mendel Reif (1910–1943) and Bronisław Schneider (1915–1943). Several of the artists, including Bickels, Reif, and Schneider, also contributed to Yiddish and Polish-language Jewish magazines.[11] Despite being based in Warsaw, many who published in the magazine were originally from Lviv, having been born under the liberal Austro-Hungarian partition.[12]

Szpilki's antifascist and anti-Sanacja profile meant that state distributors often refused to circulate the magazine. The editors were forced to use informal distribution channels, which often left them struggling. When Julian Tuwim, the popular Polish Jewish poet, joined the magazine, it was able to increase circulation from four thousand to ten thousand copies. Despite further confiscations and numerous court cases brought by its right-wing adversaries, which wreaked havoc on its finances, *Szpilki* survived until September 1939. It was reactivated in March 1945 with many returning contributors.[13] From the late 1940s onwards, *Szpilki* came to serve the socialist cause, becoming one of the longest-running and most reputable satirical magazines in the history of Polish print media.[14]

JEWISH IMMIGRATION, ECONOMIC BOYCOTT, AND "GHETTO BENCHES"

From early on, *Szpilki* published special issues that parodied competing publications. Using the special-issue format, the magazine contributed to ongoing debates on pressing concerns of the time, such as ethnonationalist calls for the elimination of Jews from all sectors of the economy and public life and appeals to remove them from the country as a whole. One such special issue, which came out on 28 November 1937, was devoted to the nonexistent state of Serdania and covered topics such as the erotic life of Serdanians, family, and leisure activities as well as providing a historical timeline of reciprocal relations between Poland and Serdania.[15] The issue was modelled on a special issue about Japan of the left-oriented cultural weekly *Wiadomości Literackie* (*Literary News*).[16] The success of the *Wiadomości* issue encouraged the magazine to use the same format to tackle more serious topical issues, many of which concerned the situation of Jews in Poland.

On 30 January 1938, *Szpilki* published another special issue that concerned the putative Jewish immigration to Madagascar. As earlier examples from the progovernment *Mucha* have shown, this was a widely discussed topic at the time; the authorities' interest in the island peaked following the fact-finding mission in spring 1937 and the presumably encouraging declarations on the issue by the French minister of the colonies, Marius Moutet.[17] The ethnonationalist press often misconstrued Moutet's diplomacy and presented his being sympathetic to the project as unconditional support.[18] This meant that exaggerated and contradictory reporting was commonplace, particularly following the group's trip to the island. According to one article in July 1937, "the French government has now agreed to accept four million Jewish farmers to the island of Madagascar."[19] Another newspaper announced in December 1937 that Madagascar was already "waiting for the Jews" and that the colony was able to absorb the entirety of Poland's Jewish population.[20] This was not the case. According to the mission report, only the central part of the island was suitable for European colonization, and the settlement would have to be of the agricultural type.[21] This meant that the majority of the Polish Jewish population, who were urban dwellers in nonagricultural professions, did not fit the bill.[22] Despite these findings, Polish nationalists continued to demand that Jews leave for Madagascar.[23] If Jews resist, some reporters advised, they should be sent there forcibly.[24]

Szpilki published the special issue on Madagascar shortly after the findings of the expedition had been made public. According to Lipiński, the right-wing debate on the colony was grist to *Szpilki*'s satirical mill; it was easy to ridicule, which led to increased readership.[25] The issue consisted of eight pages and comprised cartoons, satirical prose, and mock news pieces. The cover page presented two well-known cartoon characters, Żółtko and Eierweis [sic], after their supposed move to the island.[26] The two protagonists had made frequent appearances in *Cyrulik Warszawski*, a liberal magazine published between 1926 and 1934, on which *Szpilki* was modelled.[27] The couple was the creation of the poet Julian Tuwim, who introduced the series and wrote all dialogues, while the illustrations were drawn by the established artist Jerzy Zaruba.[28] In the special issue of *Szpilki*, the two men are placed in a barren desert landscape with camels, palm trees, and cacti in the background. Żółtko is depicted wearing shorts and a T-shirt, sweating profusely, while Eierweis wears a big coat, scarf, hat, and gloves as he had dressed for winter weather in Warsaw.[29] The cover page cartoon, drawn by Zaruba, set the tone for the whole issue, which envisioned a Jewish homeland in Madagascar and discussed the changes the mass outflow of Jews would bring to Poland.

Szpilki's imaginary political, social, and cultural setting on Madagascar was clearly modelled on the interwar Polish Republic. This being a satirical magazine meant that the contributors were able to proliferate various fantasy scenarios, while departing from factual accuracy and transgressing traditional timelines. In so doing, they provided a poignant commentary on the present.[30] For example, in a mock travel piece, poet Jerzy Kamil Weintraub took readers to the future as he reported on his putative trip to a PEN Club congress on Madagascar in June 1965. By then, the island had become a Jewish dictatorship, with an authoritarian leader named Nachum Gołębikier, who has been in power for twenty-five years. The island boasts a Polish ghetto, as well as militant ethno-nationalist groups such as the Jewish Malagasy Falanga—a reference to the antisemitic militant organization National Radical Movement (RNR), also known as Falanga—that stage regular pickets in front of Polish shops and proudly encourage tourists to visit universities equipped with special seating areas for Christian Poles. The independent press is suppressed, while disobedient editors are routinely sent to concentration camps. When asked if the Jewish people of Madagascar are not concerned about how the international community would react to the abuses, the local guide responds plainly: "The rightful inhabitants of Madagascar don't give a hoot about the world's opinion," before adding that the country has already withdrawn from the League of Nations and joined the German-Italian Alliance.[31]

Weintraub's piece was the longest one in the special issue, setting the tone for the other contributions. The accompanying poems, snippets of news, advertisements, commentaries, and cartoons picked up on some of the themes introduced in his article. For example, one of the reports by MAT—*Madagaskarska Agencja Telegraficzna*, a fictional Madagascar Telegraphic Agency—informed readers about riots in the universities, supposedly to do with Lechite (Polish) students refusing to sit in the assigned ghetto benches.[32] Another report discussed the plans to bring in additional picketing squads from Poland, recruiting from unemployed diaspora Jews, who could support the boycotting of Lechite shops.[33] In a similar way, a series of cartoons published on the last page of the issue depicted daily life on Madagascar, including the parades of "Hitler-Juden," trials of "Polaco-Communists," pickets in front of Polish shops, and ghetto benches in lecture halls, presenting gentile students standing aside as the Jewish majority remained seated.[34] In addition, the issue contained short texts about "anti-Lechite" activism that was meant to make up for one's "Aryan blood," pieces on trade exchange between Madagascar and Poland, and letters from children based on the popular Polish Jewish *Mały Przegląd* (*Little Review*) newspaper for children.[35] There were also parodies of famous literary texts, such as the poem *Beniowski* by the national bard Juliusz Słowacki. In it, the main protagonist Beniowski asked the Jews who arrived on Madagascar: "Wy tu przyjechali? / Któż został w Polszcze, aby nań złe zwalić?" (You have come here? Who remains in Poland to blame the evil on?).[36] Importantly, the special issue devoted some attention to the already "de-Judaized Warsaw" in which the nationalists embarked on a new struggle, this time against the bald.[37]

Szpilki's vision of Poland without Jews was not the only one to appear that year. In 1938, a writer for the magazine named Tadeusz Hollender began contributing installments of a satirical novel *Polska bez Żydów* (*Poland without Jews*) to the Polish-language Jewish newspaper *Nasz Przegląd*. The novel imagined the country under a militant ethno-nationalist dictatorship, modelled on existing groups such as ONR. As the group assumes power, all Jews are expelled and their property taken over by ethnic Poles. However, the liberal sections of society grieve the expulsion of Jews, fearing—as one of Hollender's characters does—that "the daily bread which we will eat alone from now will be dry and bland."[38] Here the Jews are the salt of the earth and the worthiest of people.[39]

Like Hollender's novel, *Szpilki*'s fabricated scenarios were meant to present an inverted image of the realities of 1930s Poland to emphasize the real-life hurt inflicted by antisemitic activity and show the perils of a "de-Judaized" state. The references to contemporary events were deliberately blatant to mimic the crudeness of far-right publications.[40] In the latter respect, the magazine's staff shared the view of the leftist poet and journalist of the time Antoni Słonimski, who argued that right-wing humor was churlish and clumsy since the "Muse was ill-disposed toward fascists, chauvinists, and Endeks."[41] In that, Słonimski could not be closer to present-day communications scholars cited here previously who see satire as an exclusively liberal territory.[42] In mimicking the style of such outlets, *Szpilki* also ridiculed the follies, vices, and abuses of both the ethno-nationalist Poles and Poland's increasingly authoritarian regime.

By the time the special issue was printed, many of the practices disparaged by *Szpilki*'s authors and illustrators had been in place for years. Picket lines in front of Jewish shops were notorious. Ethno-nationalist picket squads threatened Christians who patronized Jewish businesses. In some locations, Jewish stalls in the marketplace were forced into a special section to separate them from Christian vendors. In other locations, Jews were prevented from entering the market altogether.[43] Many businesses were attacked.[44] Far-right newspapers called for the end of "Jewish economic dominance," published country-wide reports in which they commented on the progress of boycotting activities, and argued that picket activists always kept to the letter of the law.[45]

Szpilki was not the only magazine to protest these events. *Kontratak* (*Counterattack*), the Polish-language weekly of the young Jewish academic community in Lviv, published cartoons by *Szpilki* regulars Jakub Bickels and Bronisław Schneider that criticized right-wing calls for a "de-Judaized" economy. One such cartoon by Schneider presented a smashed window of a Jewish store as two policemen walk past indifferently. The caption reads: "Muzyka O.N.R.-u. Symfonia demol" (ONR's Music Is a Smash Symphony), providing a word play on the verb *demolować* (to destroy) and the name of a musical scale *d-moll* (D minor) (Figure 3.1).[46] Schneider not only drew attention to violence perpetrated by young ethno-nationalist activists; he also emphasized associated police passivity, which exacerbated the problem across the country.

It is possible that, in referring to the ONR, Schneider did not necessarily mean the National Radical Camp per se. After 1934, the organization split into two factions: ONR ABC, led by Henryk Rossman, and RNR, also known as Falanga, headed by Bolesław Piasecki.[47] Nonetheless, the abbreviation

3.1. Bronisław Schneider, ONR's Music, from *Kontratak*, 20 December 1936, 4.

ONR, as well as the corresponding adjective *oenerowski*, continued to be used as a by-word for antisemitic proclamations and violence, often irrespective of actual perpetrators. According to historian Mikołaj Kunicki, the "term was applied indiscriminately to all forces behind violent anti-Semitic excesses, whether they were Endeks, Rossman's ONR ABC, or Piasecki's

RNR."[48] Indeed, the root ONR organization considered the struggle against so-called Jewish influence its chief concern, and this remained a central tenet of both factions' activity after the split.[49] As far as the latter issue was concerned, Schneider's cartoon corresponds with the findings of historian Paul Brykczynski who demonstrates that, in interwar Poland, "the inactivity of the police was not simply the result of incompetence"; rather, it pointed to "deeper sympathies with the radical nationalists within the force."[50] Brykczynski further shows that many individual officers in Warsaw, in particular, were members of the secret organization Polish Patriots' Emergency, which sympathized with Endecja.[51] Although the organization was exposed in 1924, it can be presumed that such sympathies persisted and shaped much of the institutional culture within the police force.

In a similar way to the Polish-language *Kontratak*, the Yiddish press ridiculed antisemitic utterances and actions by both central figures in the government and anonymous members of society. The former included Polish prime minister Felicjan Sławoj Składkowski, whose ill-advised inaugural address to the Sejm in 1936 was often considered an incitement to violence. Składkowski said of the economic competition against Jews, "[If you want] an economic struggle, then by all means go ahead; but [inflict] no [physical] harm."[52] In particular, *Der Moment* and *Der Mechabel* mocked Składkowski's notorious *pas de deux* of "Beating up Jews—no; economic struggle—by all means."[53] The particle *owszem* (by all means) became a byword for both top-down discrimination and the condoning of bottom-up attacks.[54] The phrasing continued to be derided in many anti-regime leftist outlets until the outbreak of the war.

By January 1938, when the special issue on Madagascar was published, mob violence in the universities had become endemic. Christian students forced their Jewish counterparts to sit in "ghetto benches" set up on the left side of lecture halls. In the words of one eyewitness, "The Jewish students strongly resisted. Instead of sitting on the 'ghetto benches,' they stood during the lectures. The antisemitic Polish students wanted to forcibly make them sit there. This led to dreadful scenes in the universities, culminating in frequent fights. They fell upon and beat the Jewish students, even women, till blood flowed."[55] According to the historian Natalia Aleksiun:

> universities in the Second Polish Republic emerged as a contested space of ethnic tension and violence. Since institutions of higher education trained the future elite of the country, the presence of Jewish students there—most visible among minorities—was challenged and decried, especially by those who imagined Poland as a nation state.

Universities, therefore, became laboratories for what many ethnic Poles perceived as a reclaiming of their country.⁵⁶

Szpilki kept a close watch on those events and returned to the theme of violence in universities in another issue that same year by publishing a cover image by illustrator Mendel Reif that portrayed a Jewish man strolling hand in hand with two Polish students, both looking happy (Figure 3.2). The cheerful gait of the characters is matched by the pastel yellow coloring of the image, which exudes a sense of calm and contentment. The telling caption, "Prima-Aprilis" (April Fools' Day), disrupts the positive message of the drawing and shows the unlikelihood of the portrayed scene. Reif intimated that, given the ongoing assaults by ethnic Polish students, peaceful coexistence between the two groups was no longer possible.⁵⁷

The drawing is built on a contrast between the tall stocky bodies of the Polish students and the slight figure of the Jewish man. Reif applied a similar visual formula in some of his other works, wherein large gentile bodies are placed side by side with frail, if not impoverished, bodies of Orthodox Jews.⁵⁸ This strategy to represent ethnic difference by contrasting body types could be read as the artist's distinct response to the realities of social inequality that he sought to redress. This is one of the reasons why his cartoons were applauded by fellow artists for displaying "formal sensitivity" as well as protesting against injustices he experienced and observed in daily life.⁵⁹

Reif was not the only one to comment on violence in universities. Cartoons in other magazines also alluded to the outlandish demands by ethnic Polish students, in particular their calls for so-called ghetto benches in lecture halls. In his drawing for the magazine *Wróble na Dachu*, illustrator Mieczysław Piotrowski proposed that seating areas in universities should be formed in a conical shape with the lecturer standing on top of the cone and the students sitting around him. This way, Piotrowski's cartoon implied, lecture halls would be no longer divided into left or right.⁶⁰

Many artists, Reif included, chose the motif of a cane or walking stick, a sign of belonging to the academic community, to comment on the unrest in universities. Canes were not only an element of student attire but could also be used as weapons. They were, at times, equipped with razor blades attached to the tip to inflict additional wounds on the victim. Numerous cartoons from liberal Polish, Polish Jewish, and Yiddish magazines focused on the cane, employing it as a useful visual metonymy for those students who wreaked violence.⁶¹ In one *Szpilki* issue, Reif portrayed a lecture hall full of canes dressed in suits. This was the future generation of *żydoznawcy* (Jewish

3.2. Mendel Reif, Prima Aprilis, from *Szpilki*, 3 April 1938, 1.

experts), tutored by some of the country's most renowned antisemites.[62] In another issue, he presented a student kissing his cane before leaving for the summer holidays. This was, as the tongue-in-cheek caption reads, "a touching farewell with education."[63] In yet another drawing, Reif depicted a group of mobster-looking youths posing for an image with canes, warning they will now fight the Freemasons.[64] Similarly, artist Karol Baraniecki drew a razor blade with two canes on either side that formed the likeness of a paragraph, an "Aryan paragraph," as the title had it.[65] Edward Szymański portrayed a calligraphy book of an aspiring ONR member. In it, words such as "cane," "mason," "nose," "Jew," and "matzo" were being neatly calligraphed.[66] The Yiddish press, too, used the cane motif as a visual formula with which to represent Christian students and, by association, to criticize Polish universities as breeding grounds for ethnic violence.[67] Both walking sticks and violence in universities were also frequent motifs in the popular magazine *Wróble na Dachu*. Importantly, canes appeared in more ominous cartoons in the ethno-nationalist magazine *Szarża*, as was the case in a menacing drawing that depicted a gang of gentile students armed with walking sticks and guarding access to the Warsaw Polytechnic.[68]

The use of metonymy, in this case with one attribute pointing to a larger group of people or their actions, has been a common strategy employed by cartoonists worldwide. According to Ilan Danjoux, metonymies tend to be "effective solutions to the cartoonist's need for visual efficiency."[69] They add ambiguity to the portrayal and allow the illustrator to move away from purely figurative representation while accommodating the pithiness of the medium. Metonymies require a degree of visual literacy on the part of the reader too; deciphering the associative links made by the artist is an integral part of the reception of cartoon art.[70]

Szpilki provided political satire of the highest caliber, criticizing the authorities and their sympathizers, as well as lambasting right-wing groups such as ONR and others responsible for anti-Jewish violence. The choice of Madagascar as a possible Jewish homeland was puzzling to many Jews and liberal non-Jews in the Second Republic, and it was that sense of bafflement that the magazine attempted to convey.[71] Although seemingly light-hearted, the fictitious issue from Madagascar allowed the magazine not only to reflect on the official discourse surrounding immigration but also to condemn other disturbing developments in the country. Growing discrimination and inequalities as well as parallels with Hitler's Germany and Mussolini's Italy were all pointed out.

Liberal leftist publications such as this one were particularly vulnerable to censorship, and *Szpilki* had a long record of confiscations by the state.[72] Although the special issue on Madagascar evaded top-down interference, other issues were not that fortunate. As I show below, *Szpilki*'s editor in chief, Zbigniew Mitzner, faced two court cases in 1937 and 1938, both of which revolved around the magazine's criticism of anti-Jewish practices and utterances.[73]

PORNOGRAPHY, FREEMASONRY, AND ANTI-JEWISH LAWS IN EUROPE

On 17 April 1938, *Szpilki* published a belated April Fools' Day issue, containing a "free anti-Jewish supplement" of two pages. The supplement was styled on flagship publications of the ONR—*ABC: Nowiny Codzienne* (*ABC: Daily News*) and *Falanga*—which corresponded with ONR's two splinter factions, ONR ABC and RNR. These organizations rejected the multicultural state and "insisted that because all nations showed distinct traits, no single state could accommodate several nationalities." In their vision, "National minorities simply had no place in Poland."[74] Given their stark layout, crude anti-Jewish rhetoric, and authoritarian vision of the state, publications such as *ABC* and *Falanga* provided an easy target for *Szpilki*'s satirists.

Szpilki's "anti-Jewish supplement" mocked the idea of a homogenous state; it presented an antisemitic manifesto, painted horrific "scenes from the Soviet paradise," and discussed recent incidents involving Jews, as well as incorporating a small ads section. One visual composition incorporated mug shots of "the lovely female and male Varsovians who patronized Jewish shops."[75] The work, although caricatural in nature, moved away from the traditional cartoon format in favor of a different innovative technique. The mug shots, which presented six Jewish customers, were the creation of artist Zenon Wasilewski who, after 1936, progressively abandoned the customary drawing in ink for hand-made plasticine figurines, which he then photographed and made into collages of various scenes.[76] In this case, Wasilewski opted for a simple grid of six photographs of plasticine heads without any additional drawing, shading, or coloring. The shots presented two women and four men whose noses, lips, and eyes were intentionally exaggerated. The use of plasticine and the sculpted look it afforded to the protagonists provided them with both lifelike and frightening qualities, all in an attempt to mimic the demonizing portrayals in the right-wing media. Although such practices were known elsewhere in Europe, including works by Czech artist Jiří Trnka, Wasilewski stood out among the caricature illustrators in Poland who opted for the traditional format of ink drawings. Although the artist continued to work with the traditional cartoon medium throughout the 1930s, his experiments with plasticine and photography marked the beginning of his interest in animation and puppet film that he pursued full-time after the Second World War.[77]

Aside from lambasting the hate-infused visual rhetoric of right-wing publications, *Szpilki*'s anti-Jewish supplement did not shy away from explicit content that state censors eventually deemed licentious. The two pieces in question included a mock press report on a case of bestiality in southern Hungary, which was said to have attracted the attention of a local Jew, Nachume Cypkin. The other piece was a fabricated ad in which a reader advertised his wish "to defile (*zhańbić*) a blonde [woman]" and "possibly also her dog."[78] Andrzej Nowicki and Eryk Lipiński, the two editors behind the supplement, were accused of spreading pornography by the representative of the commissar of Warsaw whose office was responsible for implementing censorship.[79] The hearing took place on 28 June 1938, with the two pieces forming the basis of the indictment.[80] The defendants argued that the supplement was a satire on the antisemitic press, while the ad was meant to be read as a parody of matrimonial ads from major Polish newspapers, rather than a deliberate attempt at corrupting the public.[81] Parody advertisements were not exclusive to *Szpilki*; other publications in interwar Poland published fake ads on April Fools' Day, some written by the chief humorists and doyens of satirical writing Julian Tuwim and Antoni Słonimski.[82] Irrespective of the editors' arguments, the court remained unconvinced and sentenced the two men to three months in prison. The sentence was suspended due to the lack of previous convictions.

During the trial, *Szpilki* came under attack as a garrison of moral depravity. A witness for the prosecution argued that "the defendants wrote [the pieces] in a state of titillation and were thus guilty of arousing sexual excitement."[83] This echoed some of the common anti-Jewish tropes that circulated around the time but had a longer history dating back to the early twentieth century.[84] In an antisemitic pamphlet on pornography published in 1938, the year of the trial, Catholic priest Father Stanisław Trzeciak maintained that distributing pornography was a typically Jewish enterprise and that "when one speaks about pornography, one must [naturally] speak of the Jews."[85] In the words of historian Eva Plach, "Jews were categorized as sexual degenerates and were said to possess an uncontrollable and selfish sexual lust that could not be reconciled with ideal expressions of national masculinity and femininity."[86] Such criticisms were raised not only about the press but also in relation to literature. Some Catholic commentators argued, for example, that Polish readers should be exposed to the classics, rather than the "communizing-pacifist-pornographic nonsense" of Jews and their "aryan followers and hirelings."[87] Aside from some of *Szpilki*'s own questionable content, particularly the dubious ad on "defiling a blonde," the court case shows how conflating debate on pornography with the philosemitic sympathies of a magazine could be weaponized by both the prosecution and ethnonationalist pundits alike in a wider campaign against leftist publications.[88]

Prosecuting magazines for indecent content was a common way of attempting to derail liberal leftist publications at the time, not only in Poland but elsewhere in the world.[89] In the Second Republic, particularly toward the end of the 1930s, publications that criticized manifestations of antisemitism and the position of the Catholic Church on the "Jewish question" were particularly vulnerable.[90] A significant portion of the interwar judiciary sympathized with Endecja, which meant that cases that could be subsumed under the blanket term of slander and defaming the Polish nation were zealously pursued.[91] Legal hearings against leftist liberal and anti-antisemitic outlets tended to carry an undertone of antisemitism too. In the right-wing discourse, unwelcome developments (including those that revolved around sexuality) were often categorized as "foreign," and Jews, in particular, were considered inimical to traditional Polish values.[92]

ONR newspapers followed the *Szpilki* proceedings closely. *ABC: Nowiny Codzienne* reported on the case twice. One of its headlines asked suggestively: "Fighting antisemitism or [spreading] pornography?," while the corresponding article attempted to offer extensive coverage of the trial.[93] Other right-wing outlets made no mention of the content of *Szpilki*'s supplement and focused on the offensive pieces instead, perhaps to detract attention from discussion of antisemitism. The Catholic *Mały Dziennik* (*Little Daily*) reported triumphantly that the "propagators of pornography" had now been sentenced.[94] In a similar way, the far right *Warszawski Dziennik Narodowy* (*Warsaw National Daily*) emphasized the court's revulsion at the "downright sickening (*wprost obrzydliwa*)" contents of the issue.[95] Likewise, *Słowo* (*The Word*) demanded that one must finally put an end to "Jewish jokes."[96] The conservative pro-Sanacja *Dziennik Poznański* (*Poznań Daily*) reported that the court "rightly" (*słusznie*) found the editors guilty of spreading pornography.[97]

The trial did not discourage the editors from pursuing similar topics in the future. Only one month after the hearing, on 28 July 1938, *Szpilki* published another special issue, this time devoted to the ongoing debate on Jews and their supposed links with Freemasonry.[98] While ethnonationalist commentators had often paired Jews with Freemasonry since at least the nineteenth century, the interwar debate escalated after the anti-Masonic convention of 11–12 June 1938 in Warsaw in which as many as forty sympathizing print media outlets were said to take part.[99] During the convention, the delegates pledged to undertake a concerted effort to eradicate Freemasonry in the country as well as outlining their anti-Masonic credo. This included a belief that Freemasonry served the interests of international Jewry, that it was anti-Catholic and had an aim of overthrowing the Catholic Church, that its activities were detrimental to the national struggle in Poland, and that it exerted a considerable influence in the country, being supported by four million Jews.¹⁰⁰ Many major Catholic dailies and periodicals embarked on that struggle, including *Mały Dziennik*, *Rycerz Niepokalanej* (*The Knight of the Immaculate*), and *Przegląd Katolicki* (*The Catholic Review*), among others.¹⁰¹ The conflation of antisemitism and anti-Masonic sentiment was by no means exclusive to the far right in the Poland.¹⁰² As elsewhere in Europe, here too it was part of a wider struggle against the perceived "Jewish dominance."

Szpilki's special issue was published shortly after the convention, responding to the heightened debate on Freemasonry by right-wing newspapers. The cartoon on the cover presented former Prime Minister Leon Kozłowski (1934–1935) wielding an issue of *Polityka* (*The Politics*), in which he had published that same month a (supposedly) revelatory piece on Freemasonry in Poland. Signing his text as "L.K.," the *Polityka* writer maintained that many in political life were members of the lodge. He claimed that those in the "opposition" (i.e., the liberal elites) followed the Grand Orient de France, while those in the government belonged to the Grand Lodge of Scotland. Kozłowski admitted to having seen Masonic catalogues, which were said to be widely available in Switzerland and which allegedly contained names of Polish members, including those of many influential figures.¹⁰³ *Szpilki* derided Kozłowski's purported revelations not only in the cover image but also in the final splash page, which painted an image of the two lodges—the Grand Orient consisting of snake charmers, belly dancers, and Ottomanized hookah smokers, and the Scottish lodge whose members were portrayed as wearing kilts and playing bagpipes.¹⁰⁴

In the same issue, in a characteristic cartoon by the artist Ha-Ga, appears a conversation between two protagonists that alludes to the Catholic reporting on the issue: "Mister! You are a Freemason!" says the woman. "God forbid!" responds the man. "This means that you are a Freemason because a Freemason would never admit to being a Freemason," concludes the woman resolutely (Figure 3.3).¹⁰⁵ This was *Szpilki*'s take on a typical ethno-nationalist perspective on the topic, whereby magazines advised their readers on how to recognize a Freemason, while reminding them about the secrecy of the organization and warning that, even if asked, a Freemason would never disclose his membership in the lodge.¹⁰⁶

The cartoon typifies the minimalistic style of the artist in which her *kukiełki* (little puppets) or *ludziki* (miniature persons) take center stage.¹⁰⁷ Female protagonists like the one presented here were a constant feature in Ha-Ga's drawings, often fashioned after friends whose manner also provided inspiration for the captions. The round eyes and mouth of the woman are distinctive of other characters appearing in her work in both the 1930s and later, in the course of her four-decade career as a caricaturist for *Szpilki*. The

3.3. Ha-Ga, Mister! You're a Mason!, from *Szpilki*, 28 July 1938, 3.

eyes were supposedly modelled on the artist's own eyes; her fellow artists often joked that each and every one of her cartoons was a self-portrait.[108] Despite focusing on contemporary events, the Freemason cartoon also spoke to the artist's primary interest in human interaction, rather than politics. Unlike other caricaturists working for the magazine, Ha-Ga tended to opt for social satire, shying away from strictly political commentaries. She perfected this style after the Second World War, documenting personal relationships and everyday communications, including those of her own and her husband, Eryk Lipiński.[109] The cartoon is also representative of Ha-Ga's meticulous drawing technique, which she honed over the years with a view to bringing her signature style to the generations of *ludziki*. She first drew the figures with a pencil on paper, before redrawing them on onion skin paper with pen and ink.[110]

This cartoon was not the only instance when *Szpilki* commented on the purported Masonic threat. In December that same year, the magazine alluded to the dissolution decree of 22 November 1938, issued by President Ignacy Mościcki, which declared all Masonic associations illegal. The lodges of the Jewish organization B'nai B'rith were also targeted. Eryk Lipiński responded with a small cartoon of three men playing bridge with various Jewish and Masonic symbols displayed in the background. The cartoon bore a telling caption "Bnei-Bridż" (B'nai-Bridge), deriding the suspicions of ethnonationalist pundits as to the nefarious nature of such organizations.¹¹¹ Following Mościcki's decree, anti-Masonic organizations hoped that the supposed catalogues, envisioned by "L.K.," would soon surface in Poland and solemnly pledged to continue their fight against the lodge.¹¹²

Aside from responding to developments in Poland, *Szpilki* also commented on the international situation. In the last two years before the outbreak of the Second World War, the magazine devoted a lot of space to Hitler and Mussolini. Satirical cartoons, in particular, commented on the growing sway of fascism and the rising irredentist ambitions of Nazi Germany, intimating that the future of Europe was dire. In one such cartoon, published on 13 March 1938, artist Mendel Reif portrayed Hitler pondering the fate of annexed Austria.¹¹³ In another drawing in August 1938, illustrator Franciszek Parecki presented him against a backdrop of an expanding army as the headline reported the ongoing military draft in Germany.¹¹⁴ Yet another issue depicted the German leader with a new piece of Nazi merchandise: a lighter with a map of Greater Germany.¹¹⁵

The editor, Eryk Lipiński, also captured the increasingly fraught temper of the time in his front-page cartoon "The Abduction of Europa," which was published in September 1938 (Figure 3.4).¹¹⁶ The drawing reworked the well-known myth of the kidnapping of the Phoenician princess Europa by Zeus who, transformed into a tame white bull, carried the young woman off to the island of Crete where she became his consort. The myth had been represented in several painterly renditions, including one by Titian, whose Europa was a nubile, half-naked girl sprawled on the back of the bull. In Lipiński's rendering, Europa is an elderly woman who, although portrayed unclothed, exudes a sense of despair and fear, rather than that of violated sexuality. His three-headed bull, incorporating the likenesses of Mussolini, Franco, and Hitler, is an added twist to the mythical story. Perched atop the galloping bull, Lipiński's Europa is an image of self-reproach. Like her mythical counterpart, this Europa, too, had been fooled by appearances, falling under the sway of fascism.

Similar to other cover-page caricatures in *Szpilki*, this image combines three basic colors to add detail to the visual story. In principle, it is a frameless, black-ink drawing, presented against a white backdrop. However, black does not only serve as the basic color for contour line; it is also a filling color, utilized by the artist to draw the eye to specific subjects, in this case the bull-like figure of Hitler who carries Europa off in an unknown direction. Red

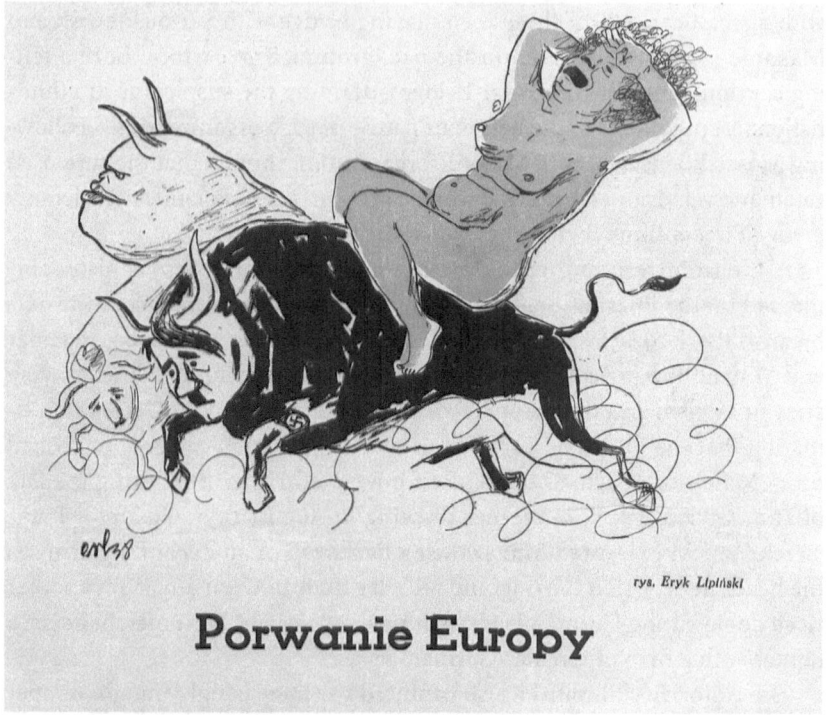

3.4. Eryk Lipiński, The Abduction of Europa, from *Szpilki*, 18 September 1938, 1.

is the third color employed by Lipiński; it introduces a sense of urgency to the page and, splashed over Europa's entire body, makes her tragedy central to the image. This use of white, black, and red enabled the artist to subject his protagonists to a certain visual hierarchy. This is particularly important when assessing the positioning of the three dictators. Although placed side by side, they are not equal. It is Hitler whom Lipiński chooses to highlight as the worst of the three evils.

While many of these drawings were somber in tone, with an almost foreboding quality, there were also cartoons that retained the lightness of *Szpilki*'s usual offerings. These included two caricatures that alluded to Hitler's visit to Italy in May 1938, a visit that, according to one historian, "captured the fascist moment when the ideology appeared in the ascendant," still basking in the glory of the Anschluss.[117] A cartoon by Zenon Wasilewski, who created the plasticine mug shots of *Szpilki*'s anti-Jewish supplement, depicted Hitler and Mussolini as a couple in love, taking a walk in the countryside, kissing and embracing lovingly, the former holding flowers in the hand, the latter wearing a light polka dot dress (Figure 3.5).[118] The strength of this cartoon

3.5. Zenon Wasilewski, Amorous May, from *Szpilki*, 15 May 1938, 2.

hinged on the element of surprise built into the reinterpretation of Hitler's Italian trip. Casting the two men as paramours and presenting the official visit as nothing more than a tryst enabled Wasilewski to toy with the basic principles of the personality cult that permitted no reflection on the sentimental, not to say sexual, side of the leader. This was also the consideration behind the cartoon by Henryk Tomaszewski published in the same issue of *Szpilki*, which presented the two dictators greeting each other in Rome, with a caption that said: "On his arrival in Rome Chancellor Hitler gave Mussolini a warm kiss, whispering: 'This is for the Anschluss.'"[119] Placed on the back page of the issue and bearing additional splashes of red, this drawing was meant to grab the attention of readers, inviting them to participate in *Szpilki*'s satirical journey to Rome. In both these cartoons, the illustrators exploited the contrasting body types of the two tyrants to achieve a comical effect. This was a popular visual strategy among interwar comic strip artists, including the creators of such well-liked duos as Pat and Patachon as well as Laurel and Hardy.

Mocking images of Hitler such as these were officially forbidden following the Polish-German press accords, but state censors were often unconcerned by antifascist imagery and erratic in penalizing publications that chose to include such content. Veiled references to the dangers of fascism, like those in Lipiński's "Abduction of Europa," might have even gone unnoticed. In that, the case of *Szpilki* is particular because it calls into question the clear-cut notions of artistic and journalistic freedoms that existed at the time. A statement by a German Jewish cartoonist and fugitive from Nazi Germany, Eric Godal, who bewailed the restrictions imposed on cartoonists across Europe in the 1930s, is one example of such misconceptions. Speaking to the American media on his arrival in New York City in 1935, Godal said that the work of political cartoonists suffered "in nearly all European countries because of censorship and dictatorial restrictions."[120] He mentioned France as the notable exception; there cartoonists were said to be free to draw without having to bow to any external pressures.

Although largely accurate, Godal's statement requires some explanation. The drawings published in *Szpilki* and elsewhere in Poland show that, even in countries veering toward authoritarianism, there were pockets of liberty in which free speech was still allowed. At the same time, even France, as romanticized as it was in Godal's account, faced its own challenges. For example, German envoys in Paris, like those in Poland, were quick to raise alarm over anti-German content, especially content that humiliated the Nazi leader. Thus, despite enjoying more freedom from state pressure, artists in France did not escape German encroachments on journalistic and artistic liberties. The case of Polish caricaturist Maja Berezowska, who worked in Paris between 1933 and 1935, is instructive in this regard. Berezowska, who was also a regular contributor to *Szpilki*, drew caricatures for several French newspapers, including *Le Figaro* and *Ici Paris*. In 1935, *Ici Paris* published a satirical article on the love affairs of Hitler that Berezowska, known for her sensual drawings, had been invited to illustrate. Her risqué caricatures of Hitler's intimate life, implying his ineptitude as a lover, caused scandal in Paris. The German embassy in France tried to block distribution of the issue, while the publisher and Berezowska were accused of libel and taken to court. The case became widely discussed in Paris intellectual circles, not least as a case of artistic autonomy, and although the caricaturist had escaped prison by then, she was not that fortunate during the Second World War. In 1942, Berezowska was arrested by the Gestapo and imprisoned in Ravensbrück. Her cartoons of Hitler were cited as the official reason for her arrest.[121]

Discussing *Szpilki*'s antifascist offerings in this wider context enables us to speculate not only about the provisional nature of state censorship in interwar Poland, but about the distinction between those cartoons that led to a serious crisis in bilateral relations and those that did not. Drawings commenting on the rise of fascism provide a useful illustration of what was allowed and what was not. The example of *Ici Paris*, as well as the earlier case of *Mucha* being forced to retract a specific issue, would suggest that it was predominantly those drawings that commented on Hitler personally, be it his looks, his supposed ethnic background, or his sexual mores, that faced angry backlash from German authorities. Other caricatures, even if critical of Nazi policies, were seen as admissible. This would explain why *Szpilki* was able to inform its readers about the various anti-Jewish laws in both Germany and Italy, a practice that was eagerly pursued by the liberal illustrators working with the magazine.

The work of Zenon Wasilewski, author of the amorous cartoon of Hitler and Mussolini and experimenter in plasticine scenes, provides one example. In a drawing published in September 1938, Wasilewski alluded to the German law on the alteration of family and personal names, passed in August 1938, which stipulated that German Jews bearing names of non-Jewish origin were obliged to adopt an additional name: "Sara" for a woman and "Israel" for a man. The law also required that all "Aryans" christen their children only with "German" names.[122] In the cartoon, Adam and Eve are presented in the moment of expulsion from the Garden of Eden, which was a punishment for their Jewish names (Figure 3.6).[123]

Wasilewski's cartoon was a modern-day reinterpretation of the biblical scene of expulsion from paradise, refashioned to reflect on the irrationality of Nazi policies. In it, the Garden of Eden is no longer divine territory; it is now ruled by Hitler, whose likeness, flanked by two swastikas, adorns the gate to paradise. Single branches of apple tree protrude from above the entrance, reminding us of the story of *Genesis* and its rendition of the original sin. The two protagonists, although supposedly gentile, are pictured with

3.6. Zenon Wasilewski, In Germany Aryans Were Forbidden from Using the Names Adam and Eva as Jewish, from *Szpilki*, 11 September 1938, 3.

stereotypical Jewish features, as if to reiterate the shared roots of Judaism and Christianity and the constant intertwining of the two in contemporary European societies.

Despite its seemingly exclusive focus on the new German law, the drawing had another dark undercurrent, which could be read as a warning to contemporary Polish readers. By picturing the expulsion from paradise, which does not follow any specific act of disobedience, the artist tells us that the world as we know it has come to an end. The theme of expulsion was highly topical at a time when Germany continued to invade the territories of its neighbors, including Austria and Czechoslovakia, portending an uncertain future to their Jewish populations. It was also during this period that Germany continued to threaten the Polish government with the banishment of Polish Jewish residents of the Reich, prompting the Polish authorities' hasty citizenship law that revoked the citizen status of all nonresidents believed to have lost connection with their home country. These bilateral tensions, in which the uncertain status of Polish Jews played a central role, were to culminate in the humanitarian catastrophe in Zbąszyń that erupted only one and a half months after Wasilewski's cartoon was published.

This cartoon is illustrative of Wasilewski's minimalistic drawing style: the cartoon is succinct, emphasizing the discord between the stark Nazi symbols and the biblical imagery. Combining the two familiar visual idioms, the language of Nazism and the language of Christianity, Wasilewski succeeded in creating an antifascist image that could be understandable to Polish and European audiences alike. In his other work, the artist advanced a similar brand of pictorial antifascism that resonated with publications elsewhere in Europe. This included the liberal Dutch magazine *De Blaasbalg*, which reprinted a four-panel strip by Wasilewski that commented on the annexation of Czech borderlands by Germany in September 1938.[124] Although it is difficult to explain how such cartoons crossed state borders, the example of *De Blaasbalg* shows that antifascist caricature was subject to similar practices of reuse as its polar opposite, the antisemitic cartoon. The fact that the strip appeared with the original signature of the artist makes it unlikely that the Dutch periodical reprinted it illegally, as magazines the likes of far-right *Pokrzywy* did. Rather, the reprint may point to cross-country networks that existed in Europe in the 1930s, both among liberal-democratic communities in general and among groups of like-minded cartoonists and journalists in particular, facilitating the spread of such imagery.

Wasilewski's fellow illustrator, Franciszek Parecki, practiced a similar style of politically engaged satire that could resonate with transnational audiences. One of Parecki's cartoons in 1938 alluded to the racial laws of Mussolini, to be introduced that same autumn. It presented the fascist leader holding an Orthodox Jew by the head and pulling single strands of hair from his beard (Figure 3.7). The caption on top of the image reads: "In Italy the struggle against Jews will happen gradually." The caption under the drawing adds: *Po włosku*, a pun that could mean "the Italian way" or "one hair after another."[125] The act of pulling hair from one man's beard was a synecdoche for the agonizing persecution of the population as a whole. The artist also employed contrast in the size of the two subjects to further emphasize the unequal power relations between the dictator and his victim. Like Wasilewski, Parecki used black ink on white paper, but his line was finer and more precise, which in this case was a fitting technique to portray the painstaking and pain-inducing antisemitic measures in Mussolini's Italy.

Parecki was renowned for his metaphorical style of drawing and the strong ideological underpinning of his work. He debuted in the liberal *Cyrulik Warszawski* in 1932, and alongside his work for *Szpilki*, he contributed drawings to the leftist political weekly *Czarno na białem* as well as writing for other periodicals of similar persuasion. In 1936, he joined the Warsaw-based

3.7. Franciszek Parecki, The Italian Way, from *Szpilki*, 4 September 1938, 3.

artists' association "Czapka Frygijska" (Phrygian Cap), which had emerged from the Communist Party of Poland (KPP) in 1934. Both Parecki and his fellow association members believed that the interwar print media were an ideal place for the leftist artist. According to Mieczysław Berman, one of the founders of the group, drawing for newspapers and magazines not only enabled the communist artist to reach mass audiences but also to perform ideological work and stimulate the aesthetic sense among the people.[126] This

3.8. Eryk Lipiński, Press Reported That . . ., from *Szpilki*, 21 August 1938, 3.

could be said about the drawing of Mussolini that both spread the antifascist message and adhered to high artistic standards.

These cartoons that focused on Germany and Italy appeared in the magazine alongside cartoons that alluded to corresponding measures being introduced in Poland. One such caricature commented on an anti-Jewish initiative from the region of Greater Poland, which was a traditional stronghold of the National Party (SN). The drawing by Eryk Lipiński presented a group of Jews standing on the right bank of the Warta river looking over to the left bank where a Christians-only beach was opened (Figure 3.8).[127] The cartoon referred to an actual strand in Puszczykowo, south of Poznań, where a "Committee for the Protection of the Polishness of Puszczykowo and the Area" leased the left bank of the river and set up a bathing spot restricted to Christian visitors only.[128] The cartoon referred not only to the rising wave of antisemitism in the conservative Poznań area; it also was a voice of protest against the right-wing discussion of the so-called Judaization of holiday resorts then raging in Poland and elsewhere.

As in his other cartoons, here Lipiński called on the knowledge of his readers to decode the built-in cultural references. In this story, the image of a group of people standing motionless on the banks of a river could be read as an allusion to the crossing of the Jordan by the Israelites escaping Egypt. In the book of Deuteronomy, this was the final leg of their journey to the Promised Land, while the river itself represented deliverance and freedom. In *Szpilki*'s cartoon, the realities of oppression and liberation are lopsided. The river is not to be crossed since the land on the other side is Christian land, which promises nothing but continued persecution. Lipiński's figures—four men, one woman, and a child, representing a people—look at that land with disbelief and despondency. This is an intentional departure from the biblical story of the crossing of the Jordan through which the artist opens up space for burning questions about the future fate of Polish Jews. Without providing answers or proposing concrete solutions, Lipiński conveys a sense of uncertainty for that future. What is to be done if the Promised Land cannot be reached?

When we compare *Szpilki* to other magazines of the time, it could seem that some of its political commentary did not differ that much from other periodicals of the 1930s. The developments described above were also satirized by other major magazines, including the pro-Sanacja *Mucha*. For example, *Mucha*'s satirical portrayal of the anti-Masonic disclosures by Leon Kozłowski in July 1938 echoed that of *Szpilki*. This was not that surprising given that Kozłowski targeted not only those on the political left but also members of the government, threatening to reveal names of the alleged Freemasons and criticizing Prime Minister Składkowski for not taking more decisive action against the organization.[129] Like *Szpilki*, *Mucha* mocked the rising German-Italian alliance, as seen in Hitler's visit to Italy in May 1938.[130] Like *Szpilki*, it also commented on the anti-Jewish laws in Germany, as in the cartoon by Bronisław Fedyszyn that presented an Orthodox Jewish man with his head trapped in a paragraph sign, uttering the words: "This collar is too tight for me" (Figure 3.9).[131] Bent half-way, straining his back to release himself from the paragraph sign, the Jewish man resembles a medieval reprobate trapped in a primitive torture device.

On the surface, neither this nor *Szpilki*'s own cartoon on the racial laws in Italy are particularly sympathetic to the Jews. Both cartoons present them as subordinate characters and do so in ways that could be seen as potentially demeaning. In the end, it was the profile of the magazine that was crucial in determining the intention behind the drawing and its actual significance. Depending on the specific outlet, satirical portrayals such as these could be interpreted as either criticizing the instigators of discriminatory policies and expressing an antifascist stance, as was the case with *Szpilki*, or expressing

3.9. The Aryan Paragraph, from *Mucha*, 18 February 1938, 5.

a moral ambivalence toward the issue so as to pander to the increasingly bigoted Sanacja government, as seen in the case of *Mucha*. Thus, it was not the satirical content per se, whether the image or the accompanying text, that was fundamental to voicing political criticism, but rather the political orientation of the magazine and its earlier record of commenting on similar issues.[132] The fact that *Mucha* devoted a lot of attention to Stalin, his crimes, and his meddling in international affairs, as well as expressing a decisive anti-Bolshevik stance, was an additional point of difference between the two magazines.[133] The personal and professional trajectories of the *Szpilki* artists also spoke volumes about their ideological engagement, distinguishing them from many other caricaturists of the time.

SZPILKI AS MENACE AND CHEAP SZMONCES

Szpilki's illustrators and writers did not only participate in the ongoing discussion about antisemitism. They also generated debate and, admittedly, emotion among right-wing pundits. To their ethnonationalist adversaries, the magazine was considered a chief platform for spreading dangerous "leftist satire," "Jewish satire," or "shmontses" (*szmonces*), all of which were said to threaten the Polish nation as well as undermine the national culture by propagating nonsense and vulgarity.

Alfred Łaszowski, a journalist for the far-right *Falanga* newspaper, was one of the most vocal and tireless opponents of leftist satire.[134] Łaszowski had an inconsistent path as a political activist, beginning as a member of the Polish Socialist Party (PPS), from which he was expelled, and later joining ONR.[135] According to Łaszowski, the type of satire disseminated by *Szpilki* and other left-wing outlets presented a serious danger to the Polish national spirit. In his words, the "crowd of jesters" who produced leftist satire tried to eradicate "the popular appeal" of the antisemitic movement. In so doing, the liberal press allegedly detracted attention from their own communist activities executed "under the guise of human and civil rights struggle."[136]

Łaszowski's articles provide an interesting insight into the ethnonationalist conceptions of leftist satire. According to one, leftist satire was to "violate everything that was sacred, in particular the national and antisemitic instincts, and ridiculed what should be inviolable for every Pole."[137] As such, *Szpilki* represented a model example of typical "Jewish audacity."[138] In Łaszowski's words, "dirty shmontses became an instrument of political struggle; it existed to 'discredit' all aspirations that were in conflict with the interests of the Jewish nation."[139] Further, Łaszowski saw daily life in the Second Republic as governed by a "race of ideas," a race that was constantly accelerating and in which "Jewish humor" was said to play too prominent a role.[140]

Łaszowski was not alone in his ideas. Other commentators, too, claimed that Jews "monopolized humor" in Poland, the same way they were said to have monopolized other areas of life. Writing songs, producing jokes, and publishing satirical press, Jews were believed to be covertly shaping the "collective national spirit."[141] These utterances show that, to some right-wing critics, leftist satire was yet another site of the supposed Jewish dominance. As in other spheres of public life, whether the economy, politics, or education, the liberal press was perceived to be governed by Jewish interests. These interests were seen as conflicting with and detrimental to Polish national "instincts," the "antisemitic instinct" in particular. To commentators like Łaszowski, antisemitism was not a shameful predilection. Rather, it was an intrinsic part of the sacrosanct national territory. It was considered a sentiment of value too, one to be safeguarded and nurtured. Leftist satire was a menace to all those perceived values. It brought the danger of laughter, which could potentially decimate the ranks of the Polish nation.

Such ideas were not new to contemporary readers. They had been voiced repeatedly throughout the 1930s in relation to the Polish press, literature, and culture more generally.[142] In particular, the idea of the "catastrophic Judaization of Polish literature and art" was widespread among right-wing commentators, as was criticism of the "hackneyed *szmonces*" that allegedly undermined Polish national culture.[143] In 1936, the issue was discussed in the Sejm. One national deputy and a veteran of the Polish Legions, Wacław Budzyński, demanded that Jews be removed from the press, radio, and diplomatic posts. While alluding to his legionnaire past, he argued that "All of us who fought for independence must strive today for the abolition of this internal occupation."[144] What Budzyński referred to was the common belief among right-wing commentators that Jews had "infiltrated" major editorial posts in the country with the aim of poisoning the reader with a non-Christian internationalist outlook.[145] Their non-Jewish hirelings, the "Judaized Aryans" (*zżydziali aryjczycy*), as the pro-Jewish Poles were described, were said to support this widespread "semiticization" of the Polish mind.[146]

Szpilki's adversaries had a reason to fear the magazine, as well as leftist satire more generally. In 1937, *Szpilki* was behind a concerted attack on two major figures of the Polish ethno-nationalist movement. The men in question, Stanisław Piasecki and Wojciech Wasiutyński, were members of ONR as well as journalists for associated outlets. The former was the editor of the far-right weekly *Prosto z mostu* (*Straight Out*), the latter one of its chief contributors and a writer for the *ABC* daily. After ONR split up, Wasiutyński became one of the chief architects behind RNR Falanga and a close colleague of Bolesław Piasecki. Aside from disseminating antisemitic content and issuing calls to deprive Jews of all political rights, these publications shamed leftist authors and artists who were Jewish. After one such attack on the acclaimed poets Julian Tuwim and Marian Hemar, the socialist daily *Walka Ludu* (*People's Struggle*), the liberal weekly *Wiadomości Literackie*, and *Szpilki* retaliated. In synchronized response to the activists, the three outlets insinuated that Tuwim's and Hemar's attackers were themselves of Jewish extraction. Indeed, both Stanisław Piasecki's mother, née Gizela Silberfeld, and Wasiutyński's maternal grandfather, painter Józef Buchbinder, were Jewish.

Szpilki's comment consisted of a damning poem by Tuwim, a topical column by Mitzner, under his usual *nom de plume* Jan Szeląg, and a satirical front-page cartoon by Lipiński.[147] The caricature presented the two Endeks sitting at a table, dressed in the traditional garb of the old Polish nobility, with their respective publications spread out in front of them. Despite trying to pass as gentile, the two activists have to confront the long line of Jewish ancestors looking at them from family portraits displayed on the wall behind. While Piasecki and Wasiutyński were drawn with Lipiński's usual subtlety, the men in the paintings are caricatures, displaying stereotypical Semitic features. The journalistic urgency of the cartoon is emphasized by the splashes of red on the men's clothing, the portraits at the back, and a stark black background that brings out and showcases the ancestral paintings.

Although the publication caused a stir in the right-wing community, Piasecki decided not to press charges and later publicly admitted that his mother was indeed Jewish.[148] In contrast, Wasiutyński accused the three publishers of slander and attempted to prove his pure "Aryan" origins.[149] The proceedings that followed went beyond a routine discussion of defamation, instead debating the essence of caricature as well as inquiring as to what constituted "Semitic features."[150] According to one Polish Jewish newspaper, this was a truly "comical trial."[151] As the art expert called by the defense was asked to compare Roman and Greek noses and comment on the similarities between Wasiutyński and the cartoon in question, the courtroom was reported to be in hysterics.[152] Following a lengthy examination of the birth and christening certificates of Wasiutyński's relatives, the court decided that investigating the actual background of the plaintiff was beyond the scope of the case.[153] After all, the judge argued, one could be "a good Pole," even if there was foreign (or even "enemy") blood flowing in their veins. He insisted that Wasiutyński was a respected member of the ethnonationalist camp and that even suppositions such as these should not be detrimental to his standing. At the same time, the final statement read, names like "Polaco-Jew" (*polakożyd*) and "Judeo-Endek" (*żydoendek*), used by some of the leftist journalists to describe the plaintiff, should be considered demeaning. In the words of the judge, these terms implied that one could be both Jewish and Polish, which was not possible. Being both was against the "spiritual essence" of a person, and implying this could be the case was slanderous. The three defendants, including *Szpilki*'s editor Mitzner, were given prison sentences of one to three months.[154]

It was not only Łaszowski, Wasiutyński, and Piasecki who reviled *Szpilki* and everything the magazine stood for. Other right-wing commentators made no secret of how *Szpilki* ranked in their hierarchy of the contemporary print media. According to one ethno-nationalist journalist named "Wan.," the magazine belonged on the Jewish street among "the indescribable noise" and "half-comprehensible gibberish" (*szwargot*) of Yiddish, among the chaos and mess (*bałagan*) of local shops and businesses, and among the omnipresent "moral decay" (*zgnilizna moralna*), "communist disease" (*zaraza komunistyczna*), and "other crimes."[155] During his "ethnographic" trip to Nalewki Street, the heart of Warsaw's Jewish district, Wan. found "a shack with newspapers," displaying *Haynt*, *Nasz Przegląd*, and other publications. On that newsstand also lay *Szpilki*, placed in a "hotchpotch" of Yiddish-language and Polish Jewish press, erotic magazines, and popular periodicals of dubious value.[156] *Szpilki* and other reputable publications, including *Haynt* and *Nasz Przegląd*, were thus categorized by this author as gutter press to be shunned, condemned, and eternally confined to "the ghetto."

To insiders and sympathizers, *Szpilki* was always "on the frontline," constituting "a heroic episode" in the history of interwar satire.[157] The magazine was said to be one of the few satirical weeklies of the time that one could read "without feeling disgusted."[158] Despite persistent censorship, it was also an outlet that succeeded in resisting the temptations of an ideological nature, particularly those that promised subsistence at a time of continuous struggle for survival.[159] *Szpilki* was not a profitable enterprise; not even the editors received pay for their work.[160] Funding was scarce.[161] At times, the magazine had to suspend activity for several weeks due to financial difficulties.[162] State censorship was ruthless. Censors assessed the content only after the issue had been printed, which meant that each confiscation could have a disastrous effect on the publication's financial situation. Few magazines survived more than three confiscations since paying printers and paper suppliers devoured much of their capital. At times, editors were forced to negotiate with censors who insisted on replacing "edgy" material with content that was "easier to digest."[163] *Szpilki* survived many such debacles.[164]

Szpilki was unequivocally pro-Jewish too. It collaborated with Jewish illustrators and authors, some of whom (notably Reif, Schneider, and Bickels) bridged the divide between Polish, Polish Jewish, and Yiddish print media, which, due to this double perspective, enabled them to provide a unique take on contemporary events. The magazine's open condemnation of what its editor described as *prasa żydożercza* (the antisemitic press) could only be matched by similar criticism expressed by a host of Yiddish-language and Polish Jewish print media.[165] Like many of their ethnonationalist adversaries, Łaszowski included, the artists and writers of *Szpilki* represented a young generation of intellectuals and activists, all born around the 1910s, who wished to put a lasting stamp on Polish cultural, social, and political life. Where the two differed was the proposed way of making that change.

Many of *Szpilki*'s contributors were recruited from the PPS, some were communist, and others were progressive intellectuals and art students, not attached to any specific faction.[166] It was precisely their inclusivity, antifascist outlook, and socialist sympathies that made them clash with their right-wing counterparts. Importantly, *Szpilki*'s critical stance on the ongoing events was not merely an intellectual position. To some of its founders and contributors, including non-Jews, the antisemitic climate of interwar Poland was deeply relatable and personal: they counted Jews among their friends and knew of antisemitic attacks first-hand.[167] According to *Szpilki*'s founder Eryk Lipiński, their political engagement was genuine too. Fighting fascism and Sanacja was their chief motivation in setting up the magazine.[168]

Well-disposed contemporaries emphasized how gifted *Szpilki*'s illustrators were.[169] Those assessing the magazine in retrospect saw it as one of the most avant-garde publications of the time and a breeding ground for new talent.[170] *Szpilki*'s content was fearless, provocative, and relevant, as many of the examples discussed in this chapter show. And yet, determining what made some interwar artists into liberal commentators and advocates of the progressive cause can pose some difficulties. Information gleaned from personal and professional biographies of the artists and writers for *Szpilki* can provide us with some insight into this question, but even those speculations should be treated with caution.

For example, the founder of the magazine, Eryk Lipiński, was born in 1908 in what was still the Austro-Hungarian city of Kraków. His father, Teodor, came from a family of Polish patriots in the Russian imperial city of Odessa. Teodor developed socialist sympathies early on, participating in the revolution of 1905 and rubbing shoulders with the likes of Vladimir Lenin and the Polish socialist Ignacy Daszyński.[171] A painter by training, Teodor exposed young Eryk to poster art, caricature drawing, and socialist banner design, all of which he himself regularly pursued. Between 1913 and 1921, the family lived in Moscow where, starting in 1917, Eryk's father oversaw the protection of Polish cultural heritage assets that had been transported to Russia in the imperial period; there the boy received his primary education.[172] Socialist ideas remained at the core of family life after the Lipiński family returned to Poland and settled in Warsaw. Teodor contributed articles to socialist outlets such as *Pobudka* (*The Awakening*) and *Robotnik* (*The Worker*) and counted many socialist activists among his close friends. Teodor's funeral in 1932 was said to be "a great demonstration," with multiple delegations flying red banners and the PPS Sejm deputy and Teodor's friend Adam Próchnik bidding him farewell.[173]

Eryk Lipiński's father was central to his growth as a political activist and artist, but so was, presumably, his academic training. Like Lipiński, several of the *Szpilki* illustrators were students at the Academy of Fine Arts in Warsaw, including Franciszek Parecki, the creator of the anti-Mussolini cartoon "One hair after another," and Ha-Ga, who drew the "Mister! You're a Mason" caricature.[174] According to Lipiński, the academy was one of the few institutions of higher learning in Poland that saw no antisemitic violence in the 1930s. He credited this to the activity of KPP's academic youth faction ZNMS "Życie" of which several of the artists discussed above were members.[175] A work by a historian of the academy, Ksawery Piwocki, corroborates this. Piwocki writes that the authorities had a zero-tolerance policy toward antisemitic excesses, but he also gives credit to the students themselves whose maturity and sentience prevented serious outbursts of violence.[176]

Although less is known of *Szpilki*'s other cartoonists and their backgrounds, basic biographical details paint a corresponding picture of professed socialists. Jakub Bickels, who was born in Lviv in 1910 or 1911, contributed illustrations to several leftist outlets, including Lviv's monthly *Sygnały* (*Signals*) and Warsaw's weekly *Wiadomości Literackie*.[177] Other artists, such as Mendel Reif and Bronisław Schneider, both born in the 1910s in Lviv or the surrounding area, had a similar record of working for the leftist print media.[178] Reif was self-taught as was Bickels, who had trained as a psychiatrist.[179] Schneider was an architect and a graduate of the Lviv Polytechnic.[180] Although less is known of their personal backgrounds, except for Reif, whose father was a melamed, it can be presumed they were a diverse group of artists who had first-hand experience of the issues they covered in their work.

Scholars have seen satire as an important cultural practice and a barometer with which to measure the ebbs and flows of democracy.[181] In late interwar Poland, right-wing pundits imagined leftist satire as the enemy within, controlled by the Jews and having the power to pollute the "true spirit" of the Polish nation. State censors and national courts suppressed and penalized it in an attempt to protect the established political and social order. As an antifascist and leftist magazine, *Szpilki* confronted political radicalization and ridiculed some of the central tenets of right-wing ideology, notably the idea of a "de-Judaized" state. The magazine satirized social ills and criticized the Sanacja government, which condoned the prevailing climate of ethnic hatred. It parodied calls for mass Jewish migration, ridiculed the struggles for ethnic economy and ethnically homogenous universities, and derided public debates on Freemasonry, as well as targeting specific antisemites, including those of Jewish extraction. Operating in a milieu that was becoming increasingly authoritarian and hostile to free speech, the magazine spoke with an engaged democratic voice. Despite coming under attack from state censors and other media outlets, as well as facing financial difficulties, the editors of

Szpilki continued to target what they saw as bigotry and philistinism. The magazine was vocal about international threats too; it criticized the growing ascendancy of fascism, as seen in some of the contemporary developments, including the annexation of Austria into the Third Reich and the proliferation of so-called racial laws. Only one week before the outbreak of the Second World War, state censors confiscated caricatures of Hitler that were to be published in the magazine, so as not to upset Nazi Germany.[182]

Szpilki's courage and steadfastness are well captured in a verse by the Polish Jewish poet Lola Szereszewska (née Rotbard), one of the regular contributors to the magazine.[183] Entitled "Przepraszam, że żyję" ("I apologise for being alive"), the poem was a powerful response to the ongoing climate of antisemitic hate and terror:

> I apologize most humbly for being Jewish
> I know it is my fault, my most grievous fault—
> I could have been born an elephant or an ant,
> any yet to spite everyone I became a Jew—
> You can punish me, you can curse me.
> I apologize most profusely, I repent and prostrate myself,
> I know it's dated to be a Semite today,
> but if a Jew digs her heels in, then God forbid,
> she'll be Jewish a long time, nothing will help her—
> I know it's rude, I know it's ugly!
> I apologize most humbly for my stubborn nose:
> the nose sticks out upwards, it does not bend downwards,
> it is supposed to be hooked but it stayed upturned—
> this is a blatant deception, inappropriate joke—
> I know it is my fault, my most grievous fault.[184]

Szpilki and its contributors were important actors in the cultural life of late interwar Poland, and depending on the political persuasion of the commentator, the magazine was either ostracized or admired. Its content was both provocative and bold. Its artists tried to redefine satire and put it in service of their socialist beliefs. This was cut short by the outbreak of the Second World War. Many of *Szpilki*'s contributors, both Jewish and gentile, did not survive the war. Jakub Bickels, Zuzanna Ginczanka, Tadeusz Hollender, Swiatopełk Karpiński, Franciszek Parecki, Mendel Reif, Bronisław Schneider, Andrzej Siemaszko, Władysław Szlengel, Jerzy Kamil Weintraub, and Lola Szereszewska, among others, did not see liberation.[185] Reif was murdered in the Janowska concentration camp in Lviv in 1943. Bickels was killed in the

Warsaw Uprising after a long period in hiding in Warsaw. Schneider fell as a soldier of the Red Army.[186]

Szpilki resumed its activity in 1945, but it was no longer a magazine of the anti-government opposition. From the late 1940s onwards, it became a flagship publication promoting "socialist satire" that served the ideological interests of the Polish People's Republic.[187] After the Communist takeover, the editors and chief contributors to the original *Szpilki*, including Zbigniew Mitzner, Eryk Lipiński, Ha-Ga, and many others, began a new chapter in their professional careers.

Chapter 4

HIDDEN IDENTITIES

On 1 July 1946, a woman named Melania Szpigiel wrote a letter to the rector of the University of Warsaw, requesting that a photograph of her late husband, Henryk Stanisław Szpigiel, which had survived the war in the university archives, be given to her. She explained that her husband, who had studied in the Faculty of Law in the 1920s, went missing during the war and that she had no photographs that could remind her of him. Since this was potentially the only surviving image of the man, Melania's wish was granted.[1] To this day, the archives of the University of Warsaw preserve a single sepia photograph of teenage Henryk Szpigiel in a military uniform, possibly a copy of the very same picture that Melania requested after the war (Figure 4.1). No other photographs and little additional information exist on the man who had been once well known in the satirical circles of interwar Warsaw.

Szpigiel's satirical career took off in the late 1920s. He initially wrote for the stage, including lyrics for popular songs that were the rave of interwar theatres and music clubs, mixing sentimental tunes with brassy sounds of jazz and tango ensembles.[2] In his writing, he wavered between different political proclivities, contributing humorous poems to far-right outlets such as *ABC* as well as writing for the leftist *Szpilki*. He was known as Harvey, Harwey, St. Harten, and Henryk Ostecki to his music audiences and V.Y., Vallin Youry, Es, S.T., and S.P. Igiel to his readers at *Szpilki*.[3] Between January and May 1937, he undertook his longest stint in satirical writing as de facto editor of the right-wing *Szarża* magazine. In *Szarża*, Szpigiel was responsible for delivering most of the textual content that appeared under various "Sarmatian-sounding pseudonyms" that evoked the old Polish nobility. This was presumably to conceal Szpigiel's Jewish family background and convince the reader of the "ethnically pure" composition of the editorial staff. For the same reason, Aleksander Dzierżawski, a deputy in the Sejm and National Party activist, was officially named the editor in chief, despite playing a minor role in the magazine.[4]

4.1. Photograph of Henryk Szpigiel, from University of Warsaw Archives.

Szarża was intended as the flagship satirical outlet of the national camp; it was created to weaken the supposed Jewish influence in satire and offset the activity of such leftist magazines as *Szpilki*.[5] Although seen as rabidly anti-Jewish by commentators of the time, including the liberal Jewish poet Antoni Słonimski and *Szpilki*'s cocreator Eryk Lipiński, the magazine was, arguably, an exercise in the pliability of satire. Henryk Szpigiel, an all-around satirical whizz, was central to this process. Using the inherent duplicity of satire as his weapon, Szpigiel was able to produce portrayals that could be read as antisemitic, while also drawing attention to the misfortune of Polish Jews that, depending on the audience, could elicit sympathy. Because it was devoid of the rabid rhetoric of magazines such as *Pokrzywy*, understanding *Szarża*'s satire hinged on the anti-Jewish predisposition of its readers since Szpigiel himself tended to avoid the usual blatancy of antisemitic satire. Although scholars generally contend that whether a portrayal is to be considered antisemitic depends on the political affiliation of the outlet and the attitude of its creators, such clear answers cannot be given about *Szarża*.[6] In fact, Szpigiel's editorial activity calls into question the intentionality on which much antisemitic representation is believed to hinge, while the history of *Szarża* adds a new perspective to our knowledge of the actors and motivations behind antisemitic satire in interwar Poland.

HENRYK STANISŁAW SZPIGIEL

Henryk Stanisław Szpigiel was born in 1903 in Warsaw to Leontyna née Neufeld and Józef Szpigiel.[7] Surviving documentation, submitted as part of his application to the University of Warsaw in 1922, including Szpigiel's handwritten curriculum vitae and a school leaving diploma, cites two dates of birth: 3 and 14 May respectively.[8] The latter date is more likely, appearing in other archival records.[9] Although Szpigiel's fellow satirists believed he was a literature graduate, the records of the University of Warsaw show that between 1922 and 1927 he was enrolled in a law degree program.[10] Like many of his young contemporaries, he struggled financially and was forced to support himself throughout his studies, which meant that his time at the Faculty of Law was replete with delays and difficulties. A letter submitted by Szpigiel to the Examination Board requesting that an exam be deferred speaks of the "demanding paid employment" in which he was involved at the time. The job was said to "weaken his eyesight," which forced him to limit his work and study time.[11] Other similar requests submitted by Szpigiel to the university authorities detail obligations toward a sick father as well as his own health issues, specifically neurosis (*nerwica serca*), a diagnosis confirmed by a doctor's note.¹²

This was likely also the time when Szpigiel embarked on a career as a satirical writer, which might have left him overcommitted and unable to cope with the university workload. Though he had a fairly modest publication record, he must have devoted a lot of time to perfecting his writer's craft. Szpigiel's only single-authored work *Ojciec zadżumionych i inne parodje polityczne* (*The Father of the Plague-Stricken and Other Political Parodies*, 1930), published under the pseudonym Henryk St. Harten (Harvey), appeared only few years after his stint at the University of Warsaw. The pamphlet of just over thirty pages contains satirical poems that Szpigiel had written for a variety of outlets, notably the literary supplement of the nationalist *ABC* daily and the antisemitic *Żółta Mucha* weekly.¹³ The pieces in the volume draw on the work of three authors: the master of eighteenth-century satire Ignacy Krasicki (1735–1801) and the two romantic poets Adam Mickiewicz (1798–1855) and Juliusz Słowacki (1809–1849). The volume's motto comes from *Monachomachia* (War of the Monks, 1778), a poem by Krasicki that criticized both the clergy and contemporary mores. The maxim read: "True virtue fears no criticism / Let the vices groan and twinge," introducing Szpigiel's poems and summarizing his own approach to satire.¹⁴

Five years later, "True virtue fears no criticism" would become the motto for the newly established *Szpilki*, which was soon to grow into a flagship satirical publication of the socialist left. According to Eryk Lipiński, it was he and *Szpilki* cofounder Zbigniew Mitzner who decided to use the excerpt from Krasicki as the motto for their magazine.¹⁵ However, a closer look at the early history of *Szpilki* also points to Henryk Szpigiel's involvement. As we have seen, the beginnings of the magazine can be traced to a group of young illustrators at the Academy of Fine Arts in Warsaw, Lipiński included, whose initial base of writers was fairly small. Szpigiel filled that void. A versatile satirist with experience in writing for other outlets, he was swift and prolific. According to one humorist of the time, "[Szpigiel] executed the job like a skilled craftsman. When assigned a topic, he would deliver what you needed in just a few minutes: be it a poem, a column, a light-hearted short story or a one-liner."¹⁶ The first issue of *Szpilki* contained satirical texts written exclusively by Szpigiel, but his true identity was hidden under various pseudonyms, which, in Lipiński's words, were supposed to make the reader think the magazine had many contributors.¹⁷ Such a strategy was necessary for creating a steady reader base in a publishing market in which many magazines were ephemeral and prone to being suspended after just a few issues. By 1936, such recognized authors as Julian Tuwim, Światopełk Karpiński,

Stanisław Jerzy Lec, and Antoni Słonimski began to regularly contribute to *Szpilki*, and Szpigiel's work became redundant. He was let go and instead became the chief contributor to the ethno-nationalist media, not least the newly established *Szarża*.

The irony of Szpigiel's move was not lost on contemporary observers. As one leftist commentator caustically remarked, the Endeks and ONR supporters "turned a blind eye to Szpigiel's prominent nose and raven hair" since his skill in satire was sorely needed in the nationalist camp.[18] Another author marveled that while the editors of *Szpilki* were Poles "without a smack of Piasecki" (the founder of the radical right group ONR), the editor of a nationalist and antisemitic magazine was essentially an "Israelite" (*Izraelita*).[19] Szpigiel's Jewish identity was an open secret, particularly among leftist and Polish Jewish commentators.[20] In contrast, the nationalists chose not to comment on his involvement in *Szarża*, and Dzierżawski figured as the sole editor of the magazine. For the sake of accuracy, however, it needs to be noted that, although Szpigiel was ethnically Jewish, he was baptized in 1913 at the age of ten, becoming a member of the Evangelical Church of Augsburg Confession, first in Kraków and starting in 1915 in Warsaw.[21] Scarce memoirs written by family acquaintances intimate that Szpigiel's father was an assimilated Jew and a Piłsudski supporter who was well liked in his local area of Wolica in the commune of Stopnica where he leased and ran the government-owned Podzamcze *folwark*.[22]

One can only speculate what the diehard ethno-nationalist illustrators made of their collaboration with Szpigiel. Given the lack of sources that would comment on the situation, it is tempting to read some of the visual material appearing in the magazine as an implicit reflection on the topic. A cutting cartoon by Włodzimierz Łukasik, who signed his works as "Ł." accompanied by a small crown, could be interpreted as one dig at the editor's ethnic background. A cover page drawing, "Popyt na nosy" ("Noses in Demand"), portrays three Jewish men visiting a fancy-dress rental (Figure 4.2). Their oversized noses, lips, and ears are meant to leave no doubt as to their ancestry. The shop, staffed by a gentile with a conspicuously small nose, leases folk and national costumes, as well as fake noses and face coverings. Interested in obtaining a set of upturned noses (*zadarte nosy*), the three men are left disappointed: these props are gone. They are told, nonetheless, they could still acquire a *kontusz* (a long robe typical for sixteenth-century Polish nobles), *siermięga* (a traditional peasant's cloak), and two types of "patriotic" caps (*konfederatka* and *maciejówka*), some of which are visible on the shelf behind the shop owner.[23] Although drawn in black ink on white paper, the cartoon uses additional plates of green and black to provide shading and a

HIDDEN IDENTITIES 125

4.2. Włodzimierz Łukasik, Noses in Demand, from *Szarża*, 7 March 1937, 1.

sense of depth to the image. This strategy was most likely copied by Szpigiel from *Szpilki* for which it was a trademark, using splashes of color for front and back cover drawings.

On the surface, the cartoon could be read as a commentary on the age-old practice of concealing Jewish looks, rhinoplasty included, in an attempt to fit in. Berlin physician Jacques Joseph, who was already conducting such surgeries in the nineteenth century, claimed that many of his patients were Jews who reduced their noses to "conceal their origins."[24] But in Łukasik's cartoon, gentile noses, let alone nasal reconstruction, are not an option. Jews are forced to make do with Sarmatian and patriotic props instead. This was also the case for Szpigiel. According to one satirical writer of the period, the Endeks disguised Szpigiel under various pseudonyms, such as "Babinicz" and "Kmicic," that brought to mind the old Polish nobility, all in an attempt to maintain the appearance that all of *Szarża*'s writers were Christian Poles.[25] The drawing could be read as a scathing portrayal of the few tools that Jews had at their disposal in trying to pass as gentiles and, possibly, as a reference to Szpigiel himself, who was both a convert to Christianity and an outlier in his immediate professional environment.

If read against corresponding cartoons by liberal artists, the mischievous drawing by Łukasik turns out to be exceedingly trivial, if not callous. In a related caricature on upturned noses published in *Szpilki* several months later, the antifascist illustrator Franciszek Parecki took on a more complex visual exercise in which he humorously commented on the supposed function of the Jewish nose. The two-image cartoon, entitled "Żydowskie podparcie" ("Jewish Underprop"), shows how uses of the hooked nose had evolved since the widespread flare-up of student violence. Both vignettes show a man sitting on a park bench. In picture one, we see a host of quotidian scenes: there is a couple in love walking hand in hand, and a mother strolling with her child. Here, the man's nose is merely a support for his left arm and hand, his right elbow resting on the lap. This is a gesture of relaxation; the man props his nose in the palm of his hand, the same way some would prop their chin. Scene two shows the same man and the same park bench, but the surroundings have changed. The usual parkgoers are gone, and the park is overrun with cane-wielding hoodlums who scrutinize the man's appearance, speculating about his ancestry. His safety in danger, the man pushes his nose up with his finger and holds still, hoping to remain unexposed as Jewish.

Parecki's cartoon attained depth through a careful mix of the comic and the tragic. Here, the upturned nose was a necessity, possibly a life-saving ploy, as the artist discussed the threat posed to Jews by ethnonationalist gangs who attack anyone they believe to be Jewish. In contrast, Łukasik omitted that aspect of the story and opted for ambiguity. Choosing to present the theme in a convention of a light-hearted dress-up play and providing little information as to the situation of his Jewish protagonists, Łukasik made readers laugh but spared them the responsibility of having to reflect on the possible predicament of his subjects. Although published only a few months apart, the two cartoons could not be more different—not only in how much the artists chose to tell about the realities of "looking Jewish" in a state overrun by violence, but also in what each artist reveals about himself, in particular his sense of compassion or lack thereof for the victims of that violence.

An indifferent cartoon like the "Noses in Demand" one was not that surprising coming from Łukasik. A staunch champion of the antisemitic drawing, Łukasik saw *Szarża* as an ideal tool with which to destroy the nation's purported enemy. His earlier drawing advertising *Szarża* in another ethnonationalist outlet presented a giant boot hanging over a party of jubilant Jews, while commenting that *Szarża* and the ONR youth were now ready to trample them into the ground.[26] The motif of a boot about to destroy a group of Jewish revelers was no doubt an allusion to the common antisemitic trope of Jews as insects that appeared in such magazines as *Pokrzywy*, both in cartoons and satirical texts. While *Pokrzywy* freely included terms such as swarms, mob, and maggots to describe its Jewish adversaries, as well as employing related imagery, Łukasik chose a less literal approach to the topic. By employing the visual metonymy of a boot about to crush the protagonists, he was able to convey both the perceived lowly status of the Jewish subjects and their perilous position in the rapidly radicalizing Polish society. This was both an expression of ethno-nationalist triumph and a warning to all opponents of the national camp.

Szpigiel was obliging: *Szarża* abounded in antisemitic content. Some of his editorial choices, including Łukasik's cartoon about noses, were clearly self-deprecating too. His own work, whether shorter poems or longer pieces of satirical journalism, adhered to the ethnonationalist ethos but were clearly addressed to a more demanding audience than the small-town offerings of such magazines as *Pokrzywy*. Bearing all the hallmarks of good satirical writing, Szpigiel's texts were detailed and well informed about the political realities in question. To convey a relevant point, they often toyed with invented realities, a strategy that was particularly popular with *Szpilki* at the time.

In one issue, Szpigiel wrote about fictional events in the provincial town of Wola Gdowska, where a local drunk accosted several Jewish merchants, accidently smashing a shop window of a certain Bajla Cynamon with a stick. Szpigiel's piece was a literary take on the popular children's whispering game, also known as "telephone," wherein a message gets garbled as it travels from one person to another. The text, "Pogrom w Polsce" ("Pogrom in Poland"), consisted of several short pieces that reported on the same event. As the reports moved from local newspapers to Warsaw dailies and on to international outlets in France and the United States, they grew increasingly sensational, inaccurate, and exaggerated. Names were distorted, and the number of victims and the hurt inflicted on them were manipulated. The text seemed to have been implying that the further from the events, the less knowledge there was about the situation at hand. In the end, it showed that what was effectively a misbehavior of a drunken individual came to be portrayed as a full-fledged pogrom that generated a wave of international protest, brought to life a multinational committee that was to explore the living conditions of Polish Jews, and elicited a charitable engagement from international organizations such as the JDC.[27]

Given the timing of the text, it can be assumed that "Pogrom w Polsce" alluded to the Przytyk events of 9 March 1936 in which two Jews were killed and many others were brutally beaten.[28] Some of the place names appearing in the article, including the fictional Ryczywół, brought to mind actual locations, such as Odrzywół in which anti-Jewish riots and boycotts of Jewish businesses took place as early as 1935.[29] Szpigiel's text showed a clear awareness of the role of the media in shaping the public opinion of contentious events. The Przytyk pogrom, in particular, engendered a flurry of media responses. Many on the political right, including the Roman Catholic Church, appeared to denounce physical violence, while condoning economic aggression against Jews. The reaction from the government was similar as both parties tended to downplay the seriousness of the events.[30] The liberal community was more decisive in condemning the violence, as were international organizations, including the JDC, which attempted to rally support for the Polish Jews in their countries.[31] Szpigiel had an excellent understanding of these disparities in representation and the political agendas that fueled them. In his piece specifically, the ongoing anti-Jewish violence was refracted in a way that glossed over the systematic campaign of hate unleashed by the ethno-nationalist right and their supporters. It minimized the targetted nature of that violence as yet another alcohol-induced brawl.[32] More importantly, it provided a damning critique of the liberal media as biased and untrustworthy.

Other pieces by Szpigiel, including "Mecz Polska-Judea" ("The Poland-Judea Match"), were more ambiguous. That text was written in the style of a report on a soccer match in which Poland plays a fictional Jewish state called Judea. There are some interesting moments in this text that reveal the author's dual perspective. Initially, the Poles are presented as the winning party, scoring one goal. The Jews are in the losing position from the start since the Polish goalpost is closed to them: the brave gentile goalkeeper "guards the post with the Aryan paragraph," a reference to anti-Jewish measures proliferating in Europe at the time. The reporting is fast-paced but somewhat fractured as the limited perspective of the broadcasting booth prevents the commentator from following the event in its entirety. As it happens, the game turns chaotic, and there is commotion on the field. Soon enough, the commentator announces that one of the Judea players was beheaded. The players take little notice of the tragic event, and the human head flies around the pitch as though it was ball. It is only when the judge challenges the winning score of the Polish team that spectators are roused. Crowds flood the soccer field. The police use water cannons to disperse the crowds. The commentator's voice disappears. His microphone is damaged by water.[33]

"Mecz Polska-Judea" is more interesting than a typical ethnonationalist piece, in terms of both the imagery and the language used. It is also less obvious in its political message than the earlier "Pogrom." In it, the usual motifs associated with soccer enable the author to allude to the existing realities of ethnic violence. In Szpigiel's text, phrasing and vocabulary are of the essence. A Polish player is described as "nationally unaware" because he passes the ball to the Jews. The Jews want to fire or score (*strzelać*), but the Polish "self-defense" (*samoobrona*) neutralizes them; then they fire for real (*strzelają*), and once that has happened, the police intervene, looking for "unknown perpetrators" (*nieznani sprawcy*). The Jews still attack the Poles, while the referee remains oblivious to the attack. In this story, the soccer field becomes a site of ethnic conflict and physical confrontation that ends in murder, police intervention, the use of water cannons, and general disorder. On a metaphorical level, the field stands for any site of Polish-Jewish confrontation and admittedly violence, whether a market place or a university hall. The referee symbolizes the state or the Sanacja government specifically, one of the major objects of the ethnonationalist offensive that saw the Jews as aggressors and the government as their ally. And yet, Szpigiel is more ambiguous than that. There are several moments of tension, including the image of the goalpost protected with the Aryan paragraph, the seemingly unimportant beheading of the Jewish player, and the general weakness of the Judea team, which is supposedly on the offensive. Here, satire allows Szpigiel to convey a more nuanced message that, if read through the liberal lens, could even be interpreted as condemning the ongoing violence and presenting the Jews as victims of the nationalist assault.

More arcane works of satire like this were interspersed in the magazine with more striking pieces that mimicked the explicitly hostile discourse of other right-wing outlets. For instance, one *jeu d'esprit* argued that, to become a successful writer in Warsaw, one had to be either Jewish or gay.[34] Another complained about the tediousness of the debate surrounding the ritual slaughter and blamed Jews for inconveniencing gentiles by opposing the proposed ban.[35] Yet another text, a verse whose poetic persona introduced himself as an "in-law" (*powinowaty*) and a "remote relative" (*daleki krewny*) of the old masters of Polish poetry, berated Jews for their alleged victim mentality.[36] There was also a piece that ridiculed the supposed Jewish penchant for the "(political) left" and wondered why they insisted on sitting on the right in universities.[37] Finally, there was a one-liner that complained about Sanacja's faltering commitment to the antisemitic sentiment.[38] All of these works focused on topical issues that were widely debated in the media and could be interpreted as an attempt to escalate existing tensions and put constant pressure on the government.

As far as Szpigiel's ethnic identity was concerned, both his writing and his editorial choices revealed an interesting interplay between staying hidden, that is trying to pass as gentile, and revealing himself as Jewish. Maintaining this kind of "dual legibility," as one historian describes it, could only happen with audiences that were able to read and recognize it properly.[39] On the one hand, Szpigiel's commissionining of such cartoons as Łukasik's "Noses in Demand" or his nuanced portrayal of the Poland-Judea game could be read as a pushback, however playful, against passing. On the other hand, his coverage of pertinent news stories (from ritual slaughter to ghetto benches) was an exercise in invisibility. Such "dual coding" meant that one could only "be openly Jewish at the right time and in the right place."[40] Longer satirical pieces afforded Szpigiel that visibility and enabled him to develop a more ambiguous writer's identity, one that would be recognizable to other Jews as well as leftist observers, particularly those who knew the real ethnicity of the editor.

It was in the best interests of the National Party to maintain the anonymity of its chief writer. After all, the "ethnic purity" of the right-wing political camp was under constant scrutiny by members of leftist progressive elites. The cases of Piasecki and Wasiutyński, discussed earlier in the context of *Szpilki*, provide chief examples of such an ongoing monitoring. At the same time, Szpigiel was not a political figure, nor was he a spokesman for the nationalist right, which effectively protected him from such targeted attacks. Spoofs among the internal circle of contributors to the publication were another matter. One other cartoon by one of *Szarża*'s contributing artists could be read as a gentle allusion to Szpigiel, drawn in the mode of Łukasik's "Noses in Demand." The drawing was produced by an illustrator identified only as "Poraj.," whose work appeared almost exclusively in *Szarża*.

The cartoon was a minimalistic drawing in black ink, presenting seven employees of the musical section of the Polish Radio at work (Figure 4.3). All of the portrayed singers as well as the piano player, visible in the background, were drawn with grotesquely large mouths and hooked noses, making the

4.3. Poraj., "'Polish' Radio," from *Szarża*, 21 February 1937, 2.

group look uniform and explicitly "Jewish." The caption "'Polskie' Radio" insinuated deception on the part of this public institution that promised to represent the titular nation of Poland.[41] Analyzed against the backdrop of existing debates, the cartoon could be read as a visual endorsement of the famous speech by Sejm delegate Wacław Budzyński, who demanded the "re-Polonization" of all cultural institutions by expunging the supposedly foreign "Jewish element."[42] The radical right saw the Polish Radio as an important battlefield for the future of national culture, all the more so since the broadcast institution underwent a rapid nationalization in mid-1930s.

By 1936, 96 percent of its shares were owned by the state.[43] Ethnonationalist pundits hoped that the government would take advantage of its position as the chief stakeholder in the Polish Radio and rise to the task of "de-Judaizing" the institution, a sentiment that appeared in some of *Szarża*'s written content too.[44] Music constituted the lion's share of all offerings on the radio. It is likely that seeing Polish Jewish musicians involved in such enterprises as the Polish Radio Orchestra, with Grzegorz Fitelberg as the principal conductor since 1935, caused much discontent in nationalist circles.[45] Importantly, the cartoon encouraged the informed reader to draw parallels between the radio and other sectors of culture. Like Szpigiel, the Jewish figures in Poraj's cartoon are hidden to the radio listeners, known only to a small group of insiders.

The scarce and fragmented historical sources that survive about Szpigiel correspond with the stories of hiding and passing told by the drawings discussed here. Much of his activity as a writer involved maintaining dual allegiances, as he vacillated between the world of the ethno-nationalist print media, which was anti-Jewish, and that of the music industry, which was largely sustained by Jewish talent. Syrena Record, the music label with which Szpigiel worked on a regular basis, was home to many Polish Jewish composers and songwriters, including Henryk Wars, Marian Hemar, Konrad Tom, and Andrzej Włast, many of whom were nonreligious or, like Szpigiel, assimilated Jews. His work for Syrena as well as his writing stints for *ABC* and later *Szarża* no doubt necessitated crossing sociocultural boundaries as well as requiring a deliberate effort to fit in. Indeed, Szpigiel's desire to succeed in writing for both sectors, paired with his attachment to the Polish literary tradition, was an ongoing exercise in reconciling identities that, given the political context, were becoming increasingly incompatible. The theme of juggling identities and ethnic mingling, whether in the past or at the time, continued to capture *Szarża*'s attention throughout much of its existence.

SZARŻA'S VISUAL POLITICS

While some of the cartoons discussed above could indeed be read as both commentaries on current events and digs at Szpigiel, other content was more heavily politicized. Polish and Jewish confluences, identity-related or otherwise, remained an important topic throughout *Szarża*'s short-lived existence. Another one of Poraj's cartoons tackled a subject that could be problematic for the ethnonationalist right: the possible Jewishness of the last king of Poland, Stanisław August Poniatowski (1732–1798). The cartoon was a reaction to an article by historian and journalist Mateusz Mieses published in the Polish Jewish daily *Nasz Przegląd*. The article was part of a larger project about Christian Poles with Jewish heritage to be published as a two-volume work the following year.⁴⁶ As Mieses stated in the foreword to his book in 1938, his research arose from concern over the spread of racial hatred in recent years. It constituted an attempt to demonstrate that the "Semitic element" had been part of Polish society, the nobility, and aristocratic circles in particular, for centuries, exerting positive influence on Polish culture.⁴⁷ He claimed that his work was also a response to such "ignorant and misleading" pamphlets as Stanisław Dider's *Rola neofitów w dziejach Polski* (*The Role of Neophytes in the History of Poland*, 1935), which used the long history of Polish and Jewish intermingling to argue for the damaging impact of "pseudo-Catholics" and Jewish converts on the Polish nation.⁴⁸ The text by Mieses went to the core of the ethno-nationalist preoccupation with so-called national purity. His preview for *Nasz Przegląd* not only pointed out the king's "Mediterranean looks" and his positive disposition toward the Jewish community, but also demonstrated that some of his ancestors were indeed Jewish.⁴⁹

The Endeks were opposed to such content, instead viewing individuals of mixed ethnicity as harmful to the "soul" of the nation and polluting Polish culture. Eradicating that influence from literature, music, the arts, and history became their chief goal.⁵⁰ At the same time, important historical and cultural figures were considered untouchable and thus in need of protection from any "accusations" of Jewishness. The cartoon by Poraj implied that if the king came back to life, he would dismiss those claims and, instead, challenge the Jews' presence. The drawing illustrates the point (Figure 4.4).⁵¹ Dressed in period attire and presented against the backdrop of royal buildings, the king strikes a Jewish man's backside with his foot, making his adversary lose balance. Like many other artists working in this genre of cartooning, Poraj uses the dichotomy of the superior gentile and his inferior Jewish counterpart, as though to emphasize the intrinsic power imbalance between the two. The artist implies that, irrespective of Mieses's efforts to prove the historical and contemporary connections between the two people, the existing situation of ethnic strife was not only natural but desirable.

Some antisemitic newspapers also responded to the article by Mieses. For example, an article in the far-right daily *Dziennik Poznański* argued that his research was yet another manifestation of "Jews wanting something" from the state. Its author advised that both Jews and other minorities needed to be educated into abstaining from such demands ("they could merely ask") because the "Polish national organism was steadily solidifying."⁵² That Jews should be considered second-class citizens could not be expressed more

4.4. Poraj., "If Kind Staś Were Alive...," from *Szarża*, 14 March 1937, 3.

clearly. Other publications used Mieses's work as grist for their antisemitic mill. In particular, *Szarża*'s sister daily, *ABC*, chose to demean King Poniatowski by admitting his cowardice, corruption, and mendacity and asking if this was the reason why the author categorized him as Jewish.[53] The following week, *ABC* reprinted Poraj's cartoon for *Szarża* as if to reemphasize its contempt for the historian's work.[54]

Szarża's visual material was not only limited to commenting on the recent news. It also focused on domestic politics, and much of that content provided a critique of contemporary political elites. As with other outlets of this kind, its main targets were Sanacja and the socialist movement. Cartoons by *Szarża*'s frequent contributor Włodzimierz Łukasik were especially critical of Sanacja. Łukasik blamed the government for not addressing more strongly the so-called Jewish question and for not taking a more decisive stance on the mass emigration of Jews. One front page cartoon showed prime minister Składkowski as a doctor (his actual profession) speaking to Składkowski in his government role. Looking through the microscope, Składkowski the doctor inspects a new strain of bacteria (*gladiolus antisemiticus*), which, according to the caption, continued to spread despite the imposed measures of isolation (Figure 4.5).[55] Like the other drawings appearing on the front page, this image employed, in the mode of the leftist *Szpilki*, additional splashes of color, in this case purple. The illustration is not particularly interesting

4.5. Włodzimierz Łukasik, Dr Sławoj-Składkowski to Sławoj-Składkowski the MP, from *Szarża*, 24 January 1937, 1.

in visual terms as the stocky Składkowski figures resemble hurriedly chiseled stone statues. It is the caption that conveys the central message of the drawing: despite striving to impose segregation, presumably by excusing economic struggle against the Jews (according to the *owszem* principle), the government failed to prevent the escalation of anti-Jewish sentiment and, as such, failed its ethnic Polish citizens by not taking a more decisive stance on the "Jewish question."

A similar undercurrent of disappointment with the government, if not sympathy for the Jewish population, was visible in yet another of Łukasik's cartoons. The drawing portrayed a rapidly deflating hot air balloon steered by Sanacja (Figure 4.6). As the balloon loses height, the pilot removes his unwanted ballast: Jews who had once acted as stabilizers. "Nothing will save this balloon anymore," reads the caption.[56] The cartoon spoke to the fragmentation of the ruling camp and the tokenistic use of Poland's ethnic minorities. It also alluded to the ongoing formation of Ozon, the militaristic and protofascist Sanacja offshoot, which was to fully launch the following month. More generally, it insinuated that Jews were pawns in the hands of political elites, a sentiment that also appeared in other cartoons published in *Szarża*.[57]

The symbolism of a deflating hot air balloon constituted a damning commentary on Sanacja's internal issues. The Jewish characters in the image, although drawn as visual types (three Orthodox and one "modern" Jew), are presented in a somewhat sympathetic manner, their predicament being an outcome of catastrophic decisions on the part of the government. This is a careful representation of a complex issue reflecting the chief purpose of the image—namely, *Szarża*'s attempt to vilify Sanacja, without drawing attention to any other social and political issues. However, this somewhat sympathetic representation of Jewish characters might also have to do with Szpigiel's involvement. It is possible that Szpigiel adhered to a common practice among editors of feeding topics to his cartoonists to create visual material that conformed with the direction of a given issue.[58] The editors of the leftist *Szpilki*, for example, often gave detailed instructions to illustrators about what they wanted to see in a drawing; this included the shape of the illustration, placement of the subjects, the use of color, and the general tone.[59] At times, the artists were given a poem or a caption to illustrate, with fewer directions as to the exact contents of the image.[60] In these ways, editors were able to ensure the illustration would reflect their perspective on the topic.

If we assume that Szpigiel discussed the content of cartoons with his illustrators, it is clear that in this case he wanted to avoid antagonizing and demonizing the Jewish community, instead directing *Szarża*'s criticism toward the authorities. That *Szarża* was noticed for its critical stance on the government can be presumed from several instances of state censorship that the magazine experienced during its brief existence.[61] At the same time, it would be incorrect to argue that Łukasik's work in general was not deliberately antisemitic. Although little is known of the artist, his earlier contributions to the anti-Jewish magazine *Żółta Mucha* in 1932–1933 and the radical

4.6. Włodzimierz Łukasik, Getting Rid of the Ballast, from *Szarża*, 24 January 1937, 4.

right ONR weekly *Prosto z Mostu* in 1937 suggest a certain continuity in the political direction of his work.[62]

Szarża's focus on contemporary events brought its contents close to those of the progovernment *Mucha*. Despite professing opposing political beliefs, both magazines wished to appeal to readers with a general interest in current affairs. Although the two outlets differed somewhat in their assessment of the Sanacja camp and its policies, the scope of their political commentary was otherwise similar. For example, both magazines commented on Sanacja's growing distancing of itself from Polish Jews. To *Mucha*, this was to mark the government's shift in viewing the "Jewish issue" as no longer a matter of internal affairs but rather a shared European problem that had to be dealt with by the League of Nations. In contrast, *Szarża*'s portrayals presented Sanacja as opportunistic side-switchers who, once dependent on support from the bloc of minorities, now disposed of the Jews to increase its political capital.

Like *Mucha*, *Szarża* devoted attention to the exploration of Madagascar as a potential location for Jewish settlement. However, while *Mucha* exploited the tropes of banishment and removal of the unwanted Jews from Poland, *Szarża* focused on the international aspect of the project instead. A humorous drawing by Poraj portrayed French prime minister Léon Blum (a Jew himself) as a latter-day Moses leading his people to the promised land of Madagascar (Figure 4.7). This was coupled with a vignette that showed the new settlers colonizing the land, mingling with the indigenous people, and adopting some of their supposed habits, including nude dancing.[63] Unlike *Mucha*'s usually hostile and blunt take on the subject, Poraj's cartoon is far from antagonistic. This modern, if whimsical, reinterpretation of the book of Exodus could be read against the backdrop of Polish interwar politics. The story of Moses, who led the Israelites out of Egypt where they had been subject to slavery, would no doubt strike a familiar chord with readers sympathetic to the Jewish cause, bringing to mind the contemporary marginalization and disenfranchisement of the group. If Blum was the latter-day Moses, then Poland was Egypt, out of which the Jews needed to be led. And yet, the cartoon is also ironic about the official policies of Jewish resettlement, ridiculing the Madagascar proposal as unrealistic. Poraj achieves this by employing the contrasting tropes of clothed and unclothed bodies, as well as the tropes of whiteness and blackness. The urban Jews who follow Blum are dressed in suits and hats that are unsuited to the heat of Africa. Likewise, the young Jewish woman in the bar scene, although naked and at ease with her indigenous dancing partner, is out of place. Poraj's racialist depiction of the Black bodies, in particular, is meant to show the incongruency of the Madagascar plan. The large lips, forehead, and gorilla-like physique of the

4.7. Poraj., PM Blum as New Moses, from *Szarża*, 14 February 1937, 2.

native man is juxtaposed with the smooth light skin and voluptuousness of the Jewish woman. To Poraj's mind, the local man is a creature of the wild, while the woman is a creation of European civilization, her features bringing to mind ideals of feminine beauty captured in Rubens's paintings. There is a certain continuity of thought between this illustration and the special issue on Madagascar published by the leftist *Szpilki* in January the following year. Toying with invented realities, the issue on Madagascar, too, derided the project, while criticizing the government for devising a plan of forced Jewish migration. It may be that the two publications differed in what they wished to criticize in Sanacja's policies, but it is also true that the usual malevolence present in much of the ethno-nationalist reporting on this issue, and in the progovernment media too, is absent from this particular portrayal in *Szarża*.

Szarża used the cartoon medium also to comment on Palestine as the potential Jewish homeland. One such illustration came close to *Mucha*'s typical pronouncements on the matter. It was a small drawing that depicted a conversation between two Jewish men. In it, one of the interlocutors reflected on whether it would be useful to call for colonies in Palestine. The other cut it short, stating categorically: "We don't have to! . . . We have Polonia."[64] The cartoon was not particularly inventive at the graphic level, using the common visual formula of two men engaged in a conversation. It was also derivative as far as ethnonationalist ideas on Jewish presence in Poland were concerned, conveying the widespread sentiment that Jews have colonized and dominated Poland. Such commentaries dovetailed with those present in other right-wing magazines and enabled *Szarża* to make a clear statement about its alliances. It was for that reason that editors of some liberal Polish Jewish publications would sometimes say that the magazine had gone too far, wishing it had never been established.[65]

Nonetheless, for each prescriptive antisemitic caricature, there was at least one other cartoon that challenged ethnonationalist readers to think of the anti-Jewish struggle in a different if not more sophisticated way. One of the most interesting cartoons in *Szarża*'s seventeen issues commented on the inauguration of the Poland-Palestine connection by Polish national airlines LOT on 5 April 1937 (Figure 4.8). The cartoon, drawn by "S. Filipski," depicted a crowded air terminal filled with travelling Jews, either boarding the plane or waiting in the queue to board. Behind the terminal building is a long line of others awaiting their turn to enter the building. The passengers constitute a cross-section of Polish Jews, comprising people of different ages, genders, and levels of assimilation. The usual trademarks of Polish jingoistic portrayals of Jews are all there: large noses, ears, and beards for the men and excessively curvy figures for the women. Drawn with three colors only—black, white, and red—the cartoon also depicts the Polish flag, flying proudly on top of the terminal building. The caption above the cartoon informs readers of the newly established air connection, while the one beneath it reads, "Safe travels!"[66]

This hectic airport scene brings to mind other portrayals of interwar urban modernity appearing elsewhere in the satirical print media, from drawings of urban traffic to illustrations of city trams.[67] Such images tended to equate modern developments, such as the increased number of motor vehicles on city streets, with Jewish crowds, both of which needed to be controlled. This is also the case in the "Safe travels!" cartoon. Not only are there several disorderly aircrafts in the sky above the airport; the passengers themselves are a confused group requiring assistance from a uniformed airport official. Like this cartoon in *Szarża*, other interwar cartoons conflated urban Jews with the tropes of overcrowding and crowd control. This was perhaps to allude to the overpopulated Jewish areas of Warsaw, Nalewki Street included, which were disparaged by the ethno-nationalist press as a hotbed of disease, backwardness, and other ills. Such images intimated that while the interwar Polish republic was well established on the path of technical progress, Jews were not—their backward ways undermining the achievements of urban modernity.

4.8. S. Filipski, One Can Already Fly from Poland to Palestine, from *Szarża*, 18 April 1937, 8.

Needless to say, the Palestine connection was a source of great pride to all Poles. In 1937 alone, as many as 181 flights were completed, carrying 676 passengers.[68] LOT also transported cargo, and the connection was said to facilitate trade between Poland and Palestine.[69] In the first year of its operation, 25,279 kilograms of cargo, including post, were carried.[70] The outgoing flights to Palestine ran three times a week: on Mondays, Wednesdays, and Fridays. The returning flights operated on Tuesdays, Thursdays, and Saturdays.[71] The flying time between Warsaw and Lydda was said to be thirteen hours, but the actual travel time came to twenty-eight hours because of an overnight stop in Bucharest.[72] Although the connection was met with much enthusiasm in both Poland and the Yishuv, some Polish Jewish commentators criticized it as deeply political, serving the interests of those who lobbied for the mass emigration of Jews.[73] This undertone could also be discerned in *Szarża*'s cartoon. The implicit message behind the exclamation of "Safe travels!" could be read as rejoicing in the outflow of Jewish people. That said, the air connection was well received by some Palestinian Jews, particularly those of Polish extraction, who appreciated the acceleration of postal service and said that it enabled them to maintain close ties with their home country.[74] Some public figures in the Yishuv, too, saw the air connection as beneficial. This included the then-mayor of Tel Aviv, Israel Rokach, who supported the influx of new immigrants and hoped that the Polish government would further facilitate Jewish settlement in Palestine.[75]

In *Szarża*, strictly local news, such as the news of the LOT connection, was often interspersed with visual commentaries on wider international developments. In particular, reflecting its anti-Communism and anti-Bolshevism, the magazine commented on the oppressive Soviet system, especially Stalin's crimes against his own population. In one cartoon for the magazine, Poraj commented on the cruel brutality of Soviet authorities. The drawing shows a Soviet official forcing the people to salute Stalin by threatening them with death (Figure 4.9). The artist found a way to incorporate antisemitic sentiment too. Reviving the traditional trope of so-called Judeo-Communism, which also featured in *Pokrzywy*, Poraj replaced the red star on the man's cap with a hexagram.[76] Elsewhere, commenting on Stalin's purges, the same illustrator depicted the Soviet leader against a backdrop of graves embellished with the Star of David (Figure 4.10). As though to imply that all of Stalin's closest collaborators, now purged, were "Judeo-Communists," Poraj also suggested that Jews were now specifically targeted by the authoritarian leader. This was conveyed by the image of Stalin trampling over the remains of the Star of David. This intricate representation was perplexing, to say the least. After all, although many Jews fell victim to Stalin's purges, they were not targeted as a specific ethnic group. To add to this confusion, the illustrator implied that the Soviet leader now hoped to become the new Napoleon.[77] Like some of the cartoons by Łukasik discussed above, this drawing by Poraj could be read as rather ambiguous, not to say confused, both conflating Jewishness with Communism and presenting Jews as victims of the totalitarian system.

Of course, given where they were published, it would be incorrect to construe some of these cartoons as sympathetic to the plight of the Jewish people. But reading such work against other antisemitic caricatures of the period gives one pause. More nuanced than the works appearing in other periodicals of similar persuasion, *Pokrzywy* including, these cartoons raise

4.9. Poraj., How to Gain Popularity among the Soviets, from *Szarża*, 4 April 1937, 3.

questions about the illustrator's intentionality. It may well be that Poraj was a culturally sensitive artist capable of operating within the Polish-Jewish contact zone. It is also likely that Szpigiel was the brains behind Poraj's creative work. I have found no conclusive evidence to support these speculations. Poraj's real name appears in no major work on Polish antisemitic caricature.[78]

"Chęć odegrania przez Stalina roli sowieckiego Napoleona staje się na tle ewolucji stosunków w ZSRR coraz wyraźniejsza." (A. B. C.)

4.10. Poraj., Stalin's Desire to Become the Soviet Napoleon, from *Szarża*, 14 February 1937, 6.

Neither have I located other instances of this pseudonym being used, with one exception. In early 1939, the alias was used in a cartoon published by the antifascist democratic weekly *Czarno na białem* (*Black on White*).[79] Although puzzling, Poraj's attempt to bridge the liberal and ethno-nationalist publications was not that unusual for struggling artists who attempted to support themselves from caricature drawing. Similarly, the use of a pseudonym would suggest that, like many others who drew antisemitic illustrations, Poraj did not necessarily identify with the content of his work. It is also likely that the alias provided a disguise for an artist who could be otherwise known in the interwar community of illustrators. Like Szpigiel, Poraj may have hidden his identity for a reason.

ALEKSANDER DZIERŻAWSKI

Szarża's official editor in chief (and publisher) was much less of a mystery than some of the magazine's contributors, including the *de facto* editor

Henryk Szpigiel and the cartoonist Poraj. Dzierżawski was born in 1890 in the Turek county in Greater Poland, which was the traditional stronghold of Endecja. In 1920, he became the district head (*starosta*) of the area and, in 1922, a deputy of the Sejm, representing Popular National Union, a party aligned with the national movement that existed between 1919 and 1928. He subsequently became affiliated with the National Party, remaining a Sejm deputy until 1935. During this period, he was an active contributor to regional and national newspapers.[80]

Little is known about the origins of *Szarża* and how far Dzierżawski's role as its publisher went. It is likely, however, that he oversaw administrative matters relating to the magazine's operations and ensured the generous financial support from the National Party for which *Szarża* was famed.[81] His commitment to the ethno-nationalist cause and his investment in political journalism were well known and made him a credible front for Szpigiel's satirical activity. In fact, according to one of the commentators of the period, Szpigiel, who had published satire for ethno-nationalist periodicals before, explicitly asked the Endeks to create a satirical magazine especially for him.[82] This is plausible, not least given the supposed lack of satirical zeal in the nationalist camp.

The practice of concealing the identity of editors and writers was not infrequent in interwar Poland. Many journalists used pseudonyms, and some editors worked incognito. One well-known case concerned the children's weekly *Gazetka Miki* (*Mickey's Little Paper*), the Polish counterpart of *Mickey Mouse Weekly*. Established in 1938, the magazine was the brainchild of Marek Przeworski, a successful publisher and bookseller of Jewish descent, who specialized in children's literature, while the editorial work in *Gazetka* was shared by three people: Wanda Wasilewska, Janina Broniewska, and Jan Marcin Szancer. The first two were well-known children's writers and former editors of the children's weekly *Płomyk* (*Little Flame*). In 1936, the weekly and Wasilewska, in particular, found themselves at the heart of a controversy, being accused by a tabloid newspaper of spreading pro-Soviet propaganda, a case that was sensationalized by the conservative media, not least because the two women were communists and socialist activists. In 1938, Wasilewska and Broniewska organized a teachers' strike, which eventually led to their dismissal from the publishing department of the Polish Teachers' Association where they had worked.[83] According to historian of the Polish print media Stanisław Borowkin, revealing the composition of the editorial board (including the identity of Szancer, who had a Jewish background) could attract criticism to *Gazetka Miki*. To avoid accusations of "Judeo-Communism," the publisher, Przeworski, established a limited liability publishing company called *Gazetka Miki*, concealing both his own involvement and the names of the actual editors.[84]

The considerations behind naming Dzierżawski the publisher and editor of *Szarża* were no doubt similar, notwithstanding the numerous differences between the two magazines. Dzierżawski was more than qualified for the role. He had a history of journalistic and editorial activity at a local level, having collaborated in 1919–1922 with *Gazeta Powiatowa* (*The District Newspaper*) of the Turek county.[85] It was then that his strong anti-socialist, anti-Communist, and anti-Soviet views were formed. In an article in 1920, he called for a struggle against so-called Bolshevism and criticized the newly created Soviet state as authoritarian. According to Dzierżawski, the Soviet Union destroyed trade, industry, and agriculture, as well as interfering in many other spheres of life.[86] His anti-Soviet stance intensified in the years to come. In 1927, he published a short pamphlet entitled *Bankructwo socjalizmu i komunizmu* (*The Bankruptcy of Socialism and Communism*). In it, he described the interwar Polish government as being under the spell of leftist agitation "aimed at destroying the Polish state."[87] He warned that by creating chaos and splitting the nation into warring factions, the communists and socialists alike (the majority of whom were supposedly Jews) intended to consolidate power and take over the country.[88] And yet, he argued further, there was an inherent "bankruptcy" to communist ideology since its many promises, including equality and common ownership, were infeasible and unrealistic.[89]

Dzierżawski's belief in the sinister machinations of clandestine Jewish forces bore all the hallmarks of nineteenth-century antisemitism. Such conspiracy theories were not exclusive to interwar Poland: after the Russian Revolution of 1917, the conviction that Jews used political influence to throw countries into disarray was widespread in Europe and the United States.[90] In that sense, Dzierżawski's take on the topic was far from original. Still, his pamphlet sheds light on him as a political actor and helps explain his later satirical work, including his first and only book of satirical poems entitled *Świnie i koryto: bajki polityczne* (*The Pigs and the Trough: Political Fables*, 1936). Using animal allegories, typical in the fables of Ignacy Krasicki, Dzierżawski provided a highly critical take on the political realities of 1930s Poland. Although the collection was deeply rooted in interwar details and is largely inaccessible to contemporary readers, reading *Świnie i koryto* against the backdrop of the author's other activities helps untangle some of the book's main concerns.

The collection developed the tropes of Jewish domination and control that the author had used in *The Bankruptcy of Socialism and Communism*, while pointing to the supposed collaboration between the Jews and the Sanacja government. The introductory poem "Świnie i koryto" ("The Pigs and the Trough") begins with a suggestive representation of pigs arguing over an empty feeder. Although once friendly, the animals turn hostile once the food runs out. In line with some of the cartoons discussed above, here Dzierżawski not only commented on Sanacja's growing disinterest in the well-being of Polish Jews, but also toyed with olfactory antisemitism, describing one of the pigs as producing "dreadful stench" of a "rotten herring," a source of complaints from the other animal.[91] That herring was one of the staples of Ashkenazi cuisine would be clear to contemporary readers. The rotten smell was meant to signify the Jews' status as unwanted visitors who outstayed their welcome.

Other poems, such as "Rozmowa świń" ("The Conversation of Pigs"), argued—using an internal rhyme—that pigs were now present in every sphere of life (*w każdej dziedzinie są świnie*).[92] In "Wywiady" ("Interviews"), the poet maintained that it was in the pig's nature to push through to the feed box, irrespective of the situation (*koniunktura*).[93] In a similar vein, in "Świnie stanu" ("Statesman Pigs"), pigs boasted about their influence that reached the highest echelons of power.[94] To emphasize the pig's qualities, the cover illustration, the only image in the book, portrayed a single pig at the trough chomping on banknotes. The drawing was authored and clearly signed by none other but Eryk Lipiński, the cocreator of the leftist *Szpilki*.

The themes of greed, domination, influence, and opportunistic side-switching were not new in global antisemitic discourse. Neither was the more local topic of Sanacja's distancing itself from the "Jewish question" uncommon for the time. The one puzzling element was Lipiński's cover design, which went against his usual liberal stance. Despite his relative success as cocreator of a new satirical magazine, in 1936 Lipiński was still a struggling art student who took casual jobs to pay his tuition and support himself. His memoirs reiterate that money was a constant worry to the young Lipiński.[95] The records of the Warsaw Academy of Arts corroborate his recollections, containing an application from Lipiński, dated 15 October 1935, to defer his tuition payment until the end of his degree. The accompanying rector's office stamp, dated 25 October, shows that Lipiński's request was not granted.[96] At the same time, collaborations that crossed the political divide were not unusual for the time. Leftist writers and illustrators sometimes lent their satirical talents to the opposing camp without detriment to their reputation as individuals engaged in the liberal cause.[97] Equally, artists who were prolific in the genre of the antisemitic cartoon were not necessarily shunned by their antifascist colleagues, as the cases of accomplished illustrators Kazimierz Grus and Jerzy Zaruba show.[98] These examples suggest that the ideological screen that separated the two camps was not necessarily inviolable and that the transfer of skills and talent was more frequent than commonly believed. Admittedly, many of these transfers went one way only, with more leftist than right-wing writers and illustrators working for the opposing faction.

Świnie i koryto was met with a warm reception, even if it was limited to like-minded publications. For example, *Szarża*'s sister daily *ABC* fêted the book as engendering the "revival of Polish humor." An *ABC* author described Dzierżawski's work as "an exceptional phenomenon" that stood out among the widespread tendency to "Judaize Polish humor." The journalist hoped that the book would be read by "every Pole who was longing for true Polish humor devoid of . . . Semitic influences."[99] In a similar way, *Kurjer Warszawski* (*Warsaw Courier*), the mouthpiece of the Christian National Party, celebrated Dzierżawski as the "new child of Aesop." Although the reviewer rightly doubted whether some of the more specific references would be understandable to future generations, he was adamant that the collection was to be relished as a work of "light, effortless, and full-bloodied humor."[100] The Kalisz-based *Pokrzywy*, too, honored Dzierżawski (who, like them, was a son of the Greater Poland region) by reprinting two of his poems, including "Świnie i koryto."[101]

The work also made it across the ocean and reached the Polish diaspora in the United States. In 1937, an anonymous Dzierżawski epigone published a collection of satirical poems explicitly modelled on *Świnie i koryto*. In the foreword, the author introduced himself as a true Pole and an enthusiast of Dzierżawski's verse, while reassuring the reader that by no means was he some "Judeo-Piłsudskite" stooge.[102] Rewriting many of the original poems (as well as reprinting others verbatim), the author commented on local Polish events in Chicago, Cleveland, and elsewhere in the United States, while criticizing both Polish émigré luminaries and the Sanacja government in Warsaw. Although the collection was published under the pseudonym "AL," which bore a close resemblance to Dzierżawski's pen name "Al," it is now commonly believed that the book was created by a diaspora priest, Father Aleksander Syski (1876–1945), who was an important figure in the Polish American community. Syski was an ardent follower of Endecja and a strong opponent of the Piłsudski camp. According to one scholar, "Syski was a prolific author, a passionate partisan, and a man of gargantuan and restless energy. He not only was an active 'builder priest,' but a national figure in Polonia political life. . . . He was reckoned by both Dmowski and Paderewski as a major figure in Polish life in the United States."[103]

The attention paid to Dzierżawski's volume by Syski and others shows that his work was known and valued in ethnonationalist circles. Such accolades and recognition were enough of a reason to name him as the editor in chief of Endecja's new flagship magazine. *Szarża*, a Polish word for "charge" or "military offensive," was to launch a concerted attack by the ethno-nationalist cavalry, its purpose being to destroy its main enemies: Sanacja and the Jews.

Some illustrated content in the magazine replicated Dzierżawski's ideas about Jewish influence. This was the case with a plaintive cartoon by artist Julian Żebrowski that claimed the Jewish "minority was the majority," while ethnic Poles were relegated to the role of servants.[104] The drawing depicts a party of seven Jewish *bon vivants*, congregated around a small bistro table, talking, drinking, and enjoying each other's company. In the background is a presumably gentile waiter at work; his day-to-day reality could not be more different from that of his customers. Here, Żebrowski's Jewish subjects represent the visual stereotype of affluent *Westjuden*, whose elegant clothing and lavish lifestyle reflect their social status. Their loquaciousness and effervescence are depicted as vices that are in discord with local mores; their spontaneous gestures are interpreted as out of place if not threatening to the ethnic Polish population. This is a cartoon that aims to malign its subjects so as to highlight social and economic imbalances and to blame these inequalities on those Jews who succeeded in business.

The caricature epitomizes Żebrowski's affinity for social satire, which he pursued in numerous drawings for other outlets, not least the rabidly xenophobic *ABC* and *Pod Pręgierz*. Some of his work attacked specific individuals, including the satirical writers Julian Tuwim and Antoni Słonimski.[105] Although loyal to the national cause as a young man in his twenties and arguably throughout much of his life, Żebrowski was embarrassed about his youthful self-righteousness later in life, viewing it as one of the darkest episodes of his journalistic career. Rationalizing his erstwhile enthusiasm for the far right, he ventured that it was the outcome of the volatile climate of the day. According to Żebrowski, given the dangers posed by Poland's neighbors, strong fascist rule seemed the only option for many in the younger generation.[106]

That such caricatures belittled and demonized Jews, as well as supporting the ideologies of the same neighbors they were supposed to fight, is unquestionable. At the same time, there was hardly any consistent effort on the part of *Szarża* to actively proliferate such portrayals. Similarly, the few cartoons on Sanacja's distancing itself from the "Jewish question," as discussed above, were not frequent enough to describe them as part of an intentional strategy. Rather, the magazine seemed to have lacked a clear editorial line, veering between various anti-Jewish topics that intersected with domestic and international affairs and other content in which Jews seemed merely incidental, such as a cartoon on filmmaking in the Polish countryside in which two Jewish fiddlers feature as exotic characters and an attractive addition to the village crowd.[107] While other right-wing outlets, such as the Kalisz-based *Pokrzywy*, were devoted to stirring up public support for the economic boycott, *Szarża* lacked a clear agenda, dividing its attention among content that glorified fascism, criticized the Soviet Union, disparaged the authorities, and ridiculed the Jewish minority.[108] In comparison to other publications of the national camp, the daily *ABC* included, some of its pieces were also more intellectual in tone. This was possibly due to Szpigiel's influence, which might have undermined some of the magazine's militant potential and compromised its potential to appeal to the mass reader.

When *Szarża* closed down in May 1937, having published only seventeen issues, liberal Polish Jewish commentators were relieved to be rid of a magazine they considered "tasteless" and "devoid of humor."[109] In a similar vein, writing about *Szarża* and other magazines of the kind many years later, *Szpilki*'s cofounder, Zbigniew Mitzner, described them as "rags" and "pathetic satirical endeavors" of the interwar right.[110] But for a while *Szarża* did pose a challenge to its counterparts on the political left. Attempting to provide quality satire, it exuded an intellectual air that was often absent from much of the right-wing discourse on the so-called Jewish question. Its writing, although overtly anti-Jewish, was the work of an accomplished author, a rarity in the ethnonationalist camp. Its antisemitic cartoons were sometimes ambiguous, while showing an insider's view of Polish Jewish affairs that was missing from other publications of this kind. Henryk Szpigiel was, no doubt, a competent and skilled editor, one whose work deserves more attention, regardless of the scarcity of sources that concern his activity.

Szarża was by no means central to Polish-language satire in the interwar period, but neither was it marginal. It was an interesting counterpart to the leftist *Szpilki*, not least because of Szpigiel's previous experience in writing for the magazine and some of the graphic techniques he copied from his previous employer, including the splashes of color in front- and back-page cartoons. Likewise, the magazine could be seen a yardstick for *Mucha*'s satirical work, with which it shared an interest in current affairs, despite taking a contrasting position on the activities of the ruling party. Importantly, the magazine was different from local satirical outlets published by SN supporters that targeted specific areas of anti-Jewish struggle.

While it is possible to trace the life trajectories of some of the illustrators who contributed to *Szarża*, this is not the case for Henryk Szpigiel. For example, Julian Żebrowski, creator of the cartoon showing a restaurant scene with a party of wealthy Jews, went on to fight in the Home Army during the Second World War as well as participating in the anti-German Warsaw Uprising in 1944.[111] Throughout the German occupation, he also contributed anti-German cartoons to the underground press.[112] No sources exist that would allow us to verify the identity of the other caricaturists who worked under the assumed names of "Poraj" and "S. Filipski." We can speculate that the aliases were a disguise for reasonably well-known illustrators of the time who drew the caricatures to earn their living. The relative gentleness of some of the representations would support that hypothesis. Some scant information exists about the war-time fate of Henryk Szpigiel. According to his wife, Melania, the author escaped Warsaw on 6 September 1939 shortly after the German attack on Poland. She reported having heard from him one more time in November 1939 after he had reached Lviv. Having no further communication about his whereabouts, she assumed him dead and requested this to be legally recognized in 1948, two years after she had asked the University of Warsaw to return the only surviving photograph of him (see Figure 4.1).[113] While we cannot be certain about what happened to Szpigiel, it is likely that he did not survive beyond 1941 when the Nazis entered Lviv.

Aleksander Dzierżawski spent the war in Warsaw. He worked for the Polish charity Central Welfare Council (Rada Główna Opiekuńcza, RGO), which provided material support for the civilian population, organizing soup kitchens, clothing provision, and medical help. He died in Warsaw in May 1944, just three months before the start of the Warsaw Uprising. Today Dzierżawski is considered one of the most deserving citizens of the Turek county. In 2014, he was awarded posthumously the honor of *Bene Meritus* for his contributions to the local commune. On 31 May 2014, a commemorative stone was placed in his birth town of Mikulice. The mayor who delivered a speech about Dzierżawski encouraged people to emulate this local hero. During the event, members of a grassroots association distributed flyers with Dzierżawski's biography and excerpts from his only book of poems, *Świnie i koryto*. His legacy lives on, setting the tone for what some would term "patriotic," "honorable," and "pro-Polish."[114]

Chapter 5

SATIRE FOR THE MASSES

After the German invasion of Poland on 1 September 1939, several Polish illustrators and satirical writers of Jewish background escaped east to Lviv where they carried on their work.[1] With the occupation of Lviv by the Wehrmacht on 30 June 1941, their fate became more precarious. Like elsewhere in Nazi-occupied Poland, a Jewish ghetto was established in the city in which those held there were forced into unpaid labor. Karol Ferster, a recognized satirical illustrator in Kraków, who had found refuge in Lviv, was now forced to use his talent to the benefit of the occupiers. As one of the registered artists working for the Jewish-run *Städtische Werkstätten* (Municipal Workshops), Ferster was assigned to produce wall paintings for the *Sicherheitspolizei* casino in the city. He was initially tasked with decorating the walls of a casino room with scenes of German folk dances. As new orders kept pouring in, he was charged with painting the hallway and staircase of the building with medieval scenes of knights. Then came a wall painting portraying a pint of beer placed alongside an ashtray with a smoking cigar, before an order to decorate the private quarters of a Gestapo officer was issued, instructing Ferster to paint a nude scene in the bathroom. His painting of a beautiful woman coming out of the bath was a success and, soon enough, the artist received an order to replicate the nude in the casino, before being assigned more graphic scenes and other "inspirational" visuals for future wall paintings.[2]

Only a few years prior, Ferster had worked for the highly popular satirical magazine *Wróble na Dachu*, producing some of the most accomplished anti-German satire in interwar Poland and entertaining the masses for whom the magazine was destined. Established in 1930, *Wróble na Dachu* was one of the most successful satirical magazines of the interwar period. It was a subsidiary of the Kraków-based print publisher and media conglomerate *Ilustrowany Kuryer Codzienny* (*Illustrated Daily Courier*), which published the tabloid newspaper also named the *Ilustrowany Kuryer Codzienny*, known as the *IKC*, as well as several other highly popular weeklies. The conglomerate was the largest of its kind in interwar Poland, receiving generous financial support from several Jewish investors in Kraków.³ *IKC*'s main shareholder, publisher and politician Marian Dąbrowski, was known for his ability to vacillate between different political camps. In 1922, he became a deputy in the Sejm for the Polish Peasant Party (PSL Piast). In 1927, he switched allegiance to represent the BBWR, which was closely aligned with Piłsudski and which ended after his death in 1935. Dąbrowski's natural savviness led him to become an important political player who understood the rules of the game and was happy to provide a platform to influential figures of the day but without committing to any particular political option.⁴ Journalists of various affiliations could find employment with the *IKC* and receive proper pay for their work. Dąbrowski also knew how to attract high-revenue advertising and how to appeal to a variety of readers.⁵

Antoni Wasilewski (1905–1975) became the artistic editor of *IKC*'s flagship satirical weekly, *Wróble na Dachu*. He was an experienced illustrator who had debuted in the Lviv satirical magazine *Szczutek* in 1923 and had had ample experience with numerous other periodicals, including the renowned *Cyrulik Warszawski*.⁶ Attractive design was of the utmost importance to Wasilewski, making the magazine stand out among other publications of the day. Thanks to the generous patronage of the *IKC*, he was able to devote more than 62 percent of *Wróble*'s content to visual material, almost twice as much as the space given to cartoons in *Szpilki* or *Pokrzywy* (36.8 percent and 32 percent respectively).⁷ *Wróble* also used more color than other satirical magazines of the time did. Of the total eight pages, half were printed in color. As the most prosperous satirical magazine in the country, *Wróble* also had the luxury of employing some of the best artists in the medium. The list of regular contributors included Karol Ferster (Charlie) (1902–1986), Jerzy Zaruba (1891–1971), Mieczysław Piotrowski (1910–1977), Jakub Bickels (1911–1944), Maksymilian Brandel (1910–1975), and Bronisław Schneider (1915–1943). Some of these illustrators collaborated regularly with other magazines. As we have seen, Bickels, Brandel, and Schneider worked for *Szpilki* as well as contributing to the Polish Jewish weekly *Kontratak*.⁸ Zaruba, once a cartoonist for *Cyrulik Warszawski*, went on to collaborate with *Szpilki* and *Wiadomości Literackie*, as well as contributing some caricatures to periodicals of other persuasions, including right-wing dailies and magazines.⁹ Others, like Piotrowski, won a prestigious cartoon competition organized by *Cyrulik Warszawski* in 1931 and became artistic pillars of the magazine before moving on to *Wróble* when the former publication closed down.¹⁰ Up until 1932, some of Piotrowski's work also appeared in the right-wing newspaper *Dziennik Bydgoski* (*The Bydgoszcz Daily*).¹¹ These various professional trajectories and ideological proclivities were often reflected in the artists' drawings for *Wróble*.

Many of those illustrators were openly anti-fascist and anti-Endek. For that reason, most of the cartoons on Jewish themes that appeared in the magazine were devoid of the hateful rhetoric characteristic of *Mucha*, *Pokrzywy*, and *Szarża*. It was owing to the deliberately vague political profile of the magazine that its artists were able to publish work that portrayed Jews in a sympathetic manner. The lack of a clear-cut political agenda meant that ideological constraints did not play a role in selecting which work was to be printed and which one was not.[12] At the same time, being a popular magazine for the masses, the publication did not shy away from stereotypical, and even fear-mongering, representations of Jews, drawn by several of its regular contributors, including the well-respected master of satire Jerzy Zaruba and the editor Antoni Wasilewski. The eye-grabbing content was matched by quality gravure printing and high-grade paper, both of which distinguished *Wróble* from other satirical weeklies of the period. Those who remembered the interwar print media recalled that the magazine "lured the passer-by with its bright colors" and rich graphic design, "leaping out" from the newsstand.[13]

It is fair to say that it was a mixture of these factors, including financial capital and human capital, that made the magazine one of the most interesting satirical outlets of late interwar Poland. Its cartoonists cocreated the very identity of the magazine. They published under their actual names, unlike many of the illustrators for *Mucha*, *Pokrzywy*, and, to some extent, *Szarża*, who resorted to using pseudonyms. On the whole, they were also able to incorporate their distinctive political agendas into their caricatures. With the exception of the leftist *Szpilki*, *Wróble* was the only magazine of the late 1930s that also showcased the artists' individual styles, promoting illustrators from various backgrounds and regions of Poland.

MILITANT SATIRE

Like the artists working for *Szpilki*, several of *Wróble*'s contributors practiced militant visual satire that condemned contemporary antisemitic violence. Its particular focus was on the ethnonationalist youth and their savage brutality, as well as the havoc they wreaked in society. Both Mieczysław Piotrowski and Charlie were at the forefront of such social critique, rebuking the barbaric attitudes and actions of ethnic Polish students and portraying the universities and urban areas as spaces that were essentially unsafe for Jews. In 1937 alone, Piotrowski referred to violence in universities and on the streets at least five times. Charlie, too, produced a number of drawings on this topic. Charlie,

5.1. M. Piotrowski, This Year's Szopka from Warsaw, from *Wróble na Dachu*, 26 December 1937, 4.

in particular, was to champion a compassionate take on Poland's "Jewish problem," which, as I will show below, was determined by his upbringing.

Piotrowski's most compelling cartoon was published at Christmas and showed an imaginary *szopka*, nativity play, in which the usual puppets were replaced with a walking stick, pitchfork, saber, and umbrella (Figure 5.1). Although seemingly random, this assemblage of props was to draw attention to the realities of violence in which innocuous objects become tools for inflicting bodily harm.[14] The reference to the Polish *szopka* was an interesting choice for Piotrowski. Traditional *szopkas* were usually performed at New Year's and blended the nativity narrative with a political and social commentary that used speeches, dialogues, and songs to discuss contemporary realities. The religious part came first: it presented the traditional nativity story using puppets. The secular part of the *szopka* followed the same format; it had no real actors but dolls introduced by the puppet master. It had a fixed set of protagonists, too, who corresponded with the various social classes and ethnicities of the population of Poland. Typical characters in the *szopka* included "the proud but seldom solvent *szlachcic* and his wife, the thrifty German burgess, a burlesque Jew and Jewess, carefree peasants, cajoling wandering artisans and pedlars, wily Gypsies, a swashbuckling Cossack and similar stock characters."[15]

The cartoon in *Wróble* reproduced many of the visual characteristics of the traditional *szopka*. There was a stage with curtain and an opening in the floor for puppets. Above the stage, the star of Bethlehem was shining bright in the evening sky. The coloring of the cartoon—pastel blue and pink—alluded to the religious part of the play, bringing a message of peace and happiness. The secular part of Piotrowski's *szopka* played out underneath and jarred with the tranquil mood of the birth of Jesus. Here, the puppets were replaced by objects that referenced the attributes of specific groups in contemporary and historical Poland: sticks were for students, pitchforks for peasants, and sabers for the nobility or the *szlachta*. The latter two were traditional characters in the Polish nativity play, and the former served as a metaphor for the contemporary violence perpetrated by ethno-nationalist youth. Aside from toying with the formula of the Polish *szopka*, Piotrowski's cartoon also brought to mind the biblical story of the birth of Jesus. In particular, portraying the props as instruments for potentially inflicting injury might have alluded to the story of the Massacre of the Innocents ordered by King Herod on learning that Jesus, the king of the Jews, had been born. As in *Szpilki*'s cartoons discussed earlier, here the cane was the most menacing attribute of all.

Piotrowski's illustration provided a heart-wrenching depiction of the intensification of anti-Jewish violence in universities and elsewhere. That year, major university cities in Poland—Warsaw, Lviv, and Vilnius—saw almost daily occurrences of vicious attacks.[16] Some reports mentioned attacks with "sticks, pistols, and bombs."[17] Others talked about Endek shock troops preventing Jewish students from entering university buildings.[18] By 1938, several Jewish students had been beaten to death, and others were perennially

5.2. M. Piotrowski, Due to Closures in Universities, from *Wróble na Dachu*, 28 March 1937, 7.

threatened.[19] To Piotrowski, the ongoing violence was equivalent to warfare. The perpetrators were young ethnonationalist men, mostly part of the ONR, and the university was one of their battlefields. In one of his other cartoons, the illustrator also commented on the ongoing "blockades" at universities. The drawing depicted a dilapidated university front with an old man in a wheelchair guarding the entrance. The caption read: "Following the blockade," as well as quoting a line from a popular song, "How quickly pass the moments," to imply the passing of time (Figure 5.2).[20]

It is likely that the cartoon alluded to the events at the University of Warsaw in November 1936 when ONR Falanga troops barricaded the entrance, calling for "ghetto benches" to be installed as well as demanding that tuition be lowered.[21] The cartoon presented a distant point in the future when the once-young man is an old war veteran, his left leg replaced with a wooden prosthetic limb and missing his right hand. Wearing dark glasses, a possible sign of blindness, Piotrowski's disabled veteran was, most likely, inspired by real-life encounters with invalid ex-combatants of the First World War. As historians of war disability have shown, the technological advances of modern warfare inflicted new kinds of injuries on the body: shrapnel wounds led to amputations, and chlorine gas caused blindness.[22] Piotrowski's ONR veteran was thus likely modelled on the familiar imagery of war disability. And yet, instead of attempting to elicit pity by showing the old man revisiting the battlefield where he was injured, Piotrowski was deliberately unsympathetic. By employing the familiar trope of an invalid ex-combatant who still wore his student cap and reminisced over the good old days, the cartoonist encouraged his audience to draw a clear line between the struggle of many real veterans of the First World War and the senseless brutality perpetrated in the name of a "de-Judaized" Poland. It could be also that Piotrowski's caricature was a response to statements by the ethnonationalist camp that equated violence in universities with historical struggles for independence, such as the anti-Russian protests in partitioned Poland, all of which attempted to add a veneer of patriotism to the current events.[23]

Like other liberal cartoonists of the time, Piotrowski was also deeply critical of the specific forms of anti-Jewish discrimination, including the so-called ghetto benches. This was a pertinent issue. In 1937, the government submitted to the demands of ethnic Polish students who wanted to see segregated lecture halls in which Jewish students would be seated on the left. Jewish students refused to obey, often standing during lectures, which enraged the Endek youth.[24] As discussed in the chapter on *Szpilki*, in his utopian proposal for resolving the issue, Piotrowski presented a new design of the lecture hall that resembled a circular cone with no left or right.[25] The illustrator ridiculed the ethnonationalist attachment to the right side of seating areas in another cartoon, which presented two students being locked up in the same cell after another violent confrontation, with the ethnic Pole demanding that the Jewish student sit on the left side of the prison bench. Piotrowski's use of the word "skirmishes" (*utarczki*) in the heading was placed in quotation marks to draw attention to the ongoing attempts by the government, university authorities, and right-wing commentators to diminish the seriousness of the events.[26]

Piotrowski's colleague Charlie also presented nationalist students as obsessed with violence. In the cartoon "Universities Introduce Mandatory Physical Exercise," he drew a group of nine youths, flexing their muscles in a calisthenics-like routine involving canes (Figure 5.3). Charlie's drawing style was minimalistic but detailed. The students' clothing consisted of simple university uniforms. Their faces were distinctively Slavic-looking, with their legs stretched sideways in a muscle-strengthening regimen. In front of them

5.3. Charlie, Universities Introduce . . ., from *Wróble na Dachu*, 24 October 1937, 7.

rested a smoking bomb, a portent of upcoming disturbances. It was the canes, however, that were at the heart of the image. Raised in unison, they were a triumphal proclamation of physical prowess.[27] Aside from alluding to the ongoing events, Charlie's cartoon reflected on the widespread nationalist cult of the body and its entanglement with a militaristic ethos. In Poland, 1937 was the year of intensified activity by the illegal fascist ONR Falanga organization, which not only operated in universities and increasingly in high schools, but also attacked Jewish businesses, newspapers, institutions, and gatherings, including the planting of bombs, attacks with petards, shootings, and beatings.[28]

Roaming gangs of ethno-nationalist youths committed random acts of violence too. In another cartoon, Charlie commented on an event in which a bearded man was attacked by a group of students (Figure 5.4). The title of the caricature, "The Happy Racist," referred to the victim himself who rejoices in having been beaten: his beard had been a decoy with which the man had tested the alertness of fascist shock troops. The delinquents, visible in the distance as they escape the crime scene, bear a close resemblance to the figures from Charlie's previous cartoon. Presented from the back,

5.4. Charlie, The Happy Racist, from *Wróble na Dachu*, 21 November 1937, 6.

the silhouettes were a study of the fascist body fulfilled. Their flying coats, above-the-ankle trousers, and sticks lifted in triumph were a visual signifier of the menace posed by the group and their lack of accountability before the law.[29] More generally, the cartoon provided a bitter reflection on a society that celebrated antisemitic violence, including random attacks on individuals who were presumed to be Jews.

Historian of the interwar period Paul Brykczynski discusses several such attacks in his book on ethnic violence in 1920s Poland. He reports that in 1922, which saw violent street demonstrations against the president-elect, Gabriel Narutowicz (who had been supported by Poland's ethnic minorities), ethnonationalist youths targeted "*all* Jews (or people identified as Jews)," but their attacks were largely haphazard and "who was and who was not a Jew was ultimately up to the rampaging youths."[30] As a result, various individuals were accosted in the streets of Warsaw and brutally beaten. These included a Catholic priest from a parish in the district of Wola and an elderly German

5.5. Wik, A Political Discussion, from *Wróble na Dachu*, 28 November 1937, 4–5.

businessman, both of whom had the misfortune to look "like a Jew."[31] Such acts of violence were often met with passivity by the police, who occasionally used water cannons to disperse the crowds. Several other drawings and texts published in *Wróble* that same year show that such incidents became widespread, while urban spaces became marked with an increased police presence.[32]

The cartoons in *Wróble* implied that the brutalization of everyday life was also transferred to other forms of social interaction. One drawing by Wik (a pseudonym of artist Ludwik Heller), the master of color illustrations of street scenes, depicted two newspaper boys scuffling on a street corner (Figure 5.5). Entitled "A Political Discussion," the cartoon portrayed the two as being of unequal strength, one of them clearly initiating the fight and dwarfing his opponent. In the background, a parallel scene has either been avoided or wound up by now: a Jewish man in traditional dress is scuttling away from a student in a long coat, his cane placed in a resting position. Wik's cartoon, which has the unmistakable quality of a documentary photograph, puts us at the heart of the event. The two boys fight, the student watches them with interest, and the Jewish man dashes away, almost disappearing from view.[33] The two panels of the image are clearly related, and the protagonists are in fact antagonists. They come in pairs, and, in both cases, they represent the existing inequalities.

Wik's placing of the Jewish man in the background is not exclusive to this cartoon. In some of his other drawings, the illustrator presented Jews as being peripheral figures. These marginal characters are somewhat disadvantaged vis-à-vis the ethnic Poles, but nonetheless inextricable from the Polish urban landscape.[34] Given the context of Wik's other work, it can be presumed that these images aimed at drawing attention to discrimination against Jews. The general tone of some of his other illustrations in the magazine supports that interpretation. Such sensitivity is noteworthy for a young artist who, most likely, came from a relatively privileged background. Born in the city of Przemyśl in 1904, Heller moved to Kraków in 1923 to pursue a degree in philosophy. His university registration form is explicit about his Polish nationality and mother tongue, as well as his "Mosaic faith" (*wyznanie mojżeszowe*). The form also states the father's name (Izydor) and profession (merchant).[35] That Heller was one of the few satirical illustrators of the interwar years who were able to leave Poland in the 1920s to study abroad would suggest that he could rely on his relations to provide for him. The municipal records of the Belgian city of Antwerp show that he arrived in Belgium in 1926 and enrolled in an art degree in the Academy of Fine Arts. In a routine interview conducted by the Belgian police, Heller declared that he held no paid job and that he was supported by his family.[36]

Wróble's Jewish illustrators were not the only ones to comment on the rising violence. Some ethnic Polish artists, too, were clear about their political allegiances, while ridiculing the discourse and actions of the antisemitic right. Piotrowski, in particular, provided a damning portrayal of the ongoing assault on small Jewish business owners. In another one of his cartoons published at Christmas, he ridiculed the ethnic Polish students of Warsaw for proclaiming they would take over the fish trade for the holiday period as a way of bolstering the national economy and undermining Jewish business owners (Figure 5.6). Using a reversal of roles, the cartoon toyed with

5.6. M. Piotrowski, Christmas "Fishing," from *Wróble na Dachu*, 26 December 1937, 9.

imagined realities. It presented local students as herring sellers, traditionally a domain of Jewish traders. Jews, in turn, assumed the role of customers.

Piotrowski's role reversal did not end there, however. He depicted the students wearing kippahs, while their Jewish patrons, dressed in black rekels and kashkets, brandish canes similar to those in the caricatures on violence in the universities. In an attempt to scare off the students, some of the Jewish customers chant, "Get out" (*Precz*) or chase the young men away using canes as weapons.[37] This role reversal was not only a scenario of what-ifs typical for satirical cartoons in general, but possibly also an attempt at eliciting empathy in readers who, no doubt, witnessed regular assaults on Jewish traders across the country. Like many liberal illustrators of the time, Piotrowski asked his readers to put themselves in the persecuted person's shoes. Imagining that person to be an ethnic Pole could be an emotive way of swaying public opinion, at least as far as the more compassionate sections of *Wróble*'s readership were concerned.[38]

While much of the visual content on pressing political issues was sympathetic to Polish Jews, the same could not be said about the satirical writing in the magazine. Some of its jokes, dialogues, and poems used a denigrating tone and vocabulary; other texts repeated antisemitic clichés in the vein of right-wing publications.[39] At the same time, there were occasional texts that matched the militant liberal agenda of the cartoons discussed above and criticized ethnonationalist follies. In one longer satirical piece, Mr. Birch describes a day in the life of "Mr. Endecki," a name derived from "Endecja," his implied political party. The text is a fantasy about life under right-wing dictates in which Jews are forced to walk on the left side of the street and sit on the left side in cafes. In the mode of Nazi Germany, where Jewish shops were marked with a yellow star and benches painted yellow, in Birch's story Jews are forced to wear yellow clothes and live in houses painted yellow. As Endecki walks through the city and observes this segregation, he feels happy and reassured. The ethnonationalist ideology prevails. When he returns home, however, he is in for a surprise. All of his furniture has been moved to the left, and all the paintings hang on the left side of the apartment. His grandmother welcomes him with an ironic smile: "Why are you so surprised?" she asks. "I used to be called Ruchla . . ., your mother's maiden name was Rabinowicz. And who is an *echt* Aryan now?"[40]

With this piece, the pseudonymous author Mr. Birch joined the nationwide discussion of the prevalence and significance of the so-called Jewish element in the lineage of many families in Poland. In his story, Mr. Birch clearly embraced the ideas of contemporary Polish Jewish historian Mateusz Mieses, discussed earlier, who proposed to fight ethnic hatred with stories of conversion and intermingling between ethnic Poles and Jews. Building on the work of Mieses, Birch warned his readers that the concept of national purity was a flawed one, particularly in a multicultural state such as the Polish Republic. At the same time, the author used the story of Endecki to contribute to a more specific debate that was raging that year, concerning two staunch advocates of the national movement: journalists and activists Stanisław Piasecki and Wojciech Wasiutyński, who had been "exposed" by the leftist *Szpilki* as having Jewish family backgrounds.[41] Like the two journalists, who had once demanded that no Jews or converts be allowed to publish in the Polish print media, the fictional Endecki wishes to see a state in which ethnic segregation is the norm. Equally, like Piasecki and Wasiutyński, he cannot escape his bloodline, which is in conflict with the politics of racial hate that he propagates. Although the fictional Endecki eventually wakes up, relieved to discover his life on the left side was only a bad dream, the cautionary tale has been told: other Piaseckis and Wasiutyńskis might not be as lucky.

Despite publishing such occasional digs at right-wing people of the day, *Wróble* rarely targeted specific parties or political figures or criticized their policies. This is corroborated by historian Olaf Bergmann who found a similar trend in the magazine over a longer period of time and in relation to other themes, whether domestic issues or international politics.[42] Although the unfavorable representation of students clearly points to ONR Falanga, the magazine seemed to have seen the organization for what it was, a terrorist grouping "of a Hitlerite sort" that had little political leverage.[43] Such a strategy was somewhat deliberate on Dąbrowski's part. This savvy politician-publisher avoided making enemies, knowing all too well that governments change. In this context, the lack of critical portrayals of Sanacja is particularly striking, distinguishing the magazine from such others as *Szpilki*, *Szarża*, and *Pokrzywy*, all of which pursued a staunch anti-Sanacja agenda and blamed many of the most challenging issues on the passivity of the government.[44]

Aside from engaging in topical issues and commenting on local events in Poland, *Wróble* also developed a strong corpus of anti-fascist cartoons that had a wider resonance. The majority of these cartoons focused on Hitler and Mussolini as well as commenting on the absurdities of life in an authoritarian state. As we have seen, other satirical magazines were more careful in publishing work that was overtly critical of Hitler. Being part of a powerful media conglomerate that was largely impervious to the financial pressures of state censorship and enjoying a degree of sympathy from the censors, *Wróble* was bold enough to comment on the rise of Europe's authoritarian leaders more often than others.[45] This approach paid off; the magazine was confiscated only twice during its nine-year operation.[46] Some historians of Polish caricature see the proliferation of anti-fascist cartoons in *Wróble* in the late 1930s as motivated by popular demand, and the ridiculing portrayals of Hitler would confirm this to be true.[47]

Wróble's antifascist cartoons veered between serious political satire and light entertainment. The serious works were drawn by some of Poland's finest illustrators, including two Polish Jewish artists from Lviv, Jakub Bickels and Bronisław Schneider, who were frequent contributors to the magazine. The lighter offerings were the domain of editor Antoni Wasilewski and others

5.7. J. Bickels, The Italian Aria, from *Wróble na Dachu*, 26 September 1937, 3.

who commented on the absurdities of Nazi policies. The drawings by Bickels, for example, looked at the growing affinity between Hitler and Mussolini, being reminiscent of similar politically engaged cartoons produced by artists for *Szpilki* (Figures 5.7 and 5.8).[48] Drawn in Bickels's characteristic style, which combined strong angular shapes, contrasting body types, and

5.8. J. Bickels, Mussolini Rode through Berlin on a White Horse, from *Wróble na Dachu*, 3 October 1937, 2.

an evocative use of black and grey shading, these cartoons are illustrative of his wider liberal stance that was also discernible in his caricatures for the Polish Jewish weekly *Kontratak*.[49]

The other group of cartoons was lighter in tone. The drawings by Wasilewski, in particular, were often printed in color and published on the

5.9. A. Wasilewski, On the Beautiful Blue Danube, from *Wróble na Dachu*, 20 March 1938, 1.

front page, commenting on the friendship between the two leaders as well as the precarious situation of Jews in Nazi Germany and, later, Austria. While most of his cartoons in 1937 avoided explicit antisemitic tropes, the drawings he produced in 1938 grew more stereotypical.[50] In his cover cartoon, for example, that portrayed the Anschluss, a group of marching Nazis causes panic among local Jews. The latter are presented scattering in all directions;

their exaggerated facial features include red hooked noses, buck teeth, and large ears that are reminiscent of more aggressive anti-Jewish caricature (Figure 5.9).[51] Such cartoons existed in the magazine side by side with those by Charlie that ridiculed Hitler's conqueror complex and poked fun at his adherents.[52] Charlie also commented on the peculiarities of the Nazi German policies and practices, from the *Lebensborn* program to the initiative of collecting human hair, organized presumably to support the textile industry.[53]

LIGHT ENTERTAINMENT

Although many of *Wróble*'s artists were stalwart supporters of the liberal cause, the magazine in essence pandered to popular audience. For that reason, many of its cartoons focused on nonpolitical and social events with a view to grabbing public attention and ensuring high readership.[54] This included abundant reporting on celebrities of the day, both Polish and foreign, as well as commenting on scandals involving the aristocracy. For example, *Wróble* devoted much attention to the Polish tenor Jan Kiepura (whose mother, incidentally, was Jewish), who had caused a sensation in Germany, France, Britain, and the US and who was much loved in his home country where he continued to perform over the years.[55] The magazine often depicted Kiepura in the act of singing, awing his audiences wherever he went.[56] *Wróble* also showed a lot of interest in foreign royals, including Edward, Duke of Windsor, the former British king who had relinquished the crown to marry the American Wallis Simpson.[57] Similarly, like much of the tabloid media in Poland, *Wróble*'s cartoonists followed Princess Juliana of the Netherlands on her honeymoon with Prince Bernhard in the mountain spa town of Krynica Zdrój in January 1937.[58]

The editor of the magazine (a successful illustrator himself), Antoni Wasilewski, exceeded in the popular cartoon genre. His cartoons were often printed in color, featured on the cover of the magazine. *Wróble*'s regular contributor Charlie also provided nonpolitical cartoons to appeal to readers. At times, the content on celebrity culture intersected with ongoing discussion about the so-called Jewish question. In 1937, one of the most hotly debated issues was the affair of prince Michał Radziwiłł of an established aristocratic family with a much younger Jewish divorcée named Judyta Suchestow. Following their first encounter in the Austrian spa town of Bad Gastein, the couple fell in love, and only a few months later, in the early autumn of 1937, Radziwiłł announced their engagement. In November, Suchestow converted to Christianity and took the name Jeanette Jadwiga. The couple's life in Radziwiłł's residence, the Antonin palace, was closely followed by the media. In no time, the relationship of the aging prince and his much younger bride-to-be—he was more than thirty years her senior—came under the spotlight. Although the engagement was eventually broken off and the affair ended the following year, it provided ample material for commentaries on Polish-Jewish intermingling.

That year *Wróble* commented on the affair at least ten times, both in cartoon form and satirical writing, with much of the reporting done in November and December 1937, the height of media interest in the couple. The most prominent cartoon on the topic was drawn by Antoni Wasilewski and appeared on the cover of the 7 November issue (Figure 5.10). It presented the happy couple on their putative wedding day. Radziwiłł, in the foreground, is in a traditional attire of old Polish nobility, including a sword. Suchestow, in the background, wears a long white dress and a veil. The prince is the active party, about to break a glass with his foot in Jewish tradition. The caption underneath the image reads: "Mazel tov, My Beloved Sir!"[59] While the good wishes intimated by the "mazel tov" exclamation were a clear reference to Suchestow's background, the "My Beloved Sir" (*Panie Kochanku!*) alluded to one of Radziwiłł's aristocratic ancestors, Karol Stanisław Radziwiłł (1734–1790), who used this informal address when speaking to others. With time, *Panie Kochanku!* came to be used as his sobriquet and a recognizable reference to the Radziwiłł family.

The cartoon emphasized the different backgrounds of the would-be newlyweds. It also conveyed a sense of surprise at the hurried nature of the union. After all, the couple met only in June, and in late September wedding preparations were already underway. What is more, the day the issue was published, news broke that Radziwiłł's previous marriage had not been yet terminated. Right-wing newspapers, in particular, reported triumphantly on the investigation launched into his putative bigamy, arguing that the prince's formal announcement of engagement was sufficient for such proceedings to commence.[60]

Wasilewski commented on the rushed nuptials in another cartoon published in the same issue. In it, the bride-to-be is depicted as a beautiful seductress with a menorah, scolding the prince for wanting to be intimate with her (Figure 5.11). As she rebuffs the "old man" for approaching her, Suchestow whispers to herself that the less she gives Radziwiłł now, the sooner she can hope to marry him.[61] The menorah was an interesting addition here. Although it is a seven-branched menorah, the symbol of Judaism, it is possible that Wasilewski was also alluding to the apocryphal story of the biblical Judith, who shared a name with Suchestow and was associated with

5.10. A. Wasilewski, Regarding a Certain Aristocratic Wedding, from *Wróble na Dachu*, 7 November 1937, 1.

the nine-branched menorah. According to the Book of Judith, the beautiful widow used her feminine charms to save the Judean city of Bethulia, besieged by the Assyrians. After seducing and inebriating the Assyrian general Holofernes, Judith beheaded him, which enabled the Jews to launch a counterattack and eventually defeat the enemy. The story of Judith is commemorated during Hanukkah, the festival of light, in which a nine-branched

5.11. A. Wasilewski, "What are you doing, old man, in God's name!," from *Wróble na Dachu*, 7 November 1937, 3.

menorah is used, while the bravery and beauty of Judith, more generally, are still cherished in the Jewish tradition.

Wasilewski was deliberate in his references to Suchestow's femininity and beauty. This was as much a comment on her ethnicity as it was a reflection on her gender and age. Here, the cartoonist tapped into a rich repertoire of gendered stereotypes of young Jewish women that existed and still exist among Jews and non-Jews. At various times in the past century, Jewish women had been depicted as exotic, beautiful, and seductive as well as being shown as "demanding and withholding."[62] Literature and popular culture have represented them as applying their feminine mystique to move upward in society, gain political influence, and advance their financial standing.[63] Thus, the enduring antisemitic stereotypes of greed, pushiness, and materialism typically attached to the Jewish male have been also projected onto Jewish women.[64]

It is fair to say that Wasilewski's drawing was built on this wider tradition of misogynistic antisemitism. Intersectional prejudice such as this also appeared in interwar pictorial culture elsewhere. Art historian Julia Secklehner shows that similar portrayals of the sexualized Jewish female were a feature of interwar satirical cartoons in Vienna.[65] Such imagery, which Secklehner describes as representing "weak" antisemitism, became normalized in many interwar societies, proliferating both casual misogyny and light-hearted antisemitism.[66] Irrespective of the context in which such representations appeared, whether the Polish popular media, Viennese interwar magazines, or American popular culture, they have consistently reproduced the stereotype of the mysterious but dangerous other. Like Judith in the apocryphal story, these women, too, have been figments of the male gaze, not least the gaze of the gentile observer.

It was not only Wasilewski who speculated on the reasons for the hasty wedding plans, while implying that Suchestow preyed on the old prince's gullibility. Commentators in other media also considered the issue, discussing explicitly the financial situation of Prince Radziwiłł. For example, one newspaper in Vilnius theorized about how much money the man would bequeath to his future wife, highlighting that the intended nuptials had been met with reservations from the Radziwiłł clan.[67] Another daily quoted an anonymous employee of the Antonin estate who alleged that Suchestow did not love the prince and was only after his wealth.[68] This was also the view of several *Wróble* authors who believed she was scamming the prince and predicted that he would lose his riches because of his childlike trust in the woman.[69] While some of these reports refashioned the stereotypes of female Jewish avarice and deceit, other articles tried to discredit Radziwiłł himself. For example, the right-wing *ABC* newspaper argued that the marriage was yet another eccentricity on his part, while listing his various antics from the ill treatment of staff to misguided decisions about the maintenance of his property.[70]

Despite the negative press, the love affair continued to captivate the public for weeks on end. Various newspapers commented on every move of the couple, from a shopping spree in Warsaw's Marszałkowska Street, where the prince was said to have bought twelve shirt collars, to his shaving off his red beard on the advice of his fiancée.[71] But it was more abstract issues that concerned many observers, in particular the issue of maintaining the purity

5.12. Marek, Prince Michał Radziwiłł with a Fiancée, from *Pokrzywy*, 7 November 1937, 1.

of the Radziwiłł bloodline. The ethnonationalist *Pokrzywy*, for example, published a cover cartoon on that topic. The drawing portrayed Suchestow with a large hooked nose and an oversized necklace of a red star with hammer and sickle (Figure 5.12). The poem accompanying the cartoon presented the union as portending the prince's imminent downfall. It shamed Radziwiłł for "Judaizing the family nest and destroying the faith of the forefathers" as

Mezalians w sferach arystokracji.

Rys. Charlie, Kraków

W galerji przodków...

5.13. Charlie, Misalliance in the Aristocratic Circles, from *Wróble na Dachu*, 14 November 1937, 7.

well as sending him the following warning: "Just you watch—you'll die like Holofernes!"[72] The references to the Book of Judith and the deceit she used to steal into the enemy camp could not be clearer.

Wróble, too, spoke out on this topic but with wit and without the usual pomposity of *Pokrzywy*. The difficulty of acknowledging Jewish additions to Poland's patrician families was humorously portrayed in a cartoon by Charlie. The cartoon depicts a portrait gallery in an aristocratic home in the process of being furnished with a painting of a Jewish elder, a new family member acquired through marriage (Figure 5.13). As the portrait is being placed on the wall, the two existing elders of the clan, dressed in the traditional "Sarmatian" fashion of Polish nobility, look out of their paintings in consternation, before trying to use physical force to scare off the unwanted addition to the family.[73]

Such a representation of the supposed misalliance (*mezalians*), as Charlie described it, was a response to hysterical reactions to the Radziwiłł affair that appeared among the ethno-nationalist pundits. As the example of *Pokrzywy* shows, some antisemites construed this Polish-Jewish affair as yet another example of Poland's supposed contamination by the Jewish race.[74] Fear-mongering visions of future Jewish offspring adulterating this eminent family appeared in satirical poems published in other outlets.[75] In stark contrast, Charlie's drawing encouraged the viewer to be critical. His was a call to undertake a mental exercise in which the so-called national purity was a construct that needed to be unpacked. Unlike Wasilewski's cartoon that replicated deeply ingrained anti-Jewish phobias, Charlie focused on the Polish psyche instead. He drew the aristocrats as rousing from their portraits, consumed by their xenophobic fury. Their supposed religious tolerance, the traditional trademark of the *Sarmacja* nobility, was exposed here as nothing but a myth, while the two men personified everything that was wrong with contemporary Poland. Specifically, the cartoon spoke of stereotypical Sarmatian vices, rowdiness and loutishness included, which clouded judgement and deepened existing ethnic divisions. In line with Mateusz Mieses's argument that Jewish blood flowed in all aristocratic families, Charlie used light entertainment to encourage his audiences to acknowledge that Jews have been and will remain a part of the Polish bloodline.

In that, Charlie was an exception among *Wróble*'s contributors, most of whom provided a largely sensationalist take on the interethnic relationship. His other work for the magazine also stood out for its strong ethical stance. In fact, both this and his other cartoons for *Wróble* could be described with the same words that those who knew him used to describe him: full of "wisdom and kindness" and averse to any form of "injustice, sham, pomposity, and deceit."[76] Charlie's engaged satire was not solely a reflection of his personality but also a by-product of his ethnicity, upbringing, and education. He was born in 1902 in Kalwaria Zebrzydowska, a town in the region of Lesser Poland. He went to school in Kraków and, in 1920, embarked on a law degree at the Jagiellonian University as well as an arts degree at the Academy of Arts in Kraków, graduating in 1924 and 1926 respectively.[77] Importantly, he identified as Jewish.[78] He came from an acculturated family of lawyer Dawid Ferster and Hermina née Jozefest; his wife, Serafina Neuman, whom he married in 1930, had a similar background.[79]

The importance of ethnicity should not be underestimated in cases such as this. Some of *Wróble*'s non-Jewish artists provided a much less thoughtful take on the Suchestow-Radziwiłł affair. For example, *Wróble*'s only female illustrator, Rena (a pseudonym for Piotrowski's then-wife, Regina Kańska),

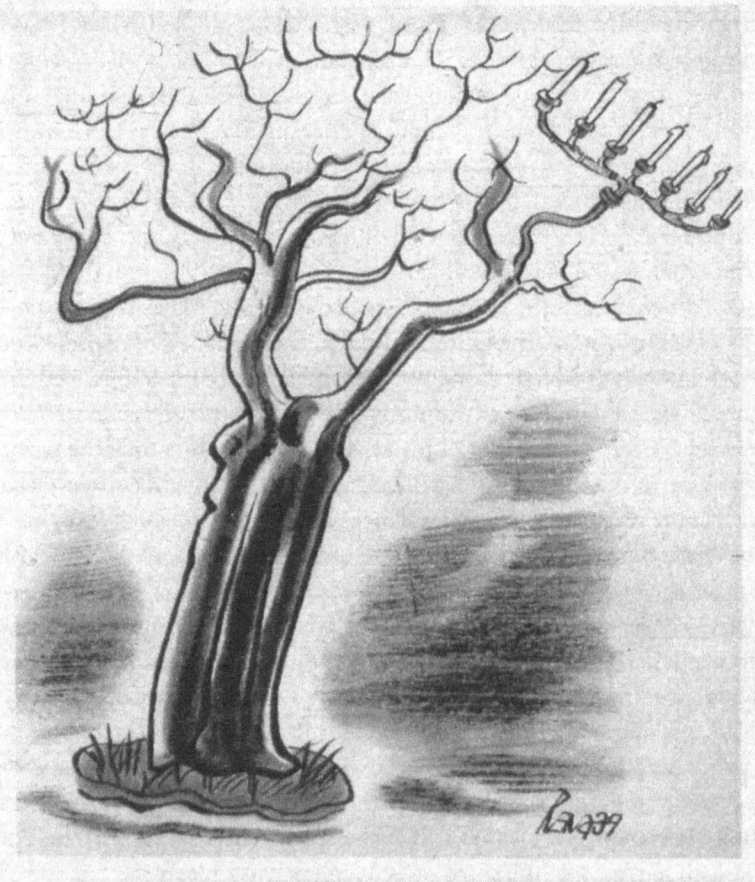

5.14. Rena, The Last Offshoot of the Genealogical Tree, from *Wróble na Dachu*, 21 November 1937, 3.

also explored the ideas of ancestry and heritage in this context but did so in a way that was wholly different from Charlie's sympathetic take on it. Rena's cartoon presented a family tree gone rogue. The tree consists of two main branches, with the right branch developing into a menorah (Figure 5.14).[80] This addition of a non-organic element suggested that this was not a natural trajectory for a family tree to take and that Judyta herself could never be absorbed into the aristocratic clan. That said, Rena was not necessarily anti-Jewish in her imagery, although the few illustrations that she drew for the magazine did little to challenge stereotypical portrayals of Jews.[81] Rather, her choice not to draw a more discursive cartoon on the topic, like the one by Charlie, could have to do with her skills and drawing style. Like Charlie and her then-husband, Mieczysław Piotrowski, she had studied arts but was not involved in the satirical media on a regular basis.[82] In 1937, when the image of the tree was published, Rena finished her studies at the Academy of Arts in Warsaw, receiving a teaching diploma that qualified her to teach drawing in high school and professional colleges.[83] Prior to her studies, she worked in the field of graphic design, possibly in advertising.[84] These professional and educational experiences, which used different aesthetics, most likely shaped her approach to the medium of cartoon.

Such differences in the tone and degree of stereotyping were not exclusive to *Wróble*'s illustrators. The writers for the magazine, a mix of commissioned authors and reader contributors, also presented different perspectives on the planned matrimony. One contributor viewed Radziwiłł's decision to marry a Jew as yet another eccentricity of the aristocracy.[85] Another took the perspective of a curious and seemingly concerned observer. As this observer comments on the recent shaving of the prince's beard, he wonders if it was his way of preventing himself from "spitting into his beard" (*pluć sobie w brodę*) when the marriage eventually fails.[86] The bon mot, translated as "to kick oneself," was yet another foreshadowing of the fiasco that was about to come. Lastly, a more extensive text by *Wróble*'s regular contributor Zbigniew Grotowski provided a satirical rewriting of Radziwiłł's tell-all interview given to one of Warsaw's newspapers. In his satire on the interview, Grotowski presented the prince as a fool in love who was on a mission to prove the world wrong, before congratulating the groom-to-be on acquiring this very first piece of "mobile Jewish property" that was successfully "transferred into the Polish hands," all narrated in the spirit of benevolent misogyny.[87]

The shorter anonymous pieces were a satirical retelling of the recent news. Written in a witty manner and presented in a concise format, they discussed minor events from the life of the couple with a view to attracting mass readers starved for recent gossip or the satirical rehashing thereof. In comparison, the longer text by Grotowski was an expression of the author's antisemitism demonstrated over time in his regular column.[88] In it, Grotowski made explicit use of the vocabulary of economic boycott, while alluding to the ethnonationalist dream of "Polonizing" Jewish property or even whole sectors of the economy. As in Wasilewski's cartoon, here Suchestow was objectified. This time she was presented as a commodity that could be freely passed on, eventually supplementing the national treasury and contributing to the creation of an ethnic Polish economy. This double othering, which underpinned Grotowski's text, went against the spirit of Radziwiłł's original interview in which the prince emphasized his egalitarian principles. In the interview, the aristocrat recalled his time spent abroad, in Britain in particular, which, in his words, turned him into a liberal who did not attach any importance to race or ethnicity and who believed in equality for all.[89] These ideals were ridiculed by Grotowski, evidencing the irreconcilability of egalitarian thinking and Polish ethnonationalist values.

Interestingly, in all of those reactions, no references were ever made to Esterka, the supposedly Jewish mistress of the Polish king Casimir the Great (1310–1370). In the Polish tradition, Esterka came to be admired for her beauty and wisdom, advising the king on important matters of the state. The legendary affair became the yardstick of other mixed-race relationships involving Poles and Jews. According to anthropologist Alina Cała, throughout much of the twentieth century the "Esterka myth" was very much alive in popular consciousness, particularly among the rural populations: this was one of the reasons why an affair between a beautiful Jewish woman and a Polish man was often associated with the aristocracy and seen in a rather positive light.[90] It seems that the "Esterka myth" was not activated in this context, and contemporary bias prevailed over the favorable retellings of the story of King Casimir and his Jewish mistress.

Wróble continued to report on the couple for the next half a year until the relationship eventually unraveled. The cartoons published during that time were topical and focused on bringing the latest news to the reader. For example, a cover cartoon in January 1938 talks about the protracted wedding preparations and the opposition from Radziwiłł's family to the potential male heir who might be born from the marriage. Here Wasilewski repurposed the earlier wedding cartoon. As previously, Suchestow is shown in a white wedding dress standing in the background, but the prince is no longer depicted crushing the wedding glass (Figure 5.15). Instead, he is portrayed as an expectant father, with a pram and a milk bottle. The exasperation of the bride-to-be is mentioned in the caption.[91] Elsewhere, Charlie commented on the couple's visit to Monte Carlo, presenting Radziwiłł as an undecided and irresponsible gambler.[92] In yet another cartoon, Rena drew a rendition of a film the couple were invited to shoot based on their love story in which they were to play themselves.[93] In it, Rena utilized her go-to imagery of menorahs and hooked-nosed Jews to represent Suchestow's world.[94] Finally, some of the last cartoons on the topic, published in late spring that year, commented on Radziwiłł's abandoning of Suchestow as well as speculating about his putative conquests in the future.[95]

5.15. A. Wasilewski, And My Rebecca..., from *Wróble na Dachu*, 16 January 1938, 1.

The majority of these later cartoons were devoid of strong antisemitic undertones, with the exception of Rena's reproducing of stereotypical antisemitic imagery, including exaggerated physical features. The last two cartoons by Wasilewski and Charlie, in particular, steered away from explicit references to Suchestow's Jewishness and, instead, offered commentary on the news at hand. The last cartoon published on the topic, drawn by Wasilewski,

5.16. A. Wasilewski, Policeman to Mrs Suchestow, from *Wróble na Dachu*, 29 May 1938, 1.

published in color, and placed on the front page, was a long way from his initial representation of the seductive and withholding Judith. In it, Suchestow is depicted as an attractive and stylish woman looking for her disappeared fiancée, her image reminiscent of illustrations of models that appeared in fashion magazines of the day (Figure 5.16).[96] Her clothing bears no references to her Jewishness; neither does she have accessories that would identify her as Jewish. This emphasis on her sophisticated style and mature beauty coincided with more sympathetic portrayals of Suchestow in the newspapers that reported on how Radziwiłł abandoned her in Monte Carlo and eloped to England with a woman named Mrs. Dawson, who had promised him a life of comfort and wealth.[97] The caption underneath the image describes how Radziwiłł "took to his heels" or "ran where the pepper grows" (*uciekać, gdzie pieprz rośnie*), as the Polish idiom has it.

It is possible that the prince's leaving of Suchestow right before the wedding and marrying a wealthier woman softened her subsequent portrayals in the Polish media, bringing about an image of a woman with hopes and plans of her own. Her plans now needed to be revised to help her escape circumstances that were said to be "pitiful."[98] In the end, it was her position as a helpless woman deserted by a man whom she had trusted that generated Wasilewski's sympathy for Suchestow. Just this once, her womanhood prevailed over her Jewishness.

BANAL ANTISEMITISM

Wróble's embracing of light entertainment was evident in many other cartoons on the Jewish theme. Despite publishing numerous cartoons that bemoaned the rise of fascism and fascist sympathies in Poland and abroad, the magazine also had a hand in spreading anti-Jewish sentiment. This was done using both "softer," banal imagery and stronger tropes that could potentially be seen as scare-mongering. One artist, Jerzy Zaruba, produced several such portrayals over the course of 1937. Born in 1891, Zaruba was older than most of his fellow illustrators, and his approach to the minority question was often old-fashioned and reminiscent of earlier interwar cartoons. Jewish individuals, as Zaruba drew them in his less-belligerent works, were mostly caricatures of traditional Jews in black clothing with large noses and oversized jaws and lips. They were by no means central characters, occupying marginal positions in the background as one of several stock characters.[99] In other portrayals by him, Jews were placed at the heart of the image and were used as the embodiment of problems with which the country was struggling, including economic underdevelopment and protracted modernization.[100]

Some of Zaruba's cartoons were rather suggestive and reproduced the old canard of Jews as vicious communists. For example, in a cartoon on recent reforms in the Red Army, the artist drew a Soviet commissar as a Jew with a thick large nose, black hair and beard, and red star on his armband (Fig-

5.17. J. Zaruba, Reforms in the Red Army, from *Wróble na Dachu*, 18 July 1937, 6.

ure 5.17). Although the topic of the cartoon suggested no connection to Poland and, as such, implied no direct threat of so-called Judeo-Communism, the placing of a Jewish protagonist in this context was far from neutral.[101] Zaruba used similar imagery in another cartoon about the Soviet Union (Figure 5.18).[102] Interestingly, all of his Jewish protagonists looked virtually the same and, barring differences in attire, could be easily transplanted from one context to another. This could either speak to the author's limited range when drawing such subjects or, more likely, his lack of interest in nuancing these portrayals. In fact, considering Zaruba's signature Jewish characters, Żółtko and Eierweiss, that he had initially created for the progressive *Cyrulik Warszawski* magazine, one can conclude that both reasons were at play here.

A corresponding cartoon by Bronisław Schneider that commented on ongoing purges in the USSR provides a striking counterexample. In it, Schneider depicted a group of eight convicts, recent victims of Stalin's terror, marching toward a firing squad (Figure 5.19). Behind them, six others

— Ten węzeł na naszym sztandarze kazałem zawiązać, ażeby nie zapomnieć, że wciąż jesteśmy krajem najbardziej postępowym na świecie...

5.18. J. Zaruba, Memento . . ., from *Wróble na Dachu*, 18 July 1937, 3.

are being executed. The artist gave equal attention to each of the characters, providing detail and variety to their facial features and making them an ethnically diverse group. The one character who could potentially be identified as Jewish is distinct from the caricatural types of Zaruba's cartoons, being drawn without unnecessary distortion or exaggeration.[103] Both this and other cartoons produced by Schneider for the magazine show that he was skilled in sketching groups. He endowed each of his characters with a distinctive personality that escapes pigeonholing and makes them a credible subject.[104] Here, as elsewhere, the artist used his characteristic soft, thick line to add clarity to the figures at the forefront and emphasize their contemplative

5.19. Br. Schneider, In the USSR, from *Wróble na Dachu*, 8 August 1937, 6.

expressions, which show a profound awareness of what is yet to come. The two sections of the image—one representing the ongoing execution, the other portraying the marching convicts—provide an eerie prediction of the destiny of the eight characters. This is a haunting image that shows people on the threshold of death.

The two artists could not be more different in their approach to Jewish characters. This difference between Zaruba and Schneider grew out of their distinctive backgrounds, both professional and personal. Zaruba spent much of his childhood and teenage years in the Russian Empire, which had a sizable and often traditional Jewish population. He grew up in a middle-class Polish-Czech family who moved a lot due to his father's military assignments. Young Zaruba was educated in Kiev: he began gymnasium in 1900, before embarking on an art degree in 1908. Following the death of his father in 1910, he transferred to art school in Warsaw, before continuing his education with Georges Braque in Paris.[105] Following the First World War, when he fought in the Russian Army, he returned to Warsaw and made the city his home until his death in 1971. Zaruba's early work was praised for displaying a keen eye for Warsaw city life, in particular the representations of "Warsaw's low-life" (*warszawski światek*), a legacy he was said to inherit from painter and caricaturist Franciszek Kostrzewski.[106] It is perhaps this interest in *typy warszawskie*, or urban stock characters, that was responsible for his attachment to visual clichés that were rarely sympathetic to Jews. It is also likely that his upbringing in the pogrom-driven atmosphere of the early twentieth-century Russian Empire was partly responsible for such stereotyping. Reminiscing about his early artistic education, Zaruba reports that he spent hours walking around Kiev, observing market stalls and tea houses and searching for exotic "types" for his drawings. The multicultural district of Podil, hosting Persian, Tatar, Jewish, and Chinese people, was to him a real "treasure-trove of impressions," providing "a richness of motifs for drawing."[107]

By comparison, Schneider, who was twenty-four years Zaruba's junior, was born in 1915 and spent most of his childhood and youth in the independent Polish state. Not much is known of his background, other than that he came from a Jewish family, studied in Lviv and Kraków, both former cities of the more liberal Austro-Hungarian Partition, and was killed on the frontlines in 1943 in the USSR fighting for the Red Army.[108] Although Jewish characters did not necessarily appear in his work more often than they did in Zaruba's, there was undoubtedly more sensitivity and depth to his portrayals. These works could be seen as an indirect response to banal antisemitism, including visual antisemitism, which was widespread in interwar Poland. Such cartoons were possibly the artist's way of visually educating the public and undoing the harm done by decades of ethnic stereotyping in cartoon art. This was not exclusive to Schneider and other illustrators like him. Art historian Matthew Baigell shows that, like some of their Polish counterparts, American Jewish artists, too, were active in countering visual othering by taking "charge of their own image" and providing more varied portrayals of their people and communities.[109]

Zaruba was by no means the only artist of the interwar period to proliferate anti-Jewish stereotyping. The work of Mieczysław Piotrowski produced in

1938 provided another interesting example of banal antisemitism. Piotrowski, author of the militant cartoons on violence in the universities in 1937, seemed to have ventured toward a less sympathetic form of caricature the following year. This reflected a wider shift in the magazine as a whole. Zaruba-style portrayals of Jews that had been fairly marginal the year before came to dominate *Wróble*'s visual satire in 1938. These shifts in direction, both within the oeuvre of one artist and in the magazine as a whole, were not that surprising for a publication that claimed to have been "impartial" and to have critiqued everyone in equal measure.[110] In reality, the impartiality of *Wróble* was a myth. The only influence to which the magazine responded was the ebbs and flows of reader satisfaction.

Indeed, Piotrowski's turn to banal antisemitism in 1938 may intimate that sales had plummeted and the editors were attempting to tweak the magazine's content to meet the changing tastes of its audience. This trend was not exclusive to interwar Poland. According to political scientist Ilan Danjoux, editors tend to favor cartoons that drive sales, while "cartoonists learn to prioritize the issues that interest their readers while avoiding frames that might offend them."[111] While no explicit evidence exists that would point to Piotrowski's self-censoring, at least three of his cartoons in 1938 were manifestly geared toward popular taste, toying with the stereotype of the "Jewish nose," both at the visual level and in the captions.[112] One of these cartoons employed the trope of the traditional Jew too.[113] Importantly, topics that could potentially be used to criticize inequities in Polish society were utilized by the artist as yet another vehicle for amusing the mass reader at the cost of the prototypical Jewish subject.

This was the case with a cartoon that communicated the ethnonationalist call for introducing separate train cars for Jewish travelers. The initiative had been championed by the right-wing newspaper *ABC*, which argued that travelling in overcrowded carriages was increasingly unpleasant for gentile passengers. "Which nation represents the innate symbiosis of such features as insolence, arrogance, rambunctiousness, boisterous gesturing, messiness, . . . and that smell," the paper suggestively asked in November 1936, while recommending immediate ghettoization.[114] Soon enough, readers were reacting to the article. Many rejoiced in the idea of separate cars and proposed that segregation be also introduced on the trams.[115] In August 1937, *ABC* reported that travelers were now petitioning for separate wagons directly with the Polish rails.[116] That summer, rumor spread that "Jewish carriages" were already introduced on the Oświęcim-Katowice line, but this was quickly repudiated.[117] *ABC* was tireless in its campaigning and, in the months to come, the newspaper claimed that its proposal was quickly spreading

W Poznaniu domagają się wprowadzenia w pociągach przedziałów dla Żydów.

Rys. M. Piotrowski, Warszawa

Specjalny wagon dla rozmawiających...

5.20. M. Piotrowski, In Poznań They Are Demanding Separate Compartments for Jews, from *Wróble na Dachu*, 20 February 1938, 7.

across the country and garnering more support. This was supposed to prove that segregated trains were an absolute necessity, "for cultural and hygienic reasons" (*ze względów kulturalnych i higienicznych*).[118] The debate continued intermittently until the outbreak of the war.

It is likely that Piotrowski's cartoon alluded to *ABC*'s proposal in depicting his own vision of the proposed wagon (Figure 5.20). The image shows a platform with no walls, doors, or windows. On it stand various Jewish characters, both Hasidic and middle-class ones, cordoned off by a low chain fence. The carriage is named "Wagon for the talking" (*Przedział dla rozmawiających*), but the passengers do not do only that. Their uninhibited gestures make it into a dynamic scene: the open-air carriage is all astir, teeming with conversation and movement. The title says nonchalantly that in Poznań demands were made for separate cars.[119] Piotrowski's Jewish characters are a perfect likeness of supposed Jewish "rambunctiousness, boisterous gesturing, [and] messiness" described by *ABC*. Such evocative descriptions of the supposedly brash and disheveled passengers could certainly provide excellent material for visual satire. At the same time, according to scholars who say cartoons are to draw attention to "evils which need to be remedied," a question arises as to what these evils were in this case.[120]

Piotrowski's ethnic stereotyping would suggest he was pointing the finger at Jewish mores, but his caption opened the door for a more liberal interpretation of the events, one that was unsympathetic to the right-wing circles of Greater Poland and Poznań. This ambiguity is puzzling given Piotrowski's decisive and politically sensitive cartoons of the previous year. His imaginative criticism of the anti-Jewish violence in 1937 went hand in hand with the respect he garnered among the leftist illustrators of *Szpilki* who invited him to contribute to the magazine that year. Eryk Lipiński described Piotrowski's work as "drawing on the finest tradition of George Grosz, being both poetic and viciously satirical."[121] Journalist Teresa Kłosiewicz called his postwar work both "philosophical" and aphoristic.[122] Others emphasised his sensitivity and sympathy for the struggles of a fellow human.[123] Admittedly, despite these accolades and his prior accomplished career with the progressive *Cyrulik Warszawski*, Piotrowski's trajectory was not as consistent as that of some of the liberal artists of the interbellum. His earlier work also included, however sparse, antisemitic cartoons drawn for the right-wing newspaper *Dziennik Bydgoski*.[124] In analyzing that other strand in Piotrowski's work, it is tempting to draw comparisons with the cartoons of his then-wife Regina Kańska, known to the readers of *Wróble* as Rena. In fact, the style of "Wagon" brings to mind some of Rena's earlier caricatures. In particular, her November 1937 cartoon commenting on disturbances in the British colonies, including the Arab revolt in Mandatory Palestine, presented a somewhat corresponding image of bundled-up bodies and heads. Rena's vision of the enmeshed Arab, Jewish, and non-white torsos and arms, resting on the back of a colonial official, is one of pandemonium (Figure 5.21). Wielding guns, knives, and other weapons, the colonial people are "The English disease," as the caption has it.[125] Although different in tone and topic, the drawing style and the visual tropes used (including outstretched arms, hooked noses, and black beards) bore close resemblance to Piotrowski's cartoon discussed above. While the theme of disease did not necessarily appear in the "Wagon" caricature, the discourse of squalor and infestation was prominent in right-wing utterances on the topic, bringing the two drawings into a shared semantic pool.[126]

It is possible that Piotrowski was inspired by Rena's earlier caricature of the British colonies, but it is also likely that the two images were produced by the same person. Like their colleague Zaruba, the putative author of the two cartoons tended to rehash familiar motifs and ways of drawing Jewish characters. A closer scrutiny of Rena's few cartoons for *Wróble* indicates that it was her, and not necessarily Piotrowski, who tended to recycle specific visual tropes in the space of two or three cartoons (barring Piotrowski's penchant for hooked noses). It is thus not unlikely that the couple collaborated more

5.21. R. Kańska, Due to Unrest in English Dominions, from *Wróble na Dachu*, 7 November 1937, 2.

5.22. Rena, The Transport of Tyrolese [Germans] to Germany, from *Wróble na Dachu*, 30 July 1939, 7.

closely than it would initially seem and that the more successful Piotrowski also lent his name to showcase the unpublished work of his wife.

Leafing through the later issues of *Wróble* brings more conclusive evidence that it was in fact Regina Kańska who created the "Wagon" drawing in February 1938. In July 1939, *Wróble* published a modified version of that cartoon, this time under Rena's name. Commenting on the immigration of Germans from South Tyrol into Nazi Germany, the drawing presents an overcrowded train platform on which waving and shouting passengers are being transported, presumably as part of the South Tyrol Option Agreement, which allowed ethnic Germans from Italy to leave the country before Italianization measures were introduced by the Mussolini government (Figure 5.22).[127] The cartoon is clearly recognizable as another rendition of the previous drawing, which would attest to Rena's growing fortune as an illustrator for *Wróble*. The two cartoons also tell us something about the artist's process. It is possible that Kańska created many drafts before choosing the right one and that the South Tyrol cartoon is one draft of the earlier "Wagon" illustration. Other caricaturists had a similar process. For example, Zuzanna Lipińska, the daughter of *Szpilki* artists Ha-Ga and Eryk Lipiński, recalls her mother's tenacity in drafting several versions of the same drawing before deciding on just one, in contrast to her father, whose process was much faster.[128]

The story of Rena is, to some extent, a story of other interwar female illustrators. Rena's oeuvre has often been sidelined by scholars, as has been the work of other women artists of the time. In fact, one recent history of Polish interwar cartoons mentions only three of the most productive and popular female cartoonists of the interbellum, the renowned artist Maja Berezowska and the *Szpilki* illustrators Ha-Ga and Irena Kuczborska. Rena or Regina Kańska is not listed at all.[129] Equally, her name is missing from the memoirs of major caricaturists of the day such as Eryk Lipiński.[130] To what extent this was a result of Rena's being eclipsed by her husband, Piotrowski, we will never know. Referring to another spousal unit of two caricature artists, that of Lipiński and Ha-Ga, art historian Katarzyna Murawska-Muthesius suggests that the male spouse tends to play a more active role in both narrating and preserving the legacy of such units, which often results in a scarcity of information on the female artist.[131] Historians of the American political cartoon show that there is a historical and transnational pattern to this dearth of research on women cartoonists. In the US, for instance, female caricaturists were underresearched for much of the twentieth century, and it was only in the 1970s that the situation began to change. The suffrage era of the 1910s, when many female illustrators emerged and pursued artistic careers in American print media, was the only notable exception.[132]

That said, Rena's contribution to the history of Polish caricature was not wholly forgotten. In 1969, Eryk Lipiński traced her to the city of Łódź where she had been living since the end of the Second World War. Lipiński requested that she complete an artist questionnaire that was later to become part of the archives of Warsaw's Museum of Caricature, alongside other similar materials. Rena's questionnaire and the accompanying letter she wrote to Lipiński from Łódź are the only record of personal and professional information on the artist that I have found, except for the university records retained in the archives of the Academy of Arts in Warsaw. According to the questionnaire, Rena was born in Kharkov (present-day Kharkiv in Ukraine) on 9 November 1906 at a time when the city was part of the Russian Empire. Like Zaruba, she later moved to Warsaw where she studied in the academy between 1932 and 1937.[133] As far as her career as a caricaturist went, Kańska might have seen it as negligible. She did not acknowledge her contributions to *Wróble* at all and mentioned only her postwar work for the Łódź-based

5.23. Rena, Commemorative Candelabra, from *Wróble na Dachu*, 24 April 1938, 3.

satirical magazine *Rózgi* (Birch Rods) in 1946–1947.[134] This omission might be to do with the fact that Kańska was an occasional contributor to *Wróble* and that most of her cartoons appeared under the pseudonym "Rena," which, although easily recognizable as her, could have implied her wish to remain anonymous. In contrast, her later illustrations in *Rózgi* are signed with her full name, many of them appearing on the front page.[135]

Unlike the oeuvre of her then-husband Piotrowski, which was fairly varied, Rena's work in the 1930s was consistently tinged with mild anti-Jewish sentiment.[136] The repurposing of specific motifs was also more frequent in her drawings than in Piotrowski's. For example, her cartoon on the planned Radziwiłł-Suchestow marriage used the motif of a tree branch evolving into a menorah. A similar visual strategy was employed in a later caricature that commented on the proposed legislation to ban ritual slaughter (Figure 5.23). The cartoon portrays a Jewish man wearing a yarmulke, reading a newspaper and smoking a pipe, with a stuffed head of an ox hanging above his chair.

As in the image of a warped genealogical tree, here too the menorah grows out of organic matter, the antlers providing a stable base for the candelabra. Aside from these visual parallels that point to continuities in Rena's style, the political message of this cartoon was equally important to and in line with her earlier work. The drawing showed a not too distant future after ritual slaughter has been prohibited and discontinued. According to the caption, the contraption was to act as a memento of a time when *shechita* had been still allowed.[137]

The ritual slaughter cartoon agreed with animal rights advocates who deemed the practice, in the words of historian Eva Plach, "a stubborn religious relic of questionable authenticity" that was "unsuited to the modern age."[138] By the time Rena's cartoon was published, the bill requiring the stunning of animals before slaughter had been in place for more than a year, but the ethno-nationalist right and activist circles demanded a complete ban, linking concerns over animal welfare with nationalist goals. In March 1938, the Sejm passed a new bill to ban the *shechita* entirely, but it was never ratified by the Senate; discussion of it died out at the outbreak of war.[139] To cite Plach, "In all of these condemnations of ritual slaughter, animal protectionists [rights advocates] relied on, benefited from and contributed to a pervasive antisemitism in interwar Poland."[140] Like those antisemitic pundits, Rena saw the practice as a sign of Jewish backwardness and welcomed the bill as heralding an imminent ban on ritual slaughter. This also was the case for Antoni Wasilewski, who, in a cover image of April 1938, intimated that the ban was a done deal.[141] Interestingly, Charlie, whose earlier drawing on the topic ridiculed Sejm deputy Janina Prystorowa, the main proponent of the ban, was the only one of the three illustrators to draw attention to the ethnic Polish political elites, instead of associating the issue solely with the Jews.

Charlie's cartoon, which depicted Prystorowa riding an untamed animal, avoided the simple stereotyping of the other two cartoons, which made it, in effect, sympathetic to Jewish campaigning against the ban (Figure 5.24).[142] As in Lipiński's later drawing of the abduction of Europa, which he drew for *Szpilki* the following year, the motif of the kidnapping was repurposed to match the realities of the present. Unlike Lipiński, Charlie used a lighthearted retelling of the mythical story in which the ox is substituted for a cow, while the exposed body of desperate Europa is replaced with the fully clothed and smiling figure of Prystorowa. Drawing her in the process of being carried away by the cow, Charlie teased the politician for her vocal and excessive involvement in the matter.

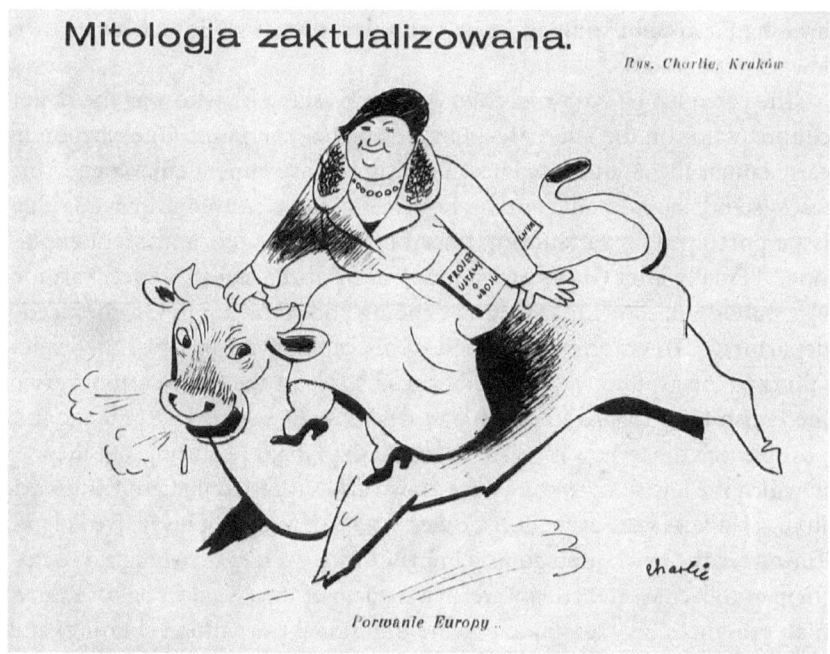

5.24. Charlie, Mythology in the Present, from *Wróble na Dachu*, 19 December 1937, 6.

Comparing how different artists responded to the same issues enables us not only to determine the fluctuations of political proclivities within one particular magazine, as was the case above, but also to trace how one topic was discussed across several satirical weeklies. Looking at how *Wróble* and others responded to important international developments says a lot about the degree and tone of their Jewish-themed satire. The introduction of anti-Jewish laws in Romania following installation of the Octavian Goga government on 28 December 1937 provides one interesting example. As seen earlier, in early 1938, the pro-government *Mucha* devoted a lot of attention to the possible influx of Romanian Jews into Poland. Much of this reporting reworked the fear-mongering trope of "enemies at the gate," impatient to enter neighboring Poland, that appeared in right-wing newspapers. *Wróble* also commented on the issue but was careful not to weaponize it. While *Mucha* focused predominantly on the affluent middle-class Jews who were supposedly about to arrive in Poland and further escalate the so-called Jewish problem, *Wróble* did not make any such connections and instead commented on Romania's fascist turn. As such, the magazine chose not to reproduce the representations of putative refugees from across the border that could have had a destabilizing effect in a country already divided over its own Jewish population.

The cartoons by editor in chief Antoni Wasilewski, who was the major commentator on the issue, are an interesting case in point. One cartoon in early January 1938 illustrated how the shift in government emboldened the fascists and caused panic among Romania's Jews.[143] Another image in that issue portrayed Goga taunting the country's Jews with imminent expulsion.[144] Finally, after Goga's resignation on 10 February 1938, a cover cartoon was published, showing two Jews dancing and rejoicing in Goga's speedy departure.[145] To emphasize the end of his cabinet, an image of the leader falling to the ground was also published.[146] Two of the three cartoons used the Polish term *szopka* in the title to describe the events in Romania. It is possible that the term was meant to emphasize Goga's posturing, but the way in which the Jewish characters were drawn also suggested that, to Wasilewski, Romanian Jews were even more exotic than the Hasidim of his native Poland. They were the stock protagonists in his Romanian *szopka*, which presented them as folk characters that were an amalgam of the visual tropes of Romanian provinces (as exemplified by the traditional Carpathian clothing) and stereotypical images of Jewish bodies. Although Wasilewski was no doubt reproducing familiar antisemitic tropes, as well as Orientalizing his characters as representatives of a "remote" Romanian culture, he made no obvious references to Poland. Thus, when compared to *Mucha*'s cartoons, these images were geared toward light entertainment and informing readers about the international situation, rather than making an ideological statement on issues that mattered to local audiences, from a possible influx of refugees to a putative transplanting of anti-Jewish laws in Poland.[147]

Most of the illustrations discussed in this chapter, although replicating existing stereotypes, managed to avoid the aggressive rhetoric of right-wing magazines. The more antagonistic portrayals that did appear, including Zaruba's references to so-called Judeo-Communism, were few and far between and largely marginal to the overall production of *Wróble*. However, cartoons that thrived on milder antisemitic tropes, including exaggerated images of the Jewish body and their supposedly alien mores, were by no means rare and must have enjoyed relative popularity with its readers, contributing to the mass appeal of the magazine.

More generally, there are several perspectives that emerge from *Wróble*'s reporting in the late 1930s. These include the engaged perspective of cartoonists who opposed anti-Jewish violence, the relatively indifferent standpoint of those who used nonpolitical stories for entertainment purposes, and the mild antisemitic stance of others who commented on current affairs involving Jews. The magazine was able to bridge these various viewpoints as part of its quest for supposed impartiality or, more likely, as an attempt to appeal to a cross-section of Polish society. It could be argued that the magazine was indeed representative of the views of the general, albeit more intellectual, public.[148] Much of *Wróble*'s content shied away from political partisanship, often verging on political indifference, and only some of its material was either explicitly liberal or blatantly antisemitic. Otherwise, the magazine avoided political extremes. Entertainment remained its chief goal. The traditional purpose of satire—to mend social ills—was present only concerning marginal players in political life, such as the ethno-nationalist youth.

The last issue of *Wróble* was published on 3 September 1939, two days after the Nazi invasion of Poland. The war-time fate of its artists was as varied as their offerings in 1930s Poland. The editor in chief, Antoni Wasilewski, joined the Polish Army and, following the fiasco of the September campaign, escaped the country through Romania and France and settled in Scotland where he remained until 1957. This is where he created a satirical magazine of the Polish military called *Werinajs* (a Polonized variant of the English phrase "very nice"), as well as contributing caricatures to other exile Polish magazines and the British press.[149] Karol Ferster, aka Charlie, fled his hometown of Kraków to Lviv at the end of September 1939. In 1942, he was imprisoned in the Janowska concentration camp at the outskirts of Lviv, from which he escaped in April 1943 before arriving in Warsaw where he survived under false identity until the end of the war.[150] Following the Nazi invasion of the USSR, Jakub Bickels also moved to Warsaw where he assumed the identity of "Jakub Biliński." He was killed in the anti-Nazi Warsaw Uprising of 1944.[151] Regina Kańska, the only female artist who contributed caricatures of Jews to *Wróble*, did not pursue a career as a cartoonist after her short stint for *Rózgi* in 1946–1947. She became the chair of the Department of Weaving and Clothing Fabrics at the Łódź Academy of Arts.[152]

Wróble na Dachu did not survive the war, but its spirit lived on in other postwar weeklies, including the progressive, outward-looking *Przekrój* (*Cross-Section*), which carved out a similar position on the market, attracting mass readership and being able to navigate the complicated milieu of Communist state censorship.[153] Many of the artists discussed here continued their work as cartoonists after the war: Charlie became a celebrated caricaturist for *Przekrój*; Mieczysław Piotrowski and Jerzy Zaruba contributed to the revived *Szpilki* that began to operate under the banner of socialist satire; and others left the country altogether, including Maksymilian Brandel who headed for New York City and continued his work as caricaturist Max Brandel for the American humor magazine *Mad*.

As in other works of journalism, the visual idiom of interwar Poland was to be replaced with a new language of pictorial expression, in which the concerns of the socialist state were to play a chief role. After the Second World War, a new narrative of postwar reconstruction was on the rise.

CONCLUSION

When cartoonists in interwar Poland portrayed Jews, they rarely meant real-life people. The Jewish figure in their drawings was a convenient metaphor with which to discuss existing realities, whether of poverty, migration, fascism, or interethnic violence. The paranoid logic that guided the most negative of those portrayals allowed the artists to spin pictorial stories of dangerous conspiracies and cartels that were said to erode the nation from within. The caricatures that were milder in tone perpetrated visual narratives of the ghetto, imbued with the perennial tropes of crime, backwardness, and destitution, in addition to evoking the cosmopolitan space beyond, inhabited by well-fed and modish-looking, albeit rootless, Jews. Only rarely did the cartoonists represent actual people, but never was this done without a purpose. From the provincial merchant to the seductive Jewish woman, these portrayals enabled the illustrators to position themselves on the pressing debates of the day, be they local or national, economic, or social in nature. There were also those artists who could be described as the do-gooders as they portrayed Jewish and non-Jewish protagonists to appeal for social justice and warn against the perils of totalitarianism.

As different as they were in their depictions of Jews and irrespective of the type and quality of their satirical endeavors, all five of the magazines discussed in this book operationalized the medium of political cartoon alongside other satirical modalities—poetry and prose in particular. Verbal satire not only provided a context in which to expand on the visual message, reinforcing the publication's political position; it also helped institute distinctive communities of humor that comprised illustrators, writers, and, as elusive as they were, readers. These communities were built around a shared understanding that, because of its proclivity for journalistic topicality and ironic detachment, the satirical end product obviated the need for factual rigor and, admittedly, prudence. As they distorted the existing realities and challenged the boundaries of correctness through humor, the makers of interwar satire were able to convey a specific political message more persuasively and more directly than the politicians of similar persuasion. Employing the "Jewish question" and the idea of a nation-state as perennial reference points, they also endorsed specific visions of citizenship and citizen participation.

Editors of each of the five periodicals envisioned that their readers engaged with politics in a particular way. *Mucha* goaded its audiences to consider the path of regime-friendly conformity. *Pokrzywy* chose the route of coercion, seeking new and direct means of imposing its political dogmas onto the provincial people. *Szpilki* castigated those ethnic Poles who chose to hate, as well as challenging readers to decode its erudite references, from the Bible to Greek mythology. *Szarża* aimed to spread anti-Jewish sentiment but, in doing so, was also self-reflective and autothematic, playing with identities and encouraging its readers to see beyond the obvious. The entrepreneurial approach of *Wróble na Dachu* meant that it strove to strike a balance between absolving its audiences from thinking about politics and reveling in escapist entertainment.

Alongside the differences in political and economic outlook, editors of the five magazines also varied in how they saw their publications in the longer tradition of satirical journalism. One school of Jewish-themed satire followed the nineteenth-century pattern of conflating the figure of the Jew with a variety of current affairs. This practice had been a response to germinating fears around modernity and capitalism that, exasperated by the uncertainties of a nascent state, led to vilification as an opportune mode of commenting on the changing times. Magazines with a nineteenth-century pedigree, such as *Mucha*, and those that subscribed to the nineteenth-century tradition of satire, including *Pokrzywy*, gravitated toward such form of discourse. The new outlets that emerged in the 1930s, notably the progressive *Szpilki* and the nonpartisan *Wróble na Dachu*, endeavored to reverse that trend. These periodicals brought about a new generation of artists and commercially minded editors who chose not to engage in antisemitic politicking, whether for ideological, personal, or economic reasons. One of the ways to do so responsibly, and to set new journalistic standards, was to deanonymize the illustrator. Unlike their conservative counterparts who, similar to their nineteenth-century predecessors, remained largely anonymous, the new generation of artists refused to hide under pseudonyms, suffusing their work with individual drawing styles, backgrounds, and value systems. Similarly, as their ethno-nationalist colleagues tended to infuse Jewish-themed drawings with caricature and stereotype, aiming to elicit and deepen negative feelings toward Jews, the liberal illustrators of the late 1930s chose to present them as fellow human beings.

CONCLUSION

Interwar political cartoons replicated tropes that were, and still are, transnational and could be deciphered by audiences elsewhere in the world. Sometimes, as was the case with *Pokrzywy*, this was done through illegal reprints from foreign magazines. From the old canard of Jewish conspirators' scheming to take over global affairs to the grassroots conceptions of Jews' supposed rapaciousness, unsocial behavior, dishonesty, and other traits, those cartoons used transnational visual motifs, including oversized body parts (such as noses, pot bellies, feet, and lips), animal motifs (for example, octopus tentacles), and others. These were not mere images. As one scholar of antisemitic caricature argues, "popular visual culture defined 'Jewishness' not only as a marker for ethnic division, but also as a signifier of modern culture and the anxieties it provoked more generally."[1] The widespread pronouncements of Jewish influence in Polish media, music, literature, and other areas of culture provided illustrative examples of this mindset, as did the conflating of technological progress, industrialization, urbanization, and various new value systems with the purported Jewish influence. These visual renditions of the familiar global tropes were not only meant to emphasize the supposed destruction Jews brought upon the Polish national "spirit" that was nineteenth century in origin, but were also representative of contemporary European visual politics that arose around the "Jewish question" following the rise of Nazi Germany.

Transnational visual tropes were not the sole domain of the most hateful of the caricatures. Those artists who campaigned for equality were also prone to engage with a pictorial idiom that could be understandable to international readers. The anti-Hitler political cartoon, in particular, operated with well-known themes that had a long visual pedigree, including scenes from the Old Testament and Greek mythology. These traditional themes, some of which saw various painterly renditions over the course of the centuries, such as the mythical scene of the Rape of Europa, were repurposed to match the contemporary political context. Like their antisemitic counterparts, anti-fascist caricatures were easily transferable from one national realm into another, as foreign reprints of some leftist artists from Poland demonstrate.

The portrayals discussed in this book were produced by a small group of people, many of whom endorsed a specific political agenda and were often consistent in doing so over the course of their lives. For example, the little we know of the artists who worked for ethnonationalist publications, such as *Szarża*'s Włodzimierz Łukasik, would suggest that some of them had a long history of drawing similar content. Relinquishing their anonymity, illustrators like Łukasik openly professed their commitment to antisemitism, viewing it presumably as an intellectual choice. This was no different for others on the far right for whom, as one fictional character of a satirical novel of the day asserted, "antisemitism was never about hate. It was [an instance of] reasoning. It was [an instance] of logic."[2] This antisemitic logic was said to be motivated by the Great Depression, the ensuing poverty among Poland's urban populations, the condoning of discrimination and xenophobia, and a religious revival that strengthened the link between nationalism and Catholicism.[3]

While illustrators such as Łukasik presented a clear example of committed antisemitism, there were others whose trajectories were more ambiguous. His *Szarża* colleague, the anonymous "Poraj.," was one such example. Henryk Szpigiel, the editor of the magazine, was another. It is precisely these cases that make us question the binary thinking of Jean-Paul Sartre's *Anti-Semite and Jew* in which "the anti-Semite and the democrat tirelessly carry on their dialogue without ever understanding one another."[4] In fact, many of those who created the ethnonationalist print media (satirical magazines or otherwise) were people in the Polish-Jewish contact zone, whether by ancestry, as was the case for some far-right activists and journalists (such as Piasecki and Wasiutyński, who were famously ridiculed for their hypocrisy by the leftist *Szpilki*), or by lineage and by choice, including *Szarża*'s de facto editor, Henryk Szpigiel. People like Szpigiel, in particular, revealed a double perspective that spoke to the inequalities of interwar Poland, the struggles of acculturation, and admittedly, the importance of Jewish talent in the advancing of satirical print media. More trivially perhaps, the trajectory of such figures tells us something about the impact of financial considerations on the cultural output of the time. Minor artists and writers, as well as those who were new to the profession, were no strangers to personal compromise. The widespread use of aliases would suggest that getting their work commissioned and published was not always an ideological choice but rather a way to earn a living in one's chosen profession.

In that respect, illustrators such as *Wróble na Dachu* contributors Jerzy Zaruba and Regina Kańska are more puzzling. Their work disseminated banal antisemitism that was supposedly neither aggressive nor inflaming in nature. Zaruba's interwar drawings, in particular, were praised for being representative of the "social left" (*lewica społeczna*), attending to the ills of society and attempting to fix them.[5] However, his stereotypical caricatures of contemporary Jews show that this was not always the case. Interestingly, both Zaruba and Kańska came from the former Russian imperial territories, Kiev and Kharkov respectively, where grassroots antisemitism was widespread and pervasive. Whether one's place of origin and adolescence affect one's visual sensibility and future artistic choices may be debated, but the two artists' demeaning portrayals of Jews certainly bore some of the hallmarks of the antisemitic climate of Tsarist Russia. That very same context was often credited with providing the model for Endecja's own anti-Jewish rhetoric and practice.[6]

The case of *Mucha*'s editor in chief, Władysław Buchner, was equally interesting, though for different reasons. Originating from an assimilated Jewish family that had rejected the religious excesses of traditional Jewry, Buchner was a second-generation proselyte for whom Jewishness was no longer an issue. Unlike Szpigiel, who commissioned relatively few antisemitic drawings in his time as editor of *Szarża*, Buchner had no reservations about perpetuating anti-Jewish stereotypes. Like his learned grandfather before him, he ridiculed those he considered the most backward or most ostentatious members of the community and, in poking fun at their mores, professed his complete sense of detachment from the Jewish masses.

The impact of one's upbringing on future professional activity is also seen in the case of *Szpilki*'s cofounder Eryk Lipiński. Lipiński came from a home with strong patriotic traditions and socialist sympathies, his father's life showing that the two could be reconciled. Despite having grown up in imperial Russia, not unlike Kańska and Zaruba, it was the influence of Lipiński's father that most likely shaped his approach to the "minority question," although his professional life was not devoid of financially driven stunts for the opposing political camp. All in all, however, the liberal group of artists who opposed antisemitism consisted of young academy and university graduates, many of them Jewish, including Karol Ferster (Charlie), Jakub Bickels, and Mendel Reif. The majority of these illustrators were born around 1910 and grew up in the independent Polish state. The more liberal territories of the Austro-Hungarian Empire, Lviv and Kraków included, featured prominently in the biographies of these artists, although some of them, like Ha-Ga, Eryk Lipiński, and Franciszek Parecki, studied in Warsaw and were part of Warsaw's artistic circles. At the same time, as some of the cases discussed here demonstrate and as one scholar of antisemitism argues with regard to another period, "not everything can be explained systematically by reference to ideological convictions. Accepting the challenge and giving testimony in difficult times was above all a matter of character and of irreducible attributes of personality."[7]

Notwithstanding that these artists' biographies can shed light on the satirical production of the day, there are also limitations to the existing sources. The velocity and emphemerality that characterized much of the interwar satirical print media meant that some of the context surrounding the production of interwar satire remained only partly recorded. For example, irrespective of the erratic nature of state censorship, we are still able to reconstruct how it operated, but there are fewer sources that speak of self-censorship and other attempts to circumvent the top-down practices. Similarly, while some insights can be drawn about the various external pressures by tracing content modifications over the course of several weeks, months, and years, less is known about how interwar editors and publishers communicated the need for such changes to the writers and illustrators on the ground. The relationship that these magazines developed with their audiences is even less tangible. Some magazines, such as *Wróble na Dachu*, recorded and archived sales figures, including fluctuations in sales, enabling us to connect low circulation with the increase in "soft" antisemitism that was meant to appeal to popular tastes and potentially attract new readership. However, no sources, such as audience surveys, exist on the impact of these representations on readers and their subsequent take on the minority question.

Except for a handful of memoirs by *Szpilki* cofounder Eryk Lipiński, personal accounts about interwar political cartooning are few and far between. The *Szpilki* group and Lipiński in particular loom large in these recollections, leaving less space for those outside their inner circle. Women artists as well as some conservative illustrators remain underrepresented in these works, despite Lipiński's systematic efforts to record the history of the political cartoon in Poland, including through the research activities of the Museum of Caricature in Warsaw, which he founded in 1978.

It was the Holocaust rather than a "Judeo-Poland," of which many in the ethno-nationalist camp had forewarned, that brought an end to the contentious visual politics that divided the interwar Polish state. After finding refuge from the Nazi invasion in exile in London, many in the Sanacja camp and nationalist circles alike were reluctant to discuss the recent past, ashamed of what one liberal poet called "their disgraceful alliances and their ideological relationship with Hitlerism."[8]

The majority of those men were to assume marginal positions in the print media of the nascent Polish People's Republic, established after the war. The leftist and socialist illustrators who had been determined to eradicate antisemitism and create an equal society for all became the leading political cartoonists of socialist Poland. Yet for all their insistence on a break with the excesses of the past, the socialist caricatures they themselves forged were soon to become a vehicle for another influential crusade of hate. After the Six-Day War of 1967, an "anti-Zionist" campaign was unleased in Poland that lead to widespread violence, purges, and mass emigration of the remaining Jewish Poles. The chief opponents of interwar antisemitism, including the *Szpilki* magazine and some of its long-time contributors, not least Eryk

Lipiński, drew caricatures that were meant to chide the state of Israel but constituted, in essence, a reproduction of familiar antisemitic tropes.[9] In that sense, the new state was fated to repeat the mistakes of the old; visual culture that sought validity in ethnic conflict was revived to accomplish the interwar dream of Poland without Jews.

NOTES

INTRODUCTION

1. "Dyskusja nad budżetem min. spraw wewn. na komisji," *Nowy Dziennik*, 26 November 1928, 2.

2. Grzegorz Krzywiec, "Antysemickie karykatury od poł. XIX w. do I wojny światowej," in *Obcy i niemili: antysemickie rysunki z prasy polskiej 1919–1939* (Warszawa: Żydowski Instytut Historyczny, 2013), 14.

3. Krzywiec, "Antysemickie karykatury od poł. XIX w. do I wojny światowej," 17.

4. Dariusz Konstantynów, "Pogromy i inne akty przemocy fizycznej wobec Żydów w zwierciadle rysunków z prasy polskiej (1919–1939)," in *Pogromy Żydów na ziemiach polskich w XIX i XX wieku, Tom I: Literatura i sztuka*, ed. Sławomir Buryła (Warszawa: Instytut Historii PAN, 2018), 321–22.

5. Joanna B. Michlic, *Poland's Threatening Other: The Image of the Jew from 1880 to the Present* (Lincoln: University of Nebraska Press, 2008), 114.

6. Ezra Mendelsohn, *The Jews of East Central Europe between the World Wars* (Bloomington: Indiana University Press, 1987), 68.

7. Dariusz Konstantynów, "Antysemickie rysunki z prasy polskiej 1919–1939," in *Obcy i niemili*, 37.

8. Konstantynów, "Pogromy i inne akty przemocy fizycznej wobec Żydów w zwierciadle rysunków z prasy polskiej," 322.

9. Adam Rusek, "Prot i Gerwazy," in *Leksykon polskich bohaterów i serii komiksowych* (Poznań: Centrala, 2010), 203–4.

10. In the early 1930s, one-fifth of the population was still illiterate. Literacy rates were highest in the western regions of Silesia and Poznań and lowest in Lviv and Vilnius. The elderly rural population was particularly plagued by illiteracy. See Cecylia Leszczyńska, "Level of Living of Polish Citizens in the Interwar Period and Its Diversification," *Roczniki Dziejów Społecznych i Gospodarczych* 76 (2016): 112–13.

11. Zofia Trębacz, "Prasa katolicka drugiej połowy lat trzydziestych wobec idei masowej emigracji żydowskiej z Polski," *Studia Historica Gedanensia* 8 (2017): 285.

12. Olaf Bergmann, "Problematyka żydowska w karykaturach polskich czasopism satyrycznych Drugiej Rzeczypospolitej," *Kwartalnik Historii Żydów* 4 (2011): 464.

13. Konstantynów, "Antysemickie rysunki z prasy polskiej," 46. See also Konstantynów, "Pogromy i inne akty przemocy fizycznej wobec Żydów w zwierciadle rysunków z prasy polskiej," 362.

14. Emanuel Melzer, *No Way Out: The Politics of Polish Jewry 1935–1939* (Cincinnati: Hebrew Union College Press, 1997), 24–25.

15. *Wiadomości Literackie* had a mixed record where the "Jewish question" was concerned. For example, while they were vocal opponents of antisemitic violence both in Poland and Germany, they also criticized Jewish nationalism and, what they described as, "separatism." See Magdalena Opalski, "*Wiadomości Literackie*: Polemics on the Jewish Question, 1924–1939," in *The Jews of Poland between Two World Wars*, ed. Yisrael Gutman et al. (Hanover, NH: University Press of New England, 1989), 434–49.

16. Agnieszka Żółkiewska, "Introduction," in *Wolny Ptak. Der Frajer Fojgl. Humor z prasy żydowskiej w Polsce niepodległej* (Warszawa: Żydowski Instytut Historyczny, 2019), 37–38.

17. See, for example, Peter Limb, "Drawing a Line between Play and Power in African Political Cartooning," in *Taking African Cartoons Seriously: Politics, Satire, and Culture*, ed. Peter Limb and Tejumola Olaniyan (East Lansing: Michigan State University Press, 2018), xiii–xlviii; Jenn Burleson Mackay, "What Does Society Owe Political Cartoonists?," *Journalism Studies* 18, no. 1 (2017): 28–44; and Juha Herkman, "Populism in Political Cartoons: Caricatures of Nordic Populist Leaders," *Popular Communication* 17, no. 3 (2019): 252–67.

18. See, for example, Christopher J. Gilbert, *Caricature and National Character: The United States at War* (University Park: Pennsylvania State University Press, 2021); and Jeffrey John Barnes, "A Dictated Policy: Cartoons and the 1936 Strike in Palestine," *Journal of Graphic Novels and Comics* 8, no. 1 (2017): 3–19.

19. Chris Lamb, *Drawn to Extremes: The Use and Abuse of Editorial Cartoons* (New York: Columbia University Press, 2004), 40, 61.

20. Lamb, *Drawn to Extremes*, 4.

21. For the work that does exist, see, for example, Matthew Baigell, *The Implacable Urge to Defame: Cartoon Jews in the American Press, 1877–1935* (Syracuse, NY: Syracuse University Press, 2017); Eva Janáčová and Jakub Hauser, eds., *Visual Antisemitism in Central Europe: Imagery of Hatred* (Oldenbourg: De Gruyter, 2021); Josée Desforges, "Anti-Semitic Caricature in 1930s Montreal: Language and National Stereotypes in Adrien Arcand's *Le Goglu* (1929–1933)," in *Sketches from an Unquiet Country: Canadian Graphic Satire, 1840–1940*, ed. Dominic Hardy, Annie Gérin, and Lora Senechal Carney (Montreal: McGill-Queen's University Press, 2018), 206–31; and David I. Kertzer and Gunnar Mokosch, "In the Name of the Cross: Christianity and Anti-Semitic Propaganda in Nazi Germany and Fascist Italy," *Comparative Studies in Society and History* 62, no. 3 (2020): 456–86, among others.

22. See, for example, John Etty, *Graphic Satire in the Soviet Union: Krokodil's Political Cartoons* (Jackson: University Press of Mississippi, 2019); Kevin J. McKenna, *All the Views Fit to Print: Changing Images of the U.S. in Pravda Political Cartoons, 1917–1991* (New York: Peter Lang Publishing, 2001); Frank Althaus and Mark Sutcliffe, eds., *Drawing the Curtain: The Cold War in Cartoons* (London: Fontanka, 2012); and Katarzyna

Murawska-Muthesius, "1956 in the Cartoonist's Gaze. Fixing the Eastern European Other and Denying the Eastern European Self," *Third Text* 20, no. 2 (2006): 189–99.

23. See, for example, Thomas Milton Kemnitz, "The Cartoon as a Historical Source," *Journal of Interdisciplinary History* 4, no. 1 (1973): 82; Henry Miller, *Politics Personified: Portraiture, Caricature and Visual Culture in Britain, c. 1830–80* (Manchester, UK: Manchester University Press, 2015), 2; and Eriks Bredovskis, "Sketching America: German Depictions of the United States and Woodrow Wilson (1914–1918)," *German Studies Review* 42, no. 3 (2019): 470.

24. Richard Scully and Marian Quartly, "Using Cartoons as Historical Evidence," in *Drawing the Line: Using Cartoons as Historical Evidence*, ed. Richard Scully and Marian Quartly (Victoria: Monash University ePress, 2009), 10. See also Richard Scully and Andrekos Varnava, "Introduction: The Importance of Cartoons, Caricature, and Satirical Art in Imperial Contexts," in *Comic Empires: Imperialism in Cartoons, Caricature, and Satirical Art*, ed. Richard Scully and Andrekos Varnava (Manchester, UK: Manchester University Press, 2020), 3.

25. W. A. Coupe, "The German Cartoon and the Revolution of 1848," *Comparative Studies in Society and History* 9, no. 2 (1967): 141.

26. Kemnitz, "Cartoon as a Historical Source," 86.

27. See the scholarship on the Danish cartoon controversy, including Jytte Klausen, *The Cartoons That Shook the World* (New Haven, CT: Yale University Press, 2009); Sune Lægaard, "The Cartoon Controversy as a Case of Multicultural Recognition," *Contemporary Politics* 13, no. 2 (2007): 147–64; and Anja Kublitz, "The Cartoon Controversy: Creating Muslims in a Danish Setting," *Social Analysis* 54, no. 3 (2010): 107–25.

28. On historical analysis that sees cartoons as intertextual sources conversant with other sources of the period, see Brandon Webb, "Laughter Louder Than Bombs? Apocalyptic Graphic Satire in Cold War Cartooning, 1946–1959," *American Quarterly* 70, no. 2 (2018): 262.

29. Olaf Bergmann, *"Prawdziwa cnota krytyk się nie boi . . .": Karykatura w czasopismach satyrycznych Drugiej Rzeczypospolitej* (Warszawa: DiG, 2012), 24–25.

30. Bohdan Piątkowski, "Uwagi o współpracownikach polskiej prasy humorystyczno-satyrycznej dwudziestolecia międzywojennego," *Rocznik Historii Czasopiśmiennictwa Polskiego* 15, no. 3 (1976): 311.

31. Bergmann, *"Prawdziwa cnota krytyk się nie boi . . .,"* 48. In contrast to Piątkowski above, Bergmann cites a much lower number of twenty-five weeklies. This is incorrect. Comparisons to other states in the region would suggest that the estimate by Piątkowski is more reliable. For example, in a much smaller state of interwar Czechoslovakia, the number of satirical and humor magazines is estimated at ninety. See Jakub Hauser, "Faithful to Tradition: Visual Depictions of Antisemitism in *Humoristické listy* in the 1920s and 1930s," in *Visual Antisemitism in Central Europe*, 147.

32. See Edward Szturm de Sztrem, ed., *Mały Rocznik Statystyczny 1937* (Warszawa: Główny Urząd Statystyczny, 1937), 326.

33. Other major languages were Ukrainian, Yiddish, Ruthenian, Belarussian, and German. Many among the Jewish and Ukrainian populations, in particular, were bilingual or

trilingual. See Celia Stopnicka Heller, *On the Edge of Destruction: Jews of Poland Between the Two World Wars* (Detroit: Wayne State University Press, 1993), 68.

34. On literacy rates, see Leszczyńska, "Level of Living of Polish Citizens," 112–13. For the specific figures of urban versus rural population, see *Pierwszy powszechny spis Rzeczypospolitej Polskiej z dnia 30 września 1921 roku* (Warszawa: Główny Urząd Statystyczny Rzeczypospolitej Polskiej, 1927), 5; and *Drugi powszechny spis ludności z dn. 9. XII. 1931 r.* (Warszawa: Główny Urząd Statystyczny Rzeczypospolitej Polskiej, 1938), 1.

35. Andrzej Paczkowski, "Prasa Drugiej Rzeczypospolitej (1918–1939): ogólna charakterystyka statystyczna," *Rocznik Historii Czasopiśmiennictwa Polskiego* 11, no. 1 (1972): 60.

36. Bergmann, *"Prawdziwa cnota krytyk się nie boi . . .,"* 54.

37. Andrzej Paczkowski, *Prasa codzienna Warszawy w latach 1918–1939* (Warszawa: Państwowy Instytut Wydawniczy, 1983), 144.

38. For example, the weekly *Mucha* cost 20 groszy per issue, but the quarterly subscription was only 3,50 zloty.

39. See Leszczyńska, "Level of Living of Polish Citizens," 103–4.

40. Bergmann, *"Prawdziwa cnota krytyk się nie boi . . .,"* 56.

41. Hanna Górska and Eryk Lipiński, *Z dziejów karykatury polskiej* (Warszawa: Wiedza Powszechna, 1977), 194.

42. Adam Rusek, *Leksykon polskich bohaterów i serii komiksowych* (Poznań: Centrala, 2010), 83–85.

43. Ignacy Witz, "O karykaturze," in *50 lat karykatury polskiej: 1900–1950*, ed. Ignacy Witz and Jerzy Zaruba (Warszawa: Wydawnictwo Arkady, 1961), 24–25.

44. Górska and Lipiński, *Z dziejów karykatury polskiej*, 213.

45. Górska and Lipiński, *Z dziejów karykatury polskiej*, 231–32.

46. Górska and Lipiński, *Z dziejów karykatury polskiej*, 225.

47. Bergmann, *"Prawdziwa cnota krytyk się nie boi . . .,"* 56.

48. Illustrator Jerzy Zaruba says that *Szpilki*'s circulation was only two thousand copies per week. See Jerzy Zaruba, "Zamiast wstępu," in *50 lat karykatury polskiej: 1900–1950*, 11. The mainstream *Mucha* and *Wróble* had a higher circulation of approximately thirty thousand to forty thousand copies each.

49. On the anonymity of *Mucha*'s artists, see Górska and Lipiński, *Z dziejów karykatury polskiej*, 229.

50. Mendelsohn, *Jews of East Central Europe*, 68.

51. Mendelsohn, *Jews of East Central Europe*, 68–69. See also Michlic, *Poland's Threatening Other*, 73–74; and Mikołaj Stanisław Kunicki, *Between the Brown and the Red: Nationalism, Catholicism, and Communism in Twentieth-Century Poland—The Politics of Bolesław Piasecki* (Athens: Ohio University Press, 2012), 17.

52. Szymon Rudnicki, "Anti-Jewish Legislation in Interwar Poland," in *Antisemitism and Its Opponents in Modern Poland*, ed. Robert Blobaum (Ithaca, NY: Cornell University Press, 2005), 160–61.

53. See, for example, Kenneth B. Moss, *An Unchosen People: Jewish Political Reckoning in Interwar Poland* (Cambridge, MA: Harvard University Press, 2021), 79.

54. Eva Plach, *The Clash of Moral Nations: Cultural Politics in Piłsudski's Poland, 1926–1935* (Athens: Ohio University Press, 2006), 150.

55. Paul Brykczynski, *Primed for Violence: Murder, Antisemitism, and Democratic Politics in Interwar Poland* (Madison: University of Wisconsin Press, 2016), 83–84.

56. For recent scholarship, see Brykczynski, *Primed for Violence*; Moss, *Unchosen People*; Natalia Aleksiun, "Jewish Students and Christian Corpses in Interwar Poland: Playing with the Language of Blood Libel," *Jewish History* 26, no. 3–4 (2012): 327–42; and Natalia Aleksiun, "Christian Corpses for Christians! Dissecting the Anti-Semitism behind the Cadaver Affair of the Second Polish Republic," *East European Politics and Societies and Cultures* 25, no. 3 (2011): 393–409.

57. Mendelsohn, *Jews of East Central Europe*, 82.

58. Brykczynski, *Primed for Violence*, 43.

59. Krzywiec, "Antysemickie karykatury od poł. XIX w. do I wojny światowej," 14.

60. See, for example, Bergmann, *"Prawdziwa cnota krytyk się nie boi . . .,"* 222–24.

61. Bergmann, *"Prawdziwa cnota krytyk się nie boi . . .,"* 63, 65, 68, 71.

62. Bergmann, *"Prawdziwa cnota krytyk się nie boi . . .,"* 220.

63. Scully and Varnava, "Introduction," 5.

64. Afaf Lutfi Al-Sayyid Marsot, "The Cartoon in Egypt," *Comparative Studies in Society and History* 13, no. 1 (1971): 15.

65. On censorship in other contexts, see, for example, Lamb, *Drawn to Extremes*, 72–73; Charles Press, *The Political Cartoon* (Madison, NJ: Fairleigh Dickinson University Press, 1981), 54; and Limb, "Drawing a Line between Play and Power," xix.

66. On anti-Judaism in earlier visual culture, see the collected edition by Mitchell B. Merback, ed., *Beyond the Yellow Badge: Anti-Judaism and Antisemitism in Medieval and Early Modern Visual Culture* (Leiden: Brill, 2008). On contemporary antisemitic cartoons that use some of these medieval tropes, see, for example, Joël Kotek, *Cartoons and Extremism: Israel and the Jews in Arab and Western Media* (Edgware: Vallentine Mitchell, 2008); and Jerome Bourdon and Sandrine Boudana, "Controversial Cartoons in the Israeli-Palestinian Conflict: Cries of Outrage and Dialogue of the Deaf," *International Journal of Press/Politics* 21, no. 2 (2018): 188–208.

67. See Scully and Varnava, "Introduction," 11.

68. See Julia Secklehner, "Simple Entertainment? Die Muskete and 'Weak' Antisemitism in Interwar Vienna," in *Visual Antisemitism in Central Europe*, 124.

CHAPTER 1: THE VOICE OF THE STATE

1. AAN, PZWDziCz, *Moje Pisemko; Mucha; Muzyka* . . . (1928–1938), sygn. 2/64/0/8, folder 148, "Notatka o zmarłej ś.p. Marji Buchnerowej," no date, p. 54.

2. AAN, PZWDziCz, *Moje Pisemko; Mucha; Muzyka*, "Notatka o Władysławie Buchnerze," no date, p. 51.

3. Eryk Lipiński, *Warszawa w karykaturze* (Warszawa: Państwowe Wydawnictwo Naukowe, 1983), 17.

4. Eryk Lipiński, *Drzewo Szpilkowe* (Warszawa: Czytelnik, 1976), 19.

5. AAN, PZWDziCz, *Moje Pisemko; Mucha; Muzyka*, Władysław Buchner, "Memorjał w sprawie ogłoszeń rządowych dla pism," 4 December 1933, p. 45.

6. Some scholars call *Mucha* "centrist"; this is certainly correct of the 1920s, but no longer the case after 1935. See Jakub Szałek, "'I śmiech niekiedy może być nauką': Polska polityka międzywojenna w czasopiśmie satyrycznym Mucha," *Media—Biznes—Kultura: Dziennikarstwo i komunikacja społeczna* 4 (2011): 112.

7. AAN, PZWDziCz, *Moje Pisemko; Mucha; Muzyka*, Letter to *Mucha* from the Polish Association of the Publishers of Daily and Periodical Press in Warsaw, 6 February 1929, p. 32.

8. AAN, PZWDziCz, *Moje Pisemko; Mucha; Muzyka*, Letter from the Administrative Department of *Mucha* to the Polish Association of the Publishers of Daily and Periodical Press in Warsaw, 8 May 1937, p. 49.

9. *Mucha* was established in 1868 by a Warsaw bookseller named Józef Kaufmann. At first, it was published intermittently, becoming a regular weekly feature in 1871. For an announcement of the first issue to be published in January 1871, see "Wiadomości z pola literatury I sztuki," *Kłosy*, 26 November-8 December 1870, 366.

10. Adam Rovner, *In the Shadow of Zion: Promised Lands Before Israel* (New York: New York University Press, 2014), 137.

11. Zofia Trębacz, *Nie tylko Palestyna: Polskie plany emigracyjne wobec Żydów 1935–1939* (Warszawa: Żydowski Instytut Historyczny, 2018), 210–11, 222.

12. "Wymiana produktów kolonialnych," *Mucha*, 7 January 1938, 4.

13. "Na Kongresie Przyjaciół Ligi Narodów," *Mucha*, 4 March 1938, 3.

14. "Kwestja żydowska na konferencji w Londynie," *Mucha*, 2 December 1938, 1.

15. For more of *Mucha*'s cartoons from the period that use national personification, see, for example, "Podział Palestyny," *Mucha*, 23 July 1937, 1; "Oszczędna Marianna," *Mucha*, 6 August 1937, 4; "Podział Palestyny," *Mucha*, 20 August 1937, 5; "Kłopoty Francji," *Mucha*, 10 December 1937, 5; "Ex-budowniczowie z Wersalu," *Mucha*, 7 October 1938, 6; "Jesienna wyprzedaż," *Mucha*, 28 October 1938, 4; and "Po aneksji Czech," *Mucha*, 24 March 1939, 3.

16. Miles Taylor, "John Bull and the Iconography of Public Opinion in England c. 1712–1929," *Past & Present* 134 (1992): 98–100.

17. Stephen Tuffnell, "'The International Siamese Twins': The Iconography of Anglo-American Inter-Imperialism," in *Comic Empires*, ed. Scully and Varnava, 116.

18. Douglas M. Klahr, "Symbiosis between Caricature and Caption at the Outbreak of War: Representations of the Allegorical Figure Marianne in 'Kladderadatsch,'" *Zeitschrift für Kunstgeschichte* 74 (2011): 546.

19. See, for example, McKenna, *All the Views Fit to Print*, 39; Bredovskis, "Sketching America," 475, 478, 488; Dobrinka Parusheva, "In the Mirror of Satire: The End of World War I in Bulgarian Caricatures," *Études Balkaniques* 2 (2019): 258; and Kees Ribbens, "Picturing Anti-Semitism in the Nazi-Occupied Netherlands: Anti-Jewish Stereotyping in a Racist Second World War Comic Strip," *Journal of Modern Jewish Studies* 17, no. 1 (2018): 12.

20. For a discussion of several recent cartoons featuring Uncle Sam, see, for example, Lamb, *Drawn to Extremes*, 1–4, 23.

21. Taylor, "John Bull and the Iconography of Public Opinion," 125.

22. David Low, "Streamlining the Cartoon," *New York Times*, 7 February 1937, 26.

23. National personification did occasionally appear in Polish Cold War cartoons, particularly among the older artists who debuted after World War I. This includes one of

the doyens of Polish caricature Jerzy Zaruba (1891–1977). See, for example, his post-World War II cartoons for *Robotnik* (*The Worker*). AMK, Jerzy Zaruba PF, Newspaper Clippings and Drawings. See cartoons "Dzikie kaczki"; "'Komedia francuska'"; "Rządy kupuję, rządy"; "Marshall—Aeroplan"; "Wolność—Równość—Braterstwo"; and "Wysypka wuja Sama."

24. Górska and Lipiński, *Z dziejów karykatury polskiej*, 229–30.
25. "Antyżydowska uchwała 'Ozonu,'" *Mucha*, 10 June 1938, 3.
26. Melzer, *No Way Out*, 30.
27. Melzer, *No Way Out*, 30.
28. For another cartoon on this, see also "Miejsce dla Żydów," *Mucha*, 9 December 1938, 5.
29. Trębacz, *Nie tylko Palestyna*, 56.
30. Mateusz Sroka, "Emigracja Żydów polskich w latach 1918–1939. Zarys problematyki," *Państwo i Społeczeństwo* 10, no. 2 (2010): 118.
31. Eli Lederhendler, "The Interrupted Chain: Traditional Receiver Countries, Migration Regimes, and the East European Jewish Diaspora, 1918–39," *East European Jewish Affairs* 44, no. 2–3 (2014): 179.
32. "Anglia nie wpuszcza Żydów do Palestyny," *Mucha*, 16 December 1938, 5.
33. "Appeal Voiced in Polish Parliament," *JTA*, 25 January 1938.
34. For studies on antisemitism in Romania, see, for example, Leon Volovici, *Nationalist Ideology and Antisemitism: The Case of Romanian Intellectuals in the 1930s* (London: Butterworth-Heinemann, 1991); William Brustein and Amy Ronnkvist, "The Roots of Anti-Semitism: Romania before the Holocaust," *Journal of Genocide Research* 4, no. 2 (2004): 211–35; and Raphael Vago, "The Traditions of Antisemitism in Romania," *Patterns of Prejudice* 27, no. 1 (1993): 107–19.
35. See cartoon "Kolonie," *Mucha*, 18 November 1938, 4.
36. Waldemar Michowicz, *Walka dyplomacji polskiej przeciwko traktatowi mniejszościowemu w Lidze Narodów w 1934 roku* (Łódź: Łódzkie Towarzystwo Naukowe, 1963), 73.
37. AAN, MSZ, Press Office, sygn. 7355, Microfilm no B23692, P.VI.N. 329/1/8/36, "Notatka z rozmowy z Geheimratem Aschmannem, odbytej w dn. 10 grudnia 1935 r. w sprawie konferencji prasowej," 20 January 1936.
38. For a discussion of these more problematic areas of representation, see, for example, AAN, MSZ, Press Office, sygn. 7360, Microfilm no B23692, MZ.3.22.10, Summary of Polish-German Press Talks, 23 October 1935.
39. AAN, MSZ, Press Office, sygn. 7360, Microfilm no B23692, P. Ztg. Pol. 708/11.36, German Embassy to Press Office of Foreign Ministry of Poland, 18 November 1936.
40. AAN, MSZ, Press Office, sygn. 7360, Microfilm no B23692, P.VI.N.320/79, Press Office of Foreign Ministry of Poland to the Polish Ministry of Interior Affairs Social and Political Office, 4 December 1936.
41. Marian Wojciechowski, *Stosunki polsko-niemieckie 1933–1938* (Poznań: Instytut Zachodni, 1965), 109.
42. "O Żydach," *Mucha*, 7 October 1938, 2.
43. "O Żydach," *Mucha*, 25 March 1938, 5.

44. Jan Meysztowicz, *Czas przeszły dokonany: wspomnienia ze służby w Ministerstwie Spraw Zagranicznych w latach 1932–1939* (Warszawa: Instytut Prasy i Wydawnictw "Novum," 1989), 115.

45. Wiktor Tomir Drymmer, "Zagadnienie żydowskie w Polsce w latach 1935–1939 (Wspomnienie z pracy w Ministerstwie Spraw Zagranicznych)," *Zeszyty historyczne* 13 (1968): 68.

46. Drymmer, "Zagadnienie żydowskie w Polsce," 70.

47. Daniel Kupfert Heller, *Jabotinsky's Children: Polish Jews and the Rise of Right-Wing Zionism* (Princeton, NJ: Princeton University Press, 2017), 227.

48. Jerzy Łazor, "Wywóz polskiego sprzętu wojskowego do Palestyny w okresie międzywojennym," in *Gospodarka i społeczeństwo a wojskowość na ziemiach polskich*, ed. Tomasz Głowiński and Krzysztof Popiński (Wrocław: Gajt, 2010), 217–18.

49. Jan Karski and Maciej Wierzyński, *Emisariusz własnymi słowami. Zapis rozmów przeprowadzonych w latach 1995–1997 w Waszyngtonie emitowanych w Głosie Ameryki* (Warszawa: PWN, 2012), 16–22.

50. "Kłusak palestyński," *Mucha*, 16 September 1938, 8.

51. "Dobry środek," *Mucha*, 3 March 1939, 2.

52. "Na Nalewkach," *Mucha*, 3 March 1939, 6.

53. Julia Secklehner, "Simple Entertainment? Die Muskete and 'Weak' Antisemitism in Interwar Vienna," in *Visual Antisemitism in Central Europe*, 126.

54. Sandy Sufian, "Anatomy of the 1936–39 Revolt: Images of the Body in Political Cartoons of Mandatory Palestine," *Journal of Palestine Studies* 37, no. 2 (2008): 27–28.

55. "Milion projektów emigracji żydowskiej," *Mucha*, 10 February 1939, 5. On a similar topic, see the satirical reworking of Mickiewicz's "Koncert nad koncertami," *Mucha*, 5 August 1938, 4.

56. Czesław Miłosz, *Wyprawa w dwudziestolecie* (Kraków: Wydawnictwo Literackie, 1999), 273.

57. Brustein and Ronnkvist, "Roots of Anti-Semitism," 211–12.

58. "Endecy już apelują do premiera o zamknięcie granicy przed Żydami z Rumunii," *5-ta rano*, 14 January 1938, 10.

59. "Nie wpuszczać żydów z Rumunii. Słuszna uchwała 'Pracy Polskiej,'" *Dziennik Wileński*, 5 January 1938, 2; "Wiec," *Kurjer Warszawski*, 31 January 1938, 5; "Akcja Stron. Narodowego przeciw przyjazdowi żydów z Rumunii," *Czas*, 1 February 1938, 4; and "Akcja Stron. Narodowego przeciw przyjazdowi żydów z Rumunii," *Pielgrzym*, 5 February 1938, 2.

60. "Zamknąć granicę rumuńską!," *ABC: Nowiny Codzienne*, 6 January 1938, 1; "Zamknięcia granicy dla żydów żąda kupiectwo płockie," *ABC: Nowiny Codzienne*, 4 February 1938, 3; and "Zamknąć granicę," *Gazeta Radomska*, 9 January 1938, 1.

61. "Bukareszt—Palestyna via Praga," *Czas*, 8 January 1938, 2; and "Dwa pociągi żydów z Rumunii przybyły do Czechosłowacji," *Dziennik Wileński*, 8 January 1938, 1.

62. "Praha Denies Influx from Rumania [sic]," *JTA*, 5 January 1938.

63. "Poland Sees No Influx from Rumania [sic]," *JTA*, 7 January 1938. For the same statement in Polish and Polish Jewish newspapers, see, for example, "Żydzi rumuńscy nie ujawniają tendencji wyjazdu do Polski," *Głos Poranny*, 6 January 1938, 1; and "Żydzi z Rumunii nie osiedlą się w Polsce," *Nasz Przegląd*, 3 February 1938, 12.

64. See, for example, "Donkiszockie protesty endeków z powodu Żydów rumuńskich," *5-ta rano*, 10 January 1938, 3.

65. "Na granicy polsko-rumuńskiej," *Mucha*, 21 January 1938, 4.

66. Eddy Portnoy, *Bad Rabbi and Other Strange but True Stories from the Yiddish Press* (Stanford, CA: Stanford University Press, 2018), 14.

67. Portnoy, *Bad Rabbi*, 14.

68. This was also implied in a short satirical text by *Mucha* that envisaged Nalewki to be the next colonial territory to be settled with Jewish refugees. See "Końcowe słowa," *Mucha*, 9 December 1938, 4.

69. "Niedziałkowski w 'Robotniku' proponuje udzielenia gościny uciekinierom z sąsiednich krajów," *Mucha*, 8 July 1938, 4.

70. The article was authored by a PPS activist and a chief journalist of the socialist *Robotnik* newspaper, Mieczysław Niedziałkowski. I was not able to locate the specific article, but Niedziałkowski was often attacked by pro-Sanacja outlets for criticizing Poland's indecisive stance toward Nazi Germany. See, for example, two articles from that period: "Wizje redaktora Niedziałkowskiego," *Dziennik Poznański*, 3 June 1938, 2; and "Dobrze mówi red. Niedziałkowski," *Dziennik Poznański*, 5 June 1938, 3. For another critique of the *Robotnik* newspaper by *Mucha*, see "Biedny 'Robotnik,'" *Mucha*, 1 July 1938, 4.

71. Drymmer, "Zagadnienie żydowskie w Polsce w latach," 65.

72. Trębacz, *Nie tylko Palestyna*, 36.

73. Drymmer, "Zagadnienie żydowskie w Polsce w latach," 65. See also Jerzy Tomaszewski, *Preludium Zagłady: Wygnanie Żydów polskich z Niemiec w 1938 r.* (Warszawa: PWN, 1998), 95.

74. "Ask Warsaw to Assist Jews of Polish Origin," *JTA*, 18 March 1938; and "Poland Enacts Law Denationalizing Thousands Living Abroad," *JTA*, 30 March 1938.

75. "Polish Jews Flee Austria; Return to Warsaw," *JTA*, 15 March 1938; and "1,500 Refugees from Reich, 25,000 Polish Jews in Austria," *JTA*, 16 March 1938.

76. "792 Jews Return to Poland from Austria," *JTA*, 2 May 1938.

77. Tatjana Lichtenstein, *Zionists in Interwar Czechoslovakia: Minority Nationalism and the Politics of Belonging* (Bloomington: Indiana University Press, 2016), 48, 126.

78. "Przyrost naturalny," *Mucha*, 22 April 1938, 7.

79. On jokes and suspension of disbelief, see Norman N. Holland, "The 'Willing Suspension of Disbelief' Revisited," *Centennial Review* 11, no. 1 (1967): 7.

80. Bonnie M. Harris, "From German Jews to Polish Refugees: Germany's Polenaktion and the Zbaszyn Deportations of October 1938," *Kwartalnik Historii Żydów* 2 (2009): 179–80.

81. Harris, "From German Jews to Polish Refugees," 179–80.

82. Harris, "From German Jews to Polish Refugees," 182.

83. Harris, "From German Jews to Polish Refugees," 187.

84. Wojciech Śleszyński, *Obóz odosobnienia w Berezie Kartuskiej: 1934–1939* (Białystok: Instytut Historii Uniwersytetu w Białymstoku, 2003), 87–88; and Michał Szreffel, "Bereza Kartuska jako przykład więzienia politycznego," *Studia Iuridica Toruniensia* 1 (2010): 218. See also "Poland Internes Refugees, Foreigners Overstaying Leave," *JTA*, 16 June 1938.

85. Alina Molisak, "Polenaktion—Zbąszyń . . . Na przykładzie dyskursu publicystycznego 'Naszego Przeglądu,'" *Kwartalnik Historii Żydów* 1, no. 273 (2020): 272.

86. Michal Frankl, "Citizenship of No Man's Land? Jewish Refugee Relief in Zbąszyń and East-Central Europe, 1938–1939," *S:I.M.O.N. Shoah: Intervention, Methods, Documentation* 8, no. 2 (2020): 46.

87. Molisak, "Polenaktion—Zbąszyń,'" 275. See also "Inferno w Zbąszyniu," *5-ta rano*, 28 November 1938, 6; and "W obozie pod Zbąszyniem," *Chwila*, 19 November 1938, 4.

88. Henryk Szalewicz, "Wskrzeszone średniowiecze," *Czarno na białem*, 4 December 1938, 7. The same article was reprinted in *Chwila*, 7 December 1938, 8.

89. Włodzimierz Lencki, "Prawda, której wstyd," *Nowy Dziennik*, 25 November 1938, 7.

90. See, for example, Małgorzata Domagalska, *Antysemityzm dla inteligencji? Kwestia żydowska w publicystyce Adolfa Nowaczyńskiego na łamach "Myśli Narodowej" (1921–1934) i "Prosto z mostu" (1935–1939) (na tle porównawczym)* (Warszawa: Żydowski Instytut Historyczny, 2004), 237.

91. See "Żydzi z Niemiec podwoili liczbę mieszkańców w Zbąszyniu," *Głos Narodowy*, 25 November 1938, 3; "W Zbąszyniu jest 6300 Żydów," *Wielkopolanin*, 27 November 1938, 1; "Awantury w obozie uchodźców w Zbąszyniu," *Czas*, 17 December 1938, 8; "Zbąszyń," *Kurier Poznański*, 7 December 1938, 8; and "W Zbąszyniu bez zmian," *Dziennik Poznański*, 1 December 1938, 4.

92. See "Żydzi z Niemiec podwoili liczbę mieszkańców w Zbąszyniu," 3.

93. "Jak Żydzi uciekają," *Mucha*, 21 October 1938, 5.

94. "Znowu," *Mucha*, 6 January 1939, 8.

95. "List Żydów do Niemców," *Mucha*, 24 February 1939, 4.

96. Trębacz, *Nie tylko Palestyna*, 38; and Molisak, "Polenaktion—Zbąszyń," 278.

97. Trębacz, *Nie tylko Palestyna*, 38; and Molisak, "Polenaktion—Zbąszyń," 278.

98. Andrei Oişteanu, *Inventing the Jew: Antisemitic Stereotypes in Romanian and Other Central-East European Cultures*, transl. Mirela Adăscăliţei, with foreword by Moshe Idel (Lincoln: University of Nebraska Press, 2009), 5.

99. On the Polonization of economic life, see Melzer, *No Way Out*, 44. On the perception of Jews as the enemy within, see Michlic, *Poland's Threatening Other*, 116.

100. "Jak powinno być w Polsce," *Mucha*, 25 March 1938, 8.

101. "O Żydach," *Mucha*, 30 September 1938, 8.

102. "Ich marzenie," *Mucha*, 12 August 1938, 2.

103. See Alina Cała, "Zapożyczenia z mowy żydowskiej w narracji antysemickiej," *Studia Litteraria et Historica* 1 (2012): 2.

104. Modras, *Catholic Church and Antisemitism*, 224–25.

105. Eugenia Prokop-Janiec, *Polish-Jewish Literature in the Interwar Years* (Syracuse, NY: Syracuse University Press, 2003), 62. See also Bernard Goldstein, *Twenty Years with the Jewish Labor Bund: A Memoir of Interwar Poland* (West Lafayette, IN: Purdue University Press, 2016), 301.

106. Yehuda Bauer, *My Brother's Keeper: A History of the American Jewish Joint Distribution Committee, 1929–1939* (Philadelphia: Jewish Publication Society of America, 1974), 190.

107. For similar examples from the 1930s print media, see David Nichols and Emily Turner-Graham, "Bluey and Sol: Antisemitic Humour in a German-Australian Outpost, 1937–1939," *Immigrants & Minorities* 33 (2015): 234. For examples from the antisemitic press in the 1940s, see Ribbens, "Picturing Anti-Semitism in the Nazi-Occupied Netherlands," 16–17.

108. On such stereotypes, see Julie L. Mell, *The Myth of the Medieval Jewish Moneylender*, vol. 1 (New York: Palgrave Macmillan, 2017), 50–55.
109. "Gąbki," *Mucha*, 3 June 1938, 5.
110. "Krwisty naród," *Mucha*, 27 January 1939, 5.
111. "Panie Salomon," *Mucha*, 2 December 1938, 8.
112. Baigell, *Implacable Urge to Defame*, 20.
113. Baigell, *Implacable Urge to Defame*, 30.
114. "Wszechstronni," *Mucha*, 3 June 1938, 3. For far-right publications that used the same stereotype, see "Czyny mówią zupełnie co innego!," *Pręgierz*, 23 April 1939, 3; and an installment of a serialized novel from the period: Stefan Kiedrzyński, "Grzech powszedni," *Polska Zbrojna*, 3 August 1938, 8.
115. "Co pisała przed wojną 'Mucha' o tak zwanych loteriach żydowskich," *Mucha*, 10 June 1938, 4.
116. "Co pisała przed wojną 'Mucha' o tak zwanych loteriach żydowskich," 4.
117. Alina Cała, *Wizerunek Żyda w polskiej kulturze ludowej* (Warszawa: Wydawnictwo Uniwersytetu Warszawskiego, 1992), 17–19.
118. Portnoy, *Bad Rabbi*, 17. See also Adam Kopciowski, "Półświatek przestępczy na łamach lubelskiej prasy jidysz (1918–1939)," *Studia Judaica* 17, no. 33 (2014): 57–84.
119. Melzer, *No Way Out*, 62, 80.
120. "Nad polskim morzem," *Mucha*, 1 July 1938, 7.
121. See, for example, Władysław Wan, "Wśród czarnych chałatów. Wrażenia z dzielnicy żydowskiej w Warszawie," *Dziennik Bydgoski*, 19 April 1936, 7.
122. Sander Gilman, *The Jew's Body* (New York: Routledge, 1991), 203.
123. "Na plaży," *Mucha*, 29 July 1938, 6.
124. See Eryk Lipiński, "Prasa doniosła . . .," *Szpilki*, 21 August 1938, 3.
125. Dariusz Konstantynów, "Gdynia i Żydzi w antysemickich rysunkach z prasy II Rzeczypospolitej," *Porta Aurea* 19 (2020): 186.
126. See Eva Janáčová, "Spa Antisemitism in Bohemia and Moravia," in *Visual Antisemitism in Central Europe*, 71, 73.
127. Daniel Tilles, *British Fascist Antisemitism and Jewish Responses, 1932–40* (London: Bloomsbury, 2015), 50. For a discussion of similar cartoons in *Puck* in the nineteenth century, see Baigell, *Implacable Urge to Defame*, 21–25.
128. Lamb, *Drawn to Extremes*, 51.
129. Lamb, *Drawn to Extremes*, 54.
130. "Jest na wszystko rada," *Mucha*, 4 February 1938, 2.
131. "Obrus," *Mucha*, 29 July 1938, 8.
132. "Po co mam czytać?," *Mucha*, 1 July 1938, 5.
133. "W cukierni na Genszegass," *Mucha*, 11 March 1938, 7; and cartoon "W Krynicy," *Mucha*, 15 July 1938, 8.
134. Mark M. Smith, "Transcending, Othering, Detecting: Smell, Premodernity, Modernity," *Postmedieval: A Journal of Medieval Cultural Studies* 3, no. 4 (2012): 385.
135. For a discussion of medieval conceptions of *foetor judaicus*, see Dan Cohn-Sherbok, *The Crucified Jew: Twenty Centuries of Christian Anti-Semitism* (London: HarperCollins, 1992), 54–55.

136. Smith, "Transcending, Othering, Detecting," 388. See also Benjamin Aldes Wurgaft, "Incensed: Food Smells and Ethnic Tension," *Gastronomica* 6, no. 2 (2006): 59.

137. Frank Felsenstein, *Anti-Semitic Stereotypes: A Paradigm of Otherness in English Popular Culture, 1660–1830* (Baltimore: Johns Hopkins University Press, 1995), 257–58.

138. Smith, "Transcending, Othering, Detecting," 385.

139. See, for example, an examination of similar discourses being perpetrated by the British Union of Fascists: Tilles, *British Fascist Antisemitism and Jewish Responses*, 46, 58–59.

140. Gilman, *The Jew's Body*, 12.

141. "Red. Miedziński stwierdził brak wspólnego języka pomiędzy Żydami a Polakami," *Mucha*, 24 June 1938, 4.

142. Gilman, *The Jew's Body*, 11.

143. Gilman, *The Jew's Body*, 20.

144. Prokop-Janiec, *Polish-Jewish Literature in the Interwar Years*, 65.

145. Prokop-Janiec, *Polish-Jewish Literature in the Interwar Years*, 48–49.

146. *Mały Rocznik Statystyczny 1939* (Warszawa: Główny Urząd Statystyczny, 1939), 23.

147. Iwo Pogonowski, *Poland: A Historical Atlas* (New York: Dorset Press, 1989), 226.

148. For a recollection about the Winersztok columns fifty years later, see Józef Retman, "O, Józek przyszedł!," *Odgłosy*, 4 June 1988, 15.

149. See, for example, "Poseł Winersztok ma głos" in *Mucha*, 13 August 1937, 7; *Mucha*, 1 October 1937, 3; *Mucha*, 5 November 1937, 3; *Mucha*, 22 April 1938, 3; *Mucha*, 23 September 1938, 7; *Mucha*, 4 November 1938, 3; and *Mucha*, 27 January 1939, 7.

150. Gilman, *The Jew's Body*, 21.

151. Maria Strycharska-Brzezina, *Polszczyzna Żydów* (Warszawa: PWN, 1986), 84.

152. Teresa Torańska, *Trzy rozmowy Teresy Torańskiej: śmierć spóźnia się o minutę* (Warszawa: Agora S.A., 2010), 110.

153. For an epigram about Jews protesting discrimination in Poland, see "Żydzi," *Mucha*, 4 November 1938, 5.

154. See also "W sądzie," *Mucha*, 15 July 1938, 7; and "Na Krakowskim Przedmieściu," *Mucha*, 31 March 1939, 2. Eugenia Prokop-Janiec shows that Polish Jewish writers for whom Polish was their first language were also accused of polluting it. See Prokop-Janiec, *Polish-Jewish Literature in the Interwar Years*, 69–70.

155. Torańska, *Trzy rozmowy Teresy Torańskiej*, 110.

156. On the "postvernacularity" of Yiddish, see Jeffrey Shandler, *Adventures in Yiddishland: Postvernacular Language and Culture* (Berkeley: University of California Press, 2008), 4–5.

157. Majer Bałaban, "Abraham Buchner," in *Polski Słownik Biograficzny. Tom III* (Kraków: Polska Akademia Umiejętności, 1937), 77.

158. For similarities with fascist discourse, see Tilles, *British Fascist Antisemitism and Jewish Responses*, 57.

159. "Czy Polacy nienawidzą Żydów?," *Mucha*, 29 July 1938, 7. See also a cartoon criticizing democratic circles who were vocal about Jewish rights: "Z gazet," *Mucha*, 25 February 1938, 5.

160. "Ghetto ghetto," *Mucha*, 23 December 1938, 4.

161. "Ghetto ghetto," 4.

162. "W cukierni na Genszegass," *Mucha*, 16 September 1938, 7.

163. See Lipiński, *Warszawa w karykaturze*, 17; and Zaruba, "Zamiast wstępu," in *50 lat karykatury polskiej: 1900–1950*, 10. See also Górska and Lipiński, *Z dziejów karykatury polskiej*, 230–31.

164. Secklehner, "Simple Entertainment?," 124.

165. Konstantynów, "Pogromy i inne akty przemocy fizycznej wobec Żydów w zwierciadle rysunków z prasy polskiej (1919–1939)," 362.

166. Górska and Lipiński, *Z dziejów karykatury polskiej*, 229.

167. AMK, Bronisław Fedyszyn PF, Personal Questionnaire (handwritten), unsigned and undated.

168. See *Obcy i niemili*, 73–75. Some sources note that his musical training took place in Russia, not Warsaw. See AMK, Bronisław Fedyszyn PF, Personal Questionnaire (handwritten), unsigned and undated.

169. *Obcy i niemili*, 73–75.

170. *Obcy i niemili*, 101. See also A. Wierzbicka and U. Makowska, "Rydygier Stanisław," in *Słownik artystów polskich*, vol. 9, ed. Małgorzata Biernacka (Warszawa: Instytut Sztuki Polskiej Akademii Nauk, 2013), 362–63.

CHAPTER 2: LOCAL STRUGGLES

1. APKa, SPK, sygn. 11/3/0/13/590, Stronnictwo Narodowe 1930–1939, Letter from the Headquarters of District Police in Kalisz (Criminal Office) to Chief Prosecutor of Magistrate Court I in Kalisz, 11 December 1935.

2. APKa, SPK, sygn. 11/3/0/13/590, Stronnictwo Narodowe 1930–1939, Letter from the Łódź District Office (Social and Political Department) to All Starosts of the Łódź District, 4 September 1935.

3. APKa, SPK, sygn. 11/3/0/13/590, Stronnictwo Narodowe 1930–1939, Note on National Party's Call to the Youth, no date.

4. Aleksander Pakentreger, *Żydzi w Kaliszu w latach 1918–1939: problemy polityczne i społeczne* (Warszawa: PIW, 1988), 59–62.

5. Konstantynów, "Antysemickie rysunki z prasy polskiej 1919–1939," 37.

6. A. L., "Teraz kolej na rząd," *Pokrzywy*, 15 August 1938, 4.

7. Bergmann, "Problematyka żydowska w karykaturach polskich czasopism satyrycznych Drugiej Rzeczypospolitej," 464.

8. Bergmann, *"Prawdziwa cnota krytyk się nie boi . . . ,"* 50.

9. Aleksander Pakentreger, "Statystyka Żydów m. Kalisza ocalałych po II wojnie światowej," *Biuletyn Żydowskiego Instytutu Historycznego* 4, no. 96 (1975): 81.

10. "Rozpogodzić śmiechem oblicza!," *Pokrzywy*, 1 June 1937, 2.

11. "Dobroczynna pokrzywa," *Pokrzywy*, 1 June 1937, 3.

12. "Zarząd miasta Kalisza na usługach żydów," *Pokrzywy*, 1 June 1937, 7.

13. "Czarna lista żydofilów," *Pokrzywy*, 1 June 1937, 7.

14. "Wróble," *Pokrzywy*, 15 June 1937, 3.

15. "Ze Zduńskiej Woli," *Pokrzywy*, 1 September 1937, 7.

16. "Ze Zduńskiej Woli," 7.
17. "Niedzielny handel—w Zd. Woli," *Pokrzywy*, 1 September 1937, 7.
18. Heber was a well-known figure in the trading community. Earlier in the 1930s, he was also active in the Łódź Chamber of Commerce. See "Obwieszczenie," *Monitor Polski*, 1 August 1931, 3.
19. Pakentreger, *Żydzi w Kaliszu w latach* 1918–1939, 60. See also Aleksander Pakentreger, "Sytuacja gospodarcza ludności żydowskiej Kalisza w latach kryzysu gospodarczego 1929–1935 i w okresie pokryzysowym," *Biuletyn Żydowskiego Instytutu Historycznego* 1–2 (1985): 63.
20. "Obrońcy żydowskich straganiarzy w Kaliszu," *Pokrzywy*, 1 August 1937, 1.
21. "Jakim prawem żydzi w Kaliszu zajmują połowę rynku?," *Pokrzywy*, 21 November 1937, 6.
22. Pakentreger, *Żydzi w Kaliszu w latach* 1918–1939, 62.
23. "Skład Komitetu Wykonawczego Tyg. Propagandy w Kaliszu," *Pokrzywy*, 21 November 1937, 7.
24. "Tydzień Propagandy," *Pokrzywy*, 21 November 1937, 7.
25. "Tydzień Propagandy," 7.
26. Pakentreger, "Sytuacja gospodarcza ludności żydowskiej Kalisza w latach kryzysu gospodarczego 1929–1935 i w okresie pokryzysowym," 61.
27. "Kiedy to nastąpi w Kaliszu?," *Pokrzywy*, 21 November 1937, 4.
28. See "Inż. Bujnicki—prezydentem Kalisza," *Kurjer Warszawski*, 1 May 1937, 4.
29. "Bujnicki Ignacy Adam," in *Czy wiesz kto to jest?*, ed. Stanisław Łoza (Warszawa: Wydawnictwa Artystyczne i Filmowe, 1983), 84.
30. "Prezydent Miasta Kalisza przy pracy 'narodowej,'" *Pokrzywy*, 21 December 1937, 5.
31. Pakentreger, "Sytuacja gospodarcza ludności żydowskiej Kalisza w latach kryzysu gospodarczego 1929–1935 i w okresie pokryzysowym," 62.
32. For examples of Heber's statements on the dire situation of Jewish traders, see "Posiedzenie Centralnego Komitetu Związku Żydowskiego Kupiectwa Detalicznego," *Nasz Przegląd*, 12 November 1937, 13; and "Obrady zjazdu drobnego kupiectwa żydowskiego w Warszawie," *Nowy Dziennik*, 12 August 1938, 1.
33. "Z wycieczki Ozonowców do Poznania," *Pokrzywy*, 27 September 1937, 2.
34. "Nie wie że będzie," *Pokrzywy*, 15 July 1938, 11.
35. "Audiencja u p. Premiera," *Pokrzywy*, 1 July 1937, 3.
36. "Sprostowanie," *Pokrzywy*, 15 July 1937, 8.
37. "Publiczne zapytanie," *Pokrzywy*, 27 September 1937, 5.
38. "Nie może obejść się bez żyda," *Pokrzywy*, 1 March 1938, 4.
39. "'Jutro będziemy pracowali' dla narodu, dzisiaj—dla żydów," *Pokrzywy*, 27 September 1937, 5.
40. "Dwulicowość niektórych kupców polskich," *Pokrzywy*, 21 November 1937, 3.
41. See, for example, "Lejbusia przyjaciele," *Pokrzywy*, 11 October 1937, 8; and "Przyjaciele żydów," *Pokrzywy*, 7 December 1937, 4.
42. "Szkodnicy polskiego handlu," *Pokrzywy*, 7 November 1937, 8.
43. "Przyjaciele żydów w Ostrowie," *Pokrzywy*, 1 September 1937, 9.
44. "Przyjaciele żydów w Kaliszu," *Pokrzywy*, 1 September 1937, 10.
45. "Czarna lista żydowskich wojtków," *Pokrzywy*, 25 January 1938, 6.

46. "Żyje z Polaków a tuczy żydów," *Pokrzywy*, 25 January 1938, 8.
47. "Sprostowanie," *Pokrzywy*, 7 February 1938, 4.
48. "Żydzi w kaliskim szpitalu," *Pokrzywy*, 7 February 1938, 2.
49. "To nieładnie," *Pokrzywy*, 21 November 1937, 6.
50. "Skandal dla polskiej wsi," *Pokrzywy*, 7 February 1938, 9.
51. "Najwyższy czas odżydzić adwokaturę w Polsce!," *Pokrzywy*, 15 March 1938, 6; and "Reforma aptekarska," *Pokrzywy*, 15 August 1938, 10.
52. Mendelsohn, *Jews of East Central Europe between the World Wars*, 73.
53. A similar hypothesis is presented in Jerzy Tomaszewski, *Zarys dziejów Żydów w Polsce w latach 1918–1939* (Warszawa: Wydawnictwa Uniwersytetu Warszawskiego, 1990), 60.
54. See "Pokrzywy—postrachem żydów i szabesgojów," *Pokrzywy*, 1 September 1937, 6.
55. Konstantynów, "Antysemickie rysunki z prasy polskiej 1919–1939," 37n4.
56. Michlic, *Poland's Threatening Other*, 78.
57. See, for example, "Z Jarocina," *Pokrzywy*, 25 January 1937, 8; "Żydowska demoralizacja," *Pokrzywy*, 7 December 1937, 9; "Lejbusia przyjaciele," *Pokrzywy*, 11 October 1937, 8; and "Ciotki żydowskie," *Pokrzywy*, 21 November 1937, 7.
58. See Jan Kostka, "Kontredans chamstwa," *Pod Pręgierz*, 30 June 1935, 3; and "Kulturalni żydofile," *Pod Pręgierz*, 9 March 1939, 3.
59. "Pomorze strasznie żydzieje!," *Pod Pręgierz*, 2 May 1937, 1.
60. Ronald Modras, *The Catholic Church and Antisemitism: Poland, 1933–1939* (London: Routledge, 1994), 227.
61. Modras, *Catholic Church and Antisemitism*, 228.
62. Goldstein, *Twenty Years with the Jewish Labor Bund*, 302.
63. Melzer, *No Way Out*, 45.
64. Grzegorz Krzywiec, "The Balance of Polish Political Antisemitism: Between 'National Revolution,' Economic Crisis, and the Transformation of the Polish Public Sphere in the 1930s," in *Right-Wing Politics and the Rise of Antisemitism in Europe 1935–1941*, ed. Frank Bajohr and Dieter Pohl (Göttingen: Wallstein Verlag, 2019), 77.
65. Jolanta Żyndul, "Cele akcji antyżydowskiej w Polsce w latach 1935–1937," *Biuletyn Żydowskiego Instytutu Historycznego* 1 (1992): 55. See also "Disorders, Boycott Unabated in Poland," *JTA*, 14 September 1937.
66. See, for example, "Disorders Continue in Poland; Traders Threatened with Death for Protesting Boycott," *JTA*, 13 September 1937; and "Boycott Gains in Poland; Mass Picketing Creates Tension, Closes Shops in Czestochowa," *JTA*, 16 December 1937.
67. "Skutki bojkotu żydów w Kaliszu," *Pokrzywy*, 25 January 1938, 9.
68. See Pakentreger, *Żydzi w Kaliszu w latach 1918–1939*, 79–80.
69. Mendelsohn, *Jews of East Central Europe between the World Wars*, 74.
70. Pakentreger, *Żydzi w Kaliszu w latach 1918–1939*, 62.
71. Pakentreger, *Żydzi w Kaliszu w latach 1918–1939*, 52. For a more general discussion of Jewish suicide in interwar Poland, see Daniel Rosenthal, "Victims of Seductive and Unfortunate Lives: Jewish Suicide in Interwar Poland," *Jewish History* 29, no. 3–4 (2015): 301–30.
72. Emphasis is mine.
73. More on this in Aleksander Hertz, *The Jews in Polish Culture* (Evanston, IL: Northwestern University Press, 1988), 14–15.

74. "Żydowskie marzenia," *Pokrzywy*, 27 September 1937, 1.

75. Krzywiec, "Antysemickie karykatury od poł. XIX w. do I wojny światowej," 21; and Konstantynów, "Antysemickie rysunki z prasy polskiej 1919–1939," fn4 37.

76. Eva Plach, "Ritual Slaughter and Animal Welfare in Interwar Poland," *East European Jewish Affairs* 45, no. 1 (2015): 15–16.

77. Żyndul, "Cele akcji antyżydowskiej w Polsce w latach 1935–1937," 57.

78. Żyndul, "Cele akcji antyżydowskiej w Polsce w latach 1935–1937," 57. See also Plach, "Ritual Slaughter and Animal Welfare," 17, 19.

79. "Żydowska rzeźnia narodów," *Pokrzywy*, 21 December 1937, 9.

80. Randall L. Bytwerk, *Julius Streicher: The Man Who Persuaded a Nation to Hate Jews* (New York: Stein and Day, 1983), 56.

81. See also the issues of 21 December 1937, 25 January 1938, 7 February 1938, 1 March 1938, and 15 September 1938.

82. Bytwerk, *Julius Streicher*, 104–5.

83. See, for example, "Nowa orkiestra ze starymi grajkami," *Pokrzywy*, 25 January 1938, 4; and "Żydowskie wychowanie," *Pokrzywy*, 30 September 1938, 6–7.

84. "Żydzi z komuną gotują zagładę światu chrześcijańskiemu," *Pokrzywy*, 25 October 1937, 2.

85. Jerzy Ziomek, *Renesans* (Warszawa: Wydawnictwo Naukowe PWN, 1999), 408–9.

86. "Łódź narodowa w walce," *Pokrzywy*, 15 March 1938, 1.

87. For a summary of the *Protocols*, see Marvin Perry and Frederick M. Schweitzer, *Antisemitism: Myth and Hate from Antiquity to the Present* (New York: Palgrave Macmillan, 2002), 98–99.

88. "Żyd wieczny-rewolucjonista," *Pokrzywy*, 15 July 1938, 10.

89. Robert S. Wistrich, *Antisemitism: The Longest Hatred* (London: Thames Methuen, 1991), 29–30.

90. Perry and Schweitzer, *Antisemitism*, 99.

91. Cała, *Wizerunek Żyda w polskiej kulturze ludowej*, 103.

92. "Żydowskie kolonie," *Pokrzywy*, 11 October 1937, 1.

93. "W żydowskiej szkole," *Pokrzywy*, 15 August 1938, 3.

94. "Karnawał w Polsce," *Pokrzywy*, 7 February 1938, 1.

95. See, for example, A. L., "Kartelomania," *Pokrzywy*, 15 September 1938, 6; "Niebezpieczeństwo zalewu Polski przez żydostwo rumuńskie," *Pokrzywy*, 25 January 1938, 1; and "Zamach na polski przemysł," *Pokrzywy*, 30 June 1938, 6.

96. In 1936, PPS supported by Bund regained control of the municipality, following a short stint by Polish and German right-wing parties in 1934–1936.

97. Kamil Piskała, "The Interwar: Democratic Politics and Modern City Between Two World Wars 1918–1923," in *From Cotton and Smoke: Łódź—Industrial City and Discourses of Asynchronous Modernity 1897–1994*, ed. Agata Zysiak et al. (Łódź: Łódź University Press, 2018), 128, 139–44.

98. Maria Piechotka and Kazimierz Piechotka, "Polish Synagogues in the Nineteenth Century," in *Polin*, ed. Antony Polonsky, vol. 2, *Jews and the Emerging Polish State* (Oxford, UK: Littman Library of Jewish Civilization, 2008), 180.

99. Szymon Rudnicki, "Jews in Poland Between the Two World Wars," *Shofar: An Interdisciplinary Journal of Jewish Studies* 29, no. 3 (2011): 6.

100. Edward Rosset, ed., *Mały rocznik statystyczny miasta Łodzi 1936* (Łódź: Zarząd Miejski w Łodzi. Wydział Statystyczny, 1938), 14.

101. Gilman, *The Jew's Body*, 189.

102. "Królowie bawełniani w Łodzi," *Pokrzywy*, 15 September 1938, 4.

103. Barabara Wachowska, "Łódź Remained Red: Elections to the City Council of 27 September 1936," in *Polin*, ed. Antony Polonsky et al., vol. 9, *Poles, Jews, Socialists: The Failure of an Ideal* (Oxford, UK: Littman Library of Jewish Civilization, 2008), 97.

104. Robert Rockaway and Arnon Gutfeld, "Demonic Images of the Jew in the Nineteenth Century United States," *American Jewish History* 89, no. 4 (2001): 380. See also Baigell, *Implacable Urge to Defame*, 46.

105. Bjoern Milbradt, "Antisemitic Metaphors and Latent Communication," in *Global Antisemitism: A Crisis of Modernity*, ed. Charles Asher Small (Leiden: Brill, 2013), 45.

106. See, for example, Kateřina Šimová, "The Image of the 'Jew' as an 'Enemy' in the Propaganda of Late Stalinism and Its Reflection in the Czechoslovak Context," *Holocaust Studies* 23, no. 1–2 (2017): 124–25; Tobias Blümel, "Antisemitism as Political Theology in Greece and Its Impact on Greek Jewry, 1967–1979," *Southeast European and Black Sea Studies*, 17, no. 2 (2017): 191; and S. Jonathon O'Donnell, "Antisemitism under Erasure: Christian Zionist Anti-Globalism and the Refusal of Cohabitation," *Ethnic and Racial Studies* 44, no. 1 (2021): 49.

107. "Dezynfekcja robotniczej Łodzi," *Pokrzywy*, 1 September 1937, 3.

108. Wachowska, "Łódź Remained Red," 101–3.

109. "Żydowska dżungla na teatralnej widowni," *Pokrzywy*, 15 July 1938, 12.

110. See, for example, "Brońmy polskiego morza!" and "Nowiny żydowskie," *Pokrzywy*, 31 August 1938, 3, 12; and Artur Lorek, "Żydowski Lwów," *Pokrzywy*, 15 September 1938, 9.

111. "Ucz się języka żydowskiego!," *Pokrzywy*, 12 May 1938, 12, and *Pokrzywy*, 30 June 1938, 9.

112. "Żydowskie wrzody na gospodarczym organiźmie Polski," *Pokrzywy*, 1 May 1938, 11.

113. "Żydowski punkt widzenia," *Pokrzywy*, 10 June 1938, 11.

114. Artur Lorek, "Mocarstwowość Polski," *Pokrzywy*, 15 September 1938, 10.

115. Lorek, "Żydowski Lwów," 9.

116. Paul Weindling, *Epidemics and Genocide in Eastern Europe, 1890–1945* (Oxford, UK: Oxford University Press, 2000), 70.

117. Weindling, *Epidemics and Genocide*, 71.

118. Weindling, *Epidemics and Genocide*, 100–2.

119. Yisrael Gutman, *The Jews of Warsaw, 1939–1943: Ghetto, Underground, Revolt*, transl. Ina Friedman (Bloomington: Indiana University Press, 1989), 54.

120. Hugh Raffles, "Jews, Lice, and History," *Public Culture* 19, no. 3 (2007): 560, 562.

121. A. L., "Sami znajdą miejsce," *Pokrzywy*, 31 July 1938, 3.

122. A. L., "Dokąd z Żydami?," *Pokrzywy*, 15 September 1938, 10.

123. A. L., "Teraz kolej na rząd," *Pokrzywy*, 15 August 1938, 4.

124. "Rozpogodzić śmiechem oblicza!," 2.

125. Quoted in Lamb, *Drawn to Extremes*, 41.

126. Peter McGraw and Joel Warner, *The Humor Code: A Global Search for What Makes Things Funny* (New York: Simon and Schuster, 2015), 111.

127. Dannagal G. Young, Benjamin E. Bagozzi, and Abigail Goldring, "Psychology, Political Ideology, and Humor Appreciation: Why Is Satire So Liberal?," *Psychology of Popular Media Culture* 8, no. 2 (2019): 136.

128. Young, Bagozzi, and Goldring, "Psychology, Political Ideology, and Humor Appreciation," 144.

129. "Do Przyjaciół 'Pokrzyw'!," *Pokrzywy*, 15 August 1937, 2.

130. "'Pokrzywy' zakwitły," *Pokrzywy*, 1 September 1937, 10.

131. APKa, SPK, sygn. 11/3/0/13/590, Stronnictwo Narodowe 1930–1939, Police Report no 89, 25 April 1938.

132. For examples of the first two, see "Pogromca 'Pokrzyw' w Kaliszu," *Pokrzywy*, 25 October 1937, 6; and "Publiczne zapytanie," 5.

133. "Wrogom 'Pokrzyw' w odpowiedzi," *Pokrzywy*, 11 October 1937, 2.

134. "Dali się wziąć na kawał," *Pokrzywy*, 11 October 1937, 5.

135. "Satyra i humor przed sądem," *Pokrzywy*, 11 October 1937, 5.

136. "Po procesie 'Pokrzyw' w Krotoszynie," *Pokrzywy*, 25 October 1937, 5.

137. "Przed wyborami," *Pokrzywy*, 31 August 1938, 2.

138. "Niemiecko—ukraińska spółdzielczość," *Pokrzywy*, 31 August 1938, 3.

139. AAN, PZWDziCz, *Konfiskaty prasowe*, sygn. 2/64/0/8, folder 250, Memo of the PZWDziCz regarding the confiscation of print media, 4 November 1932; Survey regarding the confiscation of print media, no date; Letter from Drukarnia Polska in Poznań to PZWDziCz, 24 October 1932; and Letter from *Dziennik Bydgoski* to PZWDziCz, 20 March 1936.

140. "Wolność prasy satyrycznej—dawniej a dziś," *Pokrzywy*, 31 August 1938, 1.

141. "Nowe szykany żydów," *Pokrzywy*, 10 June 1938, 8.

142. Eugeniusz Kolanko, "Do żydowskiego 'poety' J.T.," *Pokrzywy*, 15 September 1938, 11.

143. "Szukam antysemityzmu. Impreza nie impresja," *Pokrzywy*, 15 August 1938, 11.

144. See Sławomir Łotysz, *Pińskie błota: Natura, wiedza i polityka na polskim Polesiu do 1939 roku* (Kraków: Universitas, 2022), 339–73.

145. "Żydowska prasa dla głupich kobiet," *Pokrzywy*, 15 March 1938, 7.

146. "Odezwa do Przyjaciół," *Pokrzywy*, 11 October 1937, 9.

147. "'Pokrzywy' mają wrogów," *Pokrzywy*, 11 October 1937, 9.

148. "'Pokrzywy' w Warszawie," *Pokrzywy*, 31 August 1938, 11.

149. "Osobliwy jubileusz," *Pokrzywy*, 25 January 1938, 5.

150. "Lekarstwo na żydów," *Pokrzywy*, 15 September 1938, 8.

151. "Skuteczny środek na żydów," *Pokrzywy*, 31 August 1938, 9; and "Rozpowszechniajcie 'Pokrzywy!,'" *Pokrzywy*, 7 December 1937, 8.

152. "Przed lekcją w Kaliszu," *Pokrzywy*, 7 November 1937, 5.

153. For a poem on Siepka, here spelled as "Siepko," see "Ze Stawiszyna: Szabesgoje—poprawcie się," *Pokrzywy*, 21 December 1937, 3.

154. The number does not take into account survivors who settled in other locations in Poland (including Lower Silesia, Szczecin, Łódź, and Warsaw) and abroad. See Pakentreger, "Statystyka Żydów m. Kalisza ocalałych po II wojnie światowej," 91.

155. Anna Tabaka, *Ignacy Adam Nieściuszko-Bujnicki* (Kalisz: Kaliskie Towarzystwo Przyjaciół Nauk, 2016), 55.

CHAPTER 3: AGAINST ANTISEMITISM

1. AŻIH, YVC, sygn. 349/24/1455, Folder of Eryk Lipiński, Letter from Mordecai Paldiel to Eryk Lipiński, 30 June 1991.

2. AŻIH, YVC, sygn. 349/24/1455, Folder of Eryk Lipiński, Notarized letter from Lida L. Birsten, 30 June 1989.

3. AŻIH, YVC, sygn. 349/24/1455, Folder of Eryk Lipiński, Letter from Ewa Otwinowska, 10 November 1985.

4. AŻIH, Notarized letter from Lida L. Birsten. See also Eryk Lipiński, *Pamiętniki* (Warszawa: Iskry, 2016), 161, 165.

5. Eryk Lipiński, *Szpilki, 1935–1965: Coś nam zostało z tych lat* . . . (Warszawa: Wydawnictwo Artystyczno-Graficzne RSW "Prasa," 1967), 3.

6. Lipiński, *Szpilki*, 3.

7. Zbigniew Mitzner, "Historia," in *Z dziejów cnoty. Szpilki 1935–1985* (Warszawa: Krajowa Agencja Wydawnicza, 1985), 9.

8. Lipiński, *Szpilki*, 3.

9. For a complete list of contributors in the first two years of *Szpilki*'s activity, see "W ciągu dwóch lat swego istnienia . . . ," *Szpilki*, 26 December 1937, 8. For a self-reflective poem on the *Szpilki* team on the third anniversary of its creation, see Lola Szereszewska, "Do czytelników 'Szpilek,'" *Szpilki*, 25 December 1938, 7.

10. Janusz Stradecki, "Szpilki," in *Literatura polska: Przewodnik encyklopedyczny, Tom 2*, ed. Julian Krzyżanowski et al. (Warszawa: Państwowe Wydawnictwo Naukowe, 1985), 433.

11. See Żółkiewska, *Wolny Ptak*, 47–48.

12. "Warszawa i Warszawka," *Chwila: Wydanie Poranne*, 18 May 1938, 9.

13. Lipiński, *Szpilki*, 3.

14. On *Szpilki*'s Cold War reporting, see Jolanta Ślęzak, "Armia europejska czy nowy Wehrmacht? Plany utworzenia Europejskiej Wspólnoty Obronnej w karykaturze polskiej na przykładzie czasopisma satyrycznego 'Szpilki' 1950–1954," *Polityka i Społeczeństwo* 1, no. 11 (2013): 130–50; and Jolanta Ślęzak, "Obraz Czechosłowacji w karykaturach opublikowanych na łamach czasopism satyrycznych 'Mucha' i 'Szpilki' w latach 1945–1948," *Polityka i Społeczeństwo* 3, no. 11 (2013): 49–68.

15. Lipiński, *Drzewo Szpilkowe*, 165.

16. *Wiadomości Literackie* initially supported the Sanacja government. Following the Brest trials of 1931–1932 during which the government targeted its political opponents, including many PPS members, the magazine became a vocal opponent of the regime. After Piłsudski's death, it became a regular target for state censorship due to its antifascist

and pacifist agendas. See Janusz Stradecki, "Wiadomości Literackie," in *Literatura polska: Przewodnik encyklopedyczny, Tom 2*, 579.

17. Trębacz, *Nie tylko Palestyna*, 210.

18. Trębacz, *Nie tylko Palestyna*, 211.

19. "Widoki osiedlania się żydów na Madagaskarze," *Dziennik Bydgoski*, 6 July 1937. I have retained the original capitalization here. Many right-wing publications did not capitalize the ethnic term "Żyd" (Jew) and tended to use lower case instead.

20. "Madagaskar czeka na żydów," *Drwęca*, 2 December 1937.

21. Melzer, *No Way Out*, 132.

22. Trębacz, *Nie tylko Palestyna*, 234–35.

23. Rovner, *In the Shadow of Zion*, 136.

24. See Stanisław Strąbski, "Polska z żydami—to zero!," *Dziennik Bydgoski*, 1 December 1937.

25. Lipiński, *Drzewo Szpilkowe*, 167.

26. The two characters are interesting in their own right. They are the ultimate Jewish comedy duo. Their names are meant to signalize their inseparability, "Żółtko" meaning "egg yolk" and "Eierweis" referring to the Yiddish word for "egg white." The spelling "Eierweis" (instead of "Eierweiss") is retained as in the original.

27. Lipiński, *Drzewo Szpilkowe*, 19.

28. Jerzy Zaruba, *Z pamiętników bywalca* (Warszawa: Iskry, 1960), 170.

29. Jerzy Zaruba, "Żółtko i Eierweis na Madagaskarze," *Szpilki*, 30 January 1938, 1.

30. On the role of such fantasy scenarios in cartoons, see Danjoux, *Political Cartoons and the Israeli-Palestinian Conflict*, 31.

31. Jerzy Kamil Weintraub, "Moja podróż na Madagaskar," *Szpilki*, 30 January 1938, 6.

32. MAT., "Ekscesy na uniwersytecie," *Szpilki*, 30 January 1938, 7.

33. MAT., "Dalsza akcja bojkotowa," *Szpilki*, 30 January 1938, 7.

34. Mieczysław Piotrowski, "Życie codzienne na Madagaskarze," *Szpilki*, 30 January 1938, 8.

35. "Oświadczenie p. Silberfelda," "Odgłosy ekonomiczne," and "Mały Przegląd," *Szpilki*, 30 January 1938, 3.

36. Edward Szymański, "Nieznany fragment 'Beniowskiego,'" *Szpilki*, 30 January 1938, 2.

37. "A tymczasem w Warszawie," *Szpilki*, 30 January 1938, 4–5.

38. Tadeusz Hollender, *Polska bez Żydów: Powieść satyryczna* (Warszawa: Wydawnictwo "Wierch," 1938), 37. For a discussion of other similar opinions in the leftist press, see Henryk Markiewicz, "Przeciw nienawiści i pogardzie," *Teksty Drugie* 6 (2004): 107–8.

39. Hollender, *Polska bez Żydów*, 38.

40. Lipiński, *Drzewo Szpilkowe*, 167.

41. Antoni Słonimski, "Kronika tygodniowa," *Wiadomości Literackie*, 18 April 1937, 5.

42. See Young, Bagozzi, and Goldring, "Psychology, Political Ideology, and Humor Appreciation," 136.

43. Melzer, *No Way Out*, 44–47.

44. Michlic, *Poland's Threatening Other*, 126.

45. See, for example, "Nieuniknione starcie," *Dziennik Bydgoski*, 20 June 1936, 2; "Wyjaśnienie urzędowe konieczne," *Kurier Poznański*, 31 July 1937, 3; "Jarmark bez żydów,"

Samodzielność, 15 June 1937, 45; "Z całej Polski. Od korespondentów Falangi," *Falanga*, 25 January 1938, 6–7; and "Nowa Chrześcijańska Kasa Bezprocentowa," *Narodowe Życie Gospodarcze*, 23 July 1939, 7.

46. Bronisław Schneider, "Muzyka O.N.R.-u," *Kontratak*, 20 December 1936, 4.
47. See Kunicki, *Between the Brown and the Red*, 29.
48. Kunicki, *Between the Brown and the Red*, 49.
49. Kunicki, *Between the Brown and the Red*, 23.
50. Brykczynski, *Primed for Violence*, 49.
51. Brykczynski, *Primed for Violence*, 49.
52. Cited in Melzer, *No Way Out*, 21.
53. See the two cartoons in Żółkiewska, *Wolny Ptak*, 252, 253.
54. Mendelsohn, *Jews of East Central Europe between the World Wars*, 71.
55. Goldstein, *Twenty Years with the Jewish Labor Bund*, 303.
56. Natalia Aleksiun, "Crossing the Line: Violence against Jewish Women and the New Model of Antisemitism in Poland in the 1930s," *Jewish History* 33 (2020): 134.
57. Mendel Reif, "Prima-Aprilis," *Szpilki*, 3 April 1938, 1.
58. See Żółkiewska, *Wolny Ptak*, 249.
59. AŻIH, SP, Reif (Schmierer) Mendel (Mieczysław), Index card no 353, no date.
60. Mieczysław Piotrowski, "Idealne urządzenie sali wykładowej na uniwersytecie, bez . . . ," *Wróble na Dachu*, 17 October 1937, 7. See also Bergmann, "Problematyka żydowska w karykaturach polskich czasopism satyrycznych Drugiej Rzeczypospolitej," 480.
61. Bergmann, "Problematyka żydowska w karykaturach polskich czasopism satyrycznych Drugiej Rzeczypospolitej," 479. See also Konstantynów, "Pogromy i inne akty przemocy fizycznej wobec Żydów w zwierciadle rysunków z prasy polskiej (1919–1939)," 343–44; and cartoon by Bronisław Schneider, "Galanteria norymberska," *Kontratak*, 29 November 1936, 5.
62. Mendel Reif, "Wykład," *Szpilki*, 16 January 1938, 4.
63. Mendel Reif, "Na początek feryj," *Szpilki*, 4 July 1937, 7.
64. Mendel Reif, "O.Z.N. zapowiada walkę z masonerią," *Szpilki*, 1 August 1937, 2.
65. Karol Baraniecki, "Paragraf aryjski," *Szpilki*, 22 May 1938, 4.
66. Edward Szymański, "ABC młodego oenerowca," *Szpilki*, 13 November 1938, 6.
67. See, for example, cartoons from *Haynt* and *Der Moment* in Żółkiewska, *Wolny Ptak*, 245, 247, 248.
68. Julian Żebrowski, "Koniec roku akademickiego," *Szarża*, 16 May 1937, 8.
69. Danjoux, *Political Cartoons and the Israeli-Palestinian Conflict*, 23.
70. Danjoux, *Political Cartoons and the Israeli-Palestinian Conflict*, 23.
71. As one local Polish Jewish newspaper put it: "Why to Madagascar? Why not to Congo? Why not to Morocco? Why not to Abyssinia? It seems that the only reasonable answer to this question may be that no one knows Madagascar, that it is very distant and that the journey [would] be both long and pleasant and interesting." See "Złudzenia emigracyjne," *Przegląd Zachodni*, 8 April 1938, 5.
72. Lipiński, *Drzewo Szpilkowe*, 27.
73. Lipiński, *Drzewo Szpilkowe*, 211–13. In general, Mitzner, who was a contributor to other leftist outlets of the time, reported having faced more than ten political cases

involving his journalism. See BN, AM, sygn. 11934, Zbigniew Mitzner, "Życiorys," 23 September 1949.

74. Lipiński, *Drzewo Szpilkowe*, 32.

75. "Fotografie uroczych Warszawianek i sympatycznych Warszawiaków," *Szpilki: Dodatek Nadzwyczajny*, 17 April 1938, 1.

76. Andrzej Kossakowski, *Polski film animowany 1945–1974* (Wrocław: Zakład Narodowy im. Ossolińskich, Wydawnictwo PAN, 1977), 22.

77. Kossakowski, *Polski film animowany*, 21–22.

78. "Wszędzie Żyd" and "Zhańbię chętnie blondynkę," *Szpilki: Dodatek Nadzwyczajny*, 17 April 1938, 1–2.

79. For a detailed report of the trial by Polish Jewish dailies, see "A więc to była pornografia," *Nasz Przegląd*, 1 July 1938, 11; and "Redaktorzy 'Szpilek' oskarżeni o szerzenie pornografii," *5-ta rano*, 29 June 1938, 4.

80. Lipiński, *Drzewo Szpilkowe*, 216–17.

81. Lipiński, *Drzewo Szpilkowe*, 217.

82. Mariusz Urbanek, *Tuwim. Wylękniony bluźnierca* (Warszawa: Wydawnictwo Iskry, 2013), 63–64.

83. Lipiński, *Drzewo Szpilkowe*, 217.

84. See Robert Blobaum, "Criminalizing the 'Other': Crime, Ethnicity, and Antisemitism in Early Twentieth-Century Poland," in *Antisemitism and Its Opponents in Modern Poland*, 89.

85. Stanisław Trzeciak, *Pornografia narzędziem obcych agentur* (Warszawa: Biblioteka "Jutra Pracy," 1938), 5.

86. Plach, *Clash of Moral Nations*, 149.

87. Quoted in Modras, *Catholic Church and Antisemitism*, 250.

88. Discussing the case of *Wiadomości Literackie*, which was frequently vilified by ethno-nationalist media as "Judeophilic," historian Eva Plach argues that "it was simply not that paper's style to focus on particularistic regional or ethnic questions" and that "What critics referred to when they condemned the *News* as a Jewish paper had more to do with the kinds of questions its writers raised and with its general disinclination to foster a particular vision of Polish nationalism that would have affirmed the connections between Polishness and Catholicism." See Plach, *Clash of Moral Nations*, 151.

89. For such cases in Poland, see Grażyna Wrona, "'Przeciw bezwstydowi w druku i obrazku': Krakowska cenzura w walce z demoralizacją (1918–1939)," *Klio: Czasopismo poświęcone dziejom Polski i powszechnym* 2 (2011): 97–112; and Marcin Żynda, "'Wysoce demoralizująca i pornograficzna' inicjatywa wydawnicza: Obrona moralności publicznej a wolność słowa w międzywojennym Grudziądzu," *Klio: Czasopismo poświęcone dziejom Polski i powszechnym* 2 (2011): 143–48. Similarities can be found in other national contexts. For example, writing about Japan in the 1930s, Gennifer Weisenfeld argued that "Though the government brutally suppressed leftist political ideas, by far the largest portion of censored publications dealt with erotic topics, particularly those marketing sexual deviance under the larger rubric of the 'erotic-grotesque,' which were thought to pose an ongoing threat to public morality." See Weisenfeld, *Mavo: Japanese Artists and the Avant-Garde, 1905–1931* (Berkeley: University of California Press, 2002), 248.

90. Prokop-Janiec, *Polish-Jewish Literature in the Interwar Years*, 64.

91. Alina Cała, *Żyd—Wróg odwieczny? Antysemityzm w Polsce i jego źródła* (Warszawa: Wydawnictwo Nisza, 2012), 374–75.

92. Plach, *Clash of Moral Nations*, 149.

93. "Walka z antysemityzmem czy pornografia?," *ABC: Nowiny Codzienne*, 29 June 1938, 2. See also "Skazanie 'Szpilek' za pornografię," *ABC: Nowiny Codzienne*, 1 July 1938, 1.

94. "Szerzyciele pornografii skazani," *Mały Dziennik*, 2 July 1938, 5.

95. "Sąd potępił pornograficzny dodatek 'Szpilek,'" *Warszawski Dziennik Narodowy*, 1 July 1938, 7.

96. Lipiński, *Drzewo Szpilkowe*, 218.

97. "Shańbię chętnie blondynkę," *Dziennik Poznański*, 2 July 1938, 6. The incorrect spelling of the verb *zhańbić* has been retained, as in the original title of the article.

98. "Shańbię chętnie blondynkę," 167–68.

99. "Kontrofenzywa," *Agencja Antymasońska: Biuletyn* 1, no. 1 (1938): 1.

100. Modras, *Catholic Church and Antisemitism*, 70–71.

101. Modras, *Catholic Church and Antisemitism*, 70–71.

102. See, for example, Roland Clark, "Anti-Masonry as Political Protest: Fascists and Freemasons in Interwar Romania," *Patterns of Prejudice* 46, no. 1 (2012): 40–57.

103. For a summary of Kozłowski's article, see "Około 2300 masonów w Polsce?," *Dziennik Bydgoski*, 13 July 1938, 1.

104. Franciszek Parecki, "Loża Wielkiego Wschodu" and "Loża Szkocka," *Szpilki*, 28 July 1938, 8.

105. Ha-Ga, "Panie! Pan jest mason!," *Szpilki*, 28 July 1938, 3.

106. Modras, *Catholic Church and Antisemitism*, 72.

107. AMK, Anna Gosławska—Lipińska PF, Newspaper Clippings: Szymon Kobyliński, "Ha-Ga nie żyje," *Express Wieczorny*, 15 April 1975, no page.

108. AMK, Anna Gosławska—Lipińska PF, Newspaper Clippings: Jerzy S. Majewski, "Jak 'Ha-Ga' Karpuszkę stworzyła," *Gazeta Wyborcza. Magazyn Stołeczny*, 6 November 2015, 14–16.

109. AMK, Anna Gosławska—Lipińska PF, Newspaper Clippings: AP, "Hanna Gosławska Ha-Ga i Eryk Lipiński," *Retro*, [no date], 6–7.

110. Agata Napiórska, *Ha-Ga: Obrazki z życia* (Warszawa: Marginesy, 2023), 219, 226.

111. Modras, *Catholic Church and Antisemitism*, 77. See Eryk Lipiński, "Bnei-Bridż," *Szpilki*, 11 December 1938, 5.

112. "Ogłosić nazwiska masonów!," *Agencja Antymasońska: Biuletyn* 1, no. 5 (1938): 2.

113. Mendel Reif, "An der blauen Donau," *Szpilki*, 13 March 1938, 8. See also Andrzej Siemaszko, "Trzęsienie ziemi," *Szpilki*, 26 June 1938, 1.

114. Franciszek Parecki, "Zachowanie z rezerwą," *Szpilki*, 28 August 1938, 1. For a cartoon on a similar topic, see Bronisław Schneider, "Komu najpierw," *Szpilki*, 26 June 1938, 3.

115. Eryk Lipiński, "Nie igrać z ogniem!," *Szpilki*, 7 August 1938, 1.

116. Eryk Lipiński, "Porwanie Europy," *Szpilki*, 18 September 1938, 1.

117. Paul Baxa, "Capturing the Fascist Moment: Hitler's Visit to Italy in 1938 and the Radicalization of Fascist Italy," *Journal of Contemporary History* 42, no. 2 (2007): 227.

118. Zenon Wasilewski, "Majowe amory," *Szpilki*, 15 May 1938, 2.

119. Henryk Tomaszewski, "Zamieńmy się ustami...," *Szpilki*, 15 May 1938, 8.

120. "German Cartoonist Tells of Wide Curbs," *New York Times*, 19 April 1935, 11.

121. Małgorzata Czyńska, *Berezowska: Nagość dla wszystkich* (Wołowiec: Czarne, 2018), 81–87.

122. "Reich Publishes List of 'Jewish Names' Barred to 'Aryans,'" *JTA*, 24 August 1938.

123. Zenon Wasilewski, "Wygnanie z raju czyli ewakuacja," *Szpilki*, 11 September 1938, 3.

124. Kees Ribbens, "Charles Boost in een vooroorlogse beeldenstrijd: Stelling nemen tegen de NSB in De Blaasbalg," *Stripschrift*, October 2022, 25–26.

125. Franciszek Parecki, "Po włosku," *Szpilki*, 4 September 1938, 3.

126. Mieczysław Berman, "Czapka Frygijska," in *Księga wspomnień* (Warszawa: Czytelnik, 1960), 55, 82.

127. Eryk Lipiński, "Prasa doniosła...," *Szpilki*, 21 August 1938, 3.

128. For a discussion of the "Beach for Christians only" project, see a contemporary report from a fascist newspaper "Odżydzić letniska wielkopolskie," *Polska Narodowa*, 2 April 1939, 2.

129. See cartoons "Masońskie odkrycia pana Leona Kozłowskiego" and "Senator Kozłowski a masoneria," *Mucha*, 29 July 1938, 1, 4; and "Pan Kozłowski niezadowolony z pana Składkowskiego" and "Dalszy spis masonów polskich," *Mucha*, 5 August 1938, 3, 8. See also the poem Władysław Buchner, "Masoni polscy," *Mucha*, 22 July 1938, 2.

130. See cartoons "Nowa sytuacja w Europie" and "Hitler w Neapolu," *Mucha*, 6 May 1938, 3, 5.

131. Bronisław Fedyszyn, "Paragraf aryjski," *Mucha*, 18 February 1938, 5.

132. On this in another context, see Danjoux, *Political Cartoons and the Israeli-Palestinian Conflict*, 36.

133. See, for example, "Nowe procesy w Rosji," *Mucha*, 30 April 1937, 3; "Moskiewskie procesy," *Mucha*, 7 May 1937, 3; "Tuchaczewski przeniesiony został do Nadwołżańskiego Okręgu Wojennego," *Mucha*, 28 May 1937, 6; "Żarłoczny," *Mucha*, 9 July 1937, 5; "Niedźwiedzia przysługa" and "Moloch kremlowski," *Mucha*, 27 May 1938, 4, 6; "Międzynarodowa pomoc zimowa," *Mucha*, 5 February 1937, 4; "Na Morzu Śródziemnym," *Mucha*, 22 January 1937, 3; and "Rewolucja w Meksyku," *Mucha*, 3 June 1938, 5.

134. Paweł Koliński, "Bieg bez przeszkód. Do redaktora 'Sygnałów,'" *Sygnały*, 1 October 1937, 11.

135. See Tadeusz Hollender, "Sprawa byłego towarzysza Łaszowskiego," *Chwila*, 26 November 1937, 7. On his postwar trajectory, see Kunicki, *Between the Brown and the Red*, 144.

136. Alfred Łaszowski, "Rola satyry żydowskiej," *Falanga*, 5 April 1938, 4.

137. Łaszowski, "Rola satyry żydowskiej."

138. "Ohydne dowcipy lewicowych 'Szpilek,'" *Kurier Poznański*, 13 July 1937, 4.

139. Łaszowski, "Rola satyry żydowskiej," 4.

140. Alfred Łaszowski, "Dyktujemy hierarchię pojęć," *Falanga*, 18 January 1938, 3.

141. "Na marginesie," *Dziennik Bydgoski*, 22 November 1938, 3.

142. Modras, *Catholic Church and Antisemitism*, 250.

143. See, for example, "Katastrofalne zażydzenie literatury i sztuki polskiej," *Polska Karta*, 5 January 1936, 5. See also M. Nałęcz-Dobrowolski, "Jaką jest obecna polska sztuka?," *Przegląd katolicki*, 14 November 1937, 715–16; and "Dygasiński a religia—sprawa

humoru—Hoene Wroński—nowe pisma," *Tygodnik Literacki Polski Zbrojnej*, 4 December 1938, 2.

144. For a summary of Budzyński's address, see "W prasie, na placówkach dyplomatycznych i w Radjo—żydzi!," *Zbudzona Polska*, 3 January 1937, 2.

145. Modras, *Catholic Church and Antisemitism*, 250.

146. B. Malczewski, "Prasa i żydzi," *Mały Dziennik*, 9 March 1939, 6.

147. Lipiński, *Drzewo Szpilkowe*, 211–12. For the original cartoon, see Eryk Lipiński, "Okazało się, że antysemici i rasiści, panowie Stanisław Piasecki i Wojciech Wasiutyński, są pochodzenia żydowskiego," *Szpilki*, 31 January 1937, 1.

148. "Heroldowie rasizmu . . .," *Chwila*, 20 April 1937, 3.

149. "Proces o zarzut niearyjskiego pochodzenia," *Dziennik Wileński*, 17 September 1937, 4.

150. "Czy dziadek był Żydem? . . . Pierwszy proces 'rasistowski' w Warszawie," *Dzień dobry*, 20 April 1937, 5.

151. "Raz rasa!," *Nasz Przegląd*, 20 April 1937, 6.

152. "Raz rasa!," 6.

153. "Proces o pochodzenie red. Wasiutyńskiego," *Kurjer Nowogródzki*, 21 April 1937, 2.

154. "Polacy z przymieszką krwi semickiej," *Expres Zagłębia*, 23 April 1923, 2. See also "O zarzuceniu pochodzenia żydowskiego," *Kurier Poznański*, 22 April 1937, 2; and "Wyrok w sprawie z oskarżenia p. Wojciecha Wasiutyńskiego," *Gazeta Robotnicza*, 23 April 1937, 5.

155. Wan., "Wśród czarnych chałatów: Wrażenia z dzielnicy żydowskiej w Warszawie," 7.

156. Wan., "Wśród czarnych chałatów: Wrażenia z dzielnicy żydowskiej w Warszawie," 7.

157. Witz, "O karykaturze," in *50 lat karykatury polskiej: 1900–1950*, 28.

158. Witz, "O karykaturze," 26.

159. Witz, "O karykaturze," 28.

160. Lipiński, *Drzewo Szpilkowe*, 21.

161. Jan Szeląg, "Siedem dni chudych," *Szpilki*, 25 December 1938, 2.

162. See "Do czytelników i kolporterów 'Szpilek,'" *Robotnik*, 29 October 1938, 6; and "'Szpilki' i OZON," *ABC: Nowiny Codzienne*, 13 November 1938, 3.

163. Witz, "O karykaturze," 28.

164. Witz, "O karykaturze," 28.

165. Lipiński, *Drzewo Szpilkowe*, 217.

166. Lipiński, *Drzewo Szpilkowe*, 11.

167. See, for example, Lipiński's mention of how his friend Eliasz Kanarek, a painter, was attacked in the ethno-nationalist press for being a Jew: AMK, Eryk Lipiński PF 3; Newspaper Clippings: "Rozmaitości Eryka Lipińskiego," *Przegląd. Warszawa*, no date.

168. Lipiński, *Drzewo Szpilkowe*, 21.

169. See, for example, George, "O polski film rysunkowy," *Kino*, 15 January 1938, 3.

170. Witz, "O karykaturze," 28.

171. Lipiński, *Pamiętniki*, 33–35.

172. Lipiński, *Pamiętniki*, 37.

173. Lipiński, *Pamiętniki*, 40–41.

174. See AASP Warsaw, SR 1922–1939, sygn. 730, Student Folder of Eryk Lipiński; sygn. 259, Student Folder of Anna Gosławska; and sygn. 1022, Student Folder of Franciszek Parecki.

175. Lipiński, *Pamiętniki*, 96.

176. Ksawery Piwocki, *Historia Akademii Sztuk Pięknych w Warszawie 1904–1964* (Wrocław: Zakład Narodowy Imienia Ossolińskich Wydawnictwo Polskiej Akademii Nauk, 1965), 52.

177. AMK, Jakub Bickels PF, Typed biography, Undated, Signed EL.

178. Żółkiewska, *Wolny Ptak*, 47–48.

179. AŻIH, SP, Reif (Schmierer) Mendel (Mieczysław), Index card no 365, no date; AMK, Jakub Bickels PF, Typed biography, Undated, Signed EL.

180. "Bronisław Schneider," in *Czasy wojen i pokoju. Karykatura Polska 1914–1939* (Warszawa: Muzeum Karykatury im. Eryka Lipińskiego w Warszawie, 2004), 157.

181. See, for example, Martina Kessel, "Introduction: Landscapes of Humour— The History and Politics of the Comical in the Twentieth Century," in *The Politics of Humour: Laughter, Inclusion, and Exclusion in the Twentieth Century*, ed. Martina Kessel and Patrick Merziger (Toronto: Toronto University Press, 2012), 3. See also Robert Hariman, "Political Parody and Public Culture," *Quarterly Journal of Speech* 94, no. 3 (2008): 248.

182. Lipiński, *Drzewo Szpilkowe*, 11–12.

183. Today Leonia Szereszewska (1895–1943) is largely forgotten, even though she was a recognized author in the 1930s. See Emilia Gałczyńska, "Lola Szereszewska (1895–1943): zapomniana poetka pogranicza," *Narracje o Zagładzie* 5 (2019): 87–88.

184. Lola Szereszewska, "Przepraszam, że żyję," *Szpilki*, 9 January 1938, 5.

185. Lipiński, *Drzewo Szpilkowe*, 11.

186. Żółkiewska, *Wolny Ptak*, 47–48.

187. Elżbieta Sidoruk, *Granice satyry* (Białystok: Instytut Filologii Polskiej Uniwersytetu w Białymstoku, 2018), 53–54.

CHAPTER 4: HIDDEN IDENTITIES

1. AUW, University of Warsaw SR 1915–1939, sygn. 11870, Henryk Szpigiel Student Folder, Letter from Melania Szpigiel to the Rector of the University of Warsaw, 1 July 1946.

2. Tomasz Lerski, *Syrena Record: pierwsza polska wytwórnia fonograficzna 1904–1939* (Warszawa: Karin, 2003), 768.

3. Lipiński, *Drzewo Szpilkowe*, 21–22.

4. Lipiński, *Drzewo Szpilkowe*, 25.

5. Poet and leftist commentator Antoni Słonimski alluded to the newly established magazine in his weekly column for the progressive *Wiadomości Literackie*. See Antoni Słonimski, "Kronika tygodniowa," *Wiadomości Literackie*, 17 January 1937, 5.

6. See Danjoux, *Political Cartoons and the Israeli-Palestinian Conflict*, 36.

7. AUW, University of Warsaw SR 1915–1939, Henryk Szpigiel Student Folder, sygn. 11870, Birth and Christening Certificate no 563/1915, The Evangelical Church of Augsburg Confession in Warsaw, 20 December 1915, p. 2.

8. AUW, University of Warsaw SR 1915–1939, Henryk Szpigiel Student Folder, sygn. 11870, Curriculum Vitae, 11 September 1922, and School Leaving Diploma, 17 June 1922.

9. APW, SGW, Nr zesp. 655, sygn. 5/4171, Melania Teresa Szpigiel to Municipal Court in Warsaw, 20 December 1948, p. 2.

10. See, for example, Lipiński, *Drzewo Szpilkowe*, 25. Other scarce literature on Szpigiel lists the same degree, most likely after Lipiński. See Lerski, *Syrena Record*, 768. For Szpigiel's records at the University of Warsaw, see AUW, University of Warsaw SR 1915–1939, Henryk Szpigiel Student Folder, sygn. 11870, Year-by-Year Record of Completed Semesters 1922–1927.

11. AUW, University of Warsaw SR 1915–1939, Henryk Szpigiel Student Folder, sygn. 11870, Request to the Chair of Examination Board for Law Students, Course no II, No Date.

12. AUW, University of Warsaw SR 1915–1939, Henryk Szpigiel Student Folder, sygn. 11870, Letter to the Board of Law Faculty, 26 November 1924; Doctor's Note by Dr. Henryk Hellin, 26 October 1924; Letter to the Board of Law Faculty, 17 September 1927.

13. According to one contemporary commentator, toward the end of the 1920s many non-*endek* authors wrote satire for the *ABC* literary supplement. They were not necessarily expected to subscribe to the nationalist worldview. This was to change after 1934 when the daily was taken over by ONR. See Janusz Minkiewicz, "Pamiętniki. Rozdział XVI," *Nowiny Literackie* 1, no. 23 (24 August 1947): 6.

14. Henryk St. Harten (Harvey), *Ojciec zadżumionych i inne parodje polityczne* (Warszawa: Tygodnik "Placówka," 1930), 3.

15. Lipiński, *Drzewo Szpilkowe*, 21.

16. Janusz Minkiewicz quoted in Lipiński, *Drzewo Szpilkowe*, 25.

17. Lipiński, *Drzewo Szpilkowe*, 21–22.

18. Minkiewicz in Lipiński, *Drzewo Szpilkowe*, 25.

19. Antoni Słonimski, "Kronika tygodniowa," *Wiadomości Literackie*, 17 January 1937, 5.

20. Słonimski alluded to it more than once; see Antoni Słonimski, "Kronika tygodniowa," *Wiadomości Literackie*, 24 January 1937, 5. See also Maurs., "Szarża," *Kontratak*, 19 January 1937, 4.

21. AUW, University of Warsaw SR 1915–1939, Henryk Szpigiel Student Folder, sygn. 11870, Birth and Christening Certificate no 563/1915, The Evangelical Church of Augsburg Confession in Warsaw, 20 December 1915, pp. 1–4.

22. Bogumił Hetnarski, *Ze Stopnicy do Itaki. Pamiętnik chemika* (Krosno: Apla, 2009), 42.

23. Ł., "Popyt na nosy," *Szarża*, 7 March 1937, 1.

24. See Gilman, *The Jew's Body*, 187.

25. Minkiewicz in Lipiński, *Drzewo Szpilkowe*, 25.

26. The cartoon appeared in *Szarża*'s sister publication, daily *ABC*, advertising the newly created magazine. See Ł., "Młodzi idą," *ABC: Nowiny codzienne*, 24 December 1936, 5.

27. Very., "Pogrom w Polsce, czyli garść wycinków z gazet," *Szarża*, 10 January 1937, 4–5.

28. For a more contemporary discussion on the Przytyk pogrom, see Jolanta Żyndul et al., "The Sixty-Fifth Anniversary of Events in Przytyk: A Debate," in *Polin: Studies in Polish Jewry*, vol. 17, ed. Antony Polonsky (Oxford, UK: Littman Library of Jewish Civilization, 2004), 385–409.

29. Melzer, *No Way Out*, 54.

30. Michlic, *Poland's Threatening Other*, 123–24.

31. Melzer, *No Way Out*, 67.

32. Historian Jolanta Żyndul argues that such interpretations were (and still are) a common way of downplaying events that were effectively aimed at systematic destruction of one specific ethnic group. See Żyndul, "If Not a Pogrom, Then What?," in *Polin: Studies in Polish Jewry*, vol. 17, 389.

33. Witold Jocz., "Mecz Polska-Judea," *Szarża*, 17 January 1937, 7.

34. "Nie przeszarżujemy, mówiąc, że . . .," *Szarża*, 10 January 1937, 3.

35. Stanisław Grotnowski, "O ciągłych atakach prasy żydowskiej na ustawę ubojową," *Szarża*, 7 February 1937, 4.

36. Moxim A. Parker, "Sprawdzone przysłowie," *Szarża*, 18 April 1937, 2.

37. Włod., "Raz na lewo, raz na prawo," *Szarża*, 31 January 1937, 3.

38. Stanisław Grotnowski, "O antysemityźmie sanacji," *Szarża*, 21 February 1937, 3.

39. Kerry Wallach, *Passing Illusions: Jewish Visibility in Weimar Germany* (Ann Arbor: University of Michigan Press, 2017), 2.

40. Wallach, *Passing Illusions*, 2.

41. Poraj., "'Polskie' radio," *Szarża*, 21 February 1937, 2.

42. See "W prasie, na placówkach dyplomatycznych i w Radjo—żydzi!," 2.

43. Maciej Józef Kwiatkowski, "Polskie Radio 1925–1939: Mała kronika," *Pamiętnik Teatralny* 22, no. 3–4 (1973): 400.

44. See, for example, the text by Kos., "Skrzynka radiowa," *Szarża*, 10 January 1937, 6.

45. Fitelberg became the organizer and chief conductor of the Polish Radio Orchestra in 1935 following more than a decade as the principal conductor of the Warsaw Philharmonic. See "Fitelberg Grzegorz," *Encyklopedia muzyki*, ed. Andrzej Chodkowski (Warszawa: Wydawnictwo Naukowe PWN, 2001), 266.

46. For a discussion of Mieses's other work, see, for example, Jerzy Jedlicki, "Resisting the Wave: Intellectuals against Antisemitism in the Last Years of the 'Polish Kingdom,'" in *Antisemitism and Its Opponents in Modern Poland*, 74.

47. Mateusz Mieses, *Polacy-chrześcijanie pochodzenia żydowskiego: Tom 1* (Warszawa: Wydawnictwo M. Fruchtmana, 1938), V-VI.

48. Mieses, *Polacy-chrześcijanie pochodzenia żydowskiego*, V.

49. The article was published in two parts: Mateusz Mieses, "Polacy chrześcijanie pochodzenia żydowskiego (I)," *Nasz Przegląd*, 6 March 1937, 6; and Mateusz Mieses, "Polacy chrześcijanie pochodzenia żydowskiego (II)," *Nasz Przegląd*, 7 March 1937, 18.

50. Michlic, *Poland's Threatening Other*, 98.

51. Poraj., "Gdyby król Staś ożył . . .," *Szarża*, 14 March 1937, 3.

52. akl., "Ostatni król polski był Żydem . . .," *Dziennik Poznański*, 9 March 1937, 2.

53. kol., "Profesor z Tworek," *ABC: Nowiny Codzienne*, 9 March 1937, 3.

54. Poraj., "Gdyby król Staś ożył . . .," *ABC: Nowiny Codzienne*, 14 March 1937, 8.

55. Ł., "Dr. Sławoj-Składkowski do premiera Sławoj-Składkowskiego," *Szarża*, 24 January 1937, 1.

56. Ł., "Wyrzucanie balastu," *Szarża*, 24 January 1937, 4.

57. See, for example, Włodzimierz Bartoszewicz, "Sanacja, żydzi i PP.S. [sic]," *Szarża*, 31 January 1937, 3; and "Stara piosenka w wykonaniu pułk: Miedzińskiego," *Szarża*, 28 February 1937, 1.

58. On similar editorial practices in interwar Austria, see Secklehner, "Simple Entertainment?," 131.

59. BUŁ, Rękopisy, PPKG, Korespondencja Kazimierza Grusa, sygn. 5241, Letter from Zbigniew Mitzner to Kazimierz Grus, 1 September 1954; and Letter from Eryk Lipiński to Kazimierz Grus, 15 September 1954. See also AMK, Maja Berezowska PF, Newspaper Clippings: Eryk Lipiński, "Maja," *Tu i teraz*, 26 January 1983, 13.

60. BUŁ, Rękopisy, PPKG, Korespondencja Kazimierza Grusa, sygn. 5241, Letter from J. Rutkowska to Kazimierz Grus, 15 March 1954.

61. See confiscation notices in issues published on 21 and 28 February 1937.

62. There is no personal folder devoted to Łukasik in the archives of the Museum of Caricature in Warsaw, but his surname does feature in the index card register. The card devoted to him lists his surname but not first name and his collaboration with *Żółta Mucha*. No other details are provided. See AMK, ICA, Łukasik Index Card, Undated. For examples of his cartoons in *Prosto z Mostu*, see issues from 3 October and 10 October 1937.

63. Poraj., "Min. Blum jako nowy Mojżesz," *Szarża*, 14 February 1937, 2.

64. Włod., "Kawałek dla nas," *Szarża*, 21 March 1937, 7.

65. See, for example, G. Bodek, "Przeszarżowanie," *Kontratak*, 14 March 1937, 4.

66. S. Filipski, "Z Polski do Palestyny można już lecieć samolotem," *Szarża*, 18 April 1937, 8.

67. See the special issue on city trams in the magazine *Wróble na Dachu*, 12 March 1933.

68. Jerzy Łazor, "Dzieje linii lewantyńskiej Polskich Linii Lotniczych 'Lot' w latach 30.," in *Ekonomia, Społeczeństwo, Polityka: Studia ofiarowane prof. dr. hab. Januszowi Kalińskiemu w 70. rocznicę urodzin*, ed. Andrzej Zawistowski (Warszawa: Szkoła Główna Handlowa, Oficyna Wydawnicza, 2012), 290–91.

69. "Otwarcie nowej polskiej linii lotniczej," *Kolejowe Przysposobienie Wojskowe*, 25 April 1937, 14; and "Pierwszy lot na linii Palestyna-Warszawa," *Dziennik Polski*, 8 April 1937, 5.

70. Łazor, "Dzieje linii lewantyńskiej," 291.

71. "Otwarcie komunikacji pocztowo-lotniczej z Polski do Palestyny," *Nowy Dziennik*, 4 April 1937, 1.

72. "Polish-Palestine Airline Uses U.S. Planes," *JTA*, 30 April 1937.

73. Łazor, "Dzieje linii lewantyńskiej," 291.

74. "Polish Airlines as Letter Carriers," *Palestine Post*, 2 May 1937, 5.

75. "Passengers on First Polish Plane Feted in Tel Aviv," *JTA*, 8 April 1937.

76. Poraj., "Jak się robi popularność w Sowietach," *Szarża*, 4 April 1937, 3.

77. Poraj., "Chęć odegrania . . .," *Szarża*, 14 February 1937, 6.

78. See, for example, *Obcy i niemili*, 100.

79. See Poraj., "Ikona popa Wołoszyna," *Czarno na białem*, 19 February 1939, 10.

80. "Aleksander Dzierżawski," in *Czy wiesz kto to jest?*, ed. Stanisław Łoza (Warszawa: Wydawnictwa Artystyczne i Filmowe, 1983), 160.

81. Górska and Lipiński, *Z dziejów karykatury polskiej*, 223.

82. Minkiewicz in Lipiński, *Drzewo Szpilkowe*, 25.
83. Stanisław Borowkin, "'Gazetka Miki' (1938–1939)," *Kwartalnik Historii Prasy Polskiej* 27, no. 1 (1988): 42–43.
84. Aleksandra Bończa-Waśniewska appeared on the cover as the editor in chief of the weekly. See Borowkin, "'Gazetka Miki' (1938–1939)," 42.
85. Andrzej Piasecki, "'Gazeta Powiatowa' w Turku (1919–1922): zarys dziejów," *Kwartalnik Historii Prasy Polskiej* 28, no. 2 (1989): 55–56, 61, 63, 66–67.
86. Piasecki, "'Gazeta Powiatowa' w Turku (1919–1922)," 66–67.
87. Aleksander Dzierżawski, *Bankructwo socjalizmu i komunizmu* (Warszawa: Wydawnictwo Zw. Ludowo-Narodowego, 1927), 3.
88. Dzierżawski, *Bankructwo socjalizmu i komunizmu*, 12.
89. Dzierżawski, *Bankructwo socjalizmu i komunizmu*, 15.
90. Jovan Byford, "Conspiracy Theories," in *Key Concepts in the Study of Antisemitism*, ed. Sol Goldberg, Scott Ury, and Kalman Weiser (Cham: Palgrave Macmillan, 2021), 82.
91. Aleksander Dzierżawski, *Świnie i koryto: bajki polityczne* (Warszawa: Warszawskie Zakłady Graficzne, 1936), 5.
92. Dzierżawski, *Świnie i koryto*, 7.
93. Dzierżawski, *Świnie i koryto*, 14.
94. Dzierżawski, *Świnie i koryto*, 89.
95. See Lipiński, *Pamiętniki*, 87, 92, 94.
96. AASP Warsaw, SR 1922–1939, sygn. 730, Student Folder of Eryk Lipiński, Eryk Lipiński's Letter to Rector, 15 October 1935.
97. See Minkiewicz, "Pamiętniki. Rozdział XVI," 6.
98. See Lipiński's admiring comments on Grus's and Zaruba's work respectively: Lipiński, *Drzewo Szpilkowe*, 77; and Lipiński, *Pamiętniki*, 339–40.
99. J.K., "'Swinie [sic] i koryto' czyli odrodzenie humoru polskiego," *ABC: Nowiny Codzienne*, 9 February 1937, 4.
100. A. Grzymała-Siedlecki, "Nowe dziecko Ezopa," *Kurjer Warszawski*, 13 October 1936, 3.
101. A. Dzierżawski, "Świnie i koryto" and "Wilcze obietnice," *Pokrzywy*, 21 November 1937, 3.
102. AL, *Amerykańskie bajki plugawe: Niecenzuralne—tylko dla dorosłych* (New York: Polish Book Importing Co., 1937), 2.
103. The quotation comes from a review of a small book by Janusz Szczepański, *Ksiądz Aleksander Syski na Mazowszu i wśród Polonii amerykańskiej* (Ciechanów: Muzeum Okręgowe w Ciechanowie, 1994). See M. B. Biskupski, Review of *Ksiądz Aleksander Syski na Mazowszu i wśród Polonii amerykańskiej*, *Polish American Studies* 52, no. 2 (1995): 82.
104. Julian Żebrowski, "Tam, gdzie mniejszość jest większością," *Szarża*, 18 April 1937, 3.
105. For an extensive list of his antisemitic cartoons, see *Obcy i niemili*, 110–14.
106. Marek Nowakowski, *Tak zapamiętałem* (Wydawnictwo Zysk i S-ka: Poznań, 2014), 66.
107. See "Filmujemy polską wieś," *Szarża*, 21 March 1937, 6.
108. See Górska and Lipiński, *Z dziejów karykatury polskiej*, 223.
109. (ak)., "Jutro i Szarża," *Kontratak*, 6 June 1937, 2.

110. Zbigniew Mitzner, "Przedmowa," in Zbigniew Mitzner and Leon Pasternak, *Satyra prawdę mówi . . . 1918–1939* (Warszawa: Czytelnik, 1963), 14.

111. Julian Żebrowski, *Polski Londyn w karykaturach* (Brooklyn, NY: Polstar Publishing Corp., 1985).

112. Nowakowski, *Tak zapamiętałem*, 66.

113. APW, SGW, Nr zesp. 655, sygn. 5/4171, Melania Teresa Szpigiel to Municipal Court in Warsaw, 20 December 1948, p. 2.

114. Andrzej R. Tyczno, "Bene Meritus dla Aleksandra Stefana Dzierżawskiego," *Z kart historii Ziemi Dobrskiej: Stowarzyszenie Przyjaciół Ziemi Dobrskiej*, 4 September 2014, https://ziemiadobrska.wordpress.com/2014/09/04/bene-meritus-dla-aleksandra-stefana-dzierzawskiego/.

CHAPTER 5: SATIRE FOR THE MASSES

1. Janina Jaworska, *Polska sztuka walcząca 1939–1945* (Warszawa: Wydawnictwa Artystyczne i Filmowe, 1985), 209.

2. AŻIH, TJS, sygn. 301/4583, Testimony of Ferster Karol, Kraków, 13 July 1946, pp. 1–3.

3. Piotr Borowiec, "Krótka historia wydawnictwa i koncernu Ilustrowany Kurier Codzienny (1910–1939)," in *Ilustrowany Kurier Codzienny. Księga pamiątkowa w stulecie powstania dziennika i wydawnictwa (1910–1939)*, ed. Grażyna Wrona, Piotr Borowiec, and Krzysztof Woźniakowski (Kraków: "Śląsk" Wydawnictwo Naukowe, 2010), 18–19.

4. Andrzej Paczkowski, "Prasa w życiu politycznym Drugiej Rzeczypospolitej," *Dzieje Najnowsze* 10, no. 3 (1978): 44.

5. Paczkowski, "Prasa w życiu politycznym Drugiej Rzeczypospolitej," 44.

6. Witz and Zaruba, *50 lat karykatury polskiej*, 47. See also APKr, StaGK, Referat Bezpieczeństwa Publicznego, Nadzór nad drukami i ich ewidencji (czasopisma) V-Z, sygn. 29/218/277, Overview of the magazine and its editors, no date, p. 877.

7. Bergmann, *"Prawdziwa cnota krytyk się nie boi . . . ,"* 59.

8. Żółkiewska, *Wolny Ptak: Der Frajer Fojgl*, 47.

9. Witz and Zaruba, *50 lat karykatury polskiej*, 49. See also *Obcy i niemili*, 110.

10. Lipiński, *Drzewo Szpilkowe*, 106.

11. Joanna Zawadzka, "Piotrowski Mieczysław," in *Współcześni pisarze i badacze literatury: Słownik bibliograficzny, Tom 6*, ed. Jadwiga Czachowska and Alicja Szałagan (Warszawa: Wydawnictwa Szkolne i Pedagogiczne S.A., 1999), 384.

12. Bergmann, "Problematyka żydowska w karykaturach polskich czasopism satyrycznych Drugiej Rzeczypospolitej," 489.

13. Górska and Lipiński, *Z dziejów karykatury polskiej*, 225.

14. M. Piotrowski, "Tegoroczna szopka warszawska," *Wróble na Dachu*, 26 December 1937, 4.

15. L. R. Lewitter, "The Polish 'Szopka,'" *Slavonic and East European Review* 29, no. 72 (1950): 77.

16. Melzer, *No Way Out*, 73.

17. Melzer, *No Way Out*, 76.

18. Melzer, *No Way Out*, 74–75.
19. Melzer, *No Way Out*, 78. See also Michlic, *Poland's Threatening Other*, 113.
20. M. Piotrowski, "Z powodu ponownych zamknięć wyższych uczelni," *Wróble na Dachu*, 28 March 1937, 7.
21. See Antoni Dudek and Grzegorz Pytel, *Bolesław Piasecki. Próba biografii politycznej* (Londyn: Aneks, 1990), 69.
22. See Heather R. Perry, *Recycling the Disabled: Army, Medicine, and Modernity in WWI Germany* (Manchester, UK: Manchester University Press, 2014), 1.
23. Poet Antoni Słonimski explicitly criticized such historical comparisons in his weekly column for *Wiadomości Literackie*. See Słonimski, *Kroniki tygodniowe 1936–1939*, 114.
24. Michlic, *Poland's Threatening Other*, 113.
25. Piotrowski, "Idealne urządzenie sali wykładowej . . .," 7.
26. M. Piotrowski, "Gdy młodzież akademicka po 'utarczkach' zasiądzie na jednej ławie . . .," *Wróble na Dachu*, 11 April 1937, 4.
27. Charlie, "Na uniwersytetach wprowadzono obowiązkowe ćwiczenia fizyczne," *Wróble na Dachu*, 24 October 1937, 7.
28. Dudek and Pytel, *Bolesław Piasecki*, 81.
29. Charlie, "Zadowolony rasista," *Wróble na Dachu*, 21 November 1937, 6.
30. Brykczynski, *Primed for Violence*, 27.
31. Brykczynski, *Primed for Violence*, 27, 40.
32. See, for example, the following cartoons: J. Zaruba, "Wielkanoc w Polsce dzisiejszej" and Wik, "Śmigus w Grajdołku," *Wróble na Dachu*, 28 March 1937, 3, 13; Charlie, "Przewidujący uczeń," *Wróble na Dachu*, 12 December 1937, 7; and a satirical text: "Na wyższych uczelniach," *Wróble na Dachu*, 28 March 1937, 11.
33. Wik, "Dyskusja polityczna," *Wróble na Dachu*, 28 November 1937, 4–5.
34. See Wik, "Na 'zastępczej służbie wojskowej,'" *Wróble na Dachu*, 31 October 1937, 8.
35. AUJ, KGS UJ, Karta Wpisowa nr 411, Ludwik Heller, 21 September 1923.
36. SA, VD, inv. no 481/188.038, City of Antwerp Police, Ludwik Heller Registration Form, typed, signed by Ludwik Heller, 5 June 1928.
37. M. Piotrowski, "Świąteczny 'wyrąb ryb' . . .," *Wróble na Dachu*, 26 December 1937, 9.
38. Three weeks later, the Polish Jewish weekly *Kontratak* published an anonymous cartoon on the same topic. The cartoon presented a group of fish waving student canes and saying that anyone who has had experience in breaking shop windows can now sell fish. See "Ryby technickie," *Kontratak*, 14 January 1938, 4.
39. See, for example, Zbigniew Grotowski, "Berlin 1950," *Wróble na Dachu*, 26 September 1937, 2; "Siła przyzwyczajenia," *Wróble na Dachu*, 17 October 1937, 3; B. Brzez., "Światło zgasło," *Wróble na Dachu*, 21 November 1937, 6; and "Z kosza redakcyjnego: Na razie emigracja . . .," *Wróble na Dachu*, 11 April 1937, 3.
40. Mr. Birch, "Życie po lewej stronie," *Wróble na Dachu*, 24 October 1937, 7.
41. See Lipiński, *Drzewo Szpilkowe*, 211–16.
42. Bergmann, "Prawdziwa cnota krytyk się nie boi . . .," 83.
43. This is how ONR more generally was described by the PPS outlet *Robotnik*. See Kunicki, *Between the Brown and the Red*, 24.

44. Bergmann, *"Prawdziwa cnota krytyk się nie boi . . .,"* 65–66.
45. Paczkowski, "Prasa w życiu politycznym Drugiej Rzeczypospolitej," 44.
46. Borowiec, "Krótka historia," 53. See also APKr, SGK, The Prosecutor of Municipal Court in Kraków, Announcement of Confiscation of *Wróble na Dachu*, issue from 28 March 1937, sygn. 29/442/15988, 25 March 1937; and Announcement of Confiscation of *Wróble na Dachu*, issue from 26 December 1937, sygn. 29/442/16279, 20 December 1937.
47. Górska and Lipiński, *Z dziejów karykatury polskiej*, 225.
48. See, for example, J. Bickels, "Włoska arja!," *Wróble na Dachu*, 26 September 1937, 3; and J. Bickels, "Mussolini przejeżdżał przez Berlin na białym koniu," *Wróble na Dachu*, 3 October 1937, 2.
49. See, for example, J. Bickels and Mr. Homo, "Defilada czołgów przed kanclerzem," *Kontratak*, 8 November 1936, 4; J. Bickels and Homo, "Ewolucja swastyki czyli . . .," *Kontratak*, 6 June 1937, 3; and J. Bickels, "Badanie lekarskie nowowstępującego na uniwersytet," *Kontratak*, 6 October 1937, 4.
50. See, for example, A. Wasilewski, "Nasz projekt ławki," *Wróble na Dachu*, 26 September 1937, 1; and A. Wasilewski, "Kanclerz Hitler . . ." and "Trójmecz międzynarodowy," *Wróble na Dachu*, 3 October 1937, 1, 3.
51. A. Wasilewski, "Nad modrym Dunajem," *Wróble na Dachu*, 20 March 1938, 1.
52. See two color cartoons: Charlie, "Po przewrocie w Austrji," *Wróble na Dachu*, 20 March 1938, 8; and Charlie, "Zorza polarna nad Europą Środkową," *Wróble na Dachu*, 22 May 1938, 1.
53. Charlie, "W kraju propagandy rozrodczości," *Wróble na Dachu*, 28 March 1937, 13; and Charlie, "W Niemczech nakazano zbiórkę włosów," *Wróble na Dachu*, 8 August 1937, 3.
54. Bergmann, *"Prawdziwa cnota krytyk się nie boi . . .,"* 85.
55. One Polish biographer of the time described Kiepura emphatically as "the king of singers" who had "gold in his throat." See A. Rogalski, *Jan Kiepura: Król śpiewaków* (Warszawa: Universum, 1933), 3.
56. See, for example, A. Wasilewski, "Człowiek zapomniany w Polsce," *Wróble na Dachu*, 10 March 1935, 1; A. Wasilewski, "Po koncercie Kiepury" and J. Bickels, "Kiepura za 100 lat," *Wróble na Dachu*, 17 October 1937, 1, 2; Rena, "Po porywających występach cudownego dziecka Europy," *Wróble na Dachu*, 27 March 1938, 5; Rena, "Po dwóch występach chóru Dana w Kownie," *Wróble na Dachu*, 22 May 1938, 6; Charlie, "Jan Kiepura na Capri," *Wróble na Dachu*, 29 May 1938, 6; and Wik, "Na koncercie Kiepury na 'Starem Mieście,'" *Wróble na Dachu*, 9 July 1939, 5.
57. See A. Wasilewski, "Ostatni kobziarz," *Wróble na Dachu*, 10 January 1937, 8; and Charlie, "Ks. Windsor w Hollywood," *Wróble na Dachu*, 17 October 1937, 5.
58. A. Wasilewski, "Poprawki holenderskie," *Wróble na Dachu*, 10 January 1937, 7; A. Wasilewski, "Aktualne poprawki w pijalni wód," *Wróble na Dachu*, 17 January 1937, 1; and Charlie, "Z imprez zimowych w Krynicy" and M. Piotrowski, "Jak mały Jaś wyobraża sobie . . .," *Wróble na Dachu*, 24 January 1937, 1, 5.
59. A. Wasilewski, "Na temat pewnego ślubu w arystokracji," *Wróble na Dachu*, 7 November 1937, 1.
60. "Ks. Radziwiłł oskarżony o bigamię," *ABC: Nowiny Codzienne*, 7 November 1937, 4; and "Ks. Michał Radziwiłł oskarżony o bigamię?," *Kurjer Poznański*, 7 November 1937, 9.

61. A. Wasilewski, "Co wyrabiasz stary chłopie, Pana Boga się bój," *Wróble na Dachu*, 7 November 1937, 3.

62. See, for example, Rachel Josefowitz Siegel, "Antisemitism and Sexism in Stereotypes of Jewish Women," *Women & Therapy* 5, no. 2–3 (1986): 254; and Riv Ellen-Prell, "Why Jewish Princesses Don't Sweat: Desire and Consumption in Postwar American Jewish Culture," in *People of the Body: Jews and Judaism from an Embodied Perspective*, ed. Howard Eilberg-Schwartz (Albany: State University of New York Press, 1992), 341.

63. See, for example, Dana Mihăilescu, *Eastern European Jewish American Narratives, 1890–1930: Struggles for Recognition* (Lanham, MD: Lexington Books, 2018), 79; and Kazimierz Adamczyk, "Kobieta w powieściach polskich ideologów ruchu nacjonalistycznego," *Konteksty kultury* 11, no. 3 (2014): 299.

64. Sara R. Horowitz, "Gender," in *Key Concepts in the Study of Antisemitism*, 115.

65. Secklehner, "Simple Entertainment?," 133.

66. Secklehner, "Simple Entertainment?," 124.

67. "500 tys. zł. zapisał ks. Radziwiłł," *Wieczorna Gazeta Wileńska*, 11 November 1937, 3.

68. "Co mówi prosty robotnik z ordynacji ks. Radziwiłła o ślubie swego pana," *Dziennik Poznański*, 29 December 1937, 5.

69. See Felix, "Fraszki aktualne. Na pewnego księcia," *Wróble na Dachu*, 21 November 1937, 6; and Ali-Baba, "Co wiem o miłości: Książę Radziwiłł," *Wróble na Dachu*, 26 December 1937, 4.

70. "Kaprysy księcia," *ABC: Nowiny Codzienne*, 28 November 1937, 4.

71. See, for example, "Ks. Michał Radziwiłł i p. Suchestow," *Dzień dobry!*, 1 December 1937, 6; and "Ks. Michał Radziwiłł zgolił rudą brodę," *ABC: Nowiny Codzienne*, 24 November 1937, 2.

72. Marek, "Książę Michał Radziwiłł z narzeczoną," *Pokrzywy*, 7 November 1937, 1.

73. Charlie, "Mezalians w sferach arystokracji," *Wróble na Dachu*, 14 November 1937, 7.

74. For another cartoon in *Pokrzywy* that stated that explicitly, see Marek, "Judeo-Polska w Antoninie," *Pokrzywy*, 21 November 1937, 1. See also Marek, "Marzenia księcia Radziwiłła," *Pokrzywy*, 21 December 1937, 7.

75. See, for example, IPO., "Na ślub ks. Radziwiłła z Żydówką," *ABC: Nowiny Codzienne*, 5 November 1937, 3; "U pani Jenty vel Żanety Suchestow, narzeczonej ks. Michała Radziwiłła z Antonin," *Mucha*, 19 November 1937, 6; and "Korespondencja braterska," *Mucha*, 24 December 1937, 4.

76. AMK, Karol Ferster "Charlie" PF, Newspaper Clippings: Ewa Garztecka, "Rysownik Charlie," *Trybuna Ludu*, 10 August 1986.

77. AMK, Karol Ferster "Charlie" PF, Personal Questionnaire (handwritten) and typed biography. Both unsigned and undated.

78. AASP Kraków, Księga świadectw Państwowej Komisji Egzaminacyjnej przy ASP w Krakowie od roku akademickiego 1925–1926, Förster Karol, Świadectwo, 27 April 1926.

79. AMK, Karol Ferster "Charlie" PF, Personal Questionnaire.

80. Rena, "Ostatnie odgałęzienie drzewa geneologicznego," *Wróble na Dachu*, 21 November 1937, 3.

81. See, for example, Rena, "Jak sobie mały Staś . . .," *Wróble na Dachu*, 28 November 1937, 3.

82. Zawadzka, "Piotrowski Mieczysław," 384.

83. AASP Warsaw, SR 1922–1939, sygn. 429, Student Folder of Regina Kańska, Confirmation of Teaching Diploma by Rector Professor Ksawery Piwocki, 1 December 1937.

84. AASP Warsaw, SR 1922–1939, sygn. 429, Curriculum Vitae by Regina Kańska, 24 September 1932.

85. "Nawyki," *Wróble na Dachu*, 28 November 1937, 6.

86. "Rodzynki," *Wróble na Dachu*, 26 December 1937, 13.

87. Zbigniew Grotowski, "Prosiłem ją w Borysławiu . . .," *Wróble na Dachu*, 7 November 1937, 2.

88. See, for example, Grotowski, "Berlin 1950" and Zbigniew Grotowski, "Podróż do Warszawy," *Wróble na Dachu*, 12 December 1937, 2.

89. For reprints of the interview, see, for example, "Miłość moją ulegalizuję małżeństwem," *Chwila*, 30 November 1937, 8; and "Ciekawy wywiad z ks. Michałem Radziwiłłem," *Dziennik Kujawski*, 1 December 1937, 3.

90. Cała, *Wizerunek Żyda w polskiej kulturze ludowej*, 55.

91. A. Wasilewski, "A moja Rebeka," *Wróble na Dachu*, 16 January 1938, 1.

92. Charlie, "Ks. Michał Radziwiłł w Monte Carlo," *Wróble na Dachu*, 9 January 1938, 7; and Charlie, "Ruletka w oczach ks. Michała Radziwiłła," *Wróble na Dachu*, 16 January 1938, 6.

93. For a brief summary of the proposed film, see "Ks. Radziwiłł i p. Suchestow otrzymali propozycje [sic] do filmu," *Dziennik poranny*, 8 March 1938, 2.

94. Rena, "Książę Radziwiłł i pani Suchestow będą nakręcali film," *Wróble na Dachu*, 20 March 1938, 4–5.

95. A. Wasilewski, "Policjant do pani Suchestow" and Charlie, "Ks. Michał Radziwiłł w niedalekiej przyszłości," *Wróble na Dachu*, 29 May 1938, 1, 7.

96. Wasilewski, "Policjant do pani Suchestow," 1.

97. See, for example, "Nigdy nie kochałam księcia . . .," *Głos Poranny*, 27 May 1938, 5.

98. This is how Suchestow's attorney described the circumstances of her abandonment by Radziwiłł. See "Trzeci ślub ks. Radziwiłła nieważny w Polsce," *Dzień dobry!*, 24 May 1938, 9.

99. See, for example, J. Zaruba, "Główny powód," *Wróble na Dachu*, 25 July 1937, 4–5.

100. J. Zaruba, "Jak powinny wyglądać nasze stacje benzynowe," *Wróble na Dachu*, 8 August 1937, 1.

101. J. Zaruba, "Reformy w Armji Czerwonej," *Wróble na Dachu*, 18 July 1937, 6.

102. J. Zaruba, "Memento . . .," *Wróble na Dachu*, 18 July 1937, 3.

103. Br. Schneider, "W Z.S.R.R.," *Wróble na Dachu*, 8 August 1937, 6.

104. See, for example, Br. Schneider, "Przed gmachem sądu," *Wróble na Dachu*, 28 March 1937, 7. Admittedly, some of his cartoons for *Kontratak* would suggest that these sensibilities were mostly limited to the representations of white Europeans. For a cartoon on Africa, see Br. Schneider and Mr. Homo, "Niemcy szukają kolonii . . .," *Kontratak*, 8 November 1936, 5.

105. AMK, Jerzy Zaruba PF, Jerzy Zaruba (typewritten biography, signed "EL"); and Personal Questionnaire (handwritten, unsigned). Both undated and unpaginated.

106. AMK, Jerzy Zaruba PF, "Ulica Jerzego Zaruby" by Eryk Lipiński, Typescript, undated and unpaginated. See also AMK, Jerzy Zaruba PF, Newspaper clippings: "Zaruba w 'Szpilkach,'" *Życie Warszawy*, 18 February 1981.

107. Zaruba, *Z pamiętników bywalca*, 20.

108. "Bronisław Schneider," in *Czasy wojen i pokoju*, 157. See also Żółkiewska, *Wolny Ptak*, 47.

109. Baigell, *Implacable Urge to Defame*, 95.

110. Górska and Lipiński, *Z dziejów karykatury polskiej*, 225.

111. Ilan Danjoux, *Political Cartoons and the Israeli-Palestinian Conflict* (Manchester, UK: Manchester University Press, 2012), 7. See also Lamb, *Drawn to Extremes*, 22.

112. M. Piotrowski, "Bony," *Wróble na Dachu*, 15 May 1938, 1; M. Piotrowski, "Pogotowie gazowe w Pradze," *Wróble na Dachu*, 12 June 1938, 7; and M. Piotrowski, "Wkrótce ma być ogłoszony konkurs na 'polski salut,'" *Wróble na Dachu*, 20 November 1938, 6.

113. Piotrowski, "Wkrótce ma być ogłoszony. . . ."

114. Inż. H., "Wprowadzić oddzielne wagony dla żydów!," *ABC: Nowiny Codzienne*, 28 October 1936, 2.

115. "Osobne wagony dla żydów," *ABC: Nowiny Codzienne*, 29 November 1936, 2.

116. "Osobne wagony dla żydów?," *ABC: Nowiny Codzienne*, 10 August 1937, 3.

117. "Niema [sic] 'wagonów dla żydów,'" *Głos Poranny*, 15 July 1937, 4.

118. "Osobnych wagonów dla żydów żąda społeczeństwo Pomorza," *ABC: Nowiny Codzienne*, 8 February 1938, 3.

119. M. Piotrowski, "W Poznaniu domagają się wprowadzenia w pociągach przedziałów dla Żydów," *Wróble na Dachu*, 20 February 1938, 7.

120. Marsot, "Cartoon in Egypt," 14.

121. Lipiński, *Drzewo Szpilkowe*, 106.

122. Teresa Kłosiewicz, "W Galerii Interpress. Rysunek prasowy," *Trybuna Ludu*, 26 March 1980, 8.

123. See AMK, Mieczysław Piotrowski PF 2, Newspaper clippings: "W Pałacyku TPSP: Ha-Ga i Piotrowski," *Życie Warszawy*, 4 October 1985.

124. *Obcy i niemili*, 100.

125. R. Kańska, "Z powodu rozruchów w angielskich dominjach," *Wróble na Dachu*, 7 November 1937, 2.

126. See, for example, K. Nor., "Na marginesie," *Pielgrzym: pismo religijne dla ludu*, 8 March 1938, 3. For a scathing commentary from a Polish Jewish daily containing quotes from the right-wing proponents of the idea, see ESES., "ABC żąda oddzielnych wagonów dla Żydów," *5-ta Rano*, 1 July 1937, 5.

127. Rena, "Transport Tyrolczyków do Niemiec," *Wróble na Dachu*, 30 July 1939, 7.

128. AMK, Eryk Lipiński PF 3; Newspaper Clippings: "Zuzanna Lipińska, córka założyciela 'Szpilek' i rysowniczki, przywraca pamięć o dziełach rodziców," *gazeta.pl*.

129. See Bergmann, *"Prawdziwa cnota krytyk się nie boi . . . ,"* 52.

130. She is not mentioned in Lipiński's memoir *Drzewo Szpilkowe*, which also covers the 1930s.

131. Katarzyna Murawska-Muthesius, Untitled text, in Anna Gosławska-Lipińska, *Ha ha Ha-Ga* (Warszawa: Bęc Zmiana, 2015), 8.

132. Lamb, *Drawn to Extremes*, 90–92.

133. Kańska puts down 1931–1936 as the period of her studies. Here, I retain the dates I have found in her university records. See AASP Warsaw, Confirmation of Teaching Diploma by Rector Professor Ksawery Piwocki.

134. AMK, Regina Piotrowska PF, Personal Questionnaire (handwritten, unsigned, and undated); and Letter from Regina Piotrowska to Eryk Lipiński (22 May 1969). For more information on *Rózgi*, see Górska and Lipiński, *Z dziejów karykatury polskiej*, 257–59.

135. See, for example, cover illustrations in the following issues of *Rózgi*: 9 March 1947; 16 March 1947; 23 March 1947; 1 April 1947; 6 April 1947; 27 April 1947; 12 May 1947; 18 May 1947; 25 May 1947; 1 June 1947; 15 June 1947; and 31 August 1947. In addition, smaller cartoons by her appeared in other issues of the magazine, including on 13 October 1946; 27 October 1946; 17 November 1946; 15 December 1946; 22 December 1946; 1 January 1947; 26 January 1947; 2 February 1947; and 9 February 1947, among others.

136. See also Rena, "Jak sobie mały Staś . . ." and "Książę Radziwiłł i pani Suchestow będą nakręcali film."

137. Rena, "Pamiątkowy kandelaber . . .," *Wróble na Dachu*, 24 April 1938, 3.

138. Plach, "Ritual Slaughter and Animal Welfare," 19.

139. Plach, "Ritual Slaughter and Animal Welfare," 18.

140. Plach, "Ritual Slaughter and Animal Welfare," 19.

141. A. Wasilewski, "Po skasowaniu uboju rytualnego," *Wróble na Dachu*, 3 April 1938, 1.

142. See Charlie, "Mitologja zaktualizowana. Porwanie Europy . . .," *Wróble na Dachu*, 19 December 1937, 6. For more on Prystorowa's involvement in the proposal, see Plach, "Ritual Slaughter and Animal Welfare," 15–17.

143. A. Wasilewski, "Rumunja przeistacza się pod rządami premjera Gogi," *Wróble na Dachu*, 9 January 1938, 3.

144. A. Wasilewski, "Szopka rumuńska," *Wróble na Dachu*, 9 January 1938, 7.

145. A. Wasilewski, "Z rumuńskiej szopki," *Wróble na Dachu*, 20 February 1938, 1.

146. M. Piotrowski, "Po upadku gabinetu rumuńskiego, premjera Gogi—poety," *Wróble na Dachu*, 20 February 1938, 3.

147. See also the following cartoon on Romanian Jews: St. Brzozowski, "Djablik drukarski w rumuńskim komunikacie gospodarczym," *Wróble na Dachu*, 16 January 1938, 6. Although the cartoon does focus on the possible expulsion of Romanian Jews, it does not point to Poland as a possible destination. See also a satirical text that discusses Goga's plans to send the Jewish population to Madagascar: gr., "Rozmawiam z Gogą," *Wróble na Dachu*, 20 February 1938, 3.

148. This is how the publisher described the intended readership of the magazine. See APKr, StaGK, Referat Bezpieczeństwa Publicznego, Nadzór nad drukami i ich ewidencji (czasopisma) V-Z, sygn. 29/218/277, Overview of the magazine and its editors, no date, p. 875.

149. AMK, Antoni Wasilewski PF, Autobiography of Antoni Wasilewski—Tony, typed, undated; and "Antoni Wasilewski—dziennikarz, art. grafik," Biography, typed, undated.

150. Karol Ferster, *Szkice z podróży. Rysunki satyryczne* (Warszawa: Związek Polskich Artystów Plastyków Okręg Warszawski, 1978). See also USC Shoah Foundation Institute, Testimony of Serafina Ferster, VHA Interview Code: 37592, 12 November 1997.

151. AMK, Jakub Bickels PF, Letter from Eryk Lipiński to Józef Bickels, 17 May 1989.

152. Andrzej Nawrot, "Historia Katedry Ubioru Akademii Sztuk Pięknych w Łodzi," accessed 10 May 2022, http://www.ubior.asp.lodz.pl/historia_c.htm.

153. Katarzyna Wrona, "Zmiana formuły 'Przekroju' w latach 2000–2013," *Acta Universitatis Lodziensis: Folia Literaria Polonica* 2, no. 28 (2015): 222.

CONCLUSION

1. Julia Secklehner, "Belligerent Drawing? The Satirical Press in Prague and Vienna 1918–1938" (PhD thesis, Courtauld Institute of Art, 2018), 34–35.
2. Hollender, *Polska bez Żydów*, 38.
3. See Kunicki, *Between the Brown and the Red*, 16.
4. Jean-Paul Sartre, *Anti-Semite and Jew* (New York: Schocken Books, 1995), 55–56.
5. Witold Filler, "Za nami, przed nami," *Szpilki*, 5 December 1985, 2.
6. See Brykczynski, *Primed for Violence*, 96.
7. Jedlicki, "Resisting the Wave," 80.
8. Antoni Słonimski, *Wspomnienia warszawskie* (Warszawa: Wydawnictwo Agora, 2017), 114.
9. Agnieszka Skalska, *Obraz wroga w antysemickich rysunkach prasowych Marca '68* (Warszawa: Narodowe Centrum Kultury, 2007), 47–49, 67.

WORKS CITED

ARCHIVAL SOURCES

Archiwum Mitznerów (AM). Biblioteka Narodowa (BN, The National Library), Warsaw.

Artist Folders (AF); and Index Card Archive (ICA). Archiwum Muzeum Karykatury (AMK, Museum of Caricature Archives), Warsaw.

Katalog główny studentów UJ za rok szkolny 1923/1924, filozofia studenci—karty wpisowe—słuchacze zwyczajni, litery A-J (KGS UJ). Archiwum Uniwersytetu Jagiellońskiego (AUJ, The Archive of the Jagiellonian University).

Księga świadectw Państwowej Komisji Egzaminacyjnej przy ASP w Krakowie od roku akademickiego 1925–1926. Archiwum Akademii Sztuk Pięknych w Krakowie (AASP Kraków, The Academy of Arts), Kraków.

Ministerstwo Spraw Zagranicznych (MSZ); and Polski Związek Wydawców Dzienników i Czasopism (PZWDziCz). Archiwum Akt Nowch (AAN, The Archive of New Documents), Warsaw.

Private Papers of Kazimierz Grus (PPKG). Biblioteka Uniwersytetu Łódzkiego (BUŁ, The Library of the University of Łódź).

Sąd Grodzki w Krakowie (SGK); and Starostwo Grodzkie Krakowskie (StaGK). Archiwum Państwowe w Krakowie (APKr, The National Archive in Kraków).

Sąd Grodzki w Warszawie (SGW). Archiwum Państwowe w Warszawie (APW, The National Archive in Warsaw).

Starostwo Powiatowe w Kaliszu (SPK). Archiwum Państwowe w Kaliszu (APKa, The National Archive in Kalisz).

Student Records 1915–1939 (SR). Archiwum Uniwersytetu Warszawskiego (AUW, The Archive of the University of Warsaw).

Student Records 1922–1939 (SR). Archiwum Akademii Sztuk Pięknych w Warszawie (AASP Warsaw, The Academy of Arts), Warsaw.

Testimonies of Jewish Survivors of the Holocaust (TJS); Papers of Józef and Ernestyna Sandel (SP); and The Yad Vashem Collection (YVC). Archiwum Żydowskiego Instytutu Historycznego (AŻIH, Archives of Jewish Historical Institute), Warsaw.

Video Testimonies. USC Shoah Foundation Institute Visual History Archive, Los Angeles, CA.

Vreemdelingendossiers (VD). Stadsarchief Antwerpen (SA, Antwerp City Archives).

MAGAZINES AND NEWSPAPERS

ABC: Nowiny Codzienne
Agencja Antymasońska: Biuletyn
Chwila
Czarno na białem
Czas
Drwęca
Dzień dobry!
Dziennik Bydgoski
Dziennik Kujawski
Dziennik Polski
Dziennik Poranny
Dziennik Poznański
Dziennik Wileński
Expres Zagłębia
Falanga
Gazeta Radomska
Gazeta Robotnicza
Głos Narodowy
Głos Poranny
Jewish Telegraphic Agency (JTA)
Kino
Kłosy
Kolejowe Przysposobienie Wojskowe
Kontratak
Kurjer Nowogródzki
Kurjer Poznański
Kurjer Warszawski
Mały Dziennik
Monitor Polski
Mucha
Narodowe Życie Gospodarcze
Nasz Przegląd
New York Times
Nowiny Literackie
Nowy Dziennik
Odgłosy
5-ta rano
Pielgrzym: pismo religijne dla ludu
Pod Pręgierz
Pokrzywy
Polska Karta
Polska Narodowa
Polska Zbrojna
Pręgierz
Przegląd Katolicki
Przegląd Zachodni
Robotnik
Rózgi
Samodzielność
Sygnały
Szarża
Szpilki
The Palestine Post
Trybuna Ludu
Tygodnik Literacki Polski Zbrojnej
Warszawski Dziennik Narodowy
Wiadomości Literackie
Wieczorna Gazeta Wileńska
Wróble na Dachu
Zbudzona Polska

OTHER PRIMARY SOURCES

AL. *Amerykańskie bajki plugawe: Niecenzuralne: tylko dla dorosłych*. New York: Polish Book Importing Co., 1937.

Berman, Mieczysław. "Czapka Frygijska." In *Księga wspomnień*, 53–90. Warszawa: Czytelnik, 1960.

Drugi powszechny spis ludności z dn. 9. XII. 1931 r. Warszawa: Główny Urząd Statystyczny Rzeczypospolitej Polskiej), 1938.

Drymmer, Wiktor Tomir. "Zagadnienie żydowskie w Polsce w latach 1935–1939 (Wspomnienie z pracy w Ministerstwie Spraw Zagranicznych)." *Zeszyty historyczne* 13 (1968): 55–77.

Dzierżawski, Aleksander. *Bankructwo socjalizmu i komunizmu.* Warszawa: Wydawnictwo Zw. Ludowo-Narodowego, 1927.
Dzierżawski, Aleksander. *Świnie i koryto: bajki polityczne.* Warszawa: Warszawskie Zakłady Graficzne, 1936.
Ferster, Karol. *Szkice z podróży: Rysunki satyryczne.* Warszawa: Związek Polskich Artystów Plastyków Okręg Warszawski, 1978.
Harten, Henryk St. (Harvey). *Ojciec zadżumionych i inne parodje polityczne.* Warszawa: Tygodnik "Placówka," 1930.
Hetnarski, Bogumił. *Ze Stopnicy do Itaki: Pamiętnik chemika.* Krosno: Apla, 2009.
Hollender, Tadeusz. *Polska bez Żydów: Powieść satyryczna.* Warszawa: Wydawnictwo "Wierch," 1938.
Karski, Jan, and Maciej Wierzyński. *Emisariusz własnymi słowami: Zapis rozmów przeprowadzonych w latach 1995–1997 w Waszyngtonie emitowanych w Głosie Ameryki.* Warszawa: PWN, 2012.
Lipiński, Eryk. *Drzewo Szpilkowe.* Warszawa: Czytelnik, 1976.
Lipiński, Eryk. *Pamiętniki.* Warszawa: Iskry, 2016.
Lipiński, Eryk. *Szpilki, 1935–1965: Coś nam zostało z tych lat. . . .* Warszawa: Wydawnictwo Artystyczno-Graficzne RSW "Prasa," 1967.
Lipiński, Eryk. *Warszawa w karykaturze.* Warszawa: Państwowe Wydawnictwo Naukowe, 1983.
Meysztowicz, Jan. *Czas przeszły dokonany: wspomnienia ze służby w Ministerstwie Spraw Zagranicznych w latach 1932–1939.* Warszawa: Instytut Prasy i Wydawnictw "Novum," 1989.
Mieses, Mateusz. *Polacy-chrześcijanie pochodzenia żydowskiego, Tom 1.* Warszawa: Wydawnictwo M. Fruchtmana, 1938.
Mitzner, Zbigniew. "Historia." In *Z dziejów cnoty: Szpilki 1935–1985*, 9–10. Warszawa: Krajowa Agencja Wydawnicza, 1985.
Mitzner, Zbigniew. "Przedmowa." In *Satyra prawdę mówi . . . 1918–1939*, edited by Zbigniew Mitzner and Leon Pasternak, 5–16. Warszawa: Czytelnik, 1963.
Nawrot, Andrzej. "Historia Katedry Ubioru Akademii Sztuk Pięknych w Łodzi." Accessed 10 May 2022. http://www.ubior.asp.lodz.pl/historia_c.htm.
Nowakowski, Marek. *Tak zapamiętałem.* Wydawnictwo Zysk i S-ka: Poznań, 2014.
Pierwszy powszechny spis Rzeczypospolitej Polskiej z dnia 30 września 1921 roku. Warszawa: Główny Urząd Statystyczny Rzeczypospolitej Polskiej, 1927.
Rogalski, A. *Jan Kiepura: Król śpiewaków.* Warszawa: Universum, 1933.
Rosset, Edward, ed. *Mały rocznik statystyczny miasta Łodzi 1936.* Łódź: Zarząd Miejski w Łodzi. Wydział Statystyczny, 1938.
Sartre, Jean-Paul. *Anti-Semite and Jew.* New York: Schocken Books, 1995.
Słonimski, Antoni. *Kroniki tygodniowe 1936–1939, Tom 3.* Warszawa: Wydawnictwo LTW, 2005.
Słonimski, Antoni. *Wspomnienia warszawskie.* Warszawa: Wydawnictwo Agora, 2017.
Szturm de Sztrem, Edward, ed. *Mały Rocznik Statystyczny 1937.* Warszawa: Główny Urząd Statystyczny, 1937.
Szturm de Sztrem, Edward, ed. *Mały Rocznik Statystyczny 1939.* Warszawa: Główny Urząd Statystyczny, 1939.

Torańska, Teresa. *Trzy rozmowy Teresy Torańskiej: śmierć spóźnia się o minutę*. Warszawa: Agora S.A., 2010.

Trzeciak, Stanisław. *Pornografia narzędziem obcych agentur*. Warszawa: Biblioteka "Jutra Pracy," 1938.

Witz, Ignacy. "O karykaturze." In *50 lat karykatury polskiej: 1900–1950*, edited by Ignacy Witz and Jerzy Zaruba, 13–30. Warszawa: Wydawnictwo Arkady, 1961.

Zaruba, Jerzy. "Zamiast wstępu." In *50 lat karykatury polskiej: 1900–1950*, edited by Ignacy Witz and Jerzy Zaruba, 5–12. Warszawa: Wydawnictwo Arkady, 1961.

Zaruba, Jerzy. *Z pamiętników bywalca*. Warszawa: Iskry, 1960.

Żebrowski, Julian. *Polski Londyn w karykaturach*. Brooklyn, NY: Polstar Publishing Corp., 1985.

SECONDARY SOURCES

Adamczyk, Kazimierz. "Kobieta w powieściach polskich ideologów ruchu nacjonalistycznego." *Konteksty kultury* 11, no. 3 (2014): 285–301.

"Aleksander Dzierżawski." In *Czy wiesz kto to jest?*, edited by Stanisław Łoza, 160. Warszawa: Wydawnictwa Artystyczne i Filmowe, 1983.

Aleksiun, Natalia. "Christian Corpses for Christians! Dissecting the Anti-Semitism behind the Cadaver Affair of the Second Polish Republic." *East European Politics and Societies and Cultures* 25, no. 3 (2011): 393–409.

Aleksiun, Natalia. "Crossing the Line: Violence against Jewish Women and the New Model of Antisemitism in Poland in the 1930s." *Jewish History* 33 (2020): 133–62.

Aleksiun, Natalia. "Jewish Students and Christian Corpses in Interwar Poland: Playing with the Language of Blood Libel." *Jewish History* 26, no. 3–4 (2012): 327–42.

Althaus, Frank, and Mark Sutcliffe, eds. *Drawing the Curtain: The Cold War in Cartoons*. London: Fontanka, 2012.

Baigell, Matthew. *The Implacable Urge to Defame: Cartoon Jews in the American Press, 1877–1935*. Syracuse, NY: Syracuse University Press, 2017.

Bałaban, Majer. "Abraham Buchner." In *Polski Słownik Biograficzny, Tom III*, 77. Kraków: Polska Akademia Umiejętności, 1937.

Barnes, Jeffrey John. "A Dictated Policy: Cartoons and the 1936 Strike in Palestine." *Journal of Graphic Novels and Comics* 8, no. 1 (2017): 3–19.

Bauer, Yehuda. *My Brother's Keeper: A History of the American Jewish Joint Distribution Committee, 1929–1939*. Philadelphia: Jewish Publication Society of America, 1974.

Baxa, Paul. "Capturing the Fascist Moment: Hitler's Visit to Italy in 1938 and the Radicalization of Fascist Italy." *Journal of Contemporary History* 42, no. 2 (2007): 227–42.

Bergmann, Olaf. *"Prawdziwa cnota krytyk się nie boi . . .": Karykatura w czasopismach satyrycznych Drugiej Rzeczypospolitej*. Warszawa: DiG, 2012.

Bergmann, Olaf. "Problematyka żydowska w karykaturach polskich czasopism satyrycznych Drugiej Rzeczypospolitej." *Kwartalnik Historii Żydów* 4 (2011): 463–90.

Biskupski, M. B. Review of *Ksiądz Aleksander Syski na Mazowszu i wśród Polonii amerykańskiej*. *Polish American Studies* 52, no. 2 (1995): 81–83.

Blobaum, Robert. "Criminalizing the 'Other': Crime, Ethnicity, and Antisemitism in Early Twentieth-Century Poland." In *Antisemitism and Its Opponents in Modern Poland*, edited by Robert Blobaum, 81–102. Ithaca, NY: Cornell University Press, 2005.

Blümel, Tobias. "Antisemitism as Political Theology in Greece and Its Impact on Greek Jewry, 1967–1979." *Southeast European and Black Sea Studies* 17, no. 2 (2017): 181–202.

Borowiec, Piotr. "Krótka historia wydawnictwa i koncernu Ilustrowany Kurier Codzienny (1910–1939)." In *Ilustrowany Kurier Codzienny. Księga pamiątkowa w stulecie powstania dziennika i wydawnictwa (1910–1939)*, edited by Grażyna Wrona, Piotr Borowiec, and Krzysztof Woźniakowski, 17–44. Kraków: "Śląsk" Wydawnictwo Naukowe, 2010.

Borowkin, Stanisław. "'Gazetka Miki' (1938–1939)." *Kwartalnik Historii Prasy Polskiej* 27, no. 1 (1988): 39–49.

Bourdon, Jerome, and Sandrine Boudana. "Controversial Cartoons in the Israeli-Palestinian Conflict: Cries of Outrage and Dialogue of the Deaf." *International Journal of Press/Politics* 21, no. 2 (2018): 188–208.

Bredovskis, Eriks. "Sketching America: German Depictions of the United States and Woodrow Wilson (1914–1918)." *German Studies Review* 42, no. 3 (2019): 469–97.

Brustein, William, and Amy Ronnkvist. "The Roots of Anti-Semitism: Romania before the Holocaust." *Journal of Genocide Research* 4, no. 2 (2004): 211–35.

Brykczynski, Paul. *Primed for Violence: Murder, Antisemitism, and Democratic Politics in Interwar Poland*. Madison: University of Wisconsin Press, 2016.

"Bujnicki Ignacy Adam." In *Czy wiesz kto to jest?*, edited by Stanisław Łoza, 84. Warszawa: Wydawnictwa Artystyczne i Filmowe, 1983.

Burleson Mackay, Jenn. "What Does Society Owe Political Cartoonists?" *Journalism Studies* 18, no. 1 (2017): 28–44.

Byford, Jovan. "Conspiracy Theories." In *Key Concepts in the Study of Antisemitism*, edited by Sol Goldberg, Scott Ury, and Kalman Weiser, 79–92. Cham: Palgrave Macmillan, 2021.

Bytwerk, Randall L. *Julius Streicher: The Man Who Persuaded a Nation to Hate Jews*. New York: Stein and Day, 1983.

Cała, Alina. "Zapożyczenia z mowy żydowskiej w narracji antysemickiej." *Studia Litteraria et Historica* 1 (2012): 1–8.

Cała, Alina. *Wizerunek Żyda w polskiej kulturze ludowej*. Warszawa: Wydawnictwo Uniwersytetu Warszawskiego, 1992.

Cała, Alina. *Żyd—Wróg odwieczny? Antysemityzm w Polsce i jego źródła*. Warszawa: Wydawnictwo Nisza, 2012.

Clark, Roland. "Anti-Masonry as Political Protest: Fascists and Freemasons in Interwar Romania." *Patterns of Prejudice* 46, no. 1 (2012): 40–57.

Cohn-Sherbok, Dan. *The Crucified Jew: Twenty Centuries of Christian Anti-Semitism*. London: HarperCollins, 1992.

Coupe, W. A. "The German Cartoon and the Revolution of 1848." *Comparative Studies in Society and History* 9, no. 2 (1967): 137–67.

Czasy wojen i pokoju: Karykatura Polska 1914–1939. Warszawa: Muzeum Karykatury im. Eryka Lipińskiego w Warszawie, 2004.

Czyńska, Małgorzata. *Berezowska: Nagość dla wszystkich*. Wołowiec: Czarne, 2018.

Danjoux, Ilan. *Political Cartoons and the Israeli-Palestinian Conflict*. Manchester, UK: Manchester University Press, 2012.

Desforges, Josée. "Anti-Semitic Caricature in 1930s Montreal: Language and National Stereotypes in Adrien Arcand's *Le Goglu* (1929–1933)." In *Sketches from an Unquiet Country: Canadian Graphic Satire, 1840–1940*, edited by Dominic Hardy, Annie Gérin, and Lora Senechal Carney, 206–31. Montreal: McGill-Queen's University Press, 2018.

Domagalska, Małgorzata. *Antysemityzm dla inteligencji? Kwestia żydowska w publicystyce Adolfa Nowaczyńskiego na łamach "Myśli Narodowej" (1921–1934) i "Prosto z mostu" (1935–1939) (na tle porównawczym)*. Warszawa: Żydowski Instytut Historyczny, 2004.

Dudek, Antoni, and Grzegorz Pytel. *Bolesław Piasecki: Próba biografii politycznej*. Londyn: Aneks, 1990.

Ellen-Prell, Riv. "Why Jewish Princesses Don't Sweat: Desire and Consumption in Postwar American Jewish Culture." In *People of the Body: Jews and Judaism from an Embodied Perspective*, edited by Howard Eilberg-Schwartz, 329–59. Albany: State University of New York Press, 1992.

Etty, John. *Graphic Satire in the Soviet Union: Krokodil's Political Cartoons*. Jackson: University Press of Mississippi, 2019.

Felsenstein, Frank. *Anti-Semitic Stereotypes: A Paradigm of Otherness in English Popular Culture, 1660–1830*. (Baltimore: Johns Hopkins University Press, 1995.

"Fitelberg Grzegorz." In *Encyklopedia muzyki*, edited by Andrzej Chodkowski, 266. Warszawa: Wydawnictwo Naukowe PWN, 2001.

Frankl, Michal. "Citizenship of No Man's Land? Jewish Refugee Relief in Zbąszyń and East-Central Europe, 1938–1939." *S:I.M.O.N. Shoah: Intervention, Methods, Documentation* 8, no. 2 (2020): 37–49.

Gałczyńska, Emilia. "Lola Szereszewska (1895–1943): zapomniana poetka pogranicza." *Narracje o Zagładzie* 5 (2019): 85–97.

Gilbert, Christopher J. *Caricature and National Character: The United States at War*. University Park: Pennsylvania State University Press, 2021.

Gilman, Sander. *The Jew's Body*. New York: Routledge, 1991.

Goldstein, Bernard. *Twenty Years with the Jewish Labor Bund: A Memoir of Interwar Poland*. West Lafayette, IN: Purdue University Press, 2016.

Górska, Hanna, and Eryk Lipiński. *Z dziejów karykatury polskiej*. Warszawa: Wiedza Powszechna, 1977.

Gutman, Yisrael. *The Jews of Warsaw, 1939–1943: Ghetto, Underground, Revolt*. Translated by Ina Friedman. Bloomington: Indiana University Press, 1989.

Hariman, Robert. "Political Parody and Public Culture." *Quarterly Journal of Speech* 94, no. 3 (2008): 247–72.

Harris, Bonnie M. "From German Jews to Polish Refugees: Germany's Polenaktion and the Zbaszyn Deportations of October 1938." *Kwartalnik Historii Żydów* 2 (2009): 175–205.

Hauser, Jakub. "Faithful to Tradition: Visual Depictions of Antisemitism in *Humoristické listy* in the 1920s and 1930s." In *Visual Antisemitism in Central Europe: Imagery of Hatred*, edited by Eva Janáčová and Jakub Hauser, 145–70. Oldenbourg: De Gruyter, 2021.

Herkman, Juha. "Populism in Political Cartoons: Caricatures of Nordic Populist Leaders." *Popular Communication* 17, no. 3 (2019): 252–67.
Hertz, Aleksander. *The Jews in Polish Culture*. Evanston, IL: Northwestern University Press, 1988.
Holland, Norman N. "The 'Willing Suspension of Disbelief' Revisited." *Centennial Review* 11, no. 1 (1967): 1–23.
Horowitz, Sara R. "Gender." In *Key Concepts in the Study of Antisemitism*, edited by Sol Goldberg, Scott Ury, and Kalman Weiser, 195–20. Cham: Palgrave Macmillan, 2021.
Janáčová, Eva, and Jakub Hauser, eds. *Visual Antisemitism in Central Europe: Imagery of Hatred*. Oldenbourg: De Gruyter, 2021.
Janáčová, Eva. "Spa Antisemitism in Bohemia and Moravia." In *Visual Antisemitism in Central Europe: Imagery of Hatred*, edited by Eva Janáčová and Jakub Hauser, 59–98. Oldenbourg: De Gruyter, 2021.
Jaworska, Janina. *Polska sztuka walcząca 1939–1945*. Warszawa: Wydawnictwa Artystyczne i Filmowe, 1985.
Jedlicki, Jerzy. "Resisting the Wave: Intellectuals against Antisemitism in the Last Years of the 'Polish Kingdom.'" In *Antisemitism and Its Opponents in Modern Poland*, edited by Robert Blobaum, 60–80. Ithaca, NY: Cornell University Press, 2005.
Josefowitz Siegel, Rachel. "Antisemitism and Sexism in Stereotypes of Jewish Women." *Women & Therapy* 5, no. 2–3 (1986): 249–57.
Kemnitz, Thomas Milton. "The Cartoon as a Historical Source." *Journal of Interdisciplinary History* 4, no. 1 (1973): 81–93.
Kertzer, David I., and Gunnar Mokosch. "In the Name of the Cross: Christianity and Anti-Semitic Propaganda in Nazi Germany and Fascist Italy." *Comparative Studies in Society and History* 62, no. 3 (2020): 456–86.
Kessel, Martina. "Introduction: Landscapes of Humour—The History and Politics of the Comical in the Twentieth Century." In *The Politics of Humour: Laughter, Inclusion, and Exclusion in the Twentieth Century*, edited by Martina Kessel and Patrick Merziger, 3–21. Toronto: Toronto University Press, 2012.
Klahr, Douglas M. "Symbiosis between Caricature and Caption at the Outbreak of War: Representations of the Allegorical Figure Marianne in 'Kladderadatsch.'" *Zeitschrift für Kunstgeschichte* 74 (2011): 537–58.
Klausen, Jytte. *The Cartoons That Shook the World*. New Haven, CT: Yale University Press, 2009.
Konstantynów, Dariusz. "Antysemickie rysunki z prasy polskiej 1919–1939." In *Obcy i niemili: antysemickie rysunki z prasy polskiej 1919–1939*, 35–48. Warszawa: Żydowski Instytut Historyczny, 2013.
Konstantynów, Dariusz. "Gdynia i Żydzi w antysemickich rysunkach z prasy II Rzeczypospolitej." *Porta Aurea* 19 (2020): 174–91.
Konstantynów, Dariusz. "Pogromy i inne akty przemocy fizycznej wobec Żydów w zwierciadle rysunków z prasy polskiej (1919–1939)." In *Pogromy Żydów na ziemiach polskich w XIX i XX wieku, Tom I: Literatura i sztuka*, edited by Sławomir Buryła, 321–62. Warszawa: Instytut Historii PAN, 2018.

Kopciowski, Adam. "Półświatek przestępczy na łamach lubelskiej prasy jidysz (1918–1939)." *Studia Judaica* 17, no. 33 (2014): 57–84.

Kossakowski, Andrzej. *Polski film animowany 1945–1974*. Wrocław: Zakład Narodowy im. Ossolińskich, Wydawnictwo PAN, 1977.

Kotek, Joël. *Cartoons and Extremism: Israel and the Jews in Arab and Western Media*. Edgware: Vallentine Mitchell, 2008.

Krzywiec, Grzegorz. "Antysemickie karykatury od poł. XIX w. do I wojny światowej." In *Obcy i niemili: antysemickie rysunki z prasy polskiej 1919–1939*, 13–21. Warszawa: Żydowski Instytut Historyczny, 2013.

Krzywiec, Grzegorz. "The Balance of Polish Political Antisemitism: Between 'National Revolution,' Economic Crisis, and the Transformation of the Polish Public Sphere in the 1930s." In *Right-Wing Politics and the Rise of Antisemitism in Europe 1935–1941*, edited by Frank Bajohr and Dieter Pohl, 61–80. Göttingen: Wallstein Verlag, 2019.

Kublitz, Anja. "The Cartoon Controversy: Creating Muslims in a Danish Setting." *Social Analysis* 54, no. 3 (2010): 107–25.

Kunicki, Mikołaj Stanisław. *Between the Brown and the Red: Nationalism, Catholicism, and Communism in Twentieth-Century Poland—The Politics of Bolesław Piasecki*. Athens: Ohio University Press, 2012.

Kupfert Heller, Daniel. *Jabotinsky's Children: Polish Jews and the Rise of Right-Wing Zionism*. Princeton, NJ: Princeton University Press, 2017.

Kwiatkowski, Maciej Józef. "Polskie Radio 1925–1939: Mała kronika." *Pamiętnik Teatralny* 22, no. 3–4 (1973): 359–408.

Lægaard, Sune. "The Cartoon Controversy as a Case of Multicultural Recognition." *Contemporary Politics* 13, no. 2 (2007): 147–64.

Lamb, Chris. *Drawn to Extremes: The Use and Abuse of Editorial Cartoons*. New York: Columbia University Press, 2004.

Lederhendler, Eli. "The Interrupted Chain: Traditional Receiver Countries, Migration Regimes, and the East European Jewish Diaspora, 1918–39." *East European Jewish Affairs* 44, no. 2–3 (2014): 171–86.

Lerski, Tomasz. *Syrena Record: pierwsza polska wytwórnia fonograficzna 1904–1939*. Warszawa: Karin, 2003.

Leszczyńska, Cecylia. "Level of Living of Polish Citizens in the Interwar Period, and Its Diversification." *Roczniki Dziejów Społecznych i Gospodarczych* 76 (2016): 93–120.

Lewitter, L. R. "The Polish 'Szopka.'" *Slavonic and East European Review* 29, no. 72 (1950): 77–85.

Lichtenstein, Tatjana. *Zionists in Interwar Czechoslovakia: Minority Nationalism and the Politics of Belonging*. Bloomington: Indiana University Press, 2016.

Limb, Peter. "Introduction: Drawing a Line between Play and Power in African Political Cartooning." In *Taking African Cartoons Seriously: Politics, Satire, and Culture*, edited by Peter Limb and Tejumola Olaniyan, xiii–xlviii. East Lansing: Michigan State University Press, 2018.

Łazor, Jerzy. "Dzieje linii lewantyńskiej Polskich Linii Lotniczych 'Lot' w latach 30." In *Ekonomia, Społeczeństwo, Polityka: Studia ofiarowane prof. dr. hab. Januszowi Kalińskiemu w*

70. rocznicę urodzin, edited by Andrzej Zawistowski, 277–92. Warszawa: Szkoła Główna Handlowa, Oficyna Wydawnicza, 2012.

Łazor, Jerzy. "Wywóz polskiego sprzętu wojskowego do Palestyny w okresie międzywojennym." In *Gospodarka i społeczeństwo a wojskowość na ziemiach polskich*, edited by Tomasz Głowiński and Krzysztof Popiński, 215–22. Wrocław: Gajt, 2010.

Łotysz, Sławomir. *Pińskie błota: Natura, wiedza i polityka na polskim Polesiu do 1939 roku*. Kraków: Universitas, 2022.

Markiewicz, Henryk. "Przeciw nienawiści i pogardzie." *Teksty Drugie* 6 (2004): 99–119.

Marsot, Afaf Lutfi Al-Sayyid. "The Cartoon in Egypt." *Comparative Studies in Society and History* 13, no. 1 (1971): 2–15.

McGraw, Peter, and Joel Warner. *The Humor Code: A Global Search for What Makes Things Funny*. New York: Simon and Schuster, 2015.

McKenna, Kevin J. *All the Views Fit to Print: Changing Images of the U.S. in Pravda Political Cartoons, 1917–1991*. New York: Peter Lang Publishing, 2001.

Mell, Julie L. *The Myth of the Medieval Jewish Moneylender*, vol. 1. New York: Palgrave Macmillan, 2017.

Melzer, Emanuel. *No Way Out: The Politics of Polish Jewry 1935–1939*. Cincinnati: Hebrew Union College Press, 1997.

Mendelsohn, Ezra. *The Jews of East Central Europe between the World Wars*. Bloomington: Indiana University Press, 1987.

Merback, Mitchell B., ed. *Beyond the Yellow Badge: Anti-Judaism and Antisemitism in Medieval and Early Modern Visual Culture*. Leiden: Brill, 2008.

Michlic, Joanna B. *Poland's Threatening Other: The Image of the Jew from 1880 to the Present*. Lincoln: University of Nebraska Press, 2008.

Michowicz, Waldemar. *Walka dyplomacji polskiej przeciwko traktatowi mniejszościowemu w Lidze Narodów w 1934 roku*. Łódź: Łódzkie Towarzystwo Naukowe, 1963.

Mihăilescu, Dana. *Eastern European Jewish American Narratives, 1890–1930: Struggles for Recognition*. Lanham, MD: Lexington Books, 2018.

Milbradt, Bjoern. "Antisemitic Metaphors and Latent Communication." In *Global Antisemitism: A Crisis of Modernity*, edited by Charles Asher Small, 45–49. Leiden: Brill, 2013.

Miller, Henry. *Politics Personified: Portraiture, Caricature, and Visual Culture in Britain, c. 1830–80*. Manchester, UK: Manchester University Press, 2015.

Miłosz, Czesław. *Wyprawa w dwudziestolecie*. Kraków: Wydawnictwo Literackie, 1999.

Modras, Ronald. *The Catholic Church and Antisemitism: Poland, 1933–1939*. New York: Routledge, 1994.

Molisak, Alina. "Polenaktion—Zbąszyń . . . Na przykładzie dyskursu publicystycznego 'Naszego Przeglądu.'" *Kwartalnik Historii Żydów* 1, no. 273 (2020): 259–80.

Moss, Kenneth B. *An Unchosen People: Jewish Political Reckoning in Interwar Poland*. Cambridge, MA: Harvard University Press, 2021.

Murawska-Muthesius, Katarzyna. "1956 in the Cartoonist's Gaze: Fixing the Eastern European Other and Denying the Eastern European Self." *Third Text* 20, no. 2 (2006): 189–99.

Murawska-Muthesius, Katarzyna. Untitled text. In Anna Gosławska-Lipińska, *Ha ha Ha-Ga*, 7–10. Warszawa: Bęc Zmiana, 2015.

Napiórska, Agata. *Ha-Ga: Obrazki z życia*. Warszawa: Marginesy, 2023.

Nichols, David, and Emily Turner-Graham. "Bluey and Sol: Antisemitic Humour in a German-Australian Outpost, 1937–1939." *Immigrants & Minorities* 33 (2015): 231–49.

O'Donnell, S. Jonathon. "Antisemitism under Erasure: Christian Zionist Anti-Globalism and the Refusal of Cohabitation." *Ethnic and Racial Studies* 44, no. 1 (2021): 39–57.

Oişteanu, Andrei. *Inventing the Jew: Antisemitic Stereotypes in Romanian and Other Central-East European Cultures*. Translated by Mirela Adăscăliței, with foreword by Moshe Idel. Lincoln: University of Nebraska Press, 2009.

Opalski, Magdalena. "*Wiadomości Literackie*: Polemics on the Jewish Question, 1924–1939." In *The Jews of Poland between Two World Wars*, edited by Yisrael Gutman et al., 434–49. Hanover, NH: University Press of New England, 1989.

Paczkowski, Andrzej. "Prasa Drugiej Rzeczypospolitej (1918–1939): ogólna charakterystyka statystyczna." *Rocznik Historii Czasopiśmiennictwa Polskiego* 11, no. 1 (1972): 49–88.

Paczkowski, Andrzej. "Prasa w życiu politycznym Drugiej Rzeczypospolitej." *Dzieje Najnowsze* 10, no. 3 (1978): 29–55.

Paczkowski, Andrzej. *Prasa codzienna Warszawy w latach 1918–1939*. Warszawa: Państwowy Instytut Wydawniczy, 1983.

Pakentreger, Aleksander. "Statystyka Żydów m. Kalisza, ocalałych po II wojnie światowej." *Biuletyn Żydowskiego Instytutu Historycznego* 4, no. 96 (1975): 81–92.

Pakentreger, Aleksander. "Sytuacja gospodarcza ludności żydowskiej Kalisza w latach kryzysu gospodarczego 1929–1935 i w okresie pokryzysowym." *Biuletyn Żydowskiego Instytutu Historycznego* 1–2 (1985): 51–68.

Pakentreger, Aleksander. *Żydzi w Kaliszu w latach 1918–1939: problemy polityczne i społeczne*. Warszawa: PIW, 1988.

Parusheva, Dobrinka. "In the Mirror of Satire: The End of World War I in Bulgarian Caricatures." *Études Balkaniques* 2 (2019): 249–77.

Perry, Heather R. *Recycling the Disabled: Army, Medicine, and Modernity in WWI Germany*. Manchester, UK: Manchester University Press, 2014.

Perry, Marvin, and Frederick M. Schweitzer. *Antisemitism: Myth and Hate from Antiquity to the Present*. New York: Palgrave Macmillan, 2002.

Piasecki, Andrzej. "'Gazeta Powiatowa' w Turku (1919–1922): zarys dziejów." *Kwartalnik Historii Prasy Polskiej* 28, no. 2 (1989): 51–69.

Piątkowski, Bohdan. "Uwagi o współpracownikach polskiej prasy humorystyczno-satyrycznej dwudziestolecia międzywojennego." *Rocznik Historii Czasopiśmiennictwa Polskiego* 15, no. 3 (1976): 311–17.

Piechotka, Maria, and Kazimierz Piechotka. "Polish Synagogues in the Nineteenth Century." In *Polin*. Vol. 2, *Jews and the Emerging Polish State*, edited by Antony Polonsky, 179–98. Oxford, UK: Litmann Library of Jewish Civilization, 2008.

Piskała, Kamil. "The Interwar: Democratic Politics and Modern City between Two World Wars 1918–1923." In *From Cotton and Smoke: Łódź—Industrial City and Discourses of Asynchronous Modernity 1897–1994*, edited by Agata Zysiak, Kamil Śmiechowski, Kamil Piskała, Wiktor Marzec, Kaja Kaźmierska, and Jacek Burski, 101–60. Łódź: Łódź University Press, 2018.

Piwocki, Ksawery. *Historia Akademii Sztuk Pięknych w Warszawie 1904–1964*. Wrocław: Zakład Narodowy Imienia Ossolińskich Wydawnictwo Polskiej Akademii Nauk, 1965.

Plach, Eva. "Ritual Slaughter and Animal Welfare in Interwar Poland." *East European Jewish Affairs* 45, no. 1 (2015): 1–25.

Plach, Eva. *The Clash of Moral Nations: Cultural Politics in Piłsudski's Poland, 1926–1935*. Athens: Ohio University Press, 2006.

Pogonowski, Iwo. *Poland: A Historical Atlas*. New York: Dorset Press, 1989.

Portnoy, Eddy. *Bad Rabbi and Other Strange but True Stories from the Yiddish Press*. Stanford, CA: Stanford University Press, 2018.

Press, Charles. *The Political Cartoon*. Madison, NJ: Fairleigh Dickinson University Press, 1981.

Prokop-Janiec, Eugenia. *Polish-Jewish Literature in the Interwar Years*. Syracuse, NY: Syracuse University Press, 2003.

Raffles, Hugh. "Jews, Lice, and History." *Public Culture* 19, no. 3 (2007): 521–66.

Ribbens, Kees. "Charles Boost in een vooroorlogse beeldenstrijd: Stelling nemen tegen de NSB in De Blaasbalg." *Stripschrift* (October 2022): 24–27.

Ribbens, Kees. "Picturing Anti-Semitism in the Nazi-Occupied Netherlands: Anti-Jewish Stereotyping in a Racist Second World War Comic Strip." *Journal of Modern Jewish Studies* 17, no. 1 (2018): 8–23.

Rockaway, Robert, and Arnon Gutfeld. "Demonic Images of the Jew in the Nineteenth Century United States." *American Jewish History* 89, no. 4 (2001): 355–81.

Rosenthal, Daniel. "Victims of Seductive and Unfortunate Lives: Jewish Suicide in Interwar Poland." *Jewish History* 29, no. 3–4 (2015): 301–30.

Rovner, Adam. *In the Shadow of Zion: Promised Lands Before Israel*. New York: New York University Press, 2014.

Rudnicki, Szymon. "Anti-Jewish Legislation in Interwar Poland." In *Antisemitism and Its Opponents in Modern Poland*, edited by Robert Blobaum, 148–70. Ithaca, NY: Cornell University Press, 2005.

Rudnicki, Szymon. "Jews in Poland Between the Two World Wars." *Shofar: An Interdisciplinary Journal of Jewish Studies* 29, no. 3 (2011): 4–23.

Rusek, Adam. *Leksykon polskich bohaterów i serii komiksowych*. Poznań: Centrala, 2010.

Scully, Richard, and Andrekos Varnava. "Introduction: The Importance of Cartoons, Caricature, and Satirical Art in Imperial Contexts." In *Comic Empires: Imperialism in Cartoons, Caricature, and Satirical Art*, edited by Richard Scully and Andrekos Varnava, 1–27. Manchester, UK: Manchester University Press, 2020.

Scully, Richard, and Marian Quartly. "Using Cartoons as Historical Evidence." In *Drawing the Line: Using Cartoons as Historical Evidence*, edited by Richard Scully and Marian Quartly, 9–41. Victoria: Monash University ePress, 2009.

Secklehner, Julia. "Belligerent Drawing? The Satirical Press in Prague and Vienna 1918–1938." PhD thesis, Courtauld Institute of Art, 2018.

Secklehner, Julia. "Simple Entertainment? *Die Muskete* and 'Weak' Antisemitism in Interwar Vienna." In *Visual Antisemitism in Central Europe: Imagery of Hatred*, edited by Eva Janáčová and Jakub Hauser, 123–43. Oldenbourg: De Gruyter, 2021.

Shandler, Jeffrey. *Adventures in Yiddishland: Postvernacular Language and Culture.* Berkeley: University of California Press, 2008.

Sidoruk, Elżbieta. *Granice satyry.* Białystok: Instytut Filologii Polskiej Uniwersytetu w Białymstoku, 2018.

Šimová, Kateřina. "The Image of the 'Jew' as an 'Enemy' in the Propaganda of Late Stalinism and Its Reflection in the Czechoslovak Context." *Holocaust Studies* 23, no. 1–2 (2017): 112–32.

Skalska, Agnieszka. *Obraz wroga w antysemickich rysunkach prasowych Marca '68.* Warszawa: Narodowe Centrum Kultury, 2007.

Śleszyński, Wojciech. *Obóz odosobnienia w Berezie Kartuskiej: 1934–1939.* Białystok: Instytut Historii Uniwersytetu w Białymstoku, 2003.

Ślęzak, Jolanta. "Armia europejska czy nowy Wehrmacht? Plany utworzenia Europejskiej Wspólnoty Obronnej w karykaturze polskiej na przykładzie czasopisma satyrycznego 'Szpilki' 1950–1954." *Polityka i Społeczeństwo* 1, no. 11 (2013): 130–50.

Ślęzak, Jolanta. "Obraz Czechosłowacji w karykaturach opublikowanych na łamach czasopism satyrycznych 'Mucha' i 'Szpilki' w latach 1945–1948." *Polityka i Społeczeństwo* 3, no. 11 (2013): 49–68.

Smith, Mark M. "Transcending, Othering, Detecting: Smell, Premodernity, Modernity." *Postmedieval: A Journal of Medieval Cultural Studies* 3, no. 4 (2012): 380–90.

Sroka, Mateusz. "Emigracja Żydów polskich w latach 1918–1939: Zarys problematyki." *Państwo i Społeczeństwo* 10, no. 2 (2010): 109–22.

Stopnicka Heller, Celia. *On the Edge of Destruction: Jews of Poland between the Two World Wars.* Detroit: Wayne State University Press, 1993.

Stradecki, Janusz. "Szpilki." In *Literatura polska: Przewodnik encyklopedyczny, Tom 2,* edited by Julian Krzyżanowski et al., 433. Warszawa: Państwowe Wydawnictwo Naukowe, 1985.

Stradecki, Janusz. "Wiadomości Literackie." In *Literatura polska: Przewodnik encyklopedyczny, Tom 2,* edited by Julian Krzyżanowski et al., 579–80. Warszawa: Państwowe Wydawnictwo Naukowe, 1985.

Strycharska-Brzezina, Maria. *Polszczyzna Żydów.* Warszawa: PWN, 1986.

Sufian, Sandy. "Anatomy of the 1936–39 Revolt: Images of the Body in Political Cartoons of Mandatory Palestine." *Journal of Palestine Studies* 37, no. 2 (2008): 23–42.

Szałek, Jakub. "'I śmiech niekiedy może być nauką': Polska polityka międzywojenna w czasopiśmie satyrycznym Mucha." *Media—Biznes—Kultura: Dziennikarstwo i komunikacja społeczna* 4 (2011): 111–26.

Szreffel, Michał. "Bereza Kartuska jako przykład więzienia politycznego." *Studia Iuridica Toruniensia* 1 (2010): 207–19.

Tabaka, Anna. *Ignacy Adam Nieściuszko-Bujnicki.* Kalisz: Kaliskie Towarzystwo Przyjaciół Nauk, 2016.

Taylor, Miles. "John Bull and the Iconography of Public Opinion in England c. 1712–1929." *Past & Present* 134 (1992): 93–128.

Tilles, Daniel. *British Fascist Antisemitism and Jewish Responses, 1932–40.* London: Bloomsbury, 2015.

Tomaszewski, Jerzy. *Preludium Zagłady: Wygnanie Żydów polskich z Niemiec w 1938 r.* Warszawa: PWN, 1998.

Tomaszewski, Jerzy. *Zarys dziejów Żydów w Polsce w latach 1918–1939*. Warszawa: Wydawnictwa Uniwersytetu Warszawskiego, 1990.
Trębacz, Zofia. *Nie tylko Palestyna: Polskie plany emigracyjne wobec Żydów 1935–1939*. Warszawa: Żydowski Instytut Historyczny, 2018.
Trębacz, Zofia. "Prasa katolicka drugiej połowy lat trzydziestych wobec idei masowej emigracji żydowskiej z Polski." *Studia Historica Gedanensia* 8 (2017): 281–302.
Tuffnell, Stephen. "'The International Siamese Twins': The Iconography of Anglo-American Inter-Imperialism." In *Comic Empires: Imperialism in Cartoons, Caricature, and Satirical Art*, edited by Richard Scully and Andrekos Varnava, 92–133. Manchester, UK: Manchester University Press, 2020.
Tyczno, Andrzej R. "Bene Meritus dla Aleksandra Stefana Dzierżawskiego." *Z kart historii Ziemi Dobrskiej: Stowarzyszenie Przyjaciół Ziemi Dobrskiej*, 4 September 2014. https://ziemiadobrska.wordpress.com/2014/09/04/bene-meritus-dla-aleksandra-stefana-dzierzawskiego/.
Urbanek, Mariusz. *Tuwim: Wylękniony bluźnierca*. Warszawa: Wydawnictwo Iskry, 2013.
Vago, Raphael. "The Traditions of Antisemitism in Romania." *Patterns of Prejudice* 27, no. 1 (1993): 107–19.
Volovici, Leon. *Nationalist Ideology and Antisemitism: The Case of Romanian Intellectuals in the 1930s*. London: Butterworth-Heinemann, 1991.
Wachowska, Barabara. "Łódź Remained Red: Elections to the City Council of 27 September 1936." In *Polin*. Vol. 9, *Poles, Jews, Socialists: The Failure of an Ideal*, edited by Antony Polonsky, Israel Bartal, Gershon Hundert, Magdalena Opalski, and Jerzy Tomaszewski, 83–106. Oxford, UK: Litmann Library of Jewish Civilization, 2008.
Wallach, Kerry. *Passing Illusions: Jewish Visibility in Weimar Germany*. Ann Arbor: University of Michigan Press, 2017.
Webb, Brandon. "Laughter Louder Than Bombs? Apocalyptic Graphic Satire in Cold War Cartooning, 1946–1959." *American Quarterly* 70, no. 2 (2018): 235–66.
Weindling, Paul. *Epidemics and Genocide in Eastern Europe, 1890–1945*. Oxford, UK: Oxford University Press, 2000.
Weisenfeld, Gennifer. *Mavo: Japanese Artists and the Avant-Garde, 1905–1931*. Berkeley: University of California Press, 2002.
Wierzbicka, A., and U. Makowska. "Rydygier Stanisław." In *Słownik artystów polskich*, vol. 9, edited by Małgorzata Biernacka, 362–63. Warszawa: Instytut Sztuki Polskiej Akademii Nauk, 2013.
Wistrich, Robert S. *Antisemitism: The Longest Hatred*. London: Thames Methuen, 1991.
Wojciechowski, Marian. *Stosunki polsko-niemieckie 1933–1938*. Poznań: Instytut Zachodni, 1965.
Wrona, Grażyna. "'Przeciw bezwstydowi w druku i obrazku': Krakowska cenzura w walce z demoralizacją (1918–1939)." *Klio: Czasopismo poświęcone dziejom Polski i powszechnym* 2 (2011): 97–112.
Wrona, Katarzyna. "Zmiana formuły 'Przekroju' w latach 2000–2013." *Acta Universitatis Lodziensis: Folia Literaria Polonica* 2, no. 28 (2015): 231–50.
Wurgaft, Benjamin Aldes. "Incensed: Food Smells and Ethnic Tension." *Gastronomica* 6, no. 2 (2006): 57–60.

Young, Dannagal G., Benjamin E. Bagozzi, and Abigail Goldring. "Psychology, Political Ideology, and Humor Appreciation: Why Is Satire So Liberal?" *Psychology of Popular Media Culture* 8, no. 2 (2019): 134–47.

Zawadzka, Joanna. "Piotrowski Mieczysław." In *Współcześni pisarze i badacze literatury: Słownik bibliograficzny, Tom 6*, edited by Jadwiga Czachowska and Alicja Szałagan, 384. Warszawa: Wydawnictwa Szkolne i Pedagogiczne S.A., 1999.

Ziomek, Jerzy. *Renesans*. Warszawa: Wydawnictwo Naukowe PWN, 1999.

Żółkiewska, Agnieszka. "Introduction." In *Wolny Ptak: Der Frajer Fojgl—Humor z prasy żydowskiej w Polsce niepodległej*, 11–12. Warszawa: Żydowski Instytut Historyczny, 2019.

Żynda, Marcin. "'Wysoce demoralizująca i pornograficzna' inicjatywa wydawnicza: Obrona moralności publicznej a wolność słowa w międzywojennym Grudziądzu." *Klio: Czasopismo poświęcone dziejom Polski i powszechnym* 2 (2011): 143–48.

Żyndul, Jolanta, et al. "The Sixty-Fifth Anniversary of Events in Przytyk: A Debate." *Polin: Studies in Polish Jewry*, vol. 17, edited by Antony Polonsky, 385–409. Oxford, UK: Littman Library of Jewish Civilization, 2004.

Żyndul, Jolanta. "Cele akcji antyżydowskiej w Polsce w latach 1935–1937." *Biuletyn Żydowskiego Instytutu Historycznego* 1 (1992): 53–63.

INDEX

Page numbers in **bold** refer to illustrations.

ABC: Nowiny Codzienne (*ABC: Daily News*), 96, 98, 113, 120, 123, 132, 134, 148, 149, 150, 173, 187, 188, 233n13, 233n26
Abduction of Europa, 101, **102**, 104, 194, **195**
accent, Yiddish (in Polish), 41–42, 70, 73–74
advertising, 153
Aesop, 148
Aleksiun, Natalia, 92
Alfa, 61, 68
Allies, 22
Americans, perceptions of, 77
animal allegory, 20, 146–48
animation, 96
annexation of Austria. *See* Anschluss
Anschluss, 28, 65, 102, 105, 118
Antichrist, 68
antifascism, 4, 6, 9, 12, 85, 86, 104, 105, 107, 109, 110, 116, 126, 147, 154, 165, 201, 225n16
anti-Judaism, 13, 211n66
antisemitic tropes, 3, 4, 14, 27, 29, 32–34, 47, 49, 63, 168, 196; Anschluss, 101, 104; Aryan paragraph, 56, 95, **111**, 128, 129; auditory, 73–74; backwardness, 36, 140, 194, 199, 203; bathing, 36, **37, 38**, 39, 109, **109**; Berlin, 29, **167**; B'nai B'rith, 100; cane, 93–94, 126, 156, 238n38; capitalism, 34; cheder, 68; cosmopolitanism, 27, 29, 199; criminality, 32, 35, 115, 199; de-Judaization, 89–90, 117, 132; devil, 68, **70**; disease, 74, **75**, 76, 115, 140, 189;
dishonesty, 35, 39, 43, 49–50, 69, 201; domination, 4, 47, 60, 61, 66, **67**, 68–70, **70**, 73, 140, 146–48; economic boycott, 89, **163**, 163–64; folkloric, 13, 32, 68; foreignness, 10, 40, 60, 76, 196; Freemasonry, 95, 99–101, **100**, 110; Jewish influence, 27, 98, 99, 112, 146–49; insects, 71, **72**, 76, 127; ghetto benches, 89, 93, 130, 158; global conspiracy, 66, 68, 69; kashket, 19, 29, 163; League of Nations, 89; Madagascar, 88–89, 92, 95, 138, 139, 227n71; menorah, 170–72, **172**, **177**, 179, **193**, 194; merchants, 34–35, 54, 58, 127; money, 34, 66, 147; Moses, 138; National Radical Camp, 91, **91**, 95, 96, 98, 112, 113, 123, 233n13; nobility, 114, 124, 126, 174–76; parasitism, 69, 76; personal hygiene, 36, 39, 40, 188; Pickelhaube, 3; pickets, 89; Polish Radio, 130, **131**, 132; pornography, 66; public transport, 140, 187, **188**, 235n67; ritual slaughter, 61, **62**, 129, 130, **193**, 193–94; sharks, 65, **66**; sidelocks, 48, 52, 55, 68–69; Star of David, 51, 142, **143**, **144**; superhuman powers, 68; swastika, 105; tentacles, 69, 70, 71; transnational, 13, 14, 63–65, 68, 71, 83; victim mentality, 130
antisemitism: and access to professions, 56, 113; and assimilation, 6, 22, 40; and calls for emigration, 4, 31, 44, 47, 85, 117; and Catholic Church, 46, 98, 128; and

259

Christianity, 66, 68; clergymen against, 5; in comic strips, 4; and conspiracy theories, 10, 66, 199; and doctored photographs, 63; and economy, 4, 10, 14, 28, 32, 43, 46–47, 49–51, 60, 69, 71, 85, 90, 117; escalation of, 10; folkloric, 32; intellectual, 32; linguistic, 41–42; medieval-style, 68, 70; misogynistic, 173; and national symbolism, 60–61, 64–65; as patriotism, 43, 58, 112, 133, 158; and physical violence, 3, 15, 44, 46, 60, 90, 92, 129, 154, 189; in print media, 4–5; students against, 5, 117; study of, 5; socialists against, 4–5, 50; in the 1920s, 10–11; in universities, 4, 41, 92, 95, 117, 129, 130, 154, 156, **157**; and war, 27; weak, 14, 18, 43–44, 173
anti-Zionist campaign of 1967–1968, 204–5
Antwerp, 162
Arab revolt, 24, 189
Arabs, 26
Arasimowicz, Stanisław, 84
Aryan paragraph, 56
assimilation, 10, 22, 27, 41–43, 176, 202
Association of Former War Volunteers of the Polish Army, 53
Association of Small Merchants and Traders, 50
audiences, 6–7, 11, 12, 18, 20, 32, 58, 63, 68, 74, 107, 108, 122, 127, 130, 158, 169, 176, 187, 196, 200–201, 204
Auschwitz, 76
Austria, 76; fugitives from, 29, 65, 32; Nazi annexation of, 28, 65, 101, 106, 118, 168; Polish Jews in, 29–30
Austro-Hungarian Empire, 16, 86, 116, 186, 203
authoritarianism, 10, 17, 24, 80, 90, 104, 117, 146, 165, 199

Bad Gastein, 169
Baigell, Matthew, 35, 186
Bąk (*Bumblebee*), 16. See also *Mucha*
Bankructwo socjalizmu i komunizmu (*The Bankruptcy of Socialism and Communism*), 146

Baraniecki, Karol, 86, 95
Bartoszewicz, Włodzimierz, 4
Beck, Józef, 22, 25
Belgium, 162
Beniowski, 89
Bereza Kartuska Internment Camp, 30
Berezowska, Maja, 4, 104–5, 192
Bergmann, Olaf, 47, 165
Berman, Mieczysław, 108
Betar, 26
Bickels, Jakub, 9, 86, 90, 115, 153, 165, **166**, **167**, 198, 203; biography, 117, 203; drawing style, 166–67; fate in Second World War, 85, 118–19, 197. See also *Szpilki*
Birsten, Lida, 85
blood libel, 13
bloodline, 165, 174, 176
Blum, Léon, 138, **139**
Bocianowski, Bohdan, 86
body, 189; Black, 138–39, **139**; contrasting types of, 93, **103**, 104, 138, **139**, 166; cult of, 159; economic, 75; gentile, 93, 126; naked, 139, 194; representations of Jewish, 27, 36, **37**, **38**, 39, 61, 63, **67**, 68, 69, 73, 93, **109**, 124, **125**, 126, 170, 172, 174, 179–80, 182, 187, 196, 201
Bolshevism, 146
Book of Deuteronomy, 110
Book of Judith, 170–71, 175
borderlands, 81
borders: consolidation of Poland's, 8; Poland's with Romania, 27–28; and refugees, 30–31, 195
Bożko, Bazyli, 79, 84
Brandel, Maksymilian, 153, 198
Braque, Georges, 186
Brennessel, Die (*The Burning Nettle*), 47, 56
Brest trials, 225n16
Britain, 24; cartoons in, 39; personifications of, 20. See also John Bull
Broniewska, Jadwiga, 145
Brykczynski, Paul, 10, 92, 160
Bucharest, 29, 141
Buchbinder, Józef, 113
Buchner, Abraham, 42

Buchner, Władysław, 14, 16–17, 40–43, 203
Buchner, Władysław, Jr., 17
Buchnerowa, Maria (née Pajewska), 16, 17, 27, 40
Budzyński, Wacław, 53, 113, 131
Bujnicki, Ignacy, 52, 78, 83. *See also* Kalisz
Bulgaria, 20
Bund, 71, 222n96
Burzenin, 55
business: Jewish, 14, 28, 46, 48, 51–56, 58–60, 90, 115, 128, 149, 159, 162; stereotype of Jewish practices, 32, 34–35

Cała, Alina, 35, 68, 179
Camp of National Unity (Obóz Zjednoczenia Narodowego, OZN, Ozon), 10, 22, 53, 58, 136
capitalism, 69, 200
cartoonists: and bodily tropes, 39; and ethnic stereotyping, 39; as guardians of democracy, 5; female, 192; impact of readers on, 187; networks, 107; restrictions on, in 1930s' Europe, 104
cartoons: American, 35, 39, 71, 192; and audiences, 7, 11, 12, 18; and citizen mobilization, 5; in Eastern Europe, 5; exhibition of antisemitic, in Warsaw, 44; as expressing political agendas, 5, 12; German, 68, 83; as historical sources, 5, 11–12; holiday resorts in, 39, 109; as medium that reforms society, 5; and multicultural societies, 6; by painters, 7; and photography, 63; pirated, 61, 74; Poland's ethnic minorities in, 11; and Poland's reputation abroad, 3; as reason for arrest, 105; restrictions on, 104; in Second World War, 151; and social emotions, 6, 11; and the rule of law, 3; tradition of in Poland, 7; and violence, 3, 128
Casimir the Great, 179
Catholic Church, 46, 98, 128
Catholicism, 11, 47, 68, 202, 228n88
Cekóv, 55
censorship, 16; Communist, 197; and freedom of speech, 13–14, 82, 104; impact on magazines, 80; interwar, 6, 12, 13, 14, 16, 25, 77, 79–80, 82, 85, 86, 95, 97, 104, 105, 115, 117, 136, 203, 225n16; morality, 228n89; outside of Poland, 104, 211n65; self-, 203–4; workings of, 80, 97, 115
Central Welfare Council (Rada Główna Opiekuńcza, RGO), 151
Chamberlain, Neville, 22
Charlie. *See* Ferster, Karol
cheder, 42
Christianity, 107
Christian National Party (Stronnictwo Chrześcijańsko-Narodowe, SChN), 148
citizens, 29, 200
citizenship laws, 27, 29, 106; and Zbąszyń crisis, 31, 106
clergy, 79
Cold War, 5; propaganda in, 71
collage, 96
colonies, 18–19; British, 189, **190**
comic strip, 73
communism, 12, 63, 64, 71, 142, 145, 146
Communist Party of Poland (Komunistyczna Partia Polski, KPP), 4, 71, 108, 116, 145
confiscation of periodicals, 25, 79, 82, 85, 86, 115, 165, 235n61
Conrad, Paul, 78
conspiracy theories, 10, 13, 146
conversion of Jews to Christianity, 42, 124, 126, 133
crime, 35–36
culture: Polish, 32, 73, 133; visual, 5–6, 11–13, 201, 205, 211n66
Cyrulik Warszawski (*The Barber of Warsaw*), 8, 88, 107, 153, 183, 189
Czarno na białem (*Black on white*), 107, 144, 153
Czechoslovakia, 24, 28, 29, 106–7

Dąbrowski, Marian, 153, 165
Danjoux, Ilan, 95, 187
Danzig, Free City of, 29
Daszyński, Ignacy, 116
De Blaasbalg, 107

deicide, 13
de-Judaization of Poland, 4, 18, 24, 43, 47,
    50, 52–53, 56, 69, 158
democracy, 7, 13, 83, 117
Dider, Stanisław, 133
diplomacy, 18, 23, 87
Dmowski, Roman, 4, 148
Doskowski, Józef, 8
drawing process, 191–92
drawing styles, 12, 50, 51, 54, 59, 61, 68,
    72–73, 74, 93, 99–102, 107, 136, 158, 162,
    178, 189, 200
Drymmer, Wiktor Tomir, 29
Dziennik Bydgoski (*The Bydgoszcz Daily*),
    153, 189
Dziennik Poznański (*Poznań Daily*), 98, 133
Dzierżawski, Aleksander, 120, 124, 144–51

Echo Kaliskie (*The Kalisz Echo*), 79
economic boycott, 14, 28, 32, 46, 49–59, 74,
    83, 87, 150; and Christian patrons, 59,
    90; and Christian traders, 49–52, 54, **54**,
    56, 58, 59; impact of on Jews, 59–60, 90;
    on Rynek Dekerta in Kalisz, 50
editors, 6–7, 9, 15–17, 40, 237n6; aging, 14,
    16–18, 40, 42; commercially minded,
    200; concealing identity of, 12, 120–24,
    130, 145–46; court cases against, 79, 86,
    95, 97–98, 114; of *Der Stürmer*, 63; of
    far-right publications, 113, 120–24;
    father and son, 17; influence on car-
    toonists, 136, 187, 204, 235n58; negotiat-
    ing with censors, 115; on satire, 48–49,
    77–84; remuneration of, 115
Egypt, escape from, 110, 138
Eight sermons before the Sejm, 65
emigration: calls for Jewish, 4, 17, 18–20,
    22–24, 26, 31, 44, 47, 76, 134, 142, 204;
    and Revisionist Zionists, 26
Endecja, Endeks. *See* National Democracy
"Enjoyable Adventures of Two
    Globetrotters, The" ("Ucieszne przy-
    gody obieżyświatów"), 4
entertainment, 8–9, 14–15, 44, 165, 169, 176,
    182, 196–97, 200

Esterka, 179
Evangelical Church, 49, 124
exaggeration, visual, 6, 39, 184
exoticization, 150, 172, 196
exploitation, stereotype of, 3, 14, 32–34, 69
Express Ilustrowany (*The Illustrated
    Express*), 81

Falanga, 96, 112
fascism, 104–5, 116, 149–50, 182, 199; threat
    of, 5, 14, 101, 118
Fascist Italy, 17, 95, 105; racial laws in, 41,
    107, 110, 118
Fedyszyn, Bronisław, 9, 24, 28, 110;
    biography, 44; drawing style, 24, 28
Ferster, Karol, 9, 153, 178; biography, 176;
    cartoons, 158–60, 169, 175–77, 179–80,
    194–95; drawing style, 158, 176; fate in
    Second World War, 152, 197; political
    proclivities, 154, 203
Ferster, Serafina, 176
Fips, 63
First World War, 20, 27, 35, 66, 186; anti-
    typhus campaigns in, 76; disabled
    veterans of, 158
Fitelberg, Grzegorz, 132, 234n45
foetor judaicus, 40, 73–74
foreign policy, 11, 13, 17–18, 32
France, 20, 66, 99, 104–5, 127, 169, 197; per-
    sonifications of, 19–20
Franco, Francisco, 101
free speech, 5, 13, 80, 82, 104, 117
Freemasonry, 46, 68, 98–99, 117
Front Aryjski (*The Aryan Front*), 82

Gałczyński, Konstanty Ildefons, 86
Garden of Eden, 105
Gazeta Polska (*Polish Gazette*), 41
Gazeta Powiatowa (*The District
    Newspaper*), 146
Gazetka Miki (*Mickey's Little Paper*),
    145–46
Gdynia, 74
Gelbart, Jakub, 51
Genesis, 105

gentiles, 33, 39, 49, 51, 56, **57**, 66, 69, 82, 89, 93, 95, 105, 118, 124, 126, 128–30, 149, 173, 187; passing as, 114, 124–26, 130
German Empire, 20
German minority: in Poland, 49, 56, 58, 71, 222n96; in South Tyrol, 191
German–Polish nonaggression pact, 24; and press accords, 25, 80, 104
Gestapo, 30, 105, 152
geszeft, 34
ghetto benches, 41, 87, 92, 93, 157–58
ghettoization, 50–51, 61, 187
Gierymski, Aleksander, 7
Gilman, Sander, 41
Ginczanka, Zuzanna, 86, 118
Głowiński, Michał, 42
gluttony, stereotype, 27
Godal, Eric, 104
Goga, Octavian, 27, 195–96
Gosławska, Anna, 85, 86, 117, 119, 203; drawing style, 99–100, **100**; work process, 192. *See also* Lipiński, Eryk; *Szpilki*
Grand Duchy of Lithuania, 3
gravure printing, 154
Great Depression, 24
Greater Poland region, 9, 14, 39, 46–47, 50–51, 69, 81, 83, 109, 145, 148, 189
Great Terror, 66, 142
greed, stereotype, 32–33, 147, 173
Greek Junta, 71
Greek mythology, 101, 194–95, 200–201
Griniow, Paweł, 4
Grosz, George, 189
Grotowski, Zbigniew, 178–79
Gruenbaum, Yitzhak, 3
Grus, Kazimierz, 4, 8, 39, 148, 236n98

Ha-Ga. *See* Gosławska, Anna
Haman, 25
Hanukkah, 171
Harvey. *See* Szpigiel, Henryk Stanisław
Harwey. *See* Szpigiel, Henryk Stanisław
Hasidism, 42
Haynt (*Today*), 5, 115, 227n67
Heber, Josef Mosze, 50–52, 220n18

Heller, Ludwik, 161–62
Hemar, Marian, 113, 132
Heydak, Edmund, 4
Hirszhorn, Samuel, 41
history: as discipline, 5; transnational approach to, 13; visual, vii
Hitler, Adolf, 24–25, 40, 95; in cartoons, 101–3, **102**, **103**, 104, 105, 110, 118, 165–66, **166**, 169, 201
Hollender, Tadeusz, 86, 89–90, 118
Holocaust survivors, 83, 85, 225n154
Holofernes, 171, 175
Home Army, 151
human traffickers, stereotype of Jewish, 4, 35
humor: corrective, 48, 83; national, 112, 148; pro-state, 12; right-wing, 78, 90, 150

Ici Paris, 104–5
identity: hidden, 124, 130, 132, 144–45; hybrid, 143, 202; living under false, 85, 197; national, 5, 200
Ilustrowany Kuryer Codzienny (*Illustrated Daily Courier*), 152, 165
interwar cartoonists, 4, 6–7, 12, 15, 17; amateur, 50, 51, 72; anonymous, 50, 53, 83, 142–44, 151, 154; and political allegiances, 147–48, 153–54, 233n13
invented realities, 127, 163
irony, 78
Israel, state of, 26, 205
Israelites, 110, 138

Jabotinsky, Ze'ev, 26
Janowska concentration camp, 118, 197
January Uprising of 1863, 53
Jarocin, 47
Jaroni, Stefan, 84
Jerusalem, 85
Jewish Historical Institute in Warsaw, vii; exhibition of antisemitic caricature in, 44
Jewish Question, 4, 6, 10–11, 13, 15, 17–18, 21, 22, 32, 41, 47, 77, 81, 98, 134, 136, 147, 149–50, 169, 200–201, 208n15

Jews: assimilated, 24, 26–29, 124, 132, 203; and Christian helpers, 56, 61, 113; and citizenship laws, 27, 29, 106; European, 20, 24; German, 20, 24; Hasidic, 22, 82, 188, 196; linguistic Polonization of, 41; middle-class, 26–27; from Palestine, 26; in Polesie, 81; Russian-speaking, 3; spelling of the word in Polish, 226n19; traditional, 24, 28; Yiddish-speaking, 3, 41
jimski cartoons, 53
John Bull, 20, 22, 24, 26. *See also* national personifications
Joint Distribution Committee (JDC), 30, 34, 128
Jordan river, 110
Joseph, Jacques, 126
journalism, 7, 12, 53, 127, 145, 198, 200
Judaism, 66, 106, 170
Judeo-Bolshevism, 13, 61, 63, **64**, 65, **67**, 142, 145, 183, 196
Judeo-Endek, 114
Judeophilia, 12, 49, 53, 82
Judeo-Piłsudskite, 148
judiciary, 56, 69, 98
Juliana of the Netherlands (queen), 169
Jutro Pracy (The Tomorrow of Work), 53

Kajzer, Narcyz, 84
Kalisz: economic boycott in, 49–51, 59; Jews in, 47, 50–51, 60, 83; municipality of, 48, 52–53, 78–79; nationalist activity in, 46–47, 51; print media in, 47, 79, 82; survivors in, 83, 225n154; Week of Propaganda in, 51
Kalwaria Zebrzydowska, 176
Kanarek, Eliasz, 231n167
Kańska, Regina, 176–80, **190**, **191**, 192; drawing style, 189–93
Karpiński, Światopełk, 86, 118, 123
Karśnicki, Feliks, 53
keffiyeh as trope, 26
Kemnitz, Thomas Milton, 6
Kharkov, 192, 202
Kiepura, Jan, 169, 239n55

Kiev, 79, 186, 202
kippah, 51, 163, 193
Kleczewski, Łajzer, 51
Kłosiewicz, Teresa, 189
Konica, Teodor, 7
Konin, 73
Konstantynów, Dariusz, 4, 39
Kontratak (*Counterattack*), 90, 92, 238n38
Kordian, 64
Kossak, Juliusz, 7
Kostrzewski, Franciszek, 186
Kotarski, Stanisław, 82
Kozłowski, Leon, 99, 110
Kraków: Academy of Arts, 176; as hub of satire, 8–9; as imperial city, 16, 116, 203; print media in, 152–53; St. Mary's Church in, 7
Krasicki, Ignacy, 123, 146
Krotoszyn, 47, 79
Kruk (*Raven*), 16. See also *Mucha*
Krynica Zdrój, 169
Kuczborska, Irena, 192
Kukułka (*Cuckoo*), 16. See also *Mucha*
Kunicki, Mikołaj, 91
Kurier Poznański (*Poznań Courier*), 3–4
Kurjer Warszawski (*Warsaw Courier*), 148

Ł. *See* Łukasik, Włodzimierz
labor market, 28, 55
Lamb, Chris, 5, 39
language, stereotypes of Jews speaking national, 41–42, 218n154
Laurel and Hardy, 104
League for the Protection of the Rights of Man and the Citizen, 5
League of Nations, 17, 20, 25–26, 138
Lebensborn, 169
Lec, Stanisław Jerzy, 86, 124
Le Figaro, 104
Lenin, Vladimir, 116
Leski, Władysław, 9
Lichtenstein, Tatjana, 29
Lipińska, Zuzanna, 192
Lipińska-Gosławska, Anna. *See* Gosławska, Anna

Lipiński, Eryk, 9, 97, 119; activity in Second World War, 85–86; and anti-Zionist campaign of 1967–1968, 204–5; biography, 116, 203; cartoons, 102, 109, 147; drawing style, 101–2, 109–10; and Ha-Ga, 100, 192; as historian of satire, 192, 204; Righteous Among the Nations, 85. *See also* Gosławska, Anna; Mitzner, Zbigniew; *Szpilki*

Lipiński, Teodor, 116

literacy, 4, 8, 207n10; visual, 95

Litvaks, 3

LOT, Polish airlines, 140, **141**, 142

Low, David, 20–22

Lviv: antisemitic violence in, 156; as hub of satire, 8, 153; Janowska concentration camp in, 118, 152, 197; Jewish artists in, 86, 90, 117, 152, 165, 186, 197, 203; Jews in, 74; literacy in interwar, 207n10; during Second World War, 151–52, 197

Lydda, 141

Łaszowski, Alfred, 112, 114–15

Łódź, 3, 47–48, 73; Academy of Arts, 197; anti-antisemitic activity in, 5; Jews in, 3, 47, 69–71; in cartoons, **70**, 71, **72**, 73; print media in, 81; socialists in, 47–48, 69, 71, 74; textile industry in, 69, 71, 81

Łukasik, Włodzimierz, 201–2; archival records on, 235n62; cartoons, 124, **125**, 126–27, 130, 134, **135**, 136, **137**, 142

Mackiewicz, Kamil, 4, 8

Mad magazine, 198

Madagascar, 33; plan, 18, 25, 87–88

Mały Dziennik (Little Daily), 98–99

Marek, cartoons by, 52. *See also Pokrzywy*

Marianne, **19**, 20, 22. *See also* national personifications

Marx, Karl, 66

Marxists, 68, 81

Massacre of the Innocents, 156

Matejko, Jan, 7

Mechabel, Der, 92

Mendelsohn, Ezra, 10

menorah in Judaism, 170–71

merchants, Jewish, 50, 52

metaphor, Jews as, 199; visual, 6, 52, 83, 93

metonymy, 93, 95, 127

Michlic, Joanna, 58

Mickey Mouse Weekly, 145

Mickiewicz, Adam, 77, 123

Miedziński, Bogusław, 41

Mieses, Mateusz, 132–33, 164, 176

Mikulice, 151

Miłosz, Czesław, 27

Ministry of Foreign Affairs, and Jewish issues, 23, 31

Minkiewicz, Janusz, 86

misogyny, 173, 178

Mitzner, Zbigniew, 113–14, 119, 123; court cases against, 95, 114, 227–28n73; and founding of *Szpilki*, 86. *See also* Lipiński, Eryk; *Szpilki*

modernity, 29, 40, 140, 200

modernization, 6, 182

Modras, Ronald, 58

Mokotów prison, 85

Moment, Der (The Moment), 5, 92

Monachomachia (War of the Monks), 123

Morawa, Maciej, 7

Mościcki, Ignacy, 100–101

Moscow, 116

Motyl (Butterfly), 16. *See also Mucha*

Moutet, Marius, 18, 87

Mucha (Fly), 3, 16; and anti-Jewish content, 14–15, 18–19, 22–24, 27–45; and anti-Hitler content, 24–25, 105; artists, 9–10, 17, 44; circulation of, 9, 17, 210n48; comparisons with other magazines, 9, 12, 47, 59, 65, 68, 70, 74, 77, 87, 110–11, 138–39, 150, 154, 195–95, 200; criticisms of, 44; origins of, 8, 16–17, 212n9; overview, 13; percentage of cartoons about Jews in, 11; personification in, 20–22; political profile of, 8, 16–17, 212n6; price, 210n38; and Sanacja, 12–13, 16–17, 23, 111, 200

Munich Agreement, 24

Murawska-Muthesius, Katarzyna, 192

Museum of Caricature in Warsaw, 192, 235n62

Mussolini, Benito, 95, 101; cartoons, **102**, **103**, 104, 107, **108**, 109, 165

Nalewki Street, 26, 28, 34, 74, 115, 140, 215n68
Napoleon trope, 142, **144**
Narutowicz, Gabriel, 160
Nasz Przegląd (*Our Review*), 41, 80, 115, 133
National Democracy (Narodowa Demokracja, ND, Endecja), 4, 10, 90, 91, 123, 127, 133, 145, 148, 164
nationalism, 11; and Catholicism, 47, 64; and economy, 48–49, 55, 60, 216n99; and nation state, 47, 49, 92; and symbolism, 60–61, 64–65
National Party (Stronnictwo Narodowe, SN), 46, 51, 53, 109, 120, 130
national personifications, 20–22, 212–13n23
National Radical Camp (Obóz Narodowo-Radykalny, ONR), 4, 10, 58, 89, 90
National Radical Camp ABC (Obóz Narodowo-Radykalny, ONR ABC), 90, 91, 96
National Radical Movement Falanga (Ruch Narodowo-Radykalny Falanga, RNR Falanga), 88, 90, 96, 113, 165
Nazi Germany, 17, 24–25, 95, 201; and censorship in Poland, 118; embassy of in Warsaw, 25; embassy of in Paris, 104–5; irredentism, 101; Poland's indecisive stance toward, 215n70; policies in, 105, 169; Polish Jews in, 29–30; refugees from, 58, 104; and Zbąszyń, 31
Negev, 26
Netherlands, 20
networks, 107
New York City, 104, 198
Niedziałkowski, Mieczysław, 215n70
nobility, and Sarmatians, 126, 175–76
Nonpartisan Bloc for Cooperation with the Government (Bezpartyjny Blok Współpracy z Rządem, BBWR), 51–53, 153
Nowakowski, Bogdan, 4

Nowicki, Andrzej, 86, 97
Nuremberg Laws, 22, 110

Odrzywół, 128
Oişteanu, Andrei, 32
Ojciec zadżumionych i inne parodje polityczne (*The Father of the Plague-Stricken and Other Political Parodies*), 123
olfactory stereotypes, 40, 73–74, 147, 187
Orędownik (*The Spokesman*), 4, 47, 71, 79, 82, 83. *See also* Greater Poland region
Ostecki, Henryk. *See* Szpigiel, Henryk Stanisław
Ostjude, 29. *See also* Jews
Ostrów Wielkopolski, 47, 55, 79
overpopulation, 10, 19, 81, 140, 187

Paczkowski, Andrzej, 8
Pajewska, Maria. *See* Buchnerowa, Maria
Palestine: air connection between Poland and, 140, 141; Arab revolt in, 26; illegal immigration to, 26; trope, 22, 24–26, 34, 49, 55, 139
Parecki, Franciszek, 86, 101, 117, 118; drawing style, 107–9, **108**, 126
Paris, 34
parody, 87, 89, 97, 123
Partitions of Poland, 7, 16, 65, 86, 158, 186
Pasternak, Leon, 86
Pat and Patachon, 104
peasants, 35; representations of, 33
Peel Commission Plan, 25
PEN Club, 88
Pharaoh, 25
photography, 63, 96
Phrygian Cap Association, 108. *See also* Parecki, Franciszek
Piasecki, Bolesław, 90, 91, 113, 124
Piasecki, Stanisław, 113, 164–65; representations of, 114, 130
pickets, 58–59, 90
Piłsudski, Józef, 4, 10, 17, 23, 124, 225n16
Piotrowska, Regina. *See* Kańska, Regina
Piotrowski, Mieczysław, 9, 93, 197; and anti-antisemitism, 155–58, 162–64; and

antisemitic stereotyping, 186–87, 189; and Regina Kańska, 191–93
Piwocki, Ksawery, 117
Plach, Eva, 97
plasticine figurines, 96
Pleszew, 47, 55
Płomyk (*Little Flame*), 145
Pobudka (*The Awakening*), 116
Pod Pręgierz (*Under the Pillory*), 3, 13, 47, 58, 83, 149
pogroms, 46, 186, 234n32; in Grodno, 4; in Przytyk, 4, 128; as trope, 127–28
Pokrzywy (*Nettles*), 9, 122; and court cases, 79; drawing styles in, 50; percentage of cartoons about Jews in, 11, 47; readership of, 78–79; self-referential content in, 77; worldview of, 48
Polenaktion, 31. See also Zbąszyń
Polesie, 81
police, 90, 92, 128, 161
Polish Army, 197
Polish Association of the Publishers of Daily and Periodical Press in Warsaw, 16–17, 80
Polish Legions, 113
Polish-Jewish coexistence, 60, 73
Polish parliament. See Sejm
Polish Patriots' Emergency, 92. See also police
Polish Peasant Party "Piast" (Polskie Stronnictwo Ludowe "Piast," PSL Piast), 153
Polish People's Republic, 119
Polish Radio Orchestra, 132
Polish Socialist Party (Polska Partia Socjalistyczna, PPS), 4, 50, 51, 71, 81, 86, 112, 115, 116, 215n70, 222n96, 225n16
Polish-Soviet War, veterans of, 52–53
Polish Teachers' Association, 145
Polityka (*The Politics*), 99
Polonia, 19
Polska bez Żydów (*Poland without Jews*), 89. See also Hollender, Tadeusz
Poniatowski, Stanisław August, 132–33, **134**

Popular National Union (Związek Ludowo-Narodowy, ZLN), 145
Poraj, **131**, 133, **134**, 138, **139**, 142, **143**; anonymity of, 143–44, **144**, 151
pornography, 97–98
Portnoy, Eddy, 35
Poznań, 52, 69, 109
print media, 6; and anti-German rhetoric, 25; and antisemitism, 4–5, 164; Catholic, 4, 58; and censorship, 6, 25, 31, 77, 79, 82, 97, 165; and funding, 6, 165; and German-Polish press accords, 25; in interwar Poland, 7–8; Polish Jewish, 31, 41, 86, 90, 93, 115; producers of, 6; stereotyping of Jews in, 36; tabloid, 81; in Yiddish, 5, 8, 86, 92, 93, 95, 115; about Zbąszyń camp, 31
Próchnik, Adam, 116
Promised Land, 110
propaganda: anti-Jewish, 4–5, 47, 51, 59; pro-Soviet, 145; Soviet in Cold War, 71
Prosto z mostu (*Straight Out*), 113, 138
Protocols of the Learned Elders of Zion, 66, 222n87
Prystorowa, Janina, 194, **195**
Przegląd Katolicki (*The Catholic Review*), 99
Przekrój (*Cross-Section*), 197
Przeworski, Marek, 145
publishing industry, 34
puppet film, 96
Puszczykowo, 109

Quartly, Marian, 5

Radziwiłł, Karol Stanisław, 170
Radziwiłł, Michał (prince), 169–70, **171**, **172**, 173, 174, **174**, 176, 178–79, **180**, 182, 193
Raffles, Hugh, 76
Ravensbrück, 105
readers, 7–8, 12, 15, 32, 58, 153, 187, 199–200; as contributors, 178
Red Army, 119, 182, **183**, 186
Red Cross, 52
Red Sea, 26
refugees, 26, 28–31, 58, 65, 195–96, 215n68

Reif, Mendel, 9, 86, 93–95, **94**, 101, 115, 117, 118, 203
rekel, 19, 163
Rena. *See* Kańska, Regina
Republika media corporation, 81
revolution, 66
Revolution of 1905, 11, 16, 116
rhinoplasty, 125
Righteous Among the Nations, 85
ritual slaughter: and animal rights, 63, 194; laws on, 63, 194
Robotnik (*The Worker*), 116, 215n70
Rokach, Israel, 142
Rola neofitów w dziejach Polski (*The Role of Neophytes in the History of Poland*), 133
Romania, 24, 197; antisemitic laws in, 27, 195; Jews in, 196; Polish border with, 27–28, 195
Romanticism, 60, 64–65, 77, 123
Roosevelt, Franklin Delano, 22
Rossman, Henryk, 90, 91
Rothschild family, 71
Rózgi (*Birch Rods*), 193. *See also* Kańska, Regina
Rupprecht, Philipp, 63. *See also Stürmer, Der*
Russia, 61, 63; as national enemy, 11
Russian Empire, 16, 116, 186, 192; antisemitism in, 66, 202–3; pogroms in, 76, 186; protests against in partitioned Poland, 158
Russian Revolution of 1917, 146
Rycerz Niepokalanej (*The Knight of the Immaculate*), 99
Rydygier, Bronisław, 44
Rydygier, Stanisław, 9, 28–29, 44

Samoobrona Narodu (*National Self-Defense*), 3, 82
Sanacja, 10, 12, 16, 22, 139, 165; anti-Sanacja reporting, 46, 80, 86, 116, 117, 134, 136, 148–49; as trope, 129, 130, **137**, 138, 147–48
Sartre, Jean-Paul, 202
satire, 5; antifascist, 85–86, 107, 109, 165; anti-Nazi, 152; antisemitic, 14; anti-tsarist, 16; as a form of democratic expression, 13, 80, 83; autothematic, 200; centers of in interwar Poland, 8; conservative, 78; corrective function of, 48, 53–55, 58, 83, 200; discussions on, 77, 112; educational value of, 77; leftist, 78, 90, 112, 117; militant, 15, 16; protest, 85; socialist, 119; social role of, 13, 83; and the nation, 48, 112, 117; and the suspension of disbelief, 35; verbal, 199; vis-à-vis Romantic tradition, 77
satirical periodicals, 6; distribution of, 86; ephemerality of, 7, 9, 78; in interwar Poland, 7–9; liberal, 8; price of, 8; popular, 8–9
schehita. *See* ritual slaughter
Schmierer, Mieczysław. *See* Reif, Mendel
Schneider, Bronisław, 9, 86, 90–92, 115, 117, 118, 119, 165; biography, 186; drawing style, 183–85; as Jewish artist, 186
Scully, Richard, 5
Secklehner, Julia, 27, 173
Second Polish Republic, 88, 92, 112; establishment of, 7, 16; languages in, 8, 209–10n33; satirical periodicals in, 7; wages in, 8
Second World War, 20, 27, 83, 85, 105, 151, 197; German invasion of Poland, 152
Sejm, 3, 33, 113, 120, 145; Jewish MPs in, 3, 33, 41; discussions on ritual slaughter in, 61, 63
shabbes goyim, 56, **57**, 82; Polish names for, 58
Shandler, Jeffrey, 42
ship trope, 65, **66**
shmontses, 81, 112; and Polish national culture, 113
shylock stereotype, 34
Sichulski, Kazimierz, 8
Siemaszko, Andrzej, 118
Siemiatycki, Leon, 59
Siepka, Władysław, 46, 83
Sieradz, 47, 55
Sierakowski, Wincenty, 84
Silberfeld, Gizela, 113

Simpson, Wallis, 169
Six-Day War, 204
Skarga, Piotr, 65
Składkowski, Felicjan Sławoj, 50, 92, 110, 134, **135**
Słonimski, Antoni, 90, 97, 122, 124, 149, 232n5, 238n23
Słowacki, Juliusz, 64, 77, 89, 123
Słowo (*The Word*), 98
socialism, 66, 134
Soros, George, cartoons about, 71
Soviet Union, 17, 20, 61, 65, 142, 146, 150; Jews in during Second World War, 83
Spain, 63
Stalin, Joseph, 111, 142
stateless persons, 30
Stawiszyn, 46
St. Harten. *See* Szpigiel, Henryk Stanisław
Stopnica, 124
Stoss, Veit, 7
students: and antisemitic violence, 92, 156–60; attire, 93, 158, 160; trope, 89, 93, **94**, 158–59, **159**, 238n38
Stürmer, Der, 63–64
Suchestow, Judyta, 169–70, **171**, **172**, 172–74, **174**, 176, 178–82, **180**, **181**, 193, 241n93, 241n98
suicide, 60, 221n71
Świnie i koryto: bajki polityczne (*The Pigs and the Trough: Political Fables*), 146–48
Sygnały (*Signals*), 117
synecdoche, 107
Syrena Record, 132. *See also* Szpigiel, Henryk Stanisław
Syski, Aleksander, 148
Szabes Kurier (*Sabbath Courier*), 3, 4, 13
Szancer, Jan Marcin, 145
Szarża (*Charge*), 9, 95, 120, 122; criticisms of, 150, 232n5; editors, 124, 144–45, 202; and *Mucha*, 138
Szczutek (*Fillip*), 3–4, 8, 153
Szeląg, Jan. *See* Mitzner, Zbigniew
Szereszewska, Leonia, 118, 232n183
Szlengel, Władysław, 118
szopka, **155**, 155–56, 196

Szpigiel, Henryk Stanisław, 14, 120, **121**, 122–24, 132, 150–51, 202. *See also Szarża*; *Szpilki*
Szpigiel, Melania, 120, 151
Szpilki (*Pins*), 5, 120, 122; circulation of, 9, 86, 210n48; contributors, 86, 225n9; court cases against, 86, 95–97, 114, 227–28n73, 228n79; funding, 115; motto of, 123; origins of, 8, 86; percentage of cartoons about Jews in, 11
Szwajcarska Café, 86
Szymański, Edward, 95

tabloids, 81
Talmud, 66
Tel Aviv, 142
"thirteen theses," 22, 53
Titian, 101
Tom, Konrad, 132
Tomaszewski, Henryk, 104
trade: Christian, 49–52, 54, 58, 60; Jewish, 49–53, 59; as Jewish domain, 35
Trnka, Jiří, 96. *See also* Wasilewski, Zenon
Trzeciak, Stanisław, 97
Turek, 145–46, 151
Tuwim, Julian, 80, 86, 88, 97, 113, 123, 149

Ukrainian minority, 11, 79, 209n33
Uncle Sam, 20, 22
Union of Independent Socialist Youth "Life" (Związek Niezależnej Młodzieży Socjalistycznej "Życie," ZNMS "Życie"), 117
Union of Young Poland (Związek Młodej Polski, ZMP), 58
United States, 20, 23; Polish diaspora in, 148
urbanization, 6, 8, 140, 201
USSR. *See* Soviet Union
Užhorod, 28

Vienna, 29; cartoons in interwar, 173
Vilnius, 173

Walentynowicz, Marian, 4
Walka Ludu (*People's Struggle*), 113

Wars, Henryk, 132
Warsaw, 3, 8–9, 16, 74, 82, 85–86, 88; Academy of Fine Arts, 86, 117, 123, 147, 178, 192; Ghetto, 85; Philharmonic, 234n45; University of, 120, 122–23, 151; Uprising, 119, 121, 197
Warszawski Dziennik Narodowy (*Warsaw National Daily*), 98
Warta river, 109
Wasilewska, Wanda, 81, 145
Wasilewski, Antoni, 153, 165
Wasilewski, Zenon, 86, 102–3, **103**, 105–7, **106**; technique, 96. See also *Szpilki*; Trnka, Jiří
Wasiutyński, Wojciech, 113, 164–65; representations of, 114, 130
Wehrmacht, 152
Weindling, Paul, 76
Weintraub, Jerzy Kamil, 86, 88–89, 118. See also *Szpilki*
Westjude, 29, 74, 149. See also Jews
Wiadomości Literackie (*Literary News*), 5, 81, 87, 113, 117, 225n16, 228n88, 232n5
Wielkopolanin, 79
Wik, 161–62
Windsor, Edward, 169
Winersztok, 41–42, 70, 218n148. See also *Mucha*
With Fire and Sword or the Adventures of Mad Grześ (*Ogniem i mieczem, czyli przygody szalonego Grzesia*), 8

Włast, Andrzej, 132
Wojciński, Jan, 84
Wolica, 124
women, 182; cartoonists, 176, 192, 197, 204; in cartoons, 29, 96; nations as, 20; stereotype of Jewish, 140, 172–73, 199
Wróble na Dachu (*Sparrows on the Roof*), 93, 95; archival sources, 204; cartoonists, 9–10, 15, 152–53, 162, 176, 182, 192, 202; circulation of, 9, 210n48; entrepreneurial approach of, 12, 169, 200; percentage of cartoons about Jews in, 11; political profile of, 9, 165, 187, 196–97, 200; print quality, 154
Wyspiański, Stanisław, 7

Yad Vashem, 85
Yiddish language, 42, 74; perceptions of, 115
Yishuv, 26, 141–42

Zaruba, Jerzy, 88, 148, 236n98; biography, 185–86; drawing style, 182–83
Zbąszyń, refugee camp in, 30–31, 106
Zduńska Wola, 49–50, 53
Żebrowski, Julian, 4, 10, 149, 151
Zionism: print media, 5; Revisionist, 26; and support from Polish government, 26
Żółta Mucha (*Yellow Fly*), 3–4, 123, 136, 235n62
Żółtko and Eierweis, 88, 226n26

ABOUT THE AUTHOR

Ewa Stańczyk is tenured assistant professor in Modern European History at the University of Amsterdam. She is author of the award-winning monograph *Comics and Nation: Power, Pop Culture, and Political Transformation in Poland* (Ohio State University Press, 2022) and editor of *Comic Books, Graphic Novels and the Holocaust* (Routledge, 2018).

www.ingramcontent.com/pod-product-compliance
Lightning Source LLC
Chambersburg PA
CBHW022002220426
43663CB00007B/928